EDUCATING INTUITION

EDUCATING

INTUITION

Robin M. Hogarth

THE UNIVERSITY OF CHICAGO PRESS
CHICAGO AND LONDON

Robin M. Hogarth is professor at Pompeu Fabra University in Barcelona. He was formerly the Wallace W. Booth Professor of Behavioral Science in the Graduate School of Business at the University of Chicago. He is the editor of *Insights in Decision Making* and coeditor of *Rational Choice,* both published by the University of Chicago Press.

The University of Chicago Press, Chicago 60637
The University of Chicago Press, Ltd., London
© 2001 by The University of Chicago
All rights reserved. Published 2001
Printed in the United States of America

10 09 08 07 06 05 04 03 02 01   1 2 3 4 5

ISBN: 0-226-34860-1 (cloth)

Library of Congress Cataloging-in-Publication Data

Hogarth, Robin M.
    Educating intuition / Robin M. Hogarth.
        p. cm.
    Includes bibliographical references (p. ·) and index.
    ISBN 0-226-34860-1 (cloth : alk. paper)
      1. Intuition.   2. Decision making.   3. Judgment.   I. Title

    BF315.5 .H64 2001
    153.4'4—dc21

                                                            2001027562

To CP-S
. . . amb amor i il.lusió

CONTENTS

E very book or article that a person writes can be thought of as a step on a journey. Clearly, there can be several journeys, and some steps are bigger than others. I consider the present book to be a large step on my major professional journey, which, for some thirty years, has been centered on understanding, first, how people make judgments and decisions and, second, how we can help them perform these tasks better.

As part of the zeitgeist, two intellectual developments captivated most people of my generation interested in these topics. The first was the excitement generated by the development of statistical decision theory. The second was the cognitive revolution in psychology. The former provided an intellectually rigorous framework for analyzing how people should make decisions and, in particular, showed how analysis could incorporate subjective inputs. The latter legitimated the study of how people think and reason in terms of processes that, although not "observable," could at least be described. We have available today a powerful methodological arsenal derived from statistical decision theory and a huge body of detailed knowledge about many aspects of how people make certain kinds of judgments and decisions.

Yet, as someone who has now taught many courses in decision making, I sense a gap between what we teach and many characteristics of daily life. I think that there are two reasons. First, when making "real" decisions, people are sensitive to the context in which they are operating. Moreover, context tends to "engulf the mind." The effect is that people quickly forget abstract principles and react to the context in which they find themselves. If they are substantive experts, this may be effective; if they are not, the result can be "bad" decisions. This is not to say, of course, that people who are experts in decision-making techniques do not know how to use them. But most people are not experts and lack both the training and the practice necessary to become skilled in the use of formal decision-making tools. In addition, there are many situations in which time or other constraints rule out the use of formal tools.

Second, I have always been struck by the awe with which people regard "intuition" and the trust that they place in intuitive judgments. Intuition seems to have a mystical quality that cannot be explained. However, I have misgivings when people explicitly appeal to intuition. What does it really mean? Do people really have "special" knowledge, or is the whole notion just a smoke screen?

Yet, when we consider our own decision-making processes, there can be no doubt that we all make many decisions "intuitively." Indeed, we can all be thought of as possessing stocks of intuitive decision-making habits that we use many times on a daily basis. How, for example, did you decide what to wear today? Which garment, and why? Why did you automatically greet one person you saw at work but hesitate before speaking to another? And so on. In short, we constantly make many decisions on what might be called an intuitive basis. These decisions may "feel" correct to us, but we would have difficulty explaining both how and why we acted as we did.

It is clear that our intuitions affect most of the small decisions that we make on a daily basis. As such, their cumulative effect on what we experience across our lifetimes must be huge. However, our intuitions can also affect how we view and deal with major decisions—in at least two important ways. The first is how we may feel about the underlying issues even if we are unable to articulate these feelings; the second is the manner in which we approach problems. If we have developed intuitive habits for making small decisions across time, these are unlikely to be suppressed just because we are now facing an important decision.

Given that we have intuitions, where do they come from? A major contention of this book is that our intuitions are formed passively through experience. This, in turn, implies that our intuitions are partly the result of the vicarious experiences to which we have been subjected. In other words, our attitude toward acquiring the intuitions that affect such a large part of our decision making has been passive. We implicitly accept our intuitions as they are and really do not know whether they are good or bad.

In this book, I adopt a proactive attitude: *It is possible to improve your decision-making skills by taking steps to educate your intuition.* Moreover, my goal is to provide a scientifically based platform on which this can be done.

In building this platform, I examine many different sources of literature and take a position on how intuition fits into a larger picture of human information processing. This, in turn, leads to developing a framework for understanding how intuitions are acquired and used. I then use this framework to develop guidelines for educating intuition, guidelines that I make operational by a series of suggestions. I cannot, of course, claim that my guidelines have been "validated" (i.e., tested empirically). But I can claim that my guidelines and suggestions are based on a most thorough examination of the existing evidence.

I have written the book in what I call "*Scientific American* style." In other words, I expect a certain level of erudition on the part of the reader but no specialized knowledge in the psychology of decision making. For experts, on the other hand, there are numerous notes documenting literature that can be used to assess how I developed my ideas. The first chapter provides an introduction to the issues and an explicit guide to the contents of the book (see pp. 24–26). In particular, the first chapter provides my working definition of the term *intuition* and introduces five key ideas that I develop in succeeding chapters as I seek to find answers to the following questions: (1) How can psychology illuminate the nature of intuition (chap. 2)? (2) How do people acquire intuitions (chap. 3)? (3) How good are people's intuitions (chaps. 4–5)? (4) How does intuition fit into the larger picture of human information processing, and what does this imply for its education (chap. 6)? (5) How can we educate intuition (chap. 7)?

Acknowledgments

In writing this book, I have incurred many debts. The first is to the larger community of scholars that has collectively generated the literature on which this book is based. Several researchers were also kind enough to send me copies of specific articles when requested, and I am most grateful for this courtesy.

I owe further thanks to many other individuals. Selwyn Becker and Harry Davis both read and commented on an early version of the book and jointly steered me in more fruitful directions. Joshua Klayman and Michael Doherty read later versions (with the exception of chap. 8) and offered detailed comments and suggestions. Josh and Mike are masters at giving pertinent feedback, and I can only hope that I did their comments justice. Paul Slovic further provided useful comments on several portions of the manuscript and helped me see the work in context. Helpful comments were also received from Kenneth Hammond, Jack Soll, Marc Le Menestrel, Terry Connolly, and anonymous reviewers for the University of Chicago Press.

My formal work on this book started after I finished a five-year period serving as deputy dean of the Graduate School of Business at the University of Chicago. I believe that one outcome of being in that position was that I gained greater respect and empathy for people making decisions within complex organizations. Another consequence was that Dean Robert Hamada rewarded my service with a one-year sabbatical, during which the first version of this book was written. I am very grateful to Bob Hamada for both opportunities.

The book was written while I was on leave from the University of Chicago at Pompeu Fabra University in Barcelona. I thank the Department of Economics and Business at Pompeu Fabra University for the courtesies extended to me and, in particular, the two people who served as department head during my visit, Professors Andreu Mas-Collel and Albert Marcet.

Finally, I thank Geoffrey Huck and the staff at the University of Chicago Press for facilitating many of the tasks necessary for the production of a book. It is a pleasure to work with such an organization.

CHAPTER 1

The Sixth Sense

Imagine that you are watching a tennis match between two leading professionals. Their technical and physical skills are impressive. But, from time to time, you also have the impression that they demonstrate a "sixth sense" in anticipating their opponents and knowing where to place their shots. Tennis professionals, however, are not alone in demonstrating a sixth sense in what they do. To illustrate, I would like you to meet some people I know.

Kevin, the Trader. Kevin is a trader at the Chicago Board of Trade. His specialty is buying and selling pork bellies. Days are hectic. On average, he makes a good living. But there are days when he feels exposed to large potential losses, and, on occasion, he has lost a lot of money. On the other hand, there are also days when he has made a lot.

If we observe Kevin on the floor of the exchange, it is hard to see what he is actually doing. He keeps what looks like a score-card in his hand. From time to time he writes things down. He also watches what is going on around him. Sometimes, Kevin suddenly seems to become quite excited. He waves his arms, gives some hand signals, and shouts. He attracts the attention of other traders and soon makes contact with one. They communicate. Kevin writes something down. This kind of activity takes up much of Kevin's time each working day.

George, the Dermatologist. George is a leading dermatologist in a major European city. Most mornings, he is heavily involved in activities at a large university hospital. In the afternoons, he runs a private practice. He has an excellent reputation and has many patients.

Let us watch George interacting with a new patient who has a small growth just below the right eye. George starts by asking a few questions. He makes a couple of notes. Then he examines the patient closely with special eyeglasses. He steps back, tells the patient what the growth is and that he should have it removed. Within a few minutes, George removes the growth. First, he carefully injects some anesthetic; next, he removes the growth with a few deft strokes using an instrument that seems to burn away the unwanted flesh. The patient has hardly felt a thing.

Anna, the Waitress. For some time, Anna has been writing her dissertation in order to complete her Ph.D. in English literature. She is short of cash and has a part-time job at a busy restaurant in downtown Chicago. She works mainly in the evenings serving dinners.

Tips are an important part of Anna's remuneration, and she works really hard at the restaurant. The customers are varied. Many are professional people, some from out of town. They typically seem to discuss business. Other customers are stopping for a meal before going on to a cinema or some other cultural or recreational event. Many seem to be eating at the restaurant for the first time. A few are regulars. Watching Anna work, one is struck by the fact that she must constantly keep an eye on what is happening at all her tables. Yet, when the restaurant is really busy, it is not clear how she can provide good service to all her customers.

Diana, the Antiquarian. Diana is a middle-aged woman who runs a business buying and selling antiques in a large Mediterranean town. Antiques have always played an important role in Diana's life. Her father was an antiquarian, and she grew up in the business. Her brother, John, also runs an antique business in the same town.

Diana had no education beyond high school. She has always worked in the business. At first, like John, she spent many years working with her father and, then, started her own shop.

In financial terms, Diana's business is a success. On the surface, it seems simple. She has a large network of contacts and a good eye for bargains. The contacts include sources of antiques and customers—past, current, and potential. When you observe Diana working, all you can see is someone looking and talking. The good eye, it would seem, depends on an intimate knowledge of the business, something that has developed with years of experience.

In all four cases, these individuals are constantly making decisions that affect their success or failure. Kevin, for example, must decide whether a given contract is or is not priced appropriately and, then, whether he should act on this conclusion. George has to recognize what kind of growth his patient has and assess the consequences of removing it. Anna must guess how long she can ignore some customers before they become annoyed. And Diana needs to determine how much to bid for a certain piece of furniture.

How do they perform these tasks? The simple answer is that all use their judgment. Moreover, just like the professional tennis players, the success that they enjoy depends critically on the accuracy of their judgments.

Now let us ask each how they make their judgments. Kevin can tell us some facts about the general state of the market for pork bellies. Furthermore, he can tell us about past circumstances that were similar or dissimilar to what is happening currently. From time to time, he also makes some rough calculations. George, on the other hand, is more explicit. He can tell us why he thinks that a growth belongs to a certain genus or type by describing its characteristics. After all, he is used to providing such explanations to medical students at the university. On the other hand, he also says that, although he can recognize a genus quite easily, he has to make an effort to explain its characteristics and justify his judgment. Anna has a lot of difficulty telling you why she thinks she can keep some customers waiting; the people just do not seem to be in such a hurry. As for Diana, she has an excellent memory for transactions that she has conducted in the past, but she also tells us that every case is unique.

Although informative, these explanations are incomplete. There comes a point at which all four just say that they have a feeling of knowing what decision to make. They can tell us some of the factors that they considered in the process of making their judgments. But, in the final analysis, they depend on their "intuition" or "sixth sense," and this they cannot explain.

Indeed, it is hard to find anyone who does *not* have similar experiences, albeit in different circumstances. We all use intuitive judgment every day. The issues involved are typically minor, for example, deciding what clothes to wear. But we may also use it when making more important decisions, for example, when buying a car or a house. In these cases, we experience feelings about what is or is not the right decision, but the reasons that underlie these feelings often escape us. We know, but we cannot explain why. It seems as though we have an intuition or sixth sense that is beyond our own comprehension.

Intuition, or that sixth sense, is the topic of this book. My goal is to explore what, at the beginning of the twenty-first century, the science of psychology can tell us about intuition. Are there ways of finding out what my four friends cannot tell us? Or what we cannot tell ourselves?

Specifically, I shall explore such questions as, What is intuition? Where does it come from? How do people develop it? Should you trust your intuition? Under what circumstances? But, more important, I shall argue that *intuition can be explicitly educated.*

This last statement may at first strike the reader as counterintuitive. After all, if we exhibit intuition but cannot explain it, how can it be educated? Surely, either we possess intuition in a given domain, or we do not. My claim is that the scientific literature in psychology provides many clues about the nature of intuition, its genesis, and how it develops. This, in turn, leads to thinking about ways in which it can be educated. In the course of this book, I shall, of course, do more than just review the scientific literature. I shall interpret it, present my own views, and make several suggestions.

Some Approaches to the Psychology of Intuition

The topic of intuition arouses much interest when it is raised in general conversation. Moreover, even though people might be hard-pressed to define *intuition,* they typically consider it seriously, if not with some awe. Reference is often made to "women's intuition," or the notion that women are better than men at sensing what is happening in social interactions. Several books written for the popular "self-help" market exhort people to trust their intuitions and cite examples of successful people who have done just this.[1] Needless to say, examples of people who have trusted their intuitions and failed are not discussed in these kinds of books. The impression given is that our intuitions are an untapped source of wisdom and that, by "getting in touch" with these kinds of feelings, we can become more successful in life.[2] In the appendix to this chapter (see pp. 279–282),

I review four books that deal with the psychology of intuition from quite different viewpoints.

It is important to emphasize that the concept of intuition means a lot of different things to many different people and has attracted the attention of several scholars. At one end of the scale, it has been represented in some philosophical writings as the path to ultimate knowledge and has a kind of mystical status. The issue faced by these philosophers is how we humans come to know certain facts. We are not born with this knowledge. Nor can we reach it by rational or analytic arguments. Instead, there are some aspects of knowledge that we reach independently through the experience of intuition. As a consequence, this knowledge is of course "true." As an example, consider how you know that 1 + 1 = 2. It is possible to work out an analytic rationale why this must be the case. However, most people just understand this proposition to be true without having to use analysis. Indeed, the axioms underlying most logical or analytic systems are typically justified by appealing to people's intuitions.[3]

There is also a literature that discusses the role of intuition in scientific discovery, especially mathematics. In these writings, recognition is given to the notion that, in complex situations, it is not possible to explore all possible connections and that successful scientists seem to be guided by intuition or a sixth sense in determining which hypotheses to explore. Several mathematicians, for example, have written about their own discoveries and attested to finding solutions to difficult problems by following their intuitions, which they knew to be correct even before writing out the formal, analytic proofs.[4] For mathematicians as well as other scientists, both intuition and analytic methods are needed in the process of discovery.

For most people, *intuition* refers to a source of knowledge. However, the term was also used by the psychoanalytic pioneer Carl Jung in expounding his theory of personality. In this context, it refers to the ability to perceive possibilities, implications, and principles without being burdened by details.[5] According to Jung, people have four mental functions, which can vary in relative importance. Two of these, *thinking* and *feeling*, involve making judgments, the former logically and inferentially, the latter with respect to likes and dislikes. The other two mental functions are *sensation* and *intuition*. These are nonjudgmental in that the former involves perceptions of sensory data, the latter implications (see above).

Jung also postulated that people can differ in terms of attitudes that orient their thought processes internally or externally—that is, the polarities *introversion* and *extroversion*. The Myers-Briggs personality indicator, a test based on Jung's theory, allows people to assess their preferred mode of thinking and has become quite popular in parts of the business community over the last twenty-five years.[6] Many people seem to find comfort in the discovery that their preferred way of thinking falls into one of the possible Jungian categories. Whether this kind of insight is valid, however, remains open to question. On the other hand, one consequence of taking the Myers-Briggs test is that people recognize that they and others can think in different ways and that all ways of thinking are legitimate. Intuition is thus recognized as being on a par with the other ways of thinking.

Intuition, however, is not without its critics. Some claim, for example, that people appeal to intuition when they wish to avoid the costs of analytic thought and that *intuition* can be a synonym for *sloppy thinking*. However, the outputs of people's thought processes are typically not subjected to rigorous empirical testing by third parties. Thus, it is not always easy to determine, first, whether people are using intuition and, second, whether the outputs of their mental processes are valid, for example, in a predictive sense. I shall examine this issue further in chapters 4 and 5.

In scientific psychology, the topic of intuition has not attracted a great deal of attention, and it can hardly be said that there is a community of scholars dedicated to the study of intuition per se. If, for example, using the "PsychInfo" service of the American Psychological Association, you search articles published in scientific journals between 1887 and July 1999 for the key word *intuition*, you will find a mere 2,941 entries. To place this number in perspective, consider that you will also find 116,108 entries for *attitude*, 72,067 for *similarity*, 22,023 for *instinct*, 10,336 for *causality*, 9,087 for *insight*, 7,614 for *induction*, and 5,253 for *illusion*.

There are several possible reasons for the relative lack of scientific interest in intuition. One is that the concept has not been well defined. Another is that the term may cover too many phenomena. Yet another is that psychologists have not found that the concept needs to be explained in order to understand particular phenomena. I do not propose to discuss these reasons. However, I shall show in this book that examining the concept of intuition does illuminate many important psychological issues. This research also has great practical significance.

Defining *Intuition*

As noted above, the scientific literature does not provide a concise definition of the term *intuition*, yet many people (scientists included) use it with an "intuitive" understanding. *Merriam-Webster's Collegiate Dictionary* provides clues to everyday usage. It refers, in one sense, to (*a*) "immediate apprehension or cognition," (*b*) "knowledge or conviction gained by intuition," or (*c*) "the power or faculty of attaining to direct knowledge or cognition without rational thought and inference" and, in a second sense, to (*d*) "quick and ready insight."⁷ Thus, the common understanding is seen to involve elements of speed of knowing (definitions *a* and *d*) and the lack of a deliberative or rational thought process (definition *c*). In addition, there is the notion of a store of knowledge that has been built up over time through past intuitions (definition *b*). Finally, a link is made to the notion of "insight" (definition *d*).

Examining the concept of intuition in more depth, it is instructive to consider it along the dimensions *process, content,* and *correlates.*

Process

The *process* of intuition is characterized by a lack of awareness of how outcomes—or judgments—have been achieved. Kenneth Hammond, a psychologist who has made significant contributions to the study of intuition, defines *intuition* by contrasting it with analysis or logical thought. He states, "The ordinary meaning of intuition signifies the opposite—a cognitive process that somehow produces an answer, solution, or idea without the use of a conscious, logically defensible step-by-step process." In other words, intuition is seen as mysterious—it "somehow produces an answer" without the use of a "conscious" process. Note that Hammond further suggests that, in contrast to analysis or logical thought, intuition cannot be defended or justified by a "step-by-step" process.⁸ These statements, however, should not be taken to imply that logic or analysis is always right and that, if it disagrees, intuition is always wrong. What is meant is simply that nonintuitive processes are *deliberative* and can be *specified* after the fact. Logic and analysis can be made transparent. Intuition cannot.

Hammond's concept of intuition was heavily influenced by Egon Brunswik's views on perception, and it is illuminating to examine this connection.⁹ In Brunswik's model of perception, the organism "achieves" a percept by attending to and taking into account various cues that indicate the nature of what is being seen. For example, imagine the act of seeing Bill, a friend of yours, who is at some distance from you on a street. The underlying notion in Brunswik's model is that the organism identifies cues that indicate who the person might be and then weighs these cues in coming to a perceptual judgment. For instance, some cues (e.g., build) might make you tend to think that the person is John, another friend (both John and Bill are of similar build), but most other cues (e.g., hair color, way of walking, and so on) indicate Bill, and, finally, the indecision is resolved in favor of Bill.

There are several connections between perception so conceived and intuitive judgment. First, perception is covert. You do not have access to the process by which you are able to recognize Bill. Second, you cannot justify what you see in terms of a conscious, logically defensible step-by-step process (see above). Third, although you want to see who the person is (i.e., you have a *goal*), the process occurs *automatically* (i.e., with little or no effort on your part). Fourth, the process happens quickly. Finally, in achieving the perceptual judgment, you attend to and weigh the contributions of several cues or pieces of information. The perception is not achieved by attending to a single piece of information or using a deliberate formula.

In chapters 2 and 8, I shall examine Hammond's model of intuition in greater detail.

Content

I have just described aspects of the process of intuition. But what is its *content?* It is helpful to recognize that intuitive judgments are inferences that can look both backward and forward in time.[10] They can also represent outcomes of a stock of knowledge.

Backward-looking intuitive judgments are diagnostic in nature. They can be thought of as *hypotheses* or *beliefs* that have involved looking back in time and interpreting experience. Consider, for example, reaching the intuitive conclusion that a stranger to whom you have just been introduced is friendly. In essence, this involves interpreting what you observed when you met the person and then arriving at the belief that the person is friendly (you presumably perceived several cues; see above).

Of course, not all intuitive diagnoses are as simple as this. In some cases, an intuition may involve a complex domain of knowledge in which a person is an expert. For example, a biologist may have an intuition about why a certain species of plant would exhibit specific characteristics in a new environment. This intuition may then trigger the search for a more formal explanation.[11] As a further example, reconsider the process of George, the dermatologist, examining a patient.

Forward-looking intuitive inferences are predictions. They may be inferred from hypotheses or beliefs (e.g., that a stranger will respond to you in a particular way *because* he is friendly). Or they may simply be the result of extrapolation from a trend (as, say, when estimating next year's sales on the basis of both this year's budget and actual figures).

Intuition can also represent a stock of knowledge on which a person can call if necessary (see dictionary definition *b* above). The basic idea here is that we all know many things intuitively and, when questioned, can provide a response without really knowing where it came from. For example, imagine someone who has played soccer since childhood and knows a great deal about the game. He would find it difficult to explain how he knows that certain plays or tactics are better in some situations than in others. But he does have an important intuitive stock of knowledge about soccer. In this respect, he is quite similar to Diana, the antiquarian, who also has a large intuitive stock of knowledge, albeit about antiques.

More generally, it is important to recognize that what we might call our *cultural capital* is a stock or an inventory of intuitions. The idea here is that, over time, we all build up a stock of ways of interpreting the world that forms part of our cultural heritage. Moreover, we do this over years of living in a culture and are typically not aware of how we acquired the knowledge that we use daily to signal our behaviors to others or to interpret signals given by others.[12] Indeed, many people become aware of the consequences of their own cultural intuitions only when they are living in a foreign country and are confronted with interactions that leave them puzzled. For example, the way in which a person behaves at the dinner table or in a meeting varies from culture to culture, and the same questions or physical gestures can be interpreted differently in different cultures. For instance, in England, people tend to avoid confrontation. Thus, when directly questioned about a sensitive issue by, say, an American, an English person could easily take offense when none is intended. The English person intuitively interprets the American's question as rude and responds in an offhand manner. The American intuitively interprets the response as unfriendly and is puzzled by the behavior.

Two people living in the same culture, however, would not be expected to have identical stocks of cultural capital. Instead, if those stocks were compared, common and idiosyncratic components would be found. This is because no two people would have had exactly the same experiences. Nonetheless, two people who have been brought up in the same environment would be expected to have more cultural capital in common than would two people with different backgrounds.

Even though I have talked about diagnoses, predictions, and stocks of knowledge, I do not mean to imply that all intuitions are necessarily precise. On the contrary, the outcomes of intuitive processes are typically approximate and often experienced in the form of feelings as opposed, say, to words. Hypotheses or beliefs are usually not well defined (what, e.g., does *friendly* mean in operational terms?), and predictions may not even be falsifiable. (For example, the intuition that somebody will be successful in a job cannot be verified unless the criteria for success and the date by which these criteria should be met are also specified.) As will be discussed below (see esp. chap. 3), this lack of precision can affect the quality of feedback from the environment and thus the ability to learn from experience. On the other hand, even imprecise hypotheses in the form of feelings or predictions that suggest only a vague direction can be useful in many situations. For example, the sense that a situation is dangerous can save you from harm even if you are unable to specify precisely why the situation might be dangerous. As an example, imagine someone who is climbing a mountain and taking a previously unexplored route.

Correlates

The term *intuition* suggests certain *correlates*. Among these are notions of speed and confidence. For example, the dictionary definition provided above uses the terms *immediate* and *quick,* and a definition provided in a recent review of the psychological literature describes intuition as "a feeling of knowing *with certitude* on the basis of inadequate information and without conscious awareness of rational thinking" (emphasis added). In addition, this review also states, "Most writers agree that intuition is characterized by intense confidence in the intuitive feelings."[13]

However, neither speed nor certainty are necessarily correlates of intuitive thought. While it is true that we often make speedy judgments about many issues, some people report experiencing intuition as a slow realization of a state, an impression being built up over time by a succession of minor intuitions. Imagine, for example, that you are interviewing a job candidate and that, by the end of the interview, you have the "impression" (i.e., made the intuitive diagnosis) that the candidate does not have a solid background in a specific area of expertise. Yet you cannot pinpoint the moment when you first started to realize this. Instead, you just have an impression that seemed to build up during the course of the interview. On the other hand, it is probably true to state that *most* intuitions are experienced as occurring quickly.

As to certainty, there are many occasions when intuitions are uncertain. One is when you are unsure what your intuition means. For instance, most of us have had the experience of feeling uncomfortable when meeting another person for the first time yet not being able to pinpoint why and what, if anything, to do about it. Not only can one experience uncertainty about intuitions, but intuitions can themselves signal uncertainty.

There are also occasions when your intuitions are challenged, perhaps by analytic arguments, and you are not sure what to trust—intuition

EXHIBIT 1 The Müller-Lyer illusion

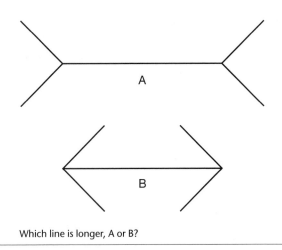

Which line is longer, A or B?

or analysis. For instance, imagine a businessperson who is considering launching a new product. An analysis based on market research and discounted cash flow may suggest that it is a good opportunity. On the other hand, intuition based on years of experience in the business, and especially contacts with customers, may suggest otherwise. There may just be a feeling that this is the wrong time to launch the product. Similarly, when interviewing a job candidate with impeccable credentials, you may experience doubts that you are unable to specify.

When confronted with a conflict between intuition and analysis, many people report greater confidence in intuition unless the dispute can be solved by appeal to a well-accepted analytic rule. This point can be illustrated by the Müller-Lyer perceptual illusion (see exhibit 1). If asked which of the two lines is longer, A or B, most people intuitively state A. However, if provided the opportunity to measure the lines, people have little difficulty accepting that there is no difference in length between them. In other words, they accept the analytic evidence offered by the opportunity of making precise measurements with a ruler even though they might still "see" the two lines as different.[14]

However, not all problems can be solved by a simple appeal to a single analytic rule. Consider, for instance, the product-launch or job-interview scenarios discussed above. Indeed, when situations become complicated, people tend to place less trust in analytic methods—for at least three reasons.

First, by definition, analytic methods imply simplification and thus cannot capture the richness of the problem context, missing details that may be important. Second, analytic methods require explicit assumptions, and these assumptions may be perceived as unrealistic. Third, people know that even the smallest mistake can invalidate the results of an analysis.[15] A recent and stunning example is the loss of an unmanned spacecraft on the planet Mars. The scientists responsible for transmitting landing instructions to the probe failed to realize that, whereas some of the underlying calculations had utilized the metric system, others were conducted in terms of imperial measures. Thus, even though intuitive solutions may not have been reached by obviously rigorous means, they have a strong appeal, an appeal based on what seem like many points of contact with the person's experience. I shall return to this issue again in chapters 5 and 8.

Insight and Intuition

The second meaning of the dictionary definition of *intuition* provided above referred to "quick and ready insight," but this begs the question of what an *insight* is. The same dictionary defines *insight* as "the power or act of seeing into a situation" or "the act or result of apprehending the inner nature of things or seeing intuitively."[16] By using the term *intuitively* in this definition, the writers of the dictionary have employed what seems like circular logic.

Unlike the situation with intuition, there is more consensus in the psychological literature about the meaning of the term *insight*. In the context of problem solving, *insight* refers to the phenomenon whereby people suddenly become aware of the solution, or part of the solution, to a problem with which they are confronted.[17] For example, consider the problem presented in exhibit 2. In thinking about this problem, many people spend considerable time trying to prove mathematically that there must be a precise point at which the monk will be present at the same time on both days. However, this approach often seems unsatisfactory.

Now consider an alternative way of looking at the problem. Imagine that there are two monks and that, starting at the same time on the *same* day, one ascends and the other descends the mountain. If both monks start at the same time, there must be a point on the path at which they cross, that is, that they both occupy at the same time. Now, transform the form of the problem from "two monks on the same day" to "one monk on two different days," and the solution becomes obvious.[18]

This is an example of what psychologists call *insight*. After work-

EXHIBIT 2   The monk problem

One morning, exactly at sunrise, a Buddhist monk began to climb a tall mountain. A narrow path, no more than a foot or two wide, spiraled around the mountain to a glittering temple at the summit. The monk ascended at varying rates of speed, stopping many times along the way to rest and eat dried fruit he carried with him. He reached the temple shortly before sunset. After several days of fasting and meditation he began his journey back along the same path, starting at sunrise and again walking at variable speeds, with many pauses along the way. His average speed descending was, of course, greater than his average climbing speed. Prove that there is a spot along the path that the monk will occupy on both trips at precisely the same time of day.

Source: Koestler (1967).

ing on a problem for some time, apparently without making progress, you find that the solution suddenly appears in consciousness.[19] The phenomenon is often illustrated by the apocryphal story of Archimedes, who, when taking a bath one day, suddenly recognized the physical principle underlying the displacement of water and, leaping from his bath and shouting "Eureka," ran naked down the street, to the amusement of his neighbors. Clearly, we have all experienced insights on occasion even though our reactions were more restrained than that of Archimedes.

A psychological explanation is that the phenomenon known as insight occurs when people have within them the knowledge necessary to solve all or part of the problem with which they are confronted. However, the solution remains obscure until the problem is viewed from a certain angle or until a certain clue, one triggering recognition of the solution, suggests itself. Think, for instance, of how the changing water level of the bath triggered Archimedes's imagination. Clearly, there would be no insight phenomenon if people were already conscious of the answer to the problem that they were facing. (In this case, Archimedes would have had no motivation to jump out of his bath.) And no insight could occur if people lacked within them the knowledge to solve the problem (e.g., had Archimedes not known how to interpret the significance of the change in the water level in his bath).

Clearly, insight and intuition are related, and the dictionary definitions of *insight* given above (i.e., "the power or act of seeing into a situation" and "the act or result of apprehending the inner nature of things or seeing intuitively") seem adequate. In most of this book, I shall talk about intuition. However, in chapter 8, I shall return to the topic of insight.

Definition Used in This Book

For the purposes of this book, I propose that the essence of intuition or intuitive responses is that *they are reached with little apparent effort, and typically without conscious awareness. They involve little or no conscious deliberation.*

Note that I do not state that intuitions are accompanied by feelings of certainty because, as pointed out above, people occasionally experience conflict between intuitive and analytic modes of thought. (Reconsider, e.g., the Müller-Lyer illusion in exhibit 1 above.) Nor have I stated that intuitions always happen quickly, even though I believe that most do.

Clearly, the definition of *intuition* provided here is not as precise as many would like. If anything, it may be too broad. However, I believe that a definition that is "approximately right" will be more useful for exploring the concept of intuition than one that is "precisely wrong." In chapter 8, I shall revisit the definition of *intuition* in the light of the issues discussed in the other chapters.

As will be seen in the following chapters, a factor that renders difficult the examination of experimental evidence is that, even if responses do involve conscious deliberation, the outcome may still depend on a set of initial intuitions. Conversely, intuition might be a result of time spent in deliberation. In addition, the working definition of *intuition* provided here might seem to cover all cognitive processes of which we are not aware. This is not meant to be the case. However, it should also be clear that processes of which we are not aware govern a huge portion of mental life.

Five Key Ideas

The major conclusion of this book is that intuition can be educated, and ways of doing so are, in fact, specified. The support for this conclusion is provided by five key ideas: (1) one organism but many information-processing systems; (2) learning shaped by experience; (3) two systems for learning and doing; (4) intuition as expertise; and (5) making scientific method intuitive.

One Organism but Many Information-Processing Systems

Although the point is obvious, it is important to emphasize that the human body, or organism, is complex.[20] It has evolved over millions of years and has demonstrated a remarkable capacity for both adapting to the environment and adapting the environment to its own needs. Compared to other species, humans are not necessarily distinguished by their physical abilities (e.g., forearm strength or speed on foot). However, they do have superior intellectual capacity.

In the past, philosophers, psychologists, and other thinkers used to think of the body and the mind as being somehow disconnected. That is, people have physical bodies, and the effects of these physical bodies interacting with their surroundings can be both seen and felt. But minds seem to be qualitatively different. Cognition, or the act of thinking, cannot be observed. Nor can you physically see or touch a thought. Yet these invisible abstract symbols and ideas can cause the body to take action. For instance, when Kevin the trader makes some rough calculations on the floor of the exchange, this can sometimes lead him to pursue different trades. In other words, the outputs of an abstract analytic process that is manipulated invisibly in the head can lead to physical actions. For Diana the antiquarian, the recognition of certain types of furniture can lead to an immediate, almost automatic assessment of value and the corresponding desire to complete a transaction. Thus, one of the tasks of science and philosophy was to resolve what was known as *the mind-body problem.* In other words, how does the abstract concept of mind fit in with the physical conception of the body?

The advent of the computer suggested an analogy that was key to resolving this issue. Both computers and humans function by processing information. In particular, the human organism (by which I mean the *whole body*) consists of a number of different systems that communicate and coordinate actions by exchanging and processing information.

At the beginning of a life, when a male's sperm fertilizes an egg from a female, information is exchanged, and the resulting DNA provides a set of instructions that determine the form that the life will take. The organism that grows from these instructions can be thought of as consisting of a complex set of systems and subsystems that need to communicate with each other in order to preserve life and meet the needs of the person.

The information-processing systems of the organism are constantly involved in processes of internal regulation and external adaptation. Some deal only with regulating internal states. For example, several organs secrete specific enzymes when they receive a signal that these are required. (Consider, e.g., the thyroid.) Other systems are more attuned to the external environment or problems of adaptation. The perceptual system, for example, is constantly sending signals to parts of the brain to update what is happening in the immediate environment of the organism.

Evolution works by retaining processes or systems that "work," that is, that provide satisfactory solutions to problems of adaptation. Thus, humans as well as other animals consist of layers of systems that have been found to "work." I use the word *layers* specifically because I want to reinforce the notion that each new process or system is added on to and does not necessarily replace what already exists.

The critical difference between humans and other animals is that the brain systems of the former are more developed. But, in considering this, it is critical to realize that the human organism (or set of systems) was not designed by some optimizing method to handle the environment that we face today. Instead, it represents a succession of developments that were successful adaptations to situations faced by our ancestors. In this, we are no different from other species. It is just that our set of adaptations has brought us to a higher level of cognitive development.

The brain itself can be thought of as a series of systems and subsystems that interacts with other parts of the body. Note well that the brain (or "mind") is not separate from the body; it is part of it. The organism is a unit composed of all these different systems and subsystems, whether located in the head or elsewhere.

Most of the information processing that is conducted within the organism is carried out in *automatic* fashion. (I shall explain this in a moment.) We do not, for example, consciously control the production of enzymes by the thyroid, we do not instruct our eyes what to do when we look at an object, and so on. In fact, many of these information-processing mechanisms are hardwired in the sense that they are part of our genetic inheritance. However, we also process information within the realm of our *consciousness*. What does this mean?[21]

To define *consciousness* and the notions of *automatic* and *nonautomatic processes,* I need first to explain what psychologists call *short-term* or *working memory* and to distinguish this from *long-term memory.*

The idea behind short-term or working memory is the following: At any given moment in time, we cannot bring to mind all the information that we possess or even all the information that is potentially available to us. (Try, e.g., to recall—without looking and verbatim—the last three sentences that you read!) Instead, we are limited in our ability to recall and process the information of which we are currently aware.[22] That information resides in working memory, and it is the contents of this working memory that define conscious experience.

By definition, therefore, conscious awareness involves only a relatively small amount of information and is also changing from moment to moment. Another way of saying this is that consciousness (or conscious awareness) is the same as *attention.* Thus, when thinking about a problem, you may imagine that you are considering a lot of information, that is, paying attention to many different aspects of the problem. However, this is only partly true. It is true only in the sense that you have brought many items of information into, and then taken them out of, working memory *over time*. The process is, in other words, sequential; these items of information are not all present simultaneously in working memory. In an important sense, short-term or working memory should be called *the conscious working space*. It is where attention is focused at any given time.

Processing information in working memory or consciousness is costly—in two senses. The first is the potential opportunity cost. Working memory has limited capacity, and thus paying attention to some information precludes paying attention to other information. Second, explicitly processing information in short-term memory takes effort. (As the reader knows, concentrating on anything is tiring!)

As for long-term memory, this is the store of information that you have accumulated over time and on which you can call. It is long term in the sense that it can contain memories acquired a long time ago, for example, of events, experiences, ideas, etc. However, operationally, long-term memory also involves information that is quite recent, for example, of events that occurred a few moments ago but have now moved out of working memory (i.e., the conscious working space).

As most people are aware, long-term memory does not work like a video or tape recorder; that is, it does not provide perfect recollection of past events. Rather, it works more by means of reconstruction and association and is heavily influenced by the meaning that people give to events. I shall return to a discussion of the nature of long-term memory and its implications for educating intuition in chapters 3 and 4.

We now have a way of defining what *automatic information processing* means. It is a process that occurs outside working memory or consciousness and, as such, does not consume attention. It should thus be clear that much of the information processing that occurs within the organism is automatic. In fact, the great majority of physical processes operate without our conscious awareness, the result of generations upon generations of evolutionary development. Consider once again the actions of the thyroid gland. However, it is also important to note that, through practice, some processes can become automatic.

The mathematician and philosopher Alfred North Whitehead once said that civilization advances by the extent to which it does *not* have to think about how to resolve problems.[23] Perhaps Whitehead should have been a psychologist because, to the extent that people can learn to process information automatically, they free attention to consider other issues and can become far more efficient.

As a simple example, consider Julie, an eleven-month-old child who is just learning to walk. Julie is at one end of the sitting room and sees her uncle at the other. She decides to walk to him. With great effort, she raises herself upright by leaning against an armchair and then begins the difficult task of walking toward her uncle. Julie makes slow but steady progress. However, when she is halfway across the room, her mother enters and says "Julie." The effect is devastating. Julie loses her balance and falls down. Why?

For Julie, walking is not an automatic process. It consumes all her attention. When her mother said her name, the recognition of it diverted her attention, and Julie lost her balance. In other words, walking and hearing her name at the same time were too much to handle.

Fortunately, Julie will soon learn to walk in a way that does not require her full attention. Through practice, the process of walking will become automatic, and Julie will not have to think about how to do it, although some attention will always be consumed in monitoring the process.

On occasion, even the little attention paid to monitoring an automatic process can be too much. To illustrate, imagine that you are walking down a street with a friend and that she suddenly gives you a really excellent idea for your work. What happens? You will probably stop walking. Indeed, the idea is so good that it stops you "dead in your tracks." In other words, when all your attention is diverted elsewhere, certain automatic processes can cease to function.

To sum up briefly, there is, in fact, no mind-body problem. The human organism is one unit that consists of many systems and subsystems for processing information. Second, these systems have developed over time through an evolutionary process and are found in layers that represent successful, successive adaptations to environmental demands. Third, many systems for processing information are automatic in the sense that they do not require conscious attention in order to operate. Furthermore, through practice, processes can become automatic, thereby lowering the cost of their operation to the organism by reducing demand on attention. As my argument in this book should make clear, intuitive processes are essentially automatic and consequently consume little or no attention. On the other hand, the fact that a process is automatic does not necessarily mean that it represents intuition. For example, when the eye is subjected to a puff of cold air, the eyelid closes automatically. This inherent reaction is more accurately characterized as instinctive rather than intuitive.

Learning Shaped by Experience

Humans learn about the world from two sources: what others tell them and their own experiences. Moreover, there is strong interaction between these two sources. What other people say can direct what people experience, and what people experience can affect how they interpret what they have been told.

It is convenient to classify *what* people learn into two categories: *content* and *rules*. *Content* refers to knowledge about the world. This includes facts, notions about how different variables are linked or associated, and so on. In brief, content is the "raw material" of long-term memory.

Rules, on the other hand, represent knowledge of how to do things. These can be thought of as sets of instructions or algorithms that the organism uses to get things done. Once learned, some rules are used to guide motor processes, such as walking—remember eleven-month-old Julie. Other rules, however, may be used simply to manipulate symbols in mental life. To illustrate, imagine that someone asks you whether the students in one class that you attended while in college were smarter than those in another. To answer, you might well try to remember the smart students in both classes and see whether it was easier to recollect smart students in one class as opposed to the other. This procedure is a rule. Given the necessary information, it provides a way of reaching an answer.[24]

The basic mechanism that enables humans to learn from experience is remarkably simple. There are two key principles. First, people learn by noticing associations or contingencies, and, on average, the more such associations are observed, the more likely they are to be remembered.[25] Second, rewards and punishments help people remember some associations better than others.

By an *association* or a *contingency*, I mean "things" that occur together.[26] These could include noticing, for example, that sugar is sweet, that coffee is generally bitter, that specific words are associated with particular objects, and so on. Associations are also made when the connection between actions and reactions is noticed, for example, recognizing that pleasure is generally expressed by those who are smiled at by another or who receive an unexpected gift or that kicking a ball in a certain way results in a certain kind of motion. Clearly, the number of potential associations that could be made is huge (even if short of infinite!).

The second principle simply says that not all associations or contingencies are equally important. Briefly, those connections that have potential costs or benefits mean more to us, and are remembered better, than those that do not. For example, after touching a flame once, a child will remember that fire burns. However, it may take several trials to learn that pencils need to be sharpened to be able to draw well.

From the viewpoint of this book, the most important fact about learning from experience is that people learn content and rules by what they experience, not by what they do *not* experience. This might seem to be a strange statement, but it has important consequences. To explain, recall my waitress friend, Anna.

When the restaurant is busy, Anna cannot serve all her customers as well as she would like. She therefore pays more attention to those customers who she believes will leave large tips. But who is likely to leave a large tip? The clue that Anna uses is dress. She believes that, on average, well-dressed customers are more likely to be wealthy and thus able to leave large tips. It is this belief that guides her actions. And, in fact, when the restaurant is busy, Anna does find that it is the better-dressed customers who leave the larger tips.

At one level, Anna is justified in her belief. She receives larger tips from the better-dressed customers. But, in a more important sense, she is fooling herself. Because she believes that well-dressed customers are likely to leave large tips, she always pays a lot of attention to them. They, in consequence, react favorably to her good treatment. However, Anna has never tested her belief and has, instead, set in motion a self-fulfilling prophecy. It is true that her belief has been reinforced by her experience, but her experience is limited. She has not given herself the opportunity of testing whether she has learned the right lesson from experience. If, for example, she started giving the poorly dressed customers special attention, they might give her even larger tips than the better dressed do.

The critical point is that, when we take action on the basis of a belief, we destroy the chance to discover whether that belief is appropriate. In fact, the feedback that we receive can be quite misleading. In later chapters, I shall explore what I call *learning structures*. By this, I mean the characteristics of the task in which people learn from experience. Some environments have favorable learning structures in that people receive quick and accurate feedback. In other learning structures, feedback can teach people the "wrong" lessons. Unfortunately, people are not always aware of the characteristics of the learning structures in which they are operating and, over time, may acquire erroneous intuitions in which they feel quite confident. (Think of Anna in the restaurant.)

In summary, the human organism is endowed with a simple mechanism for learning from experience. However, the process of most learning takes into account only what is observed. Whether people acquire the right or the wrong lessons from experience depends on the characteristics of the environments in which they have learned, that is, the learning structures.

Two Systems for Learning and Doing

As noted previously, the human organism can be thought of as consisting of many systems and subsystems that process information. What is defined as a *system*, however—the *brain system*, the *blood circulation system*, etc.—depends on a number of criteria, some possibly arbitrary. The principal reason for referring to any particular part of the organism as a system is pragmatic. Doing so helps explain, say, how the brain operates relative to other systems or how blood circulates.

For the purpose of dealing with the topic of intuition, I shall—on similar, pragmatic grounds—assume that two systems control the processes by which we learn and take action: the *tacit* system and the *deliberate* system. (It should be noted that, by *action*, I mean any response made or action taken by the organism.) While I am of course aware that more than two systems are involved (and I shall discuss this again), this twofold division is sufficiently rich to explore the topic.

The term *tacit system* is meant to encompass all processes that occur tacitly or automatically, that is, largely without use of conscious attention. It therefore includes what I previously defined as *intuition*, that is, thoughts that "*are reached with little apparent effort, and typically without conscious awareness. They involve little or no conscious deliberation*" (p. 14 above). Importantly, it also includes what is learned through experience with the expenditure of little or no conscious attention.

Note that I am not saying that the tacit system involves absolutely *no* conscious attention or deliberation. Unless automatic processes are hardwired or inherited, such as those employed in underlying biological mechanisms, there is always some level of process monitoring that is under conscious control. Consider the example cited above of how a good idea can stop people "dead in their tracks."

The term *deliberate system* is meant to encompass all processes that require effort, that is, attention and deliberation. While it includes analysis or logic, it does not exclude processes that do not conform to any known rules of analysis or logic. All that is required for a process to be considered part of the deliberate system is that it involve the explicit manipulation of cognition. Learning that takes place within the deliberate system demands explicit effort and attention.

Although I have described two mutually exclusive systems, this does not mean that only one or the other produces actions or that learning cannot involve both intuition (experience) and analysis (intellect). On the contrary, many actions and instances of learning involve both systems.

To illustrate, let us reconsider George, the dermatologist, who is examining a patient who has a growth below the right eye. When he first sees the growth, George has an immediate intuitive reaction. He has seen many growths in the past, although not necessarily below the right eye. However, the similarity between this growth and others of a particular type is striking. He just sees the resemblance without having to expend mental effort. This is George's tacit system in action. Yet George also knows that errors are made identifying growths. He therefore deliberately checks various features of this particular growth against a mental checklist in order to query his initial diagnosis. This second process is deliberative. It involves recalling details of codified medical knowledge. It involves attention and mental effort. This is the deliberate system at work.

From the viewpoint of learning, George has experienced seeing and identifying another example of one particular type of growth (an example of the tacit system at work). As a good physician, he has also noted on the patient's chart the various features characteristic of the growth, a note to which he can refer in the future, if necessary (an example of the deliberate system at work).

It should be noted that, if deliberate-system actions are repeated over time, they can move to the domain of the tacit system. Recall the example of Julie presented above. At eleven months walking is a deliberate-system activity for Julie, but for most of her life it will involve the tacit system. Also, many cognitive activities do not rely on one system alone. As we saw with George, initial thoughts in a given situation may be the product of the tacit system at work, but these thoughts may be modified, amplified, or even rejected by the deliberate system. Alternatively, an explicit calculation of your checkbook balance will be the result of efforts expended within the deliberate system. However, the outcome of the calculation will undoubtedly be compared to an intuitive guess of roughly what you think the balance should be, a guess made using the tacit system.

Finally, a useful analogy for thinking about the differences between the tacit and the deliberate systems is that of an iceberg. The deliberate system lies above the surface of the water. It can be seen and assessed. The tacit system lies below the surface. Not only is the submerged portion much larger than the exposed portion, but it cannot be seen and therefore cannot be known.

Intuition as Expertise

As stated above, the *content* of intuition can be thought of in terms of inferences that look both back and forward in time as well as a stock of knowledge. Moreover, we know that intuition is based largely on experience and that people's experience differs. Thus, whereas George, the dermatologist, has much intuitive knowledge about skin disorders, he knows almost nothing about antiques. For Diana, the antiquarian, it is the reverse.

The key notion is that intuition can be thought of as a form of expertise in the sense that it is specific to particular domains. Clearly, we all have intuitions about many different aspects of the world: the way physical and biological processes work; how humans interact in social and economic settings; and so on. These intuitions are a function of knowledge that has been acquired both intellectually (the deliberate system) and experientially (the tacit system). Thus, although we all have intuitions about many things, our relative "expertise" depends on those domains to which we have had the most exposure, mainly through experience.

In thinking about intuition, therefore, it will be instructive to consider expertise. How is expertise best acquired? What are its limits? What distinguishes those who are experts from those who are not? What distinguishes the highest levels of performance among experts?

In short, I shall show that intuition is like expertise. It is specific to particular domains. It is acquired through domain-relevant experience. And it can be improved through instruction and practice.[27]

Making Scientific Method Intuitive

As just noted, intuition is largely acquired through experiential learning and, as such, is specific to particular domains. It should therefore be clear that no book can provide the substantive content of intuitive knowledge because this will always be affected by each individual's specific experiences. But what can be done is to educate the process by which people acquire their intuitive knowledge.

The general problem of inference—or how to learn from experience—has been the subject of much discussion and debate over centuries. However, there is now remarkable agreement on the canons of scientific method. Scientists generally agree on the principles that should be followed in determining whether a conclusion can be substantiated by particular evidence, what additional evidence is necessary, and so on.

The key idea, therefore, is to help people make scientific method intuitive, in other words, to educate people's intuitive learning processes so that they more closely follow the canons of scientific method. To achieve this, two steps are necessary. First, people have to learn why and when their intuitions are or are not accurate. This involves, for example, understanding the consequences of different types of learning structures. Preferably, this instruction should be conducted in an experiential as well as an intellectual manner because the former typically has a much greater impact.[28]

Second, people need to learn how to integrate the principles of scientific method into their everyday habits. Over time, and with practice, these new habits will become more automatic and less costly to implement. In other words, they should migrate from the deliberate to the tacit system. To structure the learning process, I decompose scientific method into four stages and provide specific suggestions for educating each. The four stages are *observation, speculation, testing,* and *generalization.* They are discussed in some detail in chapter 7.

Plan of the Book

The objective of this book is to provide insights into how we can educate our intuition. My view is that, in addition to being involved in occasional, important decisions, intuition plays an enormous role in the large number of small decisions that people necessarily make every day. Thus, imagine that you could measure the quality of a person's intuitive decision-making process and improve this by just 5–10 percent. Even this small increase could have huge cumulative effects across a number of years and add considerably to the quality of the person's life.

This book consists of eight chapters. In chapters 2–5, I take the view that an educational process needs to be built on as solid a foundation as possible. For this reason, I explore what the literature in scientific psychology can tell us about intuition at the beginning of the twenty-first century. Chapters 6 and 7 present the model or framework for intuition and its education that is summarized by the five key ideas outlined above (see pp. 14–24). Chapter 6 develops a theoretical framework for understanding intuition and also develops seven guidelines for its education. Chapter 7 provides the framework as well as many specific suggestions for educating intuition. In addition to these suggestions, evidence is examined concerning the effectiveness of teaching rules for reasoning.

Chapter 8 discusses several important issues concerning intuition and also evaluates aspects of the frameworks presented in the previous chapters. This last chapter further recognizes that work on educating intuition is incomplete. Several suggestions are therefore made for future investigations.

Readers who are eager to examine my suggestions for educating intuition may wish to jump straight to chapter 6. The intervening chapters they would skip can be briefly summarized as follows.

Chapter 2 explores ways in which intuition has been treated in the psychological literature. Three different approaches are examined. The first concerns variations on the notion that people use two different modes of thought. This can be viewed as the classic distinction between intuition and analysis.

Second, I discuss the so-called cognitive or information-processing approach. Paradoxically, this approach has the least to say explicitly about intuition because much of it seeks to describe only those forms of cognition that are conscious. However, some of the models proposed do provide a way of dealing with subconscious processes, and their implications are discussed. In addition, I indicate some areas of investigation where intuition, as I define it, is beginning to play an increasingly important role in our understanding of the way in which people think.

Third, recent years have seen great interest in the link between neuroscience and cognition. I therefore also examine this literature for the light that it sheds on the role that many automatic processes play in shaping what people think.

Finally, chapter 2 discusses the link between intuition and emotion.

Chapter 3 deals with the critical issue of how people acquire intuitions. I start by considering what can be called *the genetic infrastructure of cognition*. Are we all born with the same rules for processing information, or are all such rules learned? To the extent that we all possess from birth the same rules for processing information, one could argue that part of intuition is in fact genetic in origin. As I show, many basic processes that provide important inputs to intuitive judgment either are present at birth or manifest themselves shortly thereafter in a remarkably consistent fashion across different cultures.

Chapter 3 also specifies the concept of learning structures that was described briefly above. As noted above, the basic processes underlying the way in which humans learn from experience are quite simple and typically require little effort. The concept of learning structures facilitates predicting the relative validity of intuition by characterizing the conditions under which it was acquired. This naturally leads to the topic of memory. Chapter 3 concludes with a discussion of the role of memory, distinguishing between memories that are explicit and those that are implicit.

In chapter 4, I discuss attempts to describe people's intuitions in a number of different domains. The basic approach in these studies is to compare people's judgments with the outputs of different "normative" models. Some studies examine people's intuitive understanding of physical processes, such as the effects of gravity on moving objects. However, most studies involve problems in reasoning where the standard of comparison is provided by such normative models as deductive logic and probability theory. The results of this literature have been quite controversial, and I shall provide a perspective on the nature of the controversy. In particular, I emphasize the effects of learning and how people are able to "visualize" the problems with which they are confronted.

Chapter 5 poses the question of how good intuition actually is. What are the costs and benefits of the functions that intuition performs for the organism? What does empirical evidence tell us about the accuracy of intuition—both in diagnosis and in prediction? This chapter also examines individual differences. How does intuition vary by sex and age? What is the link between expertise and intuition (discussed briefly above)? Finally, when should intuition be trusted?

To conclude, let me return to Kevin, the trader, who was introduced at the beginning of this chapter. Before writing this book, I had a conversation with Kevin in which I discussed my intention to study and explore the concept of intuition. Kevin was visibly irritated by this project. To him, intuition is something quite personal that cannot be made explicit. In fact, he prides himself on his intuition and believes that it lies at the heart of his success as a trader. I also suspect that Kevin does not like the idea that others could somehow acquire the secrets that took him so long to learn. When trading, intuition really is Kevin's sixth sense.

Kevin—and others like him—have nothing to fear. The knowledge that they have acquired intuitively will always be theirs and is not threatened by projects such as this book. By its very nature, intuition will always be personal—it is very much the product of each person's own experience. However, what third parties can do is help people acquire good intuitions in more effective ways. They can also help them realize when their intuitions might lead them astray. In other words, we can influence the rules used to think intuitively (the *how* of intuition) but not the content (the *what*). Whether or not you think of intuition as a sixth sense, judgment can always be improved.

Models of Intuition

As noted in chapter 1, the topic of intuition per se has not been the focus of much work in scientific psychology. Nonetheless, many contributions have elucidated the concept and its implications from a variety of perspectives. This chapter explores these different models or perspectives. The goal is to gain insight into how intuition might best be educated.

First, I examine the contributions of authors who have argued that people use alternative *modes of thought,* which, roughly speaking, can be characterized as analytic and intuitive. Of considerable interest, therefore, is determining why and when people use these different modes.

A second perspective is gained by examining the literature in cognitive psychology and, in particular, what is known as the *information-processing* approach. The earlier, pioneering work in this tradition did not confront the topic of intuition (as defined in chap. 1) because studies dealt mainly with the *conscious* processing of information. However, later work in different subfields has sought to study the influences of subconscious processes and is important for understanding intuition.

Another perspective is provided by examining results in *neuroscience* that are starting to identify how actual physical processes in the brain are related to psychological phenomena. Knowledge in this area is currently limited by the inability to experiment directly with human brains. However, many interesting hypotheses have been generated by studying the behavior of people suffering from different forms of brain damage and by extrapolating from studies of animals.

Finally, the chapter concludes with a discussion of the role of intuition and emotion. Emotions and feelings, it turns out, play a dual role. Sometimes, emotions and feelings *are* intuitions; that is, we have an intuition in that we sense a feeling of, say, unease. At other times, emotions and feelings affect the way in which we process information; that is, they may induce us to process information in an intuitive as opposed to an analytic mode.

Not presented in the chapter is work that examines people's abilities to make intuitive judgments as though they were experts in different areas. This will be examined as a separate topic in chapter 4, which will cover judgments involving both physical systems (e.g., the effects of gravity) and abstract reasoning schemes (e.g., probability theory and the canons of deductive logic).

Modes of Thought

As a young boy growing up in Scotland, one of my favorite family excursions was to the electric brae.[1] Situated a few miles south of the town of Ayr on the southwest coast, the electric brae is accessed from a road near the village of Dunure. The spot is called the *electric brae* because it seems to defy physical laws, as we understand them. If, for example, you leave a parked car in neutral and do not engage the emergency brake, it will start to roll uphill. If you put a ball on the ground or spill water, both will also go uphill. How can you explain such happenings?

Despite the fact that the locals call the brae *electric,* the explanation is, in fact, optical. The contours of the land surrounding the brae at that point on the road produce the illusion that objects roll uphill. However, even when you know that the phenomenon is illusory, you still have the sensation that the laws of gravity are being defied. Perhaps the brae is "electric" after all!

Like the Müller-Lyer illusion illustrated in exhibit 1 above, the electric brae phenomenon demonstrates the contrast between two modes of thought. In one, we rely on our senses. One line in exhibit 1 really is experienced as longer than the other. Objects in the electric brae really are seen to roll uphill.

In the second mode, we rely on a principle or an explicitly stated reason. We use a ruler to establish whether there is a difference in relative length. We appeal to the principle of gravity to overrule the evidence in front of our eyes that objects are rolling uphill.

Going back to antiquity, these two modes of thought, or ways of knowing about the world, are what many scholars have referred to as *intuition* and *analysis,* respectively.[2] They represent a dichotomy that has been emphasized by many and that is made clear by the examples just illustrated. We know intuitively what we mean when we say that one line in exhibit 1 is longer than the other. More precisely, we know, but we do not know *why*. We just experience it that way. On the other hand, we do know why using a ruler or appealing to the principle of gravity is an appropriate way in which to resolve an ambiguity. Doing so represents an appeal to objective criteria or principles that we can specify in the process of reaching a conclusion. Moreover, if we accept the rationale underlying the principle to which we have appealed, consistency demands that we accept the conclusion reached with its aid.

The two examples given here are instances in which intuitions are easily overruled by analysis even though, fundamentally, perceptions remain unchanged. In both these specific cases, we have greater respect for the principles on which the analysis is founded than on our senses and accordingly suppress the evidence of the latter. However, this need not be, and indeed frequently is not, the case.

It is instructive to examine the dichotomy between intuition and analysis as represented in the work of three psychologists, Jerome Bruner, Seymour Epstein, and Kenneth Hammond.

Jerome Bruner

In the intriguing essay "Two Modes of Thought," included in his book *Actual Minds, Possible Worlds,* Bruner talks of "two modes of cognitive functioning, two modes of thought, each providing distinctive ways of ordering experience, of constructing reality." One mode he calls the *paradigmatic* or *logicoscientific,* the other the *narrative.* He further notes that the two modes "(though complementary) are irreducible to one another. Efforts to reduce one mode to the other or to ignore one at the expense of the other inevitably fail to capture the rich diversity of thought."[3]

A good part of Bruner's essay examines why people find certain texts so persuasive. Whereas a good analytic argument can convince a reader of the truth of a proposition ("Yes, the laws of gravity do apply at the electric brae"), it is "lifelikeness" that convinces in the case of narrative. Good stories appeal to people in a very basic way. When they are well constructed, their context has the ability to capture a person's attention on a variety of dimensions and to involve the emotions. Arguments within the logicoscientific mode may be convincing, but only in a sharp, unidimensional sense. ("Yes, I know that it is impossible, but I still saw the car roll up the hill at the electric brae.") Statistically, people know that air travel is safer on a per passenger mile basis than traveling by road is, yet many people feel safer in a car than in an airplane. Similarly, people are more impressed by graphic descriptions of one or two specific road accidents than by accident mortality statistics.

One of the major points of Bruner's essay is that, if it is well constructed, a narrative form of explanation can be a much more powerful means of persuasion than logical argument. In particular, the narrative gains much of its force because—through context—it appeals to the implicit knowledge of the audience. In other words, the good storyteller captures and uses part of the knowledge of the reader (or listener) in creating effects. Another way of stating this is that a good story appeals to a person's stock of intuitive "cultural capital" (see chap. 1). This has two implications. First, stories have universal appeal only if they relate to themes that really are universal—in both time and space. (Consider why certain classic pieces of literature have endured for so long.) Second, stories that do not make contact with a person's intuitive cultural capital will have little impact. (This is, incidentally, one reason why children should not be forced to read certain classics. What may be considered a lack of maturity is, in fact, a lack of intuitive cultural capital. Children have not lived long enough to acquire the requisite cultural capital.)

What applies to good stories also applies to good arguments that explicitly use the narrative mode, that is, that are not based on analysis. This is a principle well understood by advertisers. The point of many advertisements is to connect with the experience of the audience and show how the product advertised can provide a needed service. Thus, advertisements for overnight mail services may contain anecdotes that suggest the consequences of packages not arriving on time.[4]

Arguments in the form of narrative are also implicit in the analogies that people use to explain things to each other. Good communicators understand their audiences and know what analogies are appropriate. Thus, for an Englishman to attempt to explain something to an American by drawing an analogy to cricket would be foolish. (What on earth is a googly?) Similarly, Englishmen are bewildered by anecdotes involving baseball. (Why is it called a *strike* when the hitter misses the ball?) In short, the effectiveness of stories, or arguments in narrative form, depends on their ability to relate to the audience's specific life experiences, that is, the audience's stock of intuitive cultural capital.

Further attesting to the power of narrative as a mode of understanding are the ideas underlying what has been called *script theory*.[5] The basic notion here is that people have intuitive understandings of the way in which certain social situations will evolve. Thus, once the initial parameters are set, the action plays itself out automatically and guides the individual's behavior. This reduces information-processing demands and allows the individual to attend to other concerns.

To illustrate the script concept, imagine what happens when eating out in a restaurant. On the basis of past experience, people expect, for example, to be shown to a table, to be given a menu, to have time to examine the menu, possibly to be told what the day's specials are, to have their order taken, etc. Thus, much of the action that occurs in the restaurant script is almost automatic or intuitive. The advantage of the quasi-automatic nature of the restaurant script is that it frees attention for other matters, for example, attending to companions, noticing who else is present in the room, and so on.

This kind of script guides the individual through the social situation of the restaurant. Other scripts may involve only oneself. Consider, for example, getting up in the morning. This can consist of quite routine, automatic behavior—moving only when the alarm clock rings; going first to the bathroom; drinking some water; and so on. Of interest in such scripts is what happens when they are interrupted in some way or a new behavior has to be integrated with the old.

Consider the example of a person who is required to take a pill each morning. At first, the behavior is quite deliberate. However, after a while, it becomes almost automatic. Indeed, there will even be occasions when the person will take a pill and then not remember having done so. This may lead to devising strategies that ensure that only one pill is taken and that it is taken at the right time. For example, a pill could be left in readiness the night before, and, if it is not there later the next day, the supposition will be that it was taken. Note that what has happened here is that the person has invented an explicit rule to overcome the inability to remember automatic behavior. In other words, the person has invoked analysis (or deliberation) to cope with a dysfunctional aspect of intuitive (or tacit) behavior.

Seymour Epstein

In developing his cognitive-experiential self-theory of personality, Epstein makes an important distinction between the two ways in which people process information.[6] One he labels *experiential,* the other *rational.* The experiential system is driven by emotions, intuitive, and automatic. It "is assumed to have a very long evolutionary history and to operate in non-human as well as human animals. . . . it is a crude system that automatically, rapidly, effortlessly, and efficiently processes information. . . . Although it represents events primarily concretely and imagistically, it is capable of generalization and abstraction through the use of prototypes, metaphors, scripts, and narratives." The rational system, on the other hand, "is a deliberative, effortful, abstract system that operates primarily in the medium of language and has a very brief evolutionary history. It is capable of very high levels of abstraction and long-term delay of gratification."[7]

From the perspective of this book, it is important to note that Epstein does not equate the experiential system with intuition but that the latter nevertheless plays an important role in the former. Epstein also stresses the role of preconscious processes and emotion in the experiential mode.[8] However, as I shall argue later (see esp. chap. 6), intuitive processes can also occur in the absence of emotion.

As evidence for the separate existence of these two modes—the rational and the experiential—Epstein points to the fact that, when emotionally aroused, people tend to eschew logical arguments, that emotions themselves may be triggered by preconscious thoughts, and that there is an important difference between learning intuitively through experience and learning intellectually through instruction or analysis (see also chap. 3). Moreover, he cites several phenomena as supporting the existence of an experiential mode of information processing that persists even though people are capable of rational analysis. These include the appeal and influence of narratives (see also my discussion of Bruner above), irrational fears, the appeal of pictures over words (e.g., pictures of accidents as opposed to accident statistics), superstitious thinking, and the ubiquity of religion. The common element in each of these phenomena is that, even when people have access to objective data, there is still a desire to place more trust in past experience. For instance, we know that certain superstitions have no rational foundations (e.g., "knock on wood") but persist in respecting them because to do so is reassuring.

In testing his contention that there are two ways in which people process information, Epstein has been heavily influenced by the work of Amos Tversky and Daniel Kahneman on the use of "heuristics" or so-called natural reasoning strategies in probabilistic thinking.[9] One of the points that Tversky and Kahneman make about these strategies is that, although they are easy to execute and often provide answers that are "good enough," they can also induce errors relative to more formal, analytic approaches.[10] But their existence provides good evidence that people can and do reason in different ways.

In one set of experiments, Epstein and his colleagues presented subjects with vignettes the outcomes of which were arbitrary and asked (1) how most people would react to the situations in the real world, (2) how they (the subjects themselves) would react, and (3) how a rational person would react.[11] One vignette involved an elaboration of a Tversky-Kahneman scenario in which two women arrive at an airport each a half hour late for a scheduled flight. One of the two women learns that her flight left on time; however, the other is told that her flight had been delayed and had only just left. Who would be more annoyed? Subjects replied that, in the real world, the second woman would be more annoyed, that they, too, would be more annoyed in the second situation, but that, from a rational viewpoint, there should be no difference in reactions because both women missed their flights. In other words, according to Epstein, people clearly recognize when they are reasoning according to different systems and that using different systems can lead to different answers.

In further experiments, Epstein and his colleagues have investigated people's willingness to choose between gambles that highlight the difference between probabilities and frequencies. In the basic paradigm, people win a prize for drawing a red jelly bean at random from a jar containing 10 percent red and 90 percent white jelly beans. The choice is between making the draw from jars containing ten or one hundred jelly beans. When the problem is presented hypothetically, most people are indifferent as to which jar to select. However, when asked actually to play the gamble, most people choose the jar containing one hundred jelly beans. Epstein interprets this result as indicating that people can reason in two ways. In the hypothetical situation, they reason analytically. Since the chances of success are the same in both jars, they are indifferent. When they play the gamble, however, a more primitive form of reasoning takes over whereby the frequency of red jelly beans (ten instead of just one) becomes more salient.[12]

It is important to note that Epstein does not say that people reason only with either the experiential or the rational mode. Typically, reasoning will start with the experiential mode and be modified by the rational, depending on circumstances. In many situations, however, modification by rational considerations could be quite minor, such as when dealing with issues in interpersonal relations.

Finally, a critical aspect of Epstein's work is to emphasize the role of the subconscious—or preconscious—in mental life. Epstein argues that Sigmund Freud was correct in emphasizing the importance of the subconscious but that, by sampling dreams, he acquired an inaccurate picture of what the subconscious does for the individual. Dreams do not reveal the functional aspects of the subconscious. Indeed, Epstein uses an evolutionary argument to make the point that the subconscious has survived precisely because it has served us well. Our subconscious feelings may often prove wiser than our rational thoughts. I shall return to this topic in chapters 5 and 8.

Switching Modes of Thought

There is, of course, much other evidence that people can switch between different modes of thought according to circumstances. For example, consider the difference between making a judgment by noticing similarity as opposed to deliberately using a definition. As an instance of the former, imagine meeting someone for the first time and immediately seeing that she strongly resembles her mother. As this example shows, judgments of similarity tend to be intuitive in that they depend on a covert cognitive process in which people match characteristics (in this case, physical features of mother and daughter). Judgment by definition, however, requires checking deliberately whether something meets certain specifications. For example, is someone old enough to drink alcohol in a public bar? This requires deliberately checking both the person's age and the regulations governing the consumption of alcohol.

The distinction between judgments made by noticing similarity and judgments made using a definition was neatly demonstrated when two groups of people were asked to imagine a circular object with a three-inch diameter.[13] One group was asked whether the object was more *similar* to a pizza than to a quarter, the other whether it was more *likely to be* a pizza or a quarter. The quarter was the majority response in the first group, the pizza in the second. In other words, whereas the object can be small *like* a quarter (an intuitive judgment), it cannot actually *be* a quarter unless it is the correct size (an analytic or rule-based judgment).

Kenneth Hammond

As noted in chapter 1, Kenneth Hammond has made important contributions to the study of intuition. Recall that Hammond's theorizing was heavily influenced by Egon Brunswik and that one of his first contributions to the study of judgment was the analogy that he made between making a judgment (largely intuitively) and the act of seeing as described by Brunswik.[14]

Hammond went on to develop means of "capturing" or describing people's judgmental processes using statistical techniques that measure how people weight different informational cues. In several cases, this has been most revealing because people are not always aware of what influences their judgments.[15] Attempts have also been made to assess how much of this process involves intuition. However, it is not clear that the statistical technique is capable of capturing what would be generally recognized as *intuition*.[16]

An interesting insight into the nature of intuition was provided by an experiment that tested Hammond's theorizing in the context of types of judgment errors. According to Hammond, intuitive judgments are the result of considering multiple, imperfect cues (see the analogy with perception made above, pp. 7–8). Analysis, on the other hand, involves the strict use of a few explicit rules. Therefore, the nature of errors that result from intuitive processes should differ from the nature of those that result from analysis.

Specifically, in a task such as the estimation of a quantity, intuitive processes should result in small errors clustered around an average value. The key idea is that intuitive judgments are like averages that result from balancing several different informational cues. Moreover, if the average is unbiased (in a statistical sense), it will be quite close to the true value. In analysis, on the other hand, errors will not cluster around a particular value but tend to be rarer and larger. Imagine, for example, estimating intuitively the total cost of the purchases that you have just made at a store. Intuitive estimation will rarely be exactly right. On the other hand, your guess is not likely to be far off the correct amount.[17] Using a calculator, you will undoubtedly be very accurate most times. But, occasionally, you could make a mistake (perhaps by inverting two figures, keying in, e.g., "91" instead of "19"), and the resulting error could be large. Indeed, in Hammond's experiment, different distributions of errors were observed when judgments were made intuitively, on the one hand, and analytically, on the other. Intuitive errors were clustered neatly around the correct figure. And, even though analysis produced fewer errors, those errors were larger, falling some distance from the correct amount.[18]

Going beyond the psychological laboratory, a striking example of the nature of error in analytic thinking can be found in the experience of the hedge fund Long Term Capital Management (LTCM) in August 1998. This fund, started in 1994, traded large sums of money in various financial instruments using sophisticated, analytic decision rules that were based on the results of research by highly qualified staff members, including two Nobel laureates. Employing about two hundred people, the fund had—until the summer of 1998—been very successful and returned large profits to investors. However, a rare combination of events not covered by the assumptions of LTCM's models struck within a couple of weeks and quickly resulted in huge losses. Fearing for the safety of the *entire* U.S. financial system, the Federal Reserve Bank of New York pressured a group of U.S. and European banks to mount a rescue plan that involved raising $3.5 billion.[19]

I shall return to the topic of errors in both intuition and analysis in chapter 5.

Whereas Hammond's work does differentiate between intuition and analysis, he does not accept a dichotomous view of judgment whereby use is made of either intuition or analysis. Instead, one of the major premises of his theoretical position is the following: "Various modes, or forms, of cognition can be ordered in relation to one another on a continuum that is identified by intuitive cognition at one pole and analytical cognition at the other."[20] In Hammond's model, people can exhibit a range of cognitive processes, most of which mix elements of intuition and analysis. He labels this intermediate form of cognition *quasi rationality* and states that judgment typically implies a *compromise* between different modes of thought as well as between different informational cues. Hammond further argues that different tasks can also be ordered on a continuum that reflects the extent to which the tasks induce intuition, analysis, or quasi rationality, and he has provided empirical evidence in support of this proposition.[21] In chapter 8, I shall discuss further aspects of Hammond's model.

Implications for Educating Intuition

There is certainly much evidence that supports the view that people can process information in two distinct modes. To simplify matters, I call one of these modes the *tacit* system, the other the *deliberate* system (see chap. 1), and, in this way, distinguish between what others broadly refer to as *intuitive* and *analytic* thinking.

The deliberate system requires effort and attention, but, when utilizing this mode, people can make explicit the bases of their reasoning. Moreover, it is clearly possible to educate the deliberate system through programs that stress such topics as logic, mathematics, deductive and probabilistic reasoning, and so on. Indeed, this is the domain of formal education.

The tacit system, on the other hand, requires little or no attention, and, when utilizing this mode, people have little awareness of how they reach their judgments. The tacit system is capable of capturing a wide range of informational inputs and connecting to a person's past experiences. It essentially operates in an automatic manner. In many cases, people's thought processes involve both the deliberate and the tacit systems. This is analogous to Hammond's concept of quasi-rational thought.

An important distinction between the deliberate and the tacit systems is that the latter is much more dependent on the context in which the reasoning is taking place. In deliberate thought, for example, the rules of arithmetic are applied in exactly the same way whether the numbers being manipulated represent people or objects. Tacit thought, on the other hand, depends much on recognizing situations and, as such, is necessarily sensitive to context. To educate intuition, therefore, we need to understand, first, more about the nature of the tacit system, second, how intuitions are acquired, and, third, how effectively our intuitive systems already guide our decisions. The remainder of this chapter is devoted to the first question. The other questions are discussed in chapters 3–5.

The Cognitive or Information-Processing Approach

In the definition provided in chapter 1, I stated "the essence of intuition or intuitive responses is that *they are reached with little apparent effort, and typically without conscious awareness. They involve little or no conscious deliberation*" (p. 14). However, on examining the history of scientific psychology in the twentieth century, it is clear that topics like intuition were not among those that mainstream psychologists wanted to elucidate. Nonetheless, a number of phenomena have been clearly demonstrated, and important contributions are being made to the study of intuition even though these may not be recognized as such. But, first, it is important to provide some historical background.

Historical Background

In thinking about the general topic of thinking, and intuition in particular, it is impossible for people not to reflect on their own thought processes or to ask others about their experiences. Recall, for example, Epstein's use of the vignette of the two women who arrived at the airport thirty minutes after the scheduled departure time of their flights. When presented with evidence of how other people answer questions about this story, few of us refrain from considering—implicitly or explicitly—how we would react and whether answers given by others "make sense." Introspection is an important stimulus to thinking in both science and everyday life.

However, there is an important distinction between using introspection to stimulate thinking, on the one hand, and using it as a means of reaching scientific conclusions, on the other. The problem of understanding the implications of this distinction has dogged much of psychology in the twentieth century.

As a reaction, in part, to earlier introspective methodologies and the vague, mentalistic concepts of the nineteenth century, scientific psychology was dominated during the first half of the twentieth century by mechanistic, stimulus-response views of human behavior. Emphasis was placed on what could be observed in as objective a manner as possible. Human behavior was thought of as occurring in a kind of "black box" whose rules could be inferred only by testing theories that related outputs to inputs, that is, responses to stimuli. As it turned out, a lot of useful research could be framed within simple stimulus-response models, and many useful findings emerged about, for example, learning.[22]

One exception to this movement was so-called Gestalt psychology. This placed great emphasis on phenomena such as pattern recognition that did not seem to fit into the simple stimulus-response models that were predominant at the time. Psychologists seemed to recognize that this was an unexplained issue, but they were not able to reconcile it with the then-prevailing mainstream.

It was also clear, however, that, in thinking about thinking, something was missing. The 1950s saw an important step forward with the start of what became known as the *cognitive revolution*. At one level, this was the notion that it is reasonable to talk about how people think and what they think about—although not in a naive, nineteenth-century manner. Cognition—or the act of thinking—was a legitimate field of study. Perhaps more important, the advent of the computer provided an analogy—as well as a language—that allowed us to describe thought as the processing of information. The notions of inputting information, storage in and retrieval from memory, a central processing unit, and programs or algorithms for processing information all provided ways of modeling and talking about mental processes.

However, there was a need to do more than just build models of thought in computers. Psychologists wanted to know how the outputs of such models would compare with the products of human thought and whether they could establish correspondence between the processes of models and those of humans. Comparing the outputs of models and humans was easy. Given the same information as input, it is no more difficult to compare the outputs of computer models and human thought processes than it is to compare the latter and any so-called black box models. It was the process comparisons that were of greater interest because, if shown to be valid, these would demonstrate that human thought could be successfully modeled by computers.[23]

Process comparisons were effected in two ways. One was to build computer models of the human thought process using the so-called think-aloud technique. For example, an expert in a particular domain, say, the stock market, would describe aloud his thoughts while engaged in picking stocks. The results (transcriptions of the verbalized thought processes) were then analyzed in detail and a program written to describe the regularities in the expert's decision rules.[24] This new model could be validated in two different ways. As noted above, one was in terms of predictive accuracy. Could the model predict how the stock market expert would value stocks that were new to him? Second, could the model predict details about the psychological information-processing system that the expert was presumed to be using? For example, how long did it take to evaluate certain kinds of stocks? What information was required? In what order was this information examined? And so on. Psychologists developed a sophisticated variety of measures to test questions about process, for example, response times, examination of eye movements, effects of presenting information in specific sequences, and so on.

The information gained from what might be called the first generation of information-processing models has proved most important. However, it did not lead directly to an illumination of the processes of intuition that are the main interest of this book. The reason is that the models primarily depicted conscious information processing in working memory. After all, the data on which the models were based were the subjects' own verbalized thoughts. In other words, in the situations examined, subjects were primarily engaged in deliberative (or analytic) as opposed to tacit (or intuitive) information processing.

However, an important finding from many of these studies was that subjects did not have access to their internal mental processes in the sense that their descriptions alone would have been adequate to build the models. Rather, investigators had to add their own assumptions about underlying processes. Whether they wanted to or not, psychologists were being forced to consider information processing that occurs at a subconscious level.

The Emergence of the Subconscious

A defining feature of intuitive processes is that they involve little or no effort. In this respect, an important conceptual point that started to be clarified in the 1970s was awareness of the distinction between so-called automatic and deliberative information-processing strategies and the domains to which automatic information processing might apply.[25]

At one level, it is clear that the human organism is involved in much unconscious and automatic information processing. For example, many acts of perception, physical movement, and the regulation of internal processes are carried out by information-processing systems that are automatic in the sense that we allocate no attention to their functioning. Moreover, we typically have no insight into *how* these processes operate. We cannot explain, for instance, what processes we invoke when we see an object or when we catch a moving object, such as a ball. We just do these things.

Work done within cognitive psychology in the 1970s, however, went beyond simple motor operations. Instead, the claim was made and substantiated that automatic processes operate across a wider range of cognitive phenomena than had at first been imagined. Experiments showed that, for familiar stimuli, people developed processing routines that worked in an almost effortless manner and that were difficult to suppress, modify, or ignore once they had been learned. In addition, investigators have been surprised at how well people are able to remember automatically certain aspects of their experience, such as frequencies and facts about spatial and temporal location. Moreover, this ability to remember automatically is not affected much by age, ability, education, or motivation.[26] The important implication of this latter statement is that it suggests that the ability to remember this kind of information is quite old in evolutionary terms and thus deeply embedded in the human operating system (to use the computer analogy once again).

Appreciation for these abilities has been incorporated in more modern information-processing models by making clearer distinctions between the domains of conscious and unconscious processing. For example, by introducing the concepts of declarative and procedural knowledge, John Anderson and his colleagues have allowed the explicit modeling of conscious and subconscious cognition.[27] Declarative knowledge represents what people know (i.e., their store of knowledge), whereas procedural knowledge is the set of procedures, rules, and strategies that operate on declarative knowledge in mental activity. Consciousness at any given point in time is equated with the declarative knowledge present in working memory; procedural knowledge, however, is assumed to operate at the subconscious level. Thus, within this framework, it is the rules that people use for processing information that are "intuitive," not the arguments on which the rules operate (i.e., declarative knowledge), provided that these arguments are in working memory.

Another approach to studying cognition, and a correspondingly different approach to considering intuition, is provided by the so-called connectionist or parallel-distributed-processing (PDP) models.[28] Here, cognition is modeled in the form of an associative network of connections that vary in strength depending on the "knowledge" that exists within the system. As new information is encountered, connections can be "excited" and responses elicited. In addition, the strengths of connections can change over time as a function of informational inputs, with the result that learning is simulated. At one level, these models seem to be "neural nets" (i.e., nets of neurons), but, in fact, no claim is made to model behavior at such a micro level.

In describing these forms of computer models, Paul Smolensky makes a distinction between what he calls *symbolic* and *subsymbolic* systems.[29] Symbolic systems are those that have been studied in "traditional" computer models of thought, such as those described above. These involve what Smolensky refers to as *conscious rule application* or the notion that cognitive operations involve the manipulation of symbols or concepts by the application of series of conscious rules—imagine, for example, the deliberative steps that you would take in thinking through a problem in logic.

Subsymbolic systems, on the other hand, are under the control of what Smolensky terms the *intuitive processor.* This controls behavior that does not involve the conscious application of rules, and, from our viewpoint, there are several interesting observations to be made. First, Smolensky notes that conclusions reached by way of intuition do not need to involve the conscious application of rules. Indeed, at this assumed intuitive level, it is "soft constraints" rather than "hard rules" that produce outcomes. Second, the intuitive processor is important because it is "presumably responsible for all animal behavior and a huge portion of human behavior."[30] Third, as people acquire more practice in certain activities over time, responsibility for information processing passes from the conscious level to the intuitive processor. And, finally, much of people's mental behavior contains elements of both symbolic and subsymbolic systems or, in other words, involves conscious and intuitive thought. The challenge that Smolensky poses to psychology is how to model the interactions between these two systems that operate according to quite different "rules."[31]

Intuitive Rules

Today, many areas of cognitive psychology can, in fact, be described as engaged in a search to specify tacit rules that explain behavior and, as such, are relevant to intuition. This is the case, for example, with work on categorization, judgments of similarity, psycholinguistics, and several models of judgment and decision making.[32] In all these fields, investigators take as given that people lack awareness of the processes that underlie their behaviors (typically judgments). The goal is to understand these implicit processes by making them explicit (at least for the investigator).

Consider judgments made in categorization or by using similarity. As for the former, investigators have sought to establish how and why people categorize objects in the way they do.[33] For example, people have little difficulty quickly categorizing robins or sparrows as birds. However, what about an ostrich or a penguin? Are these also birds? What is the basis for categorization? Some claim that categorization depends on similarity (a sparrow looks more like what a prototypical bird "should" look like than does a penguin). Others maintain that categorization reflects our "theories" about the way in which the world works. For example, we have developed a concept of what a bird is that has been useful to us (whether or not it is really valid in some objective sense). Perhaps categorization depends on both noticing similarity and referencing preconceived notions. And what about judgments of similarity? As noted above and in chapter 1, these can occur automatically and with alarming speed. Is it that we quickly notice which features two objects (or persons) have in common or which features distinguish them? Or are other, deeper processes involved?

The study of psycholinguistics also concerns many types of intuitive judgments that we make every day. Consider, for example, your judgment as to whether someone has produced a grammatically correct sentence in your native language.[34] You typically do not deliberately check people's speech for correct grammar. However, you cannot help but notice when people make certain errors. Similarly, we continually anticipate what others are about to say; we use context to understand words that might be ambiguous (e.g., the word *tank* immediately suggests one type of object when talking about military parades but quite another when the subject is storing water); and we are sensitive to the use of metaphors and images if these "ring true" to us.[35] (Recall the discussion of analogies to cricket and baseball.)

What is clear from these investigations is that these rules that we follow are functional. Good categories simplify life considerably and help avoid errors. For instance, once you have categorized an animal in a certain way, say, as a dog as opposed to a wolf, you can form expectations as to how that animal will behave, although, of course, you could be mistaken on occasion. It is also clear that most of these rules reflect the kinds of environments or contexts to which we have been exposed. Thus, as a native speaker of English, you possess good intuitions as to what does or does not constitute a grammatically correct or, at least, acceptable English sentence. Yet this intuitive skill may not help you much as you start to learn another language, for example, Russian.

From the viewpoint of intuition, these investigations highlight a critical issue. On the one hand, contextual variables and people's individual experiences clearly affect how they categorize objects, make judgments of similarity, infer sense from language, and make decisions. Yet at the same time the structure of the rules that they employ often transcends context. For instance, in many different judgment tasks, people's intuitive thoughts can be described by a rule that involves averaging different informational inputs.[36] (Imagine assessing job candidates on the basis of such different criteria as educational qualifications, length of prior work experience, social skills, and so on.) In addition, people from quite different cultural backgrounds often make analogous judgments of category membership and similarity. To what extent, therefore, are the rules that govern intuitive judgments "innate" or "context free" and how much do they reflect learning from experience? I shall consider this issue again in chapter 3.

The Mere-Exposure Effect

It is not hard to make the argument that most information processing in the human organism occurs at a subconscious level even though goals may be articulated at a conscious level, for example, to catch a ball that has been thrown to you. It is clearly functional for the unconscious to serve the needs of the conscious. However, what happens when the unconscious acts as though it has a mind of its own? Can it affect the organism in significant ways of which the person is unaware? Can it lead to behaviors that the person might not desire?

Imagine the following scenario. You have recently moved to a new city and have found an apartment in a convenient location. Each day, to go to work, you walk a few blocks and catch public transportation. At first, everything is new and, although exciting, also a little intimidating. However, you soon become familiar and comfortable with the neighborhood. One day, you need to buy an airplane ticket and decide to stop in at the travel agency that you pass each day on your way to and from work. The visit is a success: the service is friendly, and you are able to buy a ticket at a reasonable price. After leaving the travel agency, you note that your feelings toward your new surroundings are really quite positive.

This simple and seemingly ordinary scenario describes an important psychological process: the creation of positive affect through mere exposure. This process is known as the *mere-exposure effect*, and it was first clearly articulated by Robert Zajonc in 1968. Zajonc's work started with the observation that people seem to have greater positive affect for more frequently occurring objects. He illustrated this by examining words. For example, he presented people with lists of antonyms, that is, pairs of words that have opposite meanings, such as *forward/backward, high/low,* or *on/off.* He then asked his subjects to state which word in each pair had "the more favorable meaning, represented the more desirable object, event, state of affairs, characteristic, etc."[37] Zajonc also determined the frequency with which each word was used in English. His results showed a stunning relation between preferences and relative frequencies. For example, at least 97 percent of his subjects preferred *forward* to *backward, high* to *low,* and *on* to *off.* In English, the first of each of these pairs of words appears more frequently than the second. For example, *forward* is approximately 5.4 times more frequent than *backward.* The analogous figures for the other pairs are 1.4 and 8.3, respectively.[38]

Further demonstrations of this effect involved fake words said to be Turkish, Chinese-like characters, and photographs of students. In all three cases, the experimental manipulation involved showing subjects sets of stimuli that varied in frequency of exposure. Subsequently, subjects were shown all stimuli and asked to give judgments of affect. In the case of the words and characters, the question concerned "goodness" of meaning; for the photographs, subjects were asked how much they might like the person shown. In all cases, there was a strong relation between frequency of exposure and positive affect, that is, goodness of meaning or liking.

In a subsequent experiment, William Kunst-Wilson and Zajonc showed that, even when people's ability to identify stimuli is degraded to mere chance levels, positive affect is also a function of mere exposure.[39] Kunst-Wilson and Zajonc showed subjects irregular octagons in one-millisecond presentations and then asked them to express a preference between pairs of octagons, one second of viewing time being allowed for each judgment. As in the experiments described above, preference was highly correlated with frequency of prior exposure.

It could be pointed out that there is a large difference between living in and becoming accustomed to a new neighborhood and being presented with stimuli such as those used by Kunst-Wilson and Zajonc. And anyone who did so would be correct. However, consider the implication of Zajonc's findings. What he has shown is that people evaluate novel stimuli positively as a function of frequency of exposure. Moreover, this process occurs without intention and beyond conscious control. Why does it happen?

It is important to note that contact with the novel stimuli described above results in no negative consequences. Thus, one thing to be learned on first encountering them is that they are not harmful. Moreover, this idea is successively reinforced by each subsequent encounter. The argument favored by Zajonc is that increasing familiarity with stimuli that are not harmful induces positive affect through a simple process of learning. In other words, it is more important to learn when something new is potentially harmful or dangerous than when it is not. Thus, if something new is not perceived as negative, its default value is positive. Moreover, the more it is seen, the more positive affect is reinforced.

The implications of the mere-exposure effect are disturbing. Surely, we control our own thoughts and preferences? No, the mere-exposure effect suggests that our preferences are being constantly developed by our experience *independently* of what we may or may not want at some conscious level. This can mean that what we *really* like is much more a function of what we have experienced than of what *we think* we like.

On further reflection, the mere-exposure effect should not seem strange when considered in a larger, cultural context. People do prefer many things with which they are familiar. Consider, for example, food, literature, music, types of sports, and so on. Mere exposure to these stimuli from a young age can, as we all know, lead to strong preferences that are maintained throughout adult life.[40] The disturbing aspect of the mere-exposure effect is the realization that preferences in the short run, say, for one type of clothing over another, may be affected by familiarity as opposed to a more rational analysis of advantages and disadvantages.

On learning about the mere-exposure effect, many people relate the concept to subliminal advertising, the notion (discussed from time to time in the popular media) that cinemas can influence the purchasing behavior of audiences by flashing advertisements on the screen so quickly that people cannot register the information consciously. (Consider, e.g., advertisements for popcorn or soft drinks sold at the cinema.) The claim has been made that the content of these advertisements is processed at a subconscious (i.e., subliminal) level and that this affects subsequent purchasing behavior (e.g., audiences buy more popcorn). However, no scientific studies have ever shown an effect between subliminal advertising and immediate purchasing behavior.[41]

On the other hand, it should be clear from my discussion of the mere-exposure effect that advertising need not be subliminal to affect behavior. In the Western world, advertisements are very much a part of our lives and contribute to our cultural capital (see chap. 1). We are clearly more familiar with some products and prefer them over others (hence the power of brand names). Advertisements create associations between products or services and attractive images, and their appeal is often cast in the narrative mode (see the discussion of Bruner above). To the extent that products are not perceived as harmful or dangerous, familiarity leads to positive affect.[42]

In chapter 3, I explore in greater depth processes by which we learn without conscious awareness. Whereas the mere-exposure effect demonstrates the disturbing notion that each individual's preferences are shaped, in part, by idiosyncratic experiences, we shall also see that our knowledge and beliefs are similarly affected. In other words, our stocks of intuition are largely shaped implicitly by our interactions with our particular environments.

From Cognitive to Social Psychology

I started this section by stating that for many years scientific psychology in the twentieth century tried to avoid the topic of subconscious processes. However, having recognized that subconscious processing occurs even in what were considered to be the safe confines of the psychological laboratory, it was not long before investigators started examining the implications of subconscious processing in the social domain, that is, in interactions between people.

In a recent review of the effects of "automaticity" in everyday life, social psychologist John Bargh has written:

> It was one thing for reading or driving or detecting digits to be automatic and autonomous, able to operate without our conscious control, as the early automaticity research had shown. But it was another thing entirely when our understandings and judgments of ourselves and others were found to be not fully intentional or under our control. . . .
>
> . . . by now there are very few research phenomena in social psychology that have not been shown to occur at least partly automatically. A person's affective reactions to another individual are often immediate and unconscious: Attitudes toward social and nonsocial objects alike become active without conscious reflection or purpose within a quarter of a second after encountering the object. . . . And the emotional content of facial expressions is picked up outside conscious awareness and intent to influence perceptions of the target individual.[43]

In a further article, Bargh and Tanya Chartrand elaborate on this theme. Their thesis is that "most of a person's everyday life is determined not by their conscious intentions and deliberate choices but by mental processes that are put into motion by features of the environment that operate outside of conscious awareness and guidance."[44] As Bargh and Chartrand point out, this will at first be hard to accept. Think, however, about how you acquire automatic reactions in the physical domain, then about what happens in analogous social situations.

For example, think about how you acquire automatic reactions when you drive an automobile. There are two critical links: (*a*) your perception of what is happening on the road and (*b*) the actions that you take that reflect what you see. Although you guide your perceptual system (by keeping your eyes on the road), the process of perception clearly operates automatically. With practice, the actions that you take in reaction to what you see also become automatic in that they consume little or no conscious attention. (Recall the description of little Julie learning to walk that was provided in chap. 1.) Thus, your perceptual system (i.e., what you see) bypasses consciousness and triggers action.

Now make the translation from the acquisition of physical skills to learning to read and react to social situations or the behavior of others. Once again, there is automatic perception and—in many cases—ensuing automatic action. For example, Chartrand and Bargh demonstrate what they call *the chameleon effect.*[45] When people are engaged in social interaction, there is a tendency to mimic the mannerisms of others, for example, ways of sitting, hand gestures, and so on. People do this, it would seem, because it facilitates social communication. However, the important point is that people are unaware that these actions are triggered automatically by the mere perception of the behavior of others.

The kinds of automatic behavior described here can have many consequences, often unintended. Indeed, people may believe that they intended to take certain actions, but, in fact, their perceptions triggered those actions. Consider, for instance, someone who finds herself arguing vehemently with a friend about a personal issue. She may subsequently say and believe that it was her intention to argue her point, but, in fact, her words were triggered entirely by what her friend had said previously. Honestly stated intentions may simply reflect sense making; that is, we are simply trying to make sense of our own behavior.

Other phenomena can take the form of self-fulfilling processes; for example, you automatically (and unknowingly) adopt a certain tone of voice on noticing particular facial expressions. This behavior, in turn, affects that of the person with whom you are speaking, and so on.

In a fascinating book, social psychologist Robert Cialdini describes ways in which people can influence others by explicitly exploiting certain kinds of automatic reactions that tend to be elicited in social situations.[46] For example, Cialdini points out that most people do not like to feel that they are indebted to others and that, if a stranger unexpectedly does something for you, there is an immediate desire to repay the kindness. It is as though we possess social scenarios or schemata that are automatically triggered by the actions of others. Thus, for example, when two parties are engaged in negotiations and one makes even a small concession, the other usually makes a similarly conciliatory counteroffer. As Cialdini points out, con artists and salespeople have systematically exploited this side of human behavior for years. In airports, for example, travelers are sometimes induced to give charitable contributions to persons who give them flowers without asking for anything in return. (While the travelers usually throw the flowers away, the discarded flowers are not wasted. They are collected and offered to other travelers.)

Two Important Implications

In summary, intuition has not been the focus of direct attention within the cognitive or information-processing approach in psychology. However, working within these paradigms, psychologists have been forced to face the fact that much information processing does occur at a subconscious level. It therefore involves what I have defined as *intuition*. Moreover, this affects behavior in important ways.

This brief survey of the literature has at least two important implications for educating intuition. The first centers on the notion that automatic thoughts and actions can be described as either *right* or *wrong*. In other words, after the fact—and when provided with appropriate information—we can determine whether particular thoughts and actions were appropriate to the circumstances. The implication is that means need to be found to increase the ratio of right to wrong judgments. As I demonstrate in chapter 3, this depends critically on understanding the types of experiences that have honed automatic responses in the form of thoughts and actions.

Second, the literature also suggests that people may not be able to suppress intuitions in the form of automatic thoughts. As a case in point, consider prejudices based on category membership, for example, race, gender, and so on. The literature clearly highlights the fact that, through passive observation, people can acquire distinct likes and dislikes and that familiarity influences affect (the mere-exposure effect). In fact, many stereotypes are acquired in precisely this manner. However, once people become aware that they harbor certain stereotypes, steps can be taken to ensure that behavior is not governed by them. In fact, programs exist to promote awareness of stereotypes and to combat their negative effects.

I maintain that most people hold some stereotypic attitudes and that simply knowing that these attitudes are inappropriate does not automatically render them powerless. In fact, it is probably impossible to suppress some stereotypes that emerge from the operation of the *tacit* system. However, it is possible to learn to use the *deliberate* system to avoid acting on tacit prejudices. In other words, it is important to know when intuitions may be erroneous and to use deliberate thoughts to overcome perceptions that might otherwise seem to be correct. After all, I do see balls rolling uphill at the electric brae. But, given my trust in the law of gravity (a trust based both on my experience in other situations and on my knowledge of physics), I would bet a lot of money that they are not, in fact, rolling uphill. A greater ability to use our deliberate systems is what distinguishes humans from other animals. Using our deliberate systems *appropriately* is a mark of intelligence among humans.

The Neuroscientific Approach

As noted above, the analogy between the human brain and the computer has provided a useful tool for thinking about how people think. At one level, there is the abstract concept of information processing. At another level, what happens in a computer can be conceptualized in terms of physical processes. "Bits" are binary and can be turned on and off by electrical impulses; memory can be "addressed"; computational capacity and the ability to run different programs depend on the amount of memory available; caches exist that can be adjusted to allow for different sizes of operating memory; and so on.

When dealing with the human organism, however, it is not so easy to imagine information processing in actual physical terms. We would like to be able to draw a diagram of the brain that shows how everything is "wired." However, it is not clear that the "wiring" of the brain actually resembles that of a computer. Moreover, there is so much that we would need to know about the brain before we could actually construct the analogue to a wiring diagram.

Over the years, scientists have not been shy about attempting to identify which parts of the brain control which functions. In the nineteenth century, for example, the "science" (or rather pseudoscience) of phrenology established a precise map of where different functions were supposed to occur in the brain. On the basis of this mapping, claims were made that different bumps on the skull represented different capacities for thinking. Thus, it was claimed, individual profiles could be established by feeling the relative sizes of bumps on a person's head. Fortunately, the twentieth century was marked by better science and less dramatic claims.

As with work in cognitive psychology, the goal of most research on the underlying biology and neurology of the brain has not been to elucidate intuition per se. However, the knowledge gained as a result of such research helps us understand the biological system within which intuition operates and thus leads to implications for its education. To explore this system, I shall examine four topics. These are, first, the interconnections between brain, body, and mind; second, insights from the theory of evolution; third, attempts to understand how the brain functions; and, fourth, links between observable behaviors and what is known about brain functions.

The Brain-Mind-Body Link

Most psychologists work at the level of observable behaviors and do not use biological facts about the brain except in a fairly rough manner, for example, assumptions about limits on short-term or working memory. Moreover, given the current impossibility of knowing precisely how, in biological terms, the brain works, an analogical approach has proved quite useful. Nonetheless, recent interest in the underlying biology of the brain has helped both raise and clarify some important conceptual issues, including what the brain is, what the mind is, and what we mean by *state of consciousness*.

An early and attractive idea was the so-called homunculus theory of the mind. This is the notion that within each of us there is a "little person" in charge of directing information processing. In one sense, this person can be likened to the captain of a ship—standing on the bridge (at the top of a hierarchical system), receiving information, and giving orders. Unfortunately, careful examination of this theory reveals that it implies an infinite regress. To see this, ask the question, Who is directing the little person supposedly in charge of information processing? Another little person inside the first? If so, who is directing this second person? A third little person inside the second? Who then directs the third? And so on.

Today, theorists have abandoned the homunculus theory and instead conceptualize the body or organism as a unitary but complicated system of systems that has as its goal the survival of the organism (see pp. 52–54 below).[47] The tasks that these systems perform can be thought of as both internal and external. Internally, the systems must communicate with each other to handle the functioning and maintenance of the body. Externally, the systems must deal with adapting to the demands of the environment. There must, of course, also be coordination between internally and externally oriented systems.

For example, imagine that a person wants to cross a street. In this case, externally oriented perceptual systems take in information that leads to a judgment as to when it is safe to cross. Once this decision is taken, internal systems coordinate the actions that make walking in a particular direction possible. Also while walking, externally oriented systems continue to scan information that is useful to the organism—in order, perhaps, to avoid bumping into someone crossing the street in the opposite direction.

This is an example of something that happens at a particular time. But it should be clear that the body's systems are constantly monitoring a large variety of processes. Take, for example, the process by which the organism becomes aware of hunger. Here, the blood sugar level drops below a certain threshold, and information is then sent to different parts of the brain to trigger the feeling of hunger, which can lead to a conscious decision to seek food. Many other processes work in a similar fashion. What should be clear is that the organism—or systems within the body—is constantly involved in a great deal of automatic information processing. *Indeed, conscious information processing is the exception.*

Let us now consider the brain itself. While physically it may be one organ, it is more accurately thought of as a system of systems that perform different functions. Moreover, some functions—such as vision—involve different parts of the brain, that is, different systems and subsystems.[48]

What I want to emphasize is that each person is a *single organism composed of many systems and subsystems* that interact in performing tasks that regulate internal states and in providing adaptive responses to external demands. The brain, therefore, is a system within the overall system and is itself composed of many systems and subsystems that perform different functions. What, then, one might ask, is the *mind?*

Above, I equated consciousness at any given point in time with the information present in short-term or working memory. (See chap. 1 as well as pp. 39–41 above.) Clearly, however, not all the information stored in long-term memory can be brought into consciousness at any given time. On pragmatic grounds, therefore, I define *mind* as consisting of *the information that currently resides in short-term or working memory plus all the information that could be accessed in long-term memory.* It is important to note, however, that information must be available to working memory if it is to be considered part of the mind.

We can therefore describe the mind—or what is in or can be brought into consciousness—as consisting of information. However, this does not mean that all information processed in the body is in the mind. In fact, because most information processing is carried out unconsciously, most information processed by the body is *not* in the mind. The genes, for example, provide information that regulates such processes as physical growth, but this information processing is clearly achieved without conscious awareness and does not involve the mind.

Another issue raised by recent interest in the underlying biology of the brain is the form that information takes when it is in consciousness, that is, in the mind. The view used to be held that information in the human mind was strictly verbal. However, such a conception now seems too restrictive. If it were true, it would, for example, preclude infants and some primates from having states of consciousness (a position that cannot be squared with the facts). It would also exclude feelings—or the awareness of emotional states—from consciousness. While we can say what form information does *not* take in the mind, the most that we can currently say about what form it *does* take is that it is represented in the mind in the form of symbols. Much of the meaning that these symbols carry comes from an individual's past experience and from attempts to interpret current experience. Meaning may also be facilitated by innate tendencies (see chaps. 3 and 4).

Insights from the Theory of Evolution

In thinking about intuition, it is important to ask how we, as a species, came to develop the kinds of decision-making and action tendencies that we currently possess. Why do the systems that constitute our brains have their current form?

Several key ideas from the theory of evolution are relevant to this issue.[49] The first is the notion of survival. An organism is motivated to survive and to make sure that its species survives. Second, an organism evolves by finding adaptive solutions to the problems that it faces in its particular niche in the environment. Solutions are adopted if they increase the chances of survival. Those species that find and retain good solutions increase their chances of survival relative to those that do not.

Solutions that are adopted have two important characteristics. First, they are necessarily solutions to problems faced in the past. Evolution does not involve foresight; solutions are not developed for environmental circumstances that will arise only in the future. Second, evolution does not work by completely redesigning systems each time adaptations are required. Instead, adjustments are made to existing structures. In other words, evolution does not abandon existing structures; it adjusts them incrementally until current demands are met. One way to think of evolution is as a process marked by layers of development.

Many studies have examined the physical characteristics of brains across the entire phylogenetic scale. Comparisons have been made between the brains of fishes, reptiles, different animals, and primates, including, of course, humans. One resulting notion, first propagated by Paul MacLean in the 1950s, is that we humans have a *limbic* brain system that arose quite early in our evolution and that handles many visceral functions as well as emotional tasks.[50] According to MacLean, this limbic brain system is responsible for such behaviors as feeding, flight from danger, fighting, and reproduction and for producing reactions in an automatic mode. Joseph LeDoux has commented on MacLean's work as follows:

> MacLean has continued to develop and embellish the visceral brain/limbic system theory over the years. In 1970 he introduced the theory of the triune brain. The forebrain, according to MacLean, has gone through three stages of evolution: reptilian, paleomammalian, and neomammalian. He notes, "there results a remarkable linkage of three cerebrotypes which are radically different in chemistry structure and which in an evolutionary sense are eons apart. There exists, so to speak, a hierarchy of three-brains-in-one, or what I call, for short, a *triune brain.*" Each of the cerebrotypes, according to MacLean, has its own special kind of intelligence, its own special memory, its own sense of time and space, and its own motor and other functions. In humans, other primates, and advanced mammals, all three brains exist. Lower mammals lack the neomammalian brain, but have the paleomammalian and reptilian brain. All other vertebrate creatures (birds, reptiles, amphibians, and fishes) have only the reptilian brain. The paleomammalian brain, present in all mammals, is essentially the limbic system. The triune brain thus puts the limbic system into a broader evolutionary context for behaviors and mental functions of all levels of complexity.[51]

At one level, MacLean's concept of the triune brain is attractive. One can almost see evolution laying down different layers of systems that help deal with different problems. However, according to LeDoux, several details proposed by MacLean have subsequently turned out to be quite wrong. One is that some creatures that are quite primitive (on the phylogenetic scale) do have parts that meet the criteria of the neocortex, which only primates (including humans) and some advanced animals are, according to MacLean, supposed to have. Another is that parts of the human brain system that MacLean supposes regulate only the emotions have been shown to be involved in higher mental processes as well.

With the benefit of hindsight, we should not be too hard on MacLean. His ideas were consistent with both evolutionary theory and the evidence available to him. As noted by others,[52] a problem with evolutionary theory is that it is often possible to engage in imaginative reconstructions of how existing structures might have evolved. It is thus important to recognize that, while ideas borrowed from the theory of evolution can give us a general idea of how different brain systems came into existence, we are still a long way from understanding many of the particulars of the process.

Understanding How the Brain Functions

Currently, we know a great deal about the anatomy of the brain in the sense that the different parts have been identified, comparisons between the brains of different species have been made, and so on. We also know that the human brain is complex. Furthermore, we think that we know how some parts of it function. Overall, however, its complexity is baffling.

What we do know about the brain comes from several sources: observations of how the behavior of people who have suffered damage in certain areas of the brain has been affected; observations of what happens when certain parts of the brain are stimulated electrically; imaging studies that can indicate which parts of the brain are most active when people are involved in certain types of activities; and studies reporting the effects on animals of having certain parts of the brain removed surgically.

Some of the results of this research have now passed into what might be called common knowledge. For example, consider the so-called split-brain research that has led to the expressions *right-brain* and *left-brain thinking*.

In split-brain research, the same surgical procedure was performed on all subjects involved in order to attempt to control epilepsy.[53] That is, the nerve connections between the left and the right hemispheres of the brain were severed. Now, objects that are in a person's left visual field are processed in the right hemisphere, whereas objects in the right visual field are processed in the left hemisphere. Thus, in split-brain patients, obscuring objects in the left (right) visual field means that they cannot be processed or seen by the right (left) hemisphere. The experimental paradigm consisted of presenting stimuli to subjects that could be perceived only by one of the two hemispheres and then eliciting responses to see what information was available to the hemisphere from which the stimulus had been obscured. Since the two hemispheres could not communicate directly (the nerve connections had been severed), the intriguing question was whether and how one hemisphere could become aware of what the other knew.

Because language functions are typically located in the left hemisphere of the brain, it was not surprising to find that subjects could talk only about objects that the left hemisphere knew about. However, if the left hand—which is linked to the right hemisphere—was allowed to touch the obscured objects, then subjects did show awareness of what was known to the left hemisphere. The specific experimental procedure involved showing the picture of an object that was visible only to the subject's left hemisphere. The subject was then asked to touch several objects with the left hand and identify which had been seen previously. Since the left hand is linked to the right hemisphere, this was a way of asking the subject to identify an object by means of one hemisphere (the right) even though that object had been seen only by the other (the left). In further experiments, it has been found that the emotional connotations of words read by only one of the two hemispheres can be transferred to the other.

As indicated above, much effort has gone into identifying which parts of the brain are involved in which types of processing. We now know, for example, that language ability is typically located in the left hemisphere; that the sensory cortex is heavily involved in perception and short-term memory storage; that the prefrontal cortex exists only in primates, is particularly large in humans, and deals with processes of working memory and attention; and that the hippocampus is the seat of much long-term explicit memory.[54] We also know that some functions, for example, vision, seem to draw on several parts of the brain and thus that not all functions can be isolated, that is, pinned down as occurring in one or another part of the brain. Finally, we know a great deal about how connections are made between cells at the molecular level, and we are learning how certain drugs can facilitate or hinder the transmission of information between cells via those connections.

As it turned out, the tidy picture of a triune brain, in which different levels deal with different kinds of problems, is far too simple. Instead, it seems, there is considerable interaction between the various brain systems. It is to this topic that I now turn.

Observable Behavior and Brain Functions

In chapter 1, I stated that the outcomes of intuitive thought "*are reached with little apparent effort, and typically without conscious awareness. They involve little or no conscious deliberation*" (p. 14). Two sets of studies speak directly to this.

The first concerns the nature of automatic reactions to stimuli that invoke fear. As an example, imagine walking down a city street and suddenly hearing the bark of a vicious-sounding dog close behind you. The typical reaction is fear. Without thinking, you move sharply away from the sound of the dog and probably look to see where the sound is coming from. Indeed, this is precisely the kind of automatic perception-action link described previously (see pp. 46–47 above), where perception (in this case, of a sound) triggers immediate and involuntary action.

Imagine now that you see that the dog is securely tied and cannot move more than a yard or so and that it cannot therefore reach you. At this point, you relax. You know that dogs that are securely tied cannot bite you if you maintain your distance. But it takes a few moments for you to recover from the strong emotion of fear that you felt.

Joseph LeDoux and his colleagues have made extensive studies of the way in which the brain processes fear. The key is the amygdala, a small, peanut-sized organ deep in the brain that is central to many fear-related behaviors. The amygdala is connected to, among other things, the sensory thalamus, from which it receives direct information about the external world (e.g., the sound of the dog), to the nervous system (which allows the organism to take evasive action), and to the higher-level cortical regions of the brain. External information that reaches the amygdala also reaches the cortical regions, but by a different and somewhat slower route. The key point is that the amygdala acts quickly to interpret incoming information whereas the cortical region performs a slower but more thorough analysis of the situation.

From an evolutionary perspective, the operation of the amygdala can be readily interpreted. Fear signals danger, and it is better to react and move quickly out of the way than to stay and analyze the situation. Of particular interest is that, in humans, the amygdala and the cortical region work as a pair in handling fear-provoking situations: first there is an emotional reaction, which is then tempered by more deliberative thinking; that is, both the tacit and the deliberate systems are involved. Of further interest are the findings that emotional memories of fear are strongly represented in the amygdala and that there are more paths leading from the amygdala to the cortex than vice versa. Once a particular fear becomes established, it is difficult to overcome it by the means of conscious thought processes. Consider, for example, people who suffer from a fear of heights. They know full well that the fear is irrational in that they are most unlikely to lose their balance. But this knowledge does not stop them from experiencing fear when, for example, standing near the edge of a cliff. I will return to this when discussing the dual roles of emotion and cognition in producing responses (see pp. 60–65 below).

LeDoux points out that what we call the *emotion* of fear performs a function for the organism; that is, it initiates an appropriate response in the face of danger. It should not be presumed, however, that all states that we call *emotions* operate in the same way in the brain because their functions can differ. Thus, different emotions are probably supported by different brain systems. Nonetheless, LeDoux makes the point that, "at the neural level, each emotional unit can be thought of as consisting of a set of inputs, an appraisal mechanism, and a set of outputs." He goes on to state that the appraisal mechanisms are either programmed by evolution to detect what he calls *natural triggers* or, over time, acquire *learned triggers* that initiate a set of actions. Moreover, "because different kinds of problems of survival have different trigger stimuli and require different kinds of responses to deal with them, different neural systems are devoted to them."[55] In a more recent review of the literature linking intuitive responses to parts of the brain, Matthew Lieberman has suggested that, while the amygdala is involved in the automatic appraisal of negative affective stimuli, it is the basal ganglia that are involved with positive affective stimuli.[56]

The second series of studies is reported in a fascinating book by Antonio Damasio that discusses the relation between rational and emotional behavior.[57] The starting point is Damasio's observations of the behavior of people with damage in certain cortical areas of the brain (i.e., the evolutionarily newer and more "rational" component). What is interesting—and baffling—about these people is that, although they appear (remarkably) to have all their intellectual abilities intact, they are unable to make good personal and social decisions. For example, Elliot, one of Damasio's patients, suffered brain damage as the result of the surgical removal of a tumor. Before his illness, Elliot had been successful in both his business and his family life. After surgery, even though tests showed that his higher-level intellectual skills remained virtually unimpaired, Elliot was incapable of making many ordinary decisions, working slowly and failing to understand the context in which he was acting. This inefficiency led to lost jobs, failed relationships, and bankruptcy. On the surface, however, Elliot still seemed normal.

After considerable observation, Damasio reached the conclusion that Elliot had essentially "flat" emotional reactions to all that happened to him and others. In other words, although Elliot's brain damage was in the cortical or "rational" area, it seemed as though contact with the "emotional" part of the brain, which is thought to lie in other regions, had been

severed. And, Damasio concluded, it was the inability to access his emotions that led to many of Elliot's bad decisions in real life.

On the basis of these and related observations, Damasio formed
what he called the *somatic marker hypothesis*. In many ways, this is similar
to what LeDoux calls a *learned trigger*. The key idea is that, through experience with the world, people learn which emotional reactions are appropriate. This learning takes place implicitly, however, rather than explicitly,
and, over time, people develop a repertoire of actions that are triggered by
what they observe (see also chap. 3). More specifically, in the domain of
personal and social decisions, Damasio argues that people develop a capacity to recognize signals, that is, markers that warn them to be cautious.
According to Damasio, "The automated signal protects you against future
losses, without further ado, and then allows you *to choose from among fewer
alternatives*."[58] In other words, the signals warn people to avoid certain alternatives.

To test this hypothesis in an experimental setting, Damasio and his
colleagues devised a gambling task.[59] They compared the reactions of subjects who had experienced specific precortical lesions with a control group
of non-brain-damaged subjects in an experiment that required choices involving different sets of cards. In brief, subjects were presented with four
sets of cards and asked to draw cards from whichever sets they wished. Each
time they took a card, they received a positive or negative reward, that is, a
payoff. However, the risks associated with the different sets of cards varied.
Some had both higher gains and higher losses than the others. Subjects
were not given any prior information characterizing the rewards to be obtained from the various sets of cards and thus could learn only by sampling.

Separate tests of cognitive ability showed that the brain-damaged
subjects did not suffer from impaired analytic capacities relative to the
control group. Yet these subjects adopted riskier choice strategies and were
not as successful as the control subjects. The behavior of the two groups of
subjects also differed in three other ways. First, the controls exhibited
greater hesitation than the brain-damaged subjects did before making
choices involving the riskier sets of cards, even before they knew that these
choices were in fact riskier. Second, the controls exhibited heightened
physical reactions—as measured by skin conductance responses—when
making the riskier choices, whereas the brain-damaged subjects showed
no differences in their responses across sets of cards. Third, their choice
patterns indicated that the controls seemed to understand the differences
between the sets of cards before they could articulate the nature of these
differences. The brain-damaged subjects, on the other hand, showed no
evidence of such insight.

In interpreting the experimental results, Damasio and his colleagues talk about a decision-making process that occurs automatically in the control subjects and guides them, at least initially, in making wise decisions. One fascinating aspect of these results is that they suggest that rational, deliberative thinking is guided by some kind of underlying emotional sensing of situations. This is very much how many people think of intuition.

Summary and Implications

I have presented the view that, like the body, the brain is part of a single organism. This organism can be thought of as a system of systems and subsystems that, among other things, is involved in information-processing activities that support the needs of the organism. The mind, it was argued, is represented by the information that is actually in and that can be accessed by working or short-term memory. I further stated that it was useful to think of the human brain as being at the *current* end point of evolution and that it was important to realize that the adaptations fostered by evolution are in respect of problems faced in the past. Also, evolution typically works, not by constructing new solutions to problems, but by adjusting and building on current mechanisms.

Whereas we really know so very little about the operations of the brain, the last decades have provided greater insights into its complexities. One fact is clear. Many processes of which we have no conscious awareness affect what we see and learn and how we react to the world. In addition, by examining the behavior of people who suffered specific types of brain damage as well as observing the behavior of animals whose brains have been surgically treated, scientists have gained some insights into the automatic nature of emotions such as fear as well as suggesting what might be considered evidence of human intuition.

From the perspective of educating intuition, it is important to recognize the complexity of the human organism and the extent to which it already possesses inherent processes and response tendencies. Moreover, most of these tendencies are probably functional today even if they first evolved to resolve problems that arose in the past. For example, a system that warns people of potential danger may be just as valuable today in facing many of the physical complexities of urban life as it was for the dangers faced by our ancestors who were hunter-gatherers many thousands of years ago (e.g., stepping out of the way of a moving object). On the other hand, it is also likely to be deficient in that there are dangers for which its inherent properties cannot provide adequate warning (e.g., the hazards of

X-rays or carbon monoxide). At the same time, it is important to recall that evolution has worked by adjusting existing structures incrementally rather than just abandoning and replacing the previous systems. To educate intuition, therefore, it seems that a successful strategy will involve teaching people how to modify what they already do as opposed to replacing their existing processes by entirely new ones. It also suggests an incremental approach.

Intuition and Emotion

As noted in chapter 1, the notion of intuition is invariably related to feelings and emotions. Moreover, as indicated above, there is considerable evidence that emotions do play a key role in intuition. To clarify the issues, I propose to discuss three topics: What are the distinctions between feelings and emotions? What is the relation between cognition and emotion? How do feelings and emotions affect information processing? Given the close link between emotion and intuition, I also investigate whether emotions can be educated.

Distinguishing Feelings, Emotions, and Affect

Many people use the words *feelings, emotions,* and *affect* interchangeably. I think that this is a mistake.

An emotion is, first and foremost, a physical, visceral phenomenon with strong behavioral correlates. For example, when you experience fear, your heart rate increases, and you make facial gestures involuntarily. When you are joyful, your facial muscles relax. Great sadness and great happiness can both induce tears.

Interestingly, the physical expressions that accompany emotions are universal across human cultures in the sense that the same kinds of physical changes in the body are observed with the same emotions in all cultures. In addition, both humans and other primates are observed to make similar gestures when, for example, they are in states of fear. Although it is true that some people, and particularly some cultures, do not show strong emotional reactions to particular events, there is good evidence that the moderation observed represents learned behavior.[60]

Affect is like emotion in that it reflects a physical state. The difference is that affect typically creates less strong reactions than does emotion. It is more "subtle" than emotion and related to a person's general state at a given time. In this latter sense, *affect* is a synonym for *mood.*

Like emotion, however, affect can be triggered by reactions to specific stimuli. Thus, as noted above, objects can acquire positive affect through simple exposure (the mere-exposure effect). More generally, affect is associated with almost everything that we have ever experienced. It is hard, for example, to think of any object, person, or experience in life that does not evoke some degree of affect.

Feelings, I claim, differ from emotions and affect in that, whereas emotions and affect are not necessarily present in consciousness, feelings are. (Consciousness, it will be recalled, is defined as the information that is present in short-term or working memory.) What makes the relation between feelings, emotions, and affect complicated to understand is that *emotions and affect give rise to feelings.* In other words, you cannot have feelings *without an awareness* of being in some particular emotional or affective state. This means, of course, that you can experience emotions or affect without feelings but not the reverse.

Let me illustrate these points with two examples. First, consider how emotions create feelings. For instance, you are sitting quietly in your office, and you suddenly hear a loud noise that you cannot identify. You experience the emotion fear in a visceral sense (your heart rate changes), and you also *feel* frightened in the sense that you are aware of your sense of the emotion fear.

Second, consider emotion without feeling. You are talking to a friend when the topic turns to a subject that angers you. Your friend notices (although you do not) that you have become quite excited (some might say angry) and that you have started talking much more quickly. She tells you not to get so excited. Since you have not been monitoring your own behavior and are therefore not consciously aware of these changes, you reply that you are not excited. But, in fact, you are. You are experiencing an emotion without conscious awareness, that is, without that emotion stimulating the usual accompanying feelings. (Incidentally, if you think that such a scenario could not apply to you, surely you have been in the friend's situation and recognized such behavior in others.)

Now try to imagine having a feeling without having previously experienced some emotion or affect. Given my definitions of *emotions, affect,* and *feelings,* this is, I think, not possible. It is true that we can experience feelings without being able to identify the underlying emotion or affect. However, that is a separate matter and will be discussed below. The reason, I believe, that people confuse emotions, affect, and feelings is that, *in one's own awareness* of personal experiences, they are all highly correlated.

Emotion and affect can, therefore, be important inputs to intuitive thought in the sense that they can induce responses without corresponding awareness. Feelings can also be experienced as intuitions in that we are unaware of what precisely triggered the underlying emotion or affect. Moreover, precisely because feelings cannot always be reduced to rational arguments, their outputs are often experienced as intuitions when we become aware of the presence of those outputs in consciousness.

The Relation between Cognition and Emotion

I have referred above to the *cognitive revolution* in psychology. One of the consequences of this change in the scientific paradigm of psychology was to place an emphasis on explaining behavior in cognitive terms—often in cases where people thought that behavior was not cognitive in origin.

In 1962, Stanley Schachter and Jerome Singer published a paper in which they laid the foundations for cognitive interpretations of emotional phenomena. Their starting point was the notion that, whereas people may be aware that they have been aroused emotionally, they may not know what kind of emotional response is appropriate and may therefore look to social cues to interpret their feelings. In other words, cognition is explicitly used to give meaning to emotions. In their experiments, Schachter and Singer were indeed able to induce different emotions—or moods—in subjects by means of a combination of injections of adrenaline (to stimulate physical emotional symptoms) and exposure to social cues (e.g., being placed in pleasant or unpleasant situations).

The Schachter-Singer paper was considered as having established the important role that cognition plays in emotion. However, this position was challenged in 1980 by Robert Zajonc. Zajonc, it will be recalled, had established that people could form unconscious preferences (the mere-exposure effect). From this position, he argued that, because affective reactions were the root cause of preferences, emotion could be stimulated in the absence of cognition or, as he put it, that "affect has primacy." A spirited debate ensued.[61]

When they are not ridiculous, extreme positions in science—as in everyday life—tend to attract disproportionate attention. My own view is that it is unlikely that evolutionary forces accorded primacy to either affect or cognition in humans and that it is more fruitful to investigate their joint contribution to behavior. The sheer complexity of the brain suggests that, for important activities, the human organism has developed multiple systems for achieving certain functions and that we should expect some redundancy.

In 1993, Carroll Izard outlined a framework for the activation of emotion that explicitly recognizes different levels of information processing. In this framework, processes that are neural, sensorimotor, affective, or cognitive in origin can activate emotional experience. Moreover, these four levels are described as forming a loosely organized hierarchy. The neural system is at the base of the hierarchy and is the most simple and rapid. The cognitive system is at the top and is the most complex and versatile.

Izard laid a foundation for understanding that multiple paths may determine our feelings. Fear, for example, could be the result of LeDoux's natural or learned triggers, and Damasio's somatic markers might also be involved. Moreover, there is no reason why some affective states might not be interpreted cognitively exactly as Schachter and Singer described. Finally, as suggested by Zajonc, we can have emotion or affect without feelings and make choices guided by preferences even though we remain ignorant of the origins of such preferences.

How Do Feelings and Emotions Affect Information Processing?

Above I have discussed emotions and feelings as outputs; that is, my emphasis has been on how emotions and feelings arise. I now consider another question: How does being in a particular state affect information processing? For example, does being angry, joyful, or sad affect the way in which you make a decision, and, if so, are you aware that it does? A great deal of significant research has resulted from attempts to answer this question.

Much work has been done on the interaction of emotional and affective states and types of information processing. One investigator, Alice Isen, has conducted many detailed studies of the effects of mild positive moods on behavior.[62] Perhaps one of the most interesting features of her studies is how easy it is to induce mild positive moods in subjects and to affect their behavior in ways of which they are unaware. In her experiments, Isen typically obtains effects even when the mood-inducing treatment is as innocuous as giving subjects some colored candy. Now, admittedly, college students participating in a psychology experiment may not be expecting colored candy, and thus the effect could be the result of surprise. However, the outcome is also surprising to most first-time readers of Isen's work and, in itself, germane to the issue of how affect is generated and feelings arise.[63]

In summarizing her own work, Isen states clearly that affect alone does not determine what decisions people will make. Rather, affect can influence what people think about, and this clearly also reflects the context in which they find themselves. In general, people with positive affect tend to be more relaxed and open to new ideas and may therefore be more effective problem solvers. On the other hand, staying in a good mood can become one of their goals, and they may avoid actions that could endanger this.[64]

James Bettman, John Payne, and Mary Frances Luce have conducted several studies that examine the effect of the presence of negative emotion or affect on the process of choice.[65] Their general argument is that, when choosing, people trade off accuracy and effort; that is, when concerned about choosing accurately, people use strategies that involve examining more information and, as such, require more mental effort to execute. On the other hand, when accuracy is less important, it is sacrificed in order to avoid mental effort. The presence of possible negative emotion affects this trade-off. As an example, consider a situation in which resources are limited and a doctor must decide which of several needy children will obtain medical attention. In such situations—where accuracy is important—Bettman, Payne, and Luce have found that people do engage in extensive information processing. However, this processing is conducted in a way that copes indirectly with the negative emotion—by trying, for example, to process the information in a way that avoids directly confronting distressing decisions (e.g., avoiding explicit assessments of how much money would be saved were a child not given the benefit of specific medical attention).[66]

Other investigators have also researched how affective states influence the kinds of information-processing strategies that people use. Joseph Forgas, for example, has proposed a theory to account for the interaction between processing style and affect in social judgments.[67] According to Forgas, "affect infusion" in judgment is more likely to occur when judgment tasks induce "heuristic or substantive processing" as opposed to "direct access or motivated judgments." In other words, viewing these information-processing styles on a continuum ranging from the intuitive to the analytic, affect is more likely to influence intuitive than analytic modes of information processing.

In an intriguing study involving subjects who were depressed, Seymour Epstein and his colleagues found a result reminiscent of Damasio's.[68] Specifically, they investigated the decision-making strategies of clinically depressed and control subjects under two conditions: the first in trivial laboratory situations, the second in more consequential situations. Depressed subjects were found to make more optimal decisions than the controls in the trivial conditions but not in the more realistic circumstances. The depressed subjects also reported engaging in less systematic or rational information processing than the controls in the course of everyday life. Depression is clearly an emotional disorder, and, as in Damasio's studies, it seems to interfere with the ability to make good use of one's rational or analytic faculties in consequential situations.

Similarly, other studies have demonstrated interactions between mood and styles of processing, specifically, automatic and controlled processes.[69] Generally, positive mood appears to induce more automatic processing; negative moods are associated with more effortful or controlled strategies.

Finally, Paul Slovic and his colleagues have argued that, in addition to influencing information processing, affect is also used as an intuitive means of making judgments and choices.[70] They advance the idea that, because people have affective reactions to different stimuli, affect actually drives choice automatically. For example, imagine that at dinner you are faced with choosing between two dishes and that one induces positive affect whereas the other does not. In this case, a quick choice is made automatically to select the first dish. Of course, in this particular case, your affective reaction may be overruled by the deliberate system (you are controlling your diet!). But, in many other cases, affect will determine choice.[71] In chapter 5, I shall discuss intuitive choice processes in greater detail.

Educating Emotions

Emotions and affect are clearly part of our intuitive processes, and this therefore raises the question of whether they can be educated. As noted above, emotions are physical reactions to environmental stimuli, and people may or may not be aware of the extent to which they are experiencing different emotional or affective states. Moreover, emotions are triggered subconsciously and typically cannot be produced at will.[72] Actors, for example, have great difficulty learning how to simulate different emotional states, and audiences are usually quick to notice when they are not successful.[73] This suggests, therefore, that it is impractical for people to attempt to teach themselves to have emotional reactions.

On the other hand, and as noted earlier, emotions can be subject to cognitive interpretation. Thus, it is logical to believe that people can learn to interpret their own emotional states more accurately. My view—to be presented in chapter 7—is that people can and should learn to treat their emotions *as data*,[74] and I will suggest means of doing just this. Clearly, accurate insights into your emotional state can go a long way toward enabling more effective behavior. For example, you may well become angry when another driver takes what you thought was going to be your parking spot. However, before taking action, your deliberate system should weigh the costs and benefits of expressing that anger to the other driver.

Finally, recent years have seen great interest in the topic of *emotional intelligence*.[75] Although this concept is quite broad, a major component of it involves the ability to infer the emotional states of others and acting on the basis of this information. As such, emotional intelligence is typically an intuitive process, but, as I shall also discuss in chapter 7, it can be educated.

Concluding Comments

As noted in chapter 1, the concept of intuition has not been central to psychology. Yet, on reviewing the different perspectives provided in this chapter, it is clear that psychologists do have a lot to say that is germane to the topic.

Like all other human endeavors, psychology is subject to fashion and the zeitgeist. During the first half of the twentieth century, scientific psychology looked down on any attempts to describe internal, mental processes and instead concentrated on describing the relations between observable stimuli and responses, that is, what was seen and how the organism reacted.

The cognitive revolution in the 1950s rescued psychology from this impasse by recognizing that unobservable mental processes might affect behavior. Furthermore, the computer analogy provided a powerful means of describing cognitive behavior—in terms of both language and models. This, in turn, has led to exploring more explicitly processes that operate automatically and without conscious awareness. More recently, the cognitive revolution itself has been questioned as psychologists have looked to evidence of a more biological nature that has been suggested by both neuroscience and evolutionary theory. In addition, there is an increasing awareness of the role that emotion and affect play in making judgments and choices.

The various approaches reviewed in this chapter have important implications for educating intuition. First, a great deal of evidence suggests that people can and do process information in either (what I have called) the *tacit* or the *deliberate* mode. Moreover, the tacit system accounts for most mental activity.

Second, the tacit system operates *automatically*. It works at a subconscious level and consumes little or no attention. Intuitions are outputs of the tacit system. They are largely functional and greatly simplify human existence. In fact, it is hard to imagine how we could function if all our thoughts were deliberate. On the other hand, there are cases in which the outputs of the tacit system may not advance our best interests. For example, we may react foolishly on making a new acquaintance by automatically assuming that certain stereotypes hold true in this particular instance. Such errors can, however, be overcome by using the deliberate system, thereby suggesting that one key to educating intuition lies in educating the deliberate system to make appropriate interventions.

Third, the tacit system is the result of a long evolutionary process, and thus it seems hard to imagine how we could ever totally suppress its outputs. Instead, we should think of ways in which we can capitalize on our naturally occurring reactions. The emotional system, for example, is a powerful source of information. However, instead of acting immediately on the emotions that we feel, we can stop to ask what they mean, that is, start to treat our emotions as data as opposed to instructions.

Finally, I believe that cognitive psychology is today at an exciting stage in its development. In particular, there is growing awareness across all modern approaches that information processing below the level of consciousness has a far greater effect than has been previously realized. Freud, it should be added, said as much over a hundred years ago. A great deal more data, however, are available today than in Freud's time, and, as will be seen in subsequent chapters, Freud's and similar views of the subconscious can no longer be justified. Nevertheless, like Freud, I believe that we can use deliberate thought processes, or reason, to improve the outputs of the tacit system, or the subconscious.

CHAPTER 3

Acquiring Intuitions

C hapter 2 reviewed different psychological perspectives relating to intuition and, in particular, discussed several aspects of the tacit system of information processing. The goal was to gain insight into how intuition might be educated. In this chapter, I address the issue of how intuitions are acquired. I consider this a critical issue because knowledge of this process can help identify why and when our intuitions are or are not likely to be erroneous. It can also lead to improving the acquisition or learning process itself.

But what if, at the extreme, intuitions are not acquired through a process of learning but simply a consequence of our genetic inheritance? If this were the case, the implications for educating intuition would be quite different. I therefore address this issue first, and my goal is to delimit what might and might not be considered "educable."

The idea is simple to state. All normal humans are born with similar bodies: two arms, two legs, one head, the same internal organs, and the same internal circuits for the flow of blood (through the veins), information (through the nerves), and so on. In other words, we all have the same infrastructure and the same systems for regulating internal processes. However, to what extent are our systems for seeing and making sense of the world the same? Clearly, our eyes use the same physical mechanisms for seeing, and we all have the same limitations on the range of sounds that we are able to hear. But to what extent does the possession of this common equipment mean that we must all share common intuitions? To what extent are our intuitions idiosyncratic? Moreover, how does this distinction affect the ability to educate intuition?

Second, I explore the issue of learning from experience because, independent of any genetic contributions, learning clearly plays a huge role in how we acquire intuitions. In dealing with learning, I ask two questions: *What* is learned? *How* is it learned? I also introduce the concept of *learning structures*. Learning structures are important because their characteristics determine whether people are likely to learn the appropriate lessons from experience. As I shall show, learning structures affect whether people acquire good or bad intuitions.

Third, I explore the role of memory. Memory involves tasks of both recall and recognition, and I examine the processes underlying both. The human organism contains many memory systems. However, for the purposes of this book, the important distinction is between explicit and implicit systems. The former are what most of us think of as memory, that is, the ability to access information in consciousness. The latter involves information that can bypass consciousness. Most of us complain about having bad explicit memory systems. We often fail to remember things that we feel we should be able to. Paradoxically, we are unaware that our implicit memory systems are really quite effective!

Are Intuitions Innate?

Over the centuries, people have consistently asked whether human mental faculties are innate. Many years ago, a king of Scotland decided to conduct an experiment to solve part of this riddle. The issue that intrigued him was determining "man's natural tongue"—his hypothesis was that it was either Hebrew or Latin. As the ruler of an undemocratic society, he did not have to seek the approval of a human-subjects committee[1] and initiated the following experimental protocol. Two newborns were placed on an uninhabited island off the coast of Scotland under the care of two deaf-mute nursemaids. The expectation was that, since the nursemaids were not linguistic role models, the infants would eventually start to speak in "man's natural tongue." As often happens in even the best-designed experiments, an unexpected occurrence intervened. Both children died prematurely, before they could be expected to talk.

Today, we can all smile at the king's foolishness. However, the notion that some mental faculties are innate is alive and well. For example, there is considerable evidence that many intellectual abilities have a large genetic component. One way in which this is established is through studies of twins. Comparisons are made on a number of intellectual measures between pairs of monozygotic (MZ) and dyzygotic (DZ) twins. MZ twins are identical in the sense that they have exactly the same genes. DZ twins, however, have only roughly half their genes in common. Thus, if the scores of pairs of MZ twins are more similar than those of pairs of DZ twins, this is typically taken as evidence of the contribution of an underlying genetic factor.

Twin studies have been the source of much controversy. They have also been used as evidence in debates that have linked the heritability of intelligence with observed differences in intellectual achievement (e.g., IQ scores) between different racial groups.[2] Unfortunately, these debates have produced more heat than light, and they tend to confuse several issues. First, when dealing with human populations, attempts to provide a precise estimate of how much variation in, say, IQ can be explained by genetic as opposed to nongenetic or environmental factors are problematic. The reason is that precise estimates require too many assumptions that are hard to justify.[3] Second, it is not clear how one should interpret such estimates other than to say that both genes and the environment are important. At the extreme, if everyone experienced *exactly* the same environmental influences, we would have to say that *all* observed variation in IQ is due to genetic factors. Finally, the fact that a trait has been determined as partly due to genetics *within* particular groups has no bearing on any observed differences *between* groups.

One argument provides a simple way to avoid the issue of the role of genetics in understanding intuition. This argument uses the computer analogy and goes like this. The human organism is like the hardware of the computer, and it comes complete with an operating system that allows it to be programmed. (This is the analogue to the genetic component.) Over time, the computer acquires new programs or ways of doing things. It also acquires data on the basis of which its programs operate. (This corresponds to what is learned.) So it seems to be simple. We know precisely what is "genetic" and precisely what is "environmental." Clearly, intuition is not genetic. Right? Well, I'm not so sure.

I believe that the computer analogy breaks down on the following grounds. First, if it were correct, an important implication would be that the rate at which a *naive* mind learns something should not be affected by *what* is learned. As I discuss below, the primary means by which we learn through experience is by noting connections between variables. Thus, for example, we learn that a light goes on when a switch is moved into a particular position (see pp. 75–91 below). All connections, however, are not equally important in that some are more useful than others; that is, some are associated with greater benefits than others. However, even if we grant all connections equal importance, the rate of learning is still affected by *what* is learned.

For example, in a famous experiment, John B. Watson, one of psychology's pioneers in the study of learning, showed that he could condition "little Albert" (an eleven-month-old boy) to become afraid of a white rat, a rabbit, and a dog when these were paired with a startling noise.[4] However, a later study by Bregman using the same procedure failed to demonstrate learning when conventional objects, such as blocks of wood and cloth curtains, were paired with the startling noise.[5]

Martin Seligman has proposed that humans and animals are differentially "prepared" to learn connections. He has argued that there is a "continuum of preparedness" and that we are "prepared" to associate or connect some events, "unprepared" to associate others, and "counterprepared" to associate still others.[6] Studies have shown, for example, that, even after just one trial, rats can learn to associate distinctive-tasting food and a gastrointestinal illness (induced by X-rays) even though the illness does not occur at a point close in time to the ingestion of the tainted food; that is, they are prepared to associate this particular cause-effect pair.[7] On the other hand, rats appear to be "counterprepared" to associate taste with shocks administered to the feet. The argument for the continuum of preparedness is evolutionary. Countless connections can be encountered in the environment. Thus, an organism has a greater chance of survival if important connections are learned quickly and irrelevant ones ignored.

As discussed in chapter 2, evolutionary theory holds that we are the product of adaptations that occurred in response to past circumstances. An implication of the preparedness argument, therefore, is that we should still possess reactions that were useful to our ancestors but that are less meaningful today. And, in fact, this is the case with respect to certain stimuli that trigger fear. For example, we tend to fear snakes and spiders more than we do many of the real dangers of city life, such as traffic accidents and crime. In 1965, a study of Chicago schoolchildren found that among their greatest fears were lions, tigers, and snakes rather than the kinds of dangers that they were more likely to meet in their urban environment.[8]

Second, in a book entitled *The Language Instinct*, Steven Pinker has made a strong case that humans inherit "algorithms" for learning language that are operative at certain critical ages.[9] Thus, children can learn to speak a foreign language and acquire an operational understanding of its grammar (including exceptions) in a tacit or an intuitive manner, whereas adults are forced to learn in a more analytic or deliberate mode (e.g., by studying the rules of grammar, memorizing vocabulary and irregular verbs, and so on). If this is true, it poses the question of why adults lose the ability to learn languages in the same manner as children do. However, it also demonstrates that certain cognitive abilities are subject to inherent maturation or developmental processes in the same way as physical abilities and further suggests the need to distinguish between the concepts of instinct and intuition. I shall return to this issue below.

Third, it is currently impossible to identify the intellectual skills with which we are born. Yet studies of children, and sometimes quite young infants, indicate that they seem either to possess or to acquire "naturally" many abilities that facilitate higher-level information processing. For example, a recent study shows that children as young as seven months can infer linguistic rules from speech as measured by their ability to perceive patterns in nonsense syllables. For example, after being exposed to patterns that take the form A-B-A, infants are surprised when they meet a sequence in the form A-B-B.[10]

Elizabeth Spelke and her colleagues have systematically investigated the "initial knowledge" that infants appear to possess.[11] They find, for example, that infants as young as three and four months make clear distinctions between the animate and the inanimate. As far as objects are concerned, certain ideas are clear to them: they know, for example, what constitutes a whole object, that objects must move along continuous paths, and that objects affect each other only if there is contact between them. Moreover, young children are able to locate themselves by attending to geometric features of their environments that might not be salient to adults. On the other hand, the concepts of gravity and inertia are not clear to them (see also chap. 4 below).

Spelke believes that many of these cognitive abilities are innate and that what she calls *initial knowledge* is domain specific. For example, infants recognize that, unlike inanimate objects, animate objects need not be in direct contact for one to influence the other. According to Spelke, initial knowledge constitutes the core of mature knowledge and is the foundation of many adult intuitions: "Initial knowledge is central to common-sense reasoning throughout development. Intuitive knowledge of physical objects, people, sets, and places develops by enrichment around a constant core, such that the knowledge guiding infants' reasoning stands at the center of the knowledge guiding the intuitive reasoning of older children and adults."[12]

On the other hand, Spelke's views on the innate nature of initial knowledge are disputed by Renée Baillargeon, who argues that we are born, not with innate beliefs about, say, the movement of objects, but instead with "highly constrained mechanisms" that guide reasoning.[13] To return to the computer analogy introduced above, the argument being made here is that our "operating systems" are constructed in ways that limit how we process information and thus reason. It may appear as if we have innate beliefs, but this is an illusion.

Much of this research points to the domain specificity of knowledge. However, it appears that children also utilize "general algorithms" when engaged in causal thinking. They notice which variables covary; they are attentive to temporal order (where cause precedes effect); they seem to have a good understanding of contiguity in time and space; and they notice similarities. Most important, they also seem to have a good sense of what are and what are not plausible relations. For example, when considering the movements of objects, they are reluctant to attribute cause unless they can imagine how a force is transferred from one body to another.[14]

Whereas the definition and meaning of *cause* have been debated for centuries, the ability to make causal judgments undoubtedly enhances survival from an evolutionary perspective. I find it quite plausible that the "mechanism" that we use for establishing cause in our minds might well be innate. On the other hand, this is not the same thing as saying that the specific causal beliefs that we hold, even when very young, are also genetic in origin. In other words, some of the "rules" that we use to process information may well be genetic. However, the "content"—or "arguments"—of those rules is a function of experience.

This distinction can also be made using an analogy with the process of perception. We are all born with biological "equipment" that enables us to see. Moreover, this equipment can be thought of as embodying rules that translate perceptions of objects in the world into a form that can be processed by our brains. These rules are clearly part of our genetic inheritance. However, what we see—or the content of perception—is a function of our experience with the environment.[15]

So is there a genetic basis to intuition? Consider the difference between the terms *intuition* and *instinct* as I use them in this book. By definition, an instinct is a behavior that is innate. (Cats will always want to chase small birds. A puff of cold air in the eye will immediately result in the eyelid closing.) Intuitions, on the other hand, reflect largely learned behavior, although they may contain some innate components. For example, emotional reactions—like moving quickly to avoid a falling object—seem to involve instinct (to enhance survival) and can be thought of as indistinguishable from intuition as experienced by the individual. On the other hand, they could also reflect—in some measure—learned responses. Recall, for example, Antonio Damasio's experiments (discussed in chap. 2) in which people who were not brain damaged seemed to recognize subconsciously when choices they faced were or were not risky. Few would call this behavior *instinctive* (as I have defined the term), and I think that the reason that we do not is because we believe that it reflects learning that has taken place since birth. Finally, as I shall explain below, the process by which people learn from experience is definitely inherent and further confuses the distinction between intuition and instinct.

It is not my intention here to be trapped in a debate about the possible genetic basis of intuition. What should be said, however, is that we undoubtedly possess instinctive, emotional reactions (such as fear) that operate very much like intuitive processes—*"they are reached with little apparent effort, and typically without conscious awareness. They involve little or no conscious deliberation"* (p. 14 above). It is also the case that several basic, information-processing "rules" necessary for higher-level inference are present when humans are quite young, and these may also be instinctive. Thus, to the extent that these rules are employed automatically, without conscious awareness, it is clear that the procedural bases for intuitive thoughts and actions are also common, widespread, and, if not genetic in origin, then at least operational from early infancy. Predispositions to process information in specific ways must lead to similar ways of interacting with the environment. In chapters 5 and 8, I shall elaborate further on the distinctions between instinct and intuition.

What are the implications for educating intuition? The first is similar to a conclusion reached in chapter 2. You cannot repress inherent reactions, that is, instinctive behavior. Nor can you prevent intuitive reactions that are the result of much past learning (e.g., certain stereotypes). On the other hand, we can use our deliberate systems to guide us in choosing behavior. For example, even though we may have an instinctive reaction that signals hunger, most of us can learn to control this until it is the appropriate time to eat. As noted in chapter 2, we can also learn to control our stereotypic reactions.

I am not saying, however, that we would be better off if all inherent reactions (as well as some intuitions) were repressed. On the contrary, many, if not most, of our inherent reactions are functionally important. For example, pain is an important signal that there is something wrong with the body. We need to learn, however, when and when not to attend to these kinds of signals.

Second, whereas we have no choice in selecting our instincts, we do have some choice in developing our intuitions. More specifically, our inherent processes of learning from experience imply that our intuitions are shaped by the environments that we confront. But these environments need not be determined by chance. We can actively choose the environments to which we are exposed. To understand the full import of this statement, we will need to consider the processes involved in learning from experience. It is to this topic that I now turn.

Learning from Experience

As noted previously, intuitions are achieved "without conscious awareness." In addition, most learning from experience—the process by which we acquire the information on which intuitive judgments are based—also occurs automatically. In demonstrating this, I first consider *what* and *how* we learn from experience. Then I discuss *learning structures* or the conditions under which learning takes place. I shall show that the interaction of process—or *how* we learn—and *learning structures* is critical to the quality and usefulness of *what* we learn.

What and *How* We Learn from Experience

There are two simple principles underlying learning from experience. First, we make mental connections between things that happen together. Second, those connections become reinforced or strengthened in memory.[16] To clarify these notions, consider the following example.

In order to understand the first principle, imagine Mary, a child who is being brought up in an English-speaking home. When learning to speak, Mary faces the important task of acquiring vocabulary. Clearly, she does not simply memorize lists of words and their meanings. Instead, she observes what sounds are associated with particular objects. Thus, when Mary's father hands her a spoon and, in an appropriate context, says the word *spoon*, Mary can see the connection. She now knows, or has learned, what a spoon is. Note, in particular, that Mary's father used the word *spoon* in a context that involved close spatial and temporal association with the object. Indeed, this was critical for Mary to see the connection between the word and the object. For example, had her father handed her a spoon and then refrained from saying the word *spoon* until some later time and in a different context, Mary would not have made the connection.

Seeing connections is critical to learning from experience. Moreover, these connections can vary from quite simple associations between two objects to fairly complex rules that, in essence, provide instructions for doing something. Making such associations involves observing that two things are in some way connected in time and space, that is, that they occur together. The two "things" can be many different types of entities, for example, a word and an object, two different objects, a feeling and an action, and so on. Associations can also vary in complexity. More complex associations give rise to rules by means of which people can infer relations between variables. As an example, consider hitting a nail with a hammer. If you hit the nail lightly, little effect is observed; if you hit it with greater force, there is greater effect. The connection learned here is between the amount of force exerted and the effect on the nail. What you learn is a relation or function, in this case concerning the effect of exerting force.

As a further example of a rule, consider the experiment cited above in which seven-month-old children were observed to infer linguistic rules from speech by recognizing patterns in nonsense syllables. One rule learned was the pattern A-B-A, which can be obtained by generalizing that the first and third sounds are always the same. Thus, the child who learns this rule would expect the sequence E-F to be followed by E even if both these particular sounds were new. What is learned, therefore, is a principle as opposed to a particular instance. What this means is that the child who learns this rule will know how to generate similar sequences. Demonstrating the ability to learn such rules represents an important leap forward in abstract reasoning ability.[17]

The second principle—that connections are subsequently reinforced or strengthened in memory—is regulated by what I call an *importance factor*. Three variables are involved in this process: *genetic predispositions, motivation,* and *frequency.*

As noted above, a number of studies suggest that we are genetically more prepared to learn the significance of certain stimuli and that these stimuli can be ordered on a continuum that reflects the likelihood that we will make connections.[18] Fear responses that affect survival provide a case in point. Joseph LeDoux, for example, has argued that memories of frightening events connected to, say, hearing an explosion can be automatically triggered by the amygdala deep in the noncortical region of the brain when it perceives similar loud sounds.[19] It may take only one traumatic experience for the connection to be made and indelibly inscribed in emotional memory (see pp. 91–98 below). As a further example, consider a lifetime fear of dogs that results from being bitten by a dog as a child. One-connection learning is clearly functional if it helps the organism recognize danger and take appropriate action. This process, however, can also be dysfunctional if it continues to be triggered in situations in which no danger exists.

Motivation also affects the ease with which connections become established in the mind. This can be stimulated either internally or externally. *Internal motivation* is a desire to learn that resides within the person. Thus, Mary wants to learn how to talk. Learning the word *spoon* is fun for her. More important, learning provides her with a sense of competence and control over the environment. For example, she now knows how to ask for a spoon. In general, humans are motivated to learn about the environments in which they find themselves.[20] This, too, makes sense on evolutionary grounds—we need to discover how things work. If what we learn does not help us get what we want now, it could help us in the future. Curiosity is important. And it should be noted that the "things" about which we learn include, not just objects, but the social world (e.g., gestures made by others).

External motivation refers to positive or negative outcomes obtained when dealing with others or with the environment. Thus, Mary quickly learns the connections between actions and results, that is, whether what she does gets her what she wants. She learns, for example, how to approach her father when she wants his attention and how to ask her mother for special favors. She also learns to avoid doing certain things—she learns, for example, that, if she tries to play with one of his toys, her four-year-old brother reprimands her. These are all examples from the social domain. However, the principle is the same when dealing with the physical world. A good feeling rewards us when we take a hot drink on a cold day. We also learn that we hurt ourselves when we touch fire.

The frequency with which a connection is observed affects what we learn. If you dial a telephone number once, you probably will not remember it. If you dial it several times, however, you probably will. (Some people, of course, learn more quickly than others.) Mary may not learn to say some words correctly the first time, but it will not take her long to overcome such difficulties. Repetition makes a big difference—whether this involves rote learning or just seeing the same connection on a regular basis. We are all sensitive to consistency in our environments.

To summarize, we learn from observing connections in the environment, whether connections between objects or "things," connections between actions that we take and what happens (to us or to others), or connections between actions that others take and what happens (to us or to them).[21] Connections can take the form of simple associations or even complex rules that capture the relations between variables. Importance moderates the reinforcement of connections in memory. And importance is determined by inherent sensitivity to some types of events, internal and external motivation, and frequency of occurrence.

Frequency Information, Automatic Encoding, and Implicit Learning

As discussed in chapter 2, much—if not most—information processing takes place without our conscious awareness. Moreover, this is efficient in the sense that it involves many physical processes to which we would have difficulty attending consciously. What is often not realized, however, is the extent to which we are continuously processing information even when there is no apparent reason to do so. In short, the human mind continually encodes information *automatically,* that is, without conscious effort.

One phenomenon that has been studied in great detail is the manner in which humans store information about the frequencies of events that they observe in the environment. For example, ask yourself how many times you have been to, say, your favorite bookstore or the cinema in the last six months. What is typically surprising about this question is that, although we may not know the answer with precision (or without a long search through memory), we do have immediately a rough idea of the frequencies of our visits. Moreover, we probably never made conscious efforts to record the frequencies of these visits. In many ways, the human mind seems to have a built-in counter that records the frequencies of events that we observe. Moreover, this operates without effort or even the goal of paying attention to particular classes of events.

Lynn Hasher and Rose Zacks have made detailed studies of this phenomenon.[22] They show that information regarding the frequency of a wide variety of naturally occurring events is stored automatically in memory. In summarizing much evidence, they state,

> The processing of frequency of occurrence information is remarkable. Information about frequency is recorded in memory without a person's intention to do so. The information stored in this way is apparently no less fine-grained than is the information stored when intention is operating. Training and feedback do not improve the ability to encode frequency information. Unlike virtually every other cognitive skill examined in the field, memory for frequency shows a developmental invariance from early childhood through young adulthood to middle and old age. Similarly there are no effects of differences among people in motivation, intelligence, and educational background. The processing of frequency information is unaffected by reductions in cognitive capacity stemming from depression, old age or multiple task demands.[23]

As this quotation implies, the ability to attend to and store frequency information forms a basic part of our cognitive endowment. This is emphasized by the fact that the ability seems not to be influenced by age (and thus is not learned and developed over time) or by such mental conditions as depression. Hasher and Zacks point out that frequency information involves, not only "how many times" we observe certain phenomena, but also such important cognitive activities as recognizing categories of objects where we attend to the frequency of features. For example, in addition to being sensitive to how many people we meet while commuting to work, we are also sensitive to, say, how many are elderly, how many are well dressed, etc. There is no question that sensitivity to frequency plays a critical part in learning.

If, as seems likely, the ability to attend to and record frequency information automatically (i.e., without effort) is part of our genetic endowment, then one would also expect animals to have similar mechanisms. After all, it is important for all animals to understand the frequencies of many events in their natural environments. As will be discussed in chapter 4, several studies have examined the ability of animals to engage in "optimal foraging" or choosing the best strategies for finding food, a task that implicitly involves "knowing" the statistical distributions of different sources of foods. It turns out that many animals do act *as though* they know these statistical distributions. Moreover, this knowledge must be based on past observations of frequencies.

The picture that emerges from this line of research is that humans possess effortless routines for classifying—categorizing and maintaining tallies of—many different aspects of experience. Related to this is the important phenomenon of *tacit* or *implicit knowledge*—the ability to understand, after exposure (observation or interaction), how certain phenomena work even if that understanding cannot be verbalized. For example, Donald Broadbent and his colleagues have investigated people's ability to manage complex systems by having them play computer games that represent economic situations. They find that people can acquire an understanding of the games—as evinced by the actions they take—but that they are unable to articulate such knowledge.[24]

Arthur Reber has conducted detailed studies of the process that he calls *implicit learning.* In Reber's experiments, subjects are typically required to observe abstract sequences of events—strings of letters (generated by artificial grammars) or sequences of different colored lights (governed by different probabilistic processes). They may also be asked to engage in a specific cognitive task, for example, to memorize specific strings of letters. They are then asked questions designed to see whether they understand the underlying structure of the displays that they have observed. Time and time again, Reber has found that people have the ability to infer an abstract and representative understanding of quite complex phenomena—even if they cannot articulate that understanding, and even if gaining that understanding was not what they had been asked to do—and that "such knowledge is acquired independently of conscious efforts to learn."[25] Moreover, if subjects are asked to try and understand the underlying structure during the observation phase, explicit attempts to learn can sometimes lead to inferior understanding relative to implicit learning. All seems to depend on whether subjects in the explicit condition reach a correct understanding early in the learning process.[26]

Over several decades, Reber's research strategy has been to demonstrate the effects of implicit learning within a tightly controlled experimental paradigm. However, other investigators have studied implicit learning using a wider range of tasks. Pawel Lewicki and his colleagues have examined some of the implications of implicit learning in the social domain. They state that such nonconscious processing is "not limited to the housekeeping operations, such as retrieving information from memory or adjusting the level of arousal; they are directly involved in the development of interpretive categories, drawing inferences, determining emotional reactions, and other high-level cognitive operations traditionally associated with consciously controlled thinking."[27]

The concepts of the automatic recording of frequencies and the process of implicit learning are critical to understanding the content of our knowledge base. It is clear that we acquire much knowledge simply by interacting with the environment—frequently without having formed the explicit intention of doing so.[28] For example, the mere-exposure effect (discussed in chap. 2) demonstrates how preferences can be created without conscious awareness. You like certain types of music because this is what you have been exposed to. You did not choose to acquire a taste for these types of music. To take another example, we all know that we can learn by simply interacting with someone who is an expert in a specific domain, whether that person is a scientist, an artist, a craftsman, a musician, or whatever. By observing what an expert does, we seem to capture "by osmosis" what we should do in certain circumstances—even though we may not understand why. Indeed, this is one of the bases of the well-established social tradition of apprenticeship. The master does not always teach explicitly, but the apprentice learns—implicitly.

In short, we are constantly engaged in a process of learning. Moreover, we know much more than we are able to articulate. But, since much of our learning is implicit, how do we know whether the "knowledge" that we are acquiring is valid? History is full of examples of "knowledge" that has subsequently proved to be unfounded. We used to believe, for example, that the earth was at the center of the universe, that people who were ill should be "bled," and that we should "correct" those who were born left-handed. To understand the basis of our knowledge, therefore, it is important to examine the kinds of situations in which it has been acquired.

Learning from Connections

Because the process of learning from connections is so prevalent,[29] it is critical to understand its inherent strengths and weaknesses. These can be illustrated by examining a simple 2×2 table that shows how the validity of a connection can be assessed. Specifically, consider exhibit 3 and the connection established in Mary's mind between the word *spoon* and an actual spoon.

The rows of the table correspond to the word *spoon* and all other words that Mary knows, the columns to the object spoon and all other objects that she knows. Cell *a* shows the number of times Mary associates the word *spoon* with the presence of the object spoon. (The first time was when her father used the word. Other times could be when she subsequently uses a spoon and thinks of the word, and so on.) Cell *b* measures the number of times the word *spoon* is associated with an object that is *not* a spoon. Cell *c* represents the number of times a word other than *spoon* is associated with the object spoon. And cell *d* captures the number of times words other than *spoon* are associated with objects that are not spoons.

To test whether there is a valid relation between the word *spoon* and the object spoon, compare the sizes of the two ratios $a/(a + b)$ and $c/(c + d)$.

EXHIBIT 3 Learning from connections

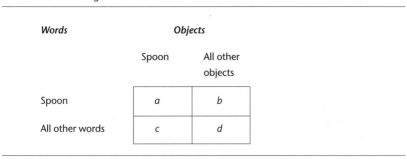

Words	*Objects*	
	Spoon	All other objects
Spoon	a	b
All other words	c	d

The validity of this relation is a function of the size of the difference between the two ratios. The first ratio can be thought of as the chances of the object being a spoon when the word *spoon* is used. The second ratio represents the chances that the object is a spoon when a word other than *spoon* is used. Consider just the first time Mary notices the connection. In this case, the ratio $a/(a + b) = 1/(1 + 0) = 1$, and the ratio $c/(c + d) = 0/(0 + k) = 0$, where k is the number of words other than *spoon* that Mary knows. Thus, even though the number of observations is so small (one!), Mary is justified in associating the word *spoon* with the object spoon.

Now, of course Mary does not actually calculate the difference between two ratios. In fact, she probably only makes a connection between the word *spoon* and the object spoon (i.e., cell *a*) and, in this context, never considers words other than *spoon* or objects other than spoons (i.e., the other cells in exhibit 3). What does happen, however, is that, by connecting the word *spoon* only to objects that are in fact spoons, Mary uses a mechanism that leads in this case to a valid relation. Moreover, the mere fact of seeing this connection many times—the effect of frequency (see above)—will reinforce the concept of a spoon in her mind.

There are two advantages of learning by connections that are reinforced. The first is that it can lead to valid knowledge, as just indicated in the case of Mary and the spoon. The second is that what we learn is intimately tied to the environment in which we live and useful to us precisely because of this. Mary, for example, lives in an English-speaking household and therefore learns English, not any other language. In other words, the organism is born with a mechanism for learning—based on connections and reinforcement—and this mechanism allows it to adapt to its particular environment. Indeed, the literature provides numerous examples of remarkable adaptation by both humans and animals.[30]

Whereas the critical advantage of learning from connections is that it benefits from what we experience or see (i.e., mainly observations in cell *a*), the critical disadvantage is that it is not possible to learn *from what is not seen*.[31] At first sight, this may seem to be a strange statement. So let us consider another example concerning Mary.

Imagine this time that Mary has noticed a connection between a way of crying and attracting her father's attention. This is shown in the 2×2 table in exhibit 4. In this table, the rows represent crying (in a special way) and not crying (in that special way), and the columns represent Mary's father paying attention to her and not paying attention to her.

By, in effect, paying attention only to cell *a*, Mary is reinforced in her belief that, by crying in a special way, she will attract her father's attention. This is a strategy that works, so she sticks with it. However, what

EXHIBIT 4 Attracting Mary's father

	Father pays attention to Mary	Father does not pay attention to Mary
Crying in a special way	*a*	*b*
Not crying in a special way	*c*	*d*

Mary fails to learn by doing this is that there may be other ways of attracting her father's attention. As long as her present strategy is successful, she is unlikely to explore other methods—she can be thought of as adhering to the adage "if it ain't broke, don't fix it."

In other words, a major disadvantage of learning by connections is that you may be "trapped" by a learned behavior or rule that is suboptimal. Mary might have been much better off had she explored other ways of attracting her father's attention. In fact, when judging the strength of relations between variables, people typically pay most attention to information represented by cell *a* and fail to seek the information represented by the other cells. They can therefore miss opportunities for further learning.[32]

To illustrate a second disadvantage of learning from observed connections, recall—from chapter 1—my friend Anna, who works part-time as a waitress in a restaurant in Chicago. Her problem is that the restaurant is often busy and that she does not know how to allocate her time in order to maximize tips. Based on a limited number of observations, she forms a hypothesis or belief that well-dressed people are good tippers and that badly dressed customers are not. The 2 × 2 table shown in exhibit 5 summarizes her situation.

The rows of the table represent actions that Anna could take—paying more attention to the well-dressed customers or paying more attention to the badly dressed. The columns represent the outcomes—big (i.e., above-average) tips or small (i.e., below-average) tips. The entries in cell *a* represent the number of above-average tips left by people who are well dressed, those in cell *b* the number of below-average tips left by the well dressed. The entries in cell *c* represent the number of above-average tips left by the badly dressed, those in cell *d* the number of below-average tips left by the badly dressed.

And now here comes the problem. Anna is pressed for time and must decide how to allocate her attention. She thinks that the well dressed

EXHIBIT 5   Anna's service to customers

Anna pays attention to	Size of tips	
	Above average	Below average
Well-dressed customers	a	b
Badly dressed customers	c	d

are bigger tippers and so deliberately allocates more time to them. What does she observe?

The better-dressed customers do leave larger tips. But that they do so may have nothing to do with the fact that they are better dressed and, as Anna presumes, therefore better able and more willing to leave large tips. It may simply reflect the fact that Anna has allocated more attention to them. In other words, because she believes that the better dressed are bigger tippers, Anna has taken actions that ensure the connection.

Thus, the critical weakness of learning by seeing connections is that *what* is learned depends on what is seen, yet accurate learning may require seeing what cannot be observed. In the present case, Anna's own behavior has prevented her from seeing what the badly dressed customers would have done had they been treated the same as the better-dressed customers. Similarly, because Mary was unwilling to try other ways of attracting her father's attention, she was unable to see whether they could be more effective than her particular way of crying.

This example of Anna illustrates two important points. The first was discussed briefly above. In order to assess *accurately* whether two variables are related, you need to be able to observe data from all four cells of tables such as that in exhibit 5. Otherwise, you cannot compare the two ratios $a/(a + b)$ and $c/(c + d)$. In exhibit 5, for example, the relation examined was that between paying attention to two different classes of customers, on the one hand, and the generosity of tips left (above or below average), on the other. Moreover, this model can be generalized to any situation in which you are testing the relation between two variables.[33] For example, one could test the relation between, say, handedness (right and left) and drawing skill (above and below average) or weight and height.

The second point is related to Anna's belief that well-dressed customers leave larger tips. By acting on this belief, Anna sets in motion a *self-fulfilling prophecy*.[34] When the restaurant is busy, well-dressed customers do leave above-average tips, and badly dressed customers do not, precisely because of the differential level of service that Anna provides. Had Anna wanted to test her belief, she should have conducted an experiment in which she randomly provided good service to well- and badly dressed customers alike! The resulting data would have told her whether there really is a relation between dress and tipping behavior.

Whereas this example of a self-fulfilling prophecy might seem innocuous, consider Lewis Thomas's description of the diagnostic activities of an early twentieth-century physician:

> The physician enjoyed the reputation of a diagnostician, with a particular skill in diagnosing typhoid fever, then the commonest disease on the wards of New York's hospitals. He placed particular reliance on the appearance of the tongue, which was universal in the medicine of that day (now entirely inexplicable, long forgotten). He believed he could detect significant differences by palpating that organ. The ward rounds conducted by this man were, essentially, tongue rounds; each patient would stick out his tongue while the eminence took it between thumb and forefinger, feeling its textures and irregularities, then moving from bed to bed, diagnosing typhoid fever in its earliest stages over and over again, and turning out a week or so later to have been right, to everyone's amazement. He was a more effective carrier, using only his hands, than Typhoid Mary.[35]

The ability to notice connections is a powerful means of learning, but it does not guarantee that what you learn will be appropriate. The process that leads to acquiring valid beliefs about the world is the same process that leads to acquiring superstitions and other erroneous beliefs. Indeed, it is quite probable that the physician that Thomas describes was thought by his many admirers to possess great clinical intuition. In addition, the physician himself undoubtedly believed in his own intuition.

In a fascinating series of experiments, Barry Schwartz showed how human subjects can find themselves trapped by their own strategies for learning and how this process is exacerbated when rewards are involved.[36] In Schwartz's experiments, subjects were seated in front of panels that took the form of 5×5 matrices. In addition, each element of the matrix contained a bulb that could be lit by pressing one of two keys, left and right. Each trial began with one bulb (the upper left) lit, and subjects soon learned that pressing the left key would turn off the bulb currently lit and activate the bulb below it and that pressing the right key would also turn off the bulb currently lit but activate the bulb to the right. The subjects were told, not what to do, but that they would be rewarded when they did the right thing. Moreover, that they did the right thing would be signaled by a red light going on. This occurred after subjects touched both the left and the right keys exactly four times each. Once, however, they touched the same key five times on a given trial, that trial ended, and they were not rewarded. The task was designed in such a way that, at the end of a successful trial, the bulb in the lower-right matrix would be lit. In all, seventy different routes (i.e., all possible combinations of pressing the left key four times and the right key four times) could be taken that would leave that lower-right bulb lit.

Subjects played this game over the course of many trials. The main result was that, once subjects discovered one sequence of key presses that proved successful, they persisted in using this and failed to discover that there were alternative ways of being rewarded. (Recall the example given above of how Mary failed to discover that there were other, possibly more effective ways of attracting her father's attention.) Of course, the subjects in Schwartz's experiments did discover a strategy that worked and were accordingly rewarded. What they failed to do was discover the general rule for gaining rewards. Moreover, when subjects in one group were also instructed to discover what the general rule was, they took longer and were less proficient than those in another group who played the same game but were not rewarded for successful trials.

It seems that, once a connection has been reinforced by an external reward (e.g., a payment of some sort), people (like Anna the waitress) are reluctant to change their behavior and seek other, possibly more effective strategies. Schwartz refers to this as *reinforcement-induced behavioral stereotypy*. This stereotypy may be effective in the short term, but it is clear that it inhibits more generalized forms of learning and can be dysfunctional if conditions in the environment change.

Social Sources of Beliefs

It is important to emphasize that connections are established in people's minds not only by what they see but also by what they have been told by others. For example, imagine that a friend had told Anna, the waitress, that well-dressed customers tend to leave good tips. In this case, Anna would have contributed to her friend's belief being affirmed.

More generally, the world is complicated, and, rather than being founded on our own observations, many of our beliefs are social in origin; that is, we seek information about possible connections from others and also transmit our "knowledge" to others. Thus, even when we observe something that could correct a socially acquired but erroneous belief, we do not always make use of this information. For example, a parent may tell a child to be wary of certain kinds of strangers, and the obedient child may never seek to test this belief or even consider evidence that could disconfirm it.

Whereas this last example is quite explicit, the social transmission of beliefs operates through many subtle and tacit mechanisms; for example, even a small smile from a parent can be a strong form of reinforcement. Much of our cultural capital (cf. chap. 1) is the result of social interactions that both suggest connections and reward socially appropriate behavior. Given the complexity of the environments in which we live, however, there can be no doubt that our stocks of cultural capital contain many invalid as well as valid beliefs.

Learning Structures

Three statements can summarize the discussion and examples just provided. First, we learn from observing connections. Second, the connections that we see may not provide the evidence necessary to infer valid conclusions. Third, by taking action, we may prevent ourselves from learning the right lessons from experience. Another way of stating the second and third points is that feedback from the environment does not necessarily help us learn the *right* lessons. We often need to be able to learn from what we do *not* see as opposed to what we *do* see. The second and third points are especially critical because people generally believe that feedback corrects errors. Clearly, this is often true. However, it is also true that feedback can both create and maintain false beliefs. It all depends on what I call the *learning structure.*

Exhibit 6 helps illustrate the concept of the learning structure. It takes account of two variables that affect how we learn. One is the quality of feedback, and the other is the consequence of errors. Both affect the connections that we see and the importance that we attach to those connections. In exhibit 6, these two variables are crossed to indicate the ways in which the task environment affects learning. The horizontal axis represents the quality of feedback, which can vary from relevant (on the left) to irrelevant (on the right).[37] With speedy and accurate feedback, we can learn both easily and accurately. However, when feedback is noisy, delayed, or characterized by uncertainty, the process of learning by connections and reinforcement can break down (i.e., what we learn may not be valid).

The vertical axis of exhibit 6 represents the extent to which errors experienced during learning are consequential and thus how "good" intu-

EXHIBIT 6   The learning structure

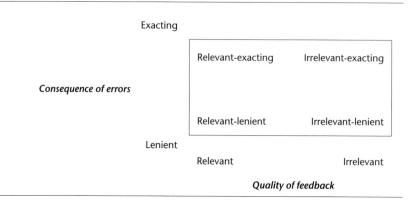

ition needs to be. Some environments (those at the bottom) are lenient, others (those at the top) exacting. Sometimes intuitive judgments do not need to be highly accurate. When walking down a corridor, for example, intuitive judgment needs to indicate only a general direction because corrective feedback, received in real time, will be sufficient to mitigate any incorrect judgments.[38] In this case, the environment—or learning structure—is lenient, providing rough but appropriate feedback on the accuracy of judgment. Other times, however, intuitive judgment must be highly accurate. The judgments made by a brain surgeon, for example, must be precisely accurate because even small errors can have serious consequences.[39] In this case, the learning structure is exacting, providing detailed feedback on the accuracy of judgment.

Consider now the implications of learning in environments characterized by different quadrants of exhibit 6. Accurate learning is easy when feedback is relevant, and it will increase in precision as tasks move from lenient to more exacting conditions. The notion here is that, with good feedback, you can see the costs of errors and your judgment will adapt accordingly. In other words, judgment will be more accurate when errors are more costly.

When feedback is irrelevant, however, learning may not be appropriate. And, when the environment is lenient, you may not realize that you have learned the wrong things. In many cases, this may not be too important. For example, much superstitious behavior takes place in the irrelevant-lenient quadrant—consider the tennis player who believes that, for good luck, he should always tie his right shoe before his left (after all, that is what he did once when he beat a very good player). The danger of learning in this quadrant, however, is gaining unfounded confidence.

An important source of irrelevant feedback lies in the random nature of outcomes observed. For example, imagine being faced with choosing one of two job candidates. You make the correct choice, but was that the result of skill (i.e., the way in which you conducted the interviews), or were you just lucky? Were both skill and luck involved? If so, in what proportions? Chance generally plays an important role in determining the outcomes of the decisions that we make and therefore in determining the feedback that we receive. Unfortunately, because its relevance is difficult to assess, its role is frequently underestimated.

Irrelevant-exacting environments can be quite dangerous. The physician described above, who diagnosed patients by feeling their tongues, provides a case in point. The outcomes observed were directly tied to his actions, but, because his errors were not apparent, he maintained his belief in his erroneous judgment, the outcomes in fact reinforcing his confidence.

Irrelevant-exacting environments can also be confusing. Consider cases in which errors have been made but the feedback is misleading. This can occur, for example, when there is a lag between action and outcome but it is not known how long that lag is. The result is that the outcome could be the result of any number of factors other than the original action. Such a situation arises in many business settings. As a case in point, consider a special advertising campaign conducted over a long period of time. The resulting sales (the outcome) are disappointing, but, because of the time lag, the cause is not apparent: sales may have been affected by any number of factors (competitors' campaigns, unexpected price changes, etc.) other than the campaign itself.

In general, you can think of learning structures as being favorable or unfavorable to accurate learning—that is, *kind* or *wicked*. An important contention of this book is that the quality of your intuitions depends on the kinds of learning structures that prevailed when these were acquired. *Kind learning structures lead to good intuitions; wicked ones do not.*

The difference between kind and wicked learning structures can be nicely illustrated by the examples of the early twentieth-century physician described above and a professional tennis player. Clearly, the physician acquired his intuitions concerning the diagnosis of typhoid fever in a *wicked* learning structure. The feedback that he received was extremely misleading. The professional tennis player, however, has played tennis almost every day since she was a child and has developed her intuitions about where to hit the ball on the basis of highly accurate feedback from coaches, personal experience in many matches (where the consequences of various shots are immediately and unmistakably apparent), and watching and analyzing other players' matches. Consequently, all her intuitions have been acquired within kind learning structures. There is no doubt in my mind that, during matches, her intuitions will be valid. (This does not mean, of course, that her choices will always be correct or that she will always execute shots precisely as she intends.)

Summary and Implications

Intuitions are acquired through experience. The process by which we learn is largely tacit. We are typically unaware of the fact that we are constantly learning—updating our impressions of the frequencies with which we make observations, making new connections, and generally building on our existing stock of explicit and implicit knowledge. Moreover, much of this learning does not even involve the intent to learn.

The process of learning through experience is simple. In fact, it is automatic. We see connections, and these are reinforced in memory by their importance to us. Importance reflects genetic predisposition, motivation, and frequency. We learn from *what we see,* but not necessarily from *what we do not see.* The advantage of this system is that our learning is adapted to the particulars of our environment. The disadvantage is that *valid* learning often requires knowing things that we cannot see.

The concept of *learning structure* is critical to the quality of intuitions that people acquire through experience. Learning structures determine a person's ability to acquire valid intuitions through the automatic connection-reinforcement learning mechanisms described above. In brief, some learning structures are *kind* in the sense that they allow people to learn the appropriate lessons from experience; others are *wicked* in that they teach the wrong lessons. I claim that the validity of a person's intuition depends on the kind of learning structure in which that intuition was acquired.

The concept of learning structures has important implications for educating intuition. First, it provides a framework for assessing the validity of intuitions. Second, it suggests the kinds of environments that should be sought in order to develop good intuitions. These two points will be explored in depth in chapter 7.

In ending this section, it is instructive to make an analogy between the processes of natural selection in evolution and learning through experience as described above. Both mechanisms are like "hill-climbing" algorithms in the sense that what is selected or learned is modified by feedback; that is, adaptations that work are retained, as are connections that are reinforced. However, without being able to use what is not observed, neither system knows whether it has reached a maximum in the sense of finding the optimal design (in evolution) or determining the best action for achieving a goal (in learning through experience). To extend the hill-climbing analogy, neither knows whether it has reached the summit of the appropriate mountain or just the top of a nearby hill.

The process of learning from experience—involving connections and reinforcement—is basic to both human and animal species. As one moves up the phylogenetic scale, however, great differences in the process can be observed. What is especially noteworthy is that humans—and some primates—have a capacity for imagination that allows them to visualize alternative scenarios and thus move beyond evidence that can be seen only physically. In other words, imagination offers another way of seeing. Indeed, there is strong evidence that in some cases humans engage automatically in counterfactual thinking in response to negative emotional experiences.[40] For example, imagine hearing that a good friend has had an accident. One common automatic reaction is to imagine circumstances under which the accident would not have occurred. For example, what if he had taken a taxi home instead of driving himself? Clearly, it is easy to construct an argument as to why such an automatic reaction evolved: it enhances the ability to understand the causes of life-threatening events and therefore increases the chances of survival. There are, however, many more situations for which evolution has not prepared us to engage in counterfactual thinking, and these require the active use of the deliberate system. It is the failure to invest effort in imagination that is one of the greatest barriers to learning from experience.

Learning correctly requires that one be skilled at both observation and imagination. In chapter 7, I shall explore both in the context of educating intuition.

The Role of Memory

The role that memory plays in intuition can be illustrated by comparing once again the physician and the professional tennis player. Intuition is acquired through experience and thus is specific to particular domains and particular people, residing in memory. In other words, the physician does not have the tennis player's (valid) intuitions about where to hit the ball, and she does not have his (erroneous) intuitions about the diagnosis of typhoid fever.

We tend to experience memory in two distinct ways: recall and recognition. Let us consider each.

Recall

Recall often involves attempting to find or identify a particular piece of information. For example, we may be trying to remember a specific date when a significant event occurred or how a certain film ended. Recall tasks vary in the ease with which they can be achieved. Sometimes they take no effort at all. (For instance, we can all recall our names without effort.) At other times, they require our full attention—just what were the last two lines of that poem you used to like so much?

In the early part of the twentieth century, recall tasks were the focus of much psychological research. Memory was investigated by asking subjects to remember so-called nonsense syllables—series of letters that had no meaning (e.g., *zog*). This line of research turned out to be useful only in a limited way—it showed that there are limits to short-term or working memory—only a limited number of such syllables can be retained for long. This research also failed to discover how recall from long-term memory works.[41]

Recall from long-term memory works by way of reconstruction.[42] To appreciate this, reflect for a moment on the way in which you tell a joke. It is highly unlikely that you try to commit jokes to memory verbatim. Instead, you keep in mind the skeleton of the story—the main characters and details of the situation—and, as you tell the joke, you elaborate the scenes and the story line extemporaneously by a process of reconstruction. (Also, if you are like most people, you will be hoping that you remember and deliver the punch line effectively.)

Many different cues can be used in the reconstruction process. Moreover, reconstruction is facilitated when you already possess a lot of knowledge about the context in which the object of recall is embedded. Thus, it is easier for a sports fan to remember specific statistics about players or the details of a given match than it is to remember facts about political events in which he has little interest. The network of possible connections for sports is much thicker than for politics for this particular individual.

However, because our memories do not work like tape or video recorders, distortions can be introduced, intentionally or unintentionally. For example, extensive evidence exists that the testimony of eyewitnesses can be affected by the way in which questions are asked. For example, a question such as, "Did you see the accused hitting the policeman?" implies that the policeman was, indeed, hit by the accused, whereas this might be a fact that remains to be established.[43]

In discussing the early twentieth-century physician and the professional tennis player above, I made the point that each had a unique stock of intuitions that pertained to their specific areas of expertise. Another way of stating this is that their memories—or stocks of intuitions—represent an important part of their expertise (although one can legitimately question the validity of the physician's expertise). There is an important and obvious link between expertise and intuition in that experts possess much domain-specific knowledge that they use intuitively. In fact, I would go so far as to say that we are all "experts" in the sense that we possess idiosyncratic knowledge that we use intuitively. (Unfortunately, most of us are not the kind of expert who gets paid for using his knowledge!) Thus, it is instructive to look at the psychology of expertise to gain some insights into the topic of intuition.

When developing recently a theory of the effects of expertise on recall, Kim Vicente and JoAnne Wang made the point that the memory of experts is facilitated because they observe constraints that limit the complexity of what they are trying to understand or remember.[44] Vicente and Wang call this *the constraint attunement hypothesis.* The key idea here is that experts are sensitive to constraints in particular situations that are relevant to goals. As I shall show, this helps not only the task of recall but also that of recognition.

Let me illustrate by comparing again the physician and the tennis player. Imagine that they have both just observed a long rally in a tennis match and that they are asked to recall what happened. The physician's ability to recall is poor. He thinks hard and can remember who served, who finally won the point, roughly how many times each player hit the ball, and some details of the winning shot. The tennis player, however, can remember much more—in greater detail and with greater accuracy—about the rally because she has a mental structure that places everything in a context. She knows a lot about how the two players play. She knows where they stand in the match and can make good guesses about the kinds of tactics that they are likely to use. She understands immediately how the type of serve and the subsequent return set up the shots that follow, how the players' individual strengths and weaknesses affect their responses to particular kinds of shots, and so on. In other words, the tennis professional's knowledge directed her attention to specific aspects of the match. It constrained what she saw but subsequently aided her ability to recall what actually happened. Indeed, although she saw exactly the same physical stimulus as the physician, the way in which she saw it was much better structured by the constraints imposed by the prior knowledge that she possessed.

To appreciate this point from another perspective, imagine a situation in which both the physician and the tennis professional are watching what is stated to be a point from a game of tennis. In fact, there are two players on a court with a ball and racquets, but the rules of the game that they are actually playing—call it "Martian tennis"—are unknown to all observers and extremely difficult to extrapolate. In this case, the tennis professional's knowledge will not impose appropriate constraints on what she sees. Her memory of the point is unlikely to be better than that of the physician.[45]

Recognition

The mental effort involved in recall can vary from a little (or none) to a lot. For example, recalling many things (your name, the names of family and friends, details of the work in which you are currently engaged) takes next to no effort, but recalling precisely the details of an accident or what someone said can often take a great deal of effort. Recognition, in contrast, is a process that seems to work with little conscious awareness or effort. Either you recognize something or someone, or you do not. True, you cannot always identify—that is, give names or labels to—what you recognize, but the fact of recognition remains. What seems to happen is a matching between an external stimulus and an internal representation. Moreover, at times you are aware that you have recognized "something"; at other times you are not.

Constraints (see above) and judgments of similarity facilitate the process of recognition. In general, similarity plays an important role in mental life. In its simplest form, it can be thought of as involving a feature-matching process. Two objects are judged to be similar to the extent that they share common features.[46] Indeed, this is why they "look alike." As noted in chapter 2, judgments of similarity are made quickly and, it would seem, intuitively. (Recall the question about whether a circular object with a three-inch diameter was more similar to a pizza or to a quarter.) Moreover, as mentioned at the beginning of this chapter, similarity plays an important role in causal reasoning—perceived similarity can be used to infer a causal link.

In chapter 2, I discussed Jerome Bruner's two modes of cognitive functioning (or knowing)—the paradigmatic and the narrative. The narrative mode takes its strength—its ability to convince—from "lifelikeness" or "verisimilitude"; that is, narrative gains much of its force because, through context, it appeals to the implicit knowledge of the audience. Clearly, the speed and ease of understanding achieved through stories depend on your being able to see immediately the resemblance between aspects of the story and (your) reality. At the same time, elements of the story create links with different parts of your memory and thereby engage further connections in your mind. In other words, through similarity, a story can make many links with the mind, something a more explicit, rational explanation cannot do.

Consider also the power of analogies, which depend on principles of similarity. When explaining phenomena to children, for example, or when trying to understand complex phenomena, we typically resort to analogies. The computer analogy, for example, has been critical to our understanding of human information processing (see chap. 2).

Clearly, the process by which we make similarity judgments—and use analogies—relies heavily on intuitive thought processes and the accessing of information in memory. That making judgments of similarity depends on memory can be illustrated by simple thought experiments. In order to determine whether two things are similar, you must know which features to consider. First, given differential past experience, people will not necessarily attend to the same common and distinguishing features. Second, analogies that some people find illuminating will be totally meaningless to those who lack the knowledge or the experience on which those analogies draw. Sports analogies, for instance, are very culture specific.

Wendell Garner nicely encapsulated the importance of constraints in recognition in the title of his 1970 paper "Good Patterns Have Few Alternatives." In other words, there is no ambiguity in perception when you can make only a single interpretation of the stimulus object—usually because constraints (perhaps self-imposed on the basis of past experience) do not allow you to see anything else. Garner talked specifically about the way in which redundancy imposes constraints on what people see and thus determines how good their judgment of patterns will be. For example, circles or squares form good patterns in the sense that, once part of the figure is recognized, the rest can be determined—there are no perceptual alternatives. On the other hand, an inkblot can take many shapes, and the whole cannot be inferred from exposure to only part.

Recognition, and therefore memory, is clearly enhanced by expertise since expertise depends largely on understanding redundancies. For example, a chess master's knowledge suggests constraints on, or redundancies in, the relations between the pieces when he or she is watching a match. And this ability to recognize constraints helps him or her reconstruct, or remember, previous moves as well as postulate various ways in which the game might develop. The knowledge of the novice chess player, however, would not impose such constraints on perception, and his or her memory of previous moves will not be as accurate as that of the master.[47]

Both the Garner and the Vicente-Wang frameworks suggest that recognition (through memory) is greatly aided by the constraints imposed on perception by experience. This clearly has implications for the education of intuition, implications that I shall explore below (see chap. 7).

As noted above, intuition can be thought of as a form of expertise in the sense that it is specific to particular domains. It is therefore illuminating to consider some findings about the memories of experts in their domains. In a recent review of the literature, Anders Ericsson and A. C. Lehmann emphasize the advantages that experts possess. These include being able to recognize domain-specific stimuli (see also above) and the relative speed with which this is done as well as a greater capacity for incidental learning related to their expertise. Even experts have limits, however; Ericsson and Lehmann propose "that experts' superior memory is not general across all types of information in a domain but reflects selective encoding of relevant information and mechanisms acquired to expand the functional capacity of the experts' working memory."[48] In other words, expertise affects not only the *content* of memory (the information that is stored) but also the *process*. In dealing with domains with which we are familiar, we learn to combat the limitations of short-term or working memory more effectively.

Ericsson and Lehmann also point out that not all expert performance is intuitive in the sense of being automatic. Expert memory is not an "automatic consequence of domain-specific experience but requires the acquisition of specific memory skills tailored to the demands of working memory by the particular activity."[49] On the other hand, some of the experts' memory skills do become automatic.

In chapter 5, I shall discuss further implications of the role that recognition plays in the intuitive skills of experts. Moreover, in chapter 7, I shall again emphasize that intuition has much in common with expertise. Thus, deliberately developing specific memory skills is also important in educating intuition.

Types of Memory

In preceding chapters, I emphasized that the human organism consists of many systems and subsystems that evolved to enhance survival. Moreover, the human organism has developed over the ages in an incremental fashion. Adaptation is a gradual, step-by-step process. New or improved mechanisms are added to existing structures; they are not built from scratch. It should therefore come as little surprise that we possess different types of memory and that these different types handle different functions. Moreover, there is no reason why memory should reside entirely in one location in the body.

Clearly, certain kinds of physical memory—those that regulate internal physical processes—operate outside conscious awareness, and we are all better off for this. For example, we do not need to remind our thyroid gland to secrete hormones at certain times. A healthy gland "knows" when to do this. From our viewpoint, it acts exactly like a thermostat that "remembers" to set in motion the process that warms a house when the temperature drops below a certain level. This kind of physical memory is not the concern of this book. On the other hand, other physical memory systems are involved in how we adapt to the environment and, because they also bypass consciousness, are relevant to our concerns.

In the area of the emotions—and especially fear—Joseph LeDoux has made a nice distinction between what he calls *implicit* and *explicit* memories. He illustrates this distinction with a story about a brain-damaged patient in France at the beginning of the twentieth century who was examined by a physician named Claparède. Apparently, the damage was such that the patient had lost the ability to create new memories:

> Each time Claparède walked into the room he had to introduce himself to her, as she had no recollection of having seen him before. The memory problem was so severe that if Claparède left the room and returned a few minutes later, she wouldn't remember having seen him.
>
> One day, he tried something new. He entered the room, and, as on every other day, he held out his hand to greet her. In typical fashion she shook his hand. But when their hands met, she quickly pulled hers back, for Claparède had concealed a tack in his palm and had pricked her with it. The next time he returned to the room to greet her, she still had no recognition of him, but she refused to shake his hand. She could not tell him why she would not shake hands with him, but she wouldn't do it.[50]

On the basis of research conducted since Claparède's day, LeDoux argues that this incident shows the distinction between implicit *emotional memory* (the prick to the hand) and explicit *memory of emotions* (knowing or remembering that the hand had been pricked). The former is an implicit memory that—in the case of fear—is registered automatically in the amygdala and can initiate behavior without involving the higher-level cortical regions of the brain. The latter is an explicit memory maintained in the cortical region. It must be assumed that, as a result of her brain damage, Claparède's patient lacked this latter form of memory. Nevertheless, she still clearly retained a functional subconscious emotional memory system.

Another example of implicit emotional memory is the fact that some people remember odors and, sometimes, music extraordinarily well. Such memories are visceral and emotional. They recur without effort, sometimes after many years have passed, and the ease with which they are recognized is surprising. Sometimes such memories are associated with specific, emotionally meaningful events—say, eating a special dish at your grandparents' house—in which case both implicit emotional memory and the explicit memory of emotions are involved.

Many of us complain about our memories. When we do so, it is with respect to our explicit memories, which reflect our higher-level cognitive processes. What we fail to notice is that we all have large implicit memories. Learning is a constant human activity. Much, however, happens below the level of consciousness. At the conscious level, we just don't know how much we know.

Summary

This chapter started by asking whether our intuitions are, in any way, genetic in origin. This question is difficult to answer, in part because, at the behavioral level, intuitions are often experienced as though they are instincts—they are initiated automatically without conscious awareness. Also, because the *processes* by which we acquire many intuitions are inherent, it is difficult to define the respective contributions of our genetic endowments and the environments with which those endowments interact. However, it is also abundantly clear that each of our individual stocks of intuition reflects our own, idiosyncratic cultural capital. It is therefore important to examine carefully the processes of learning.

Learning is an activity in which the human organism is constantly engaged. We possess automatic processes and are always tacitly updating our inventory of knowledge through observation. We can, of course, use our deliberate system to learn explicitly—in a rational, academic sense—but doing so requires effort, and learning that occurs in this fashion is the exception rather than the rule.

Learning from experience involves noticing connections that are reinforced by subsequent experience. Feedback is essential, yet feedback can often mislead us. I introduced the concepts of kind and wicked learning structures in order to make the point that characteristics of the environment in which learning takes place affect the validity of what is learned. In kind learning structures, people receive good feedback, and the right lessons can be learned from experience. In wicked learning environments, feedback can be misleading, and the right lessons are not always learned. In order therefore to determine whether intuitions are valid, the situations in which those intuitions were acquired must be examined. The concept of learning structures clearly has important implications for educating intuition. It can help us determine whether intuitions are likely to be valid, and it can also suggest the kinds of environments that should be sought in order to develop appropriate intuitions.

I went on to make the point that intuition can be thought of as a form of expertise, acquired through experience and thus specific to a particular domain. However, expertise in one domain does not guarantee expertise in another. Similarly, the fact that some of your intuitions are valid in one domain does not guarantee that they will be valid in others.

The chapter concluded with a discussion of memory. The key point was that there are many types of memory. These different types of memory are a legacy of the way in which we have evolved over millions of years. Our different memory systems appear to handle different functions. From the viewpoint of intuition, there is an important distinction between our implicit and our explicit memory systems. Explicit memory is what you and I typically think of when we invoke the term *memory*—it is what we can access in consciousness. Implicit memory is acquired automatically and provides the basis of many of our intuitions. Many of us complain about our memories, meaning our explicit memory systems. Little do we realize how effective our implicit memory systems in fact are. Paradoxically, we know more than we think we know.

CHAPTER 4

People as Intuitive "Experts"

If we were to assume that intuitive judgment is always correct, there would be no need to educate intuition since we could with safety always act in accordance with our intuitions. On the other hand, if we were to assume that intuitive judgment is always incorrect, there would likewise be no need to educate intuition since we could simply ignore our intuitions and act in a more deliberate, rational manner. Neither strategy, however, seems reasonable or even possible.

In 1967, Cameron Peterson and Lee Roy Beach published a paper entitled "Man as an Intuitive Statistician." The paper was a review of the literature that examined studies in which people had made judgments in tasks in which responses could be compared to the outputs of formal statistical models. As implied by the title of the paper, the intent was to assess whether people make judgments as though their intuitions are consistent with the principles of statistical reasoning. For example, one conclusion was that people have good intuitions about averages but not the statistical concept of variance.

This paper is typical of a large literature that compares the judgments that people make with the results obtained from models based either on physical processes (e.g., the physical laws of motion) or on abstract schemes of reasoning (e.g., probability theory). The results of such research are important for our concerns because examining the quality of intuition in different kinds of settings leads to further implications for its education. Therefore, in this chapter, I review what these studies tell us about the quality of human intuitions—how "good" they are. I further interpret the kinds of results that have been observed and comment on some of the controversies in the literature. In chapter 5, I examine other dimensions of "goodness."

When Are Responses Intuitive?

Before discussing the literature, I must first point out that, in many psychological studies of *intuitive* judgment, it is not clear whether responses have been made in an intuitive or an analytic manner. Most investigators simply record their subjects' responses, and no attempts are made to determine whether these responses involved explicit deliberation or were *"reached with little apparent effort, and typically without conscious awareness"* (p. 14 above).

On the other hand, investigators are well aware that subjects may respond to questions in intuitive or nonintuitive ways. For example, in the paper "On the Study of Statistical Intuitions," Daniel Kahneman and Amos Tversky made their understanding of intuition clear:

> The terms *intuition* and *intuitive* are used in three senses. First, a judgment is called intuitive if it is reached by an informal and unstructured mode of reasoning, without the use of analytic methods or deliberate calculation. . . . Second, a formal rule or fact of nature is called intuitive if it is compatible with our lay model of the world. . . . Third, a rule or procedure is said to be part of our repertoire of intuitions when we apply the rule or follow the procedure in our normal conduct. The rules of grammar, for example, are part of the intuitions of a native speaker.[1]

Moreover, in an important paper published in 1983, Tversky and Kahneman make the point that the way a problem is presented can trigger different ways of responding. Specifically, they suggested that "seemingly inconsequential cues" can bring "extensional" (or nonintuitive) considerations to mind, and they concluded, "A comprehensive account of human judgment must reflect the tension between compelling logical rules and seductive nonextensional intuitions."[2]

Thus, although studies do not typically control whether subjects are responding in "intuitive" ways, it is usually assumed that they are responding in ways that are natural to them and that do not involve artificial aids, such as calculators or paper and pencil.[3] Moreover, as the quotation from Tversky and Kahneman's 1983 paper makes clear, investigators recognize that people may respond to questions using different modes of thought (see also chap. 2).

Finally, it should also be noted that the problems with which subjects are presented can be structured in such a way as to require (albeit unintentionally) less intuitive and more deliberative responses—or vice versa. Take judgments about physical phenomena as an example. If subjects are asked to predict the precise trajectory of a moving body, their responses will necessarily be deliberative (even though an intuitive understanding of the phenomenon may be invoked). If, however, subjects are asked to judge which of two depictions of the trajectory of a moving object is anomalous, perceptual reactions will be invoked that are far more intuitive. I shall return to these issues below.

How Good Can or Should Our Intuitions Be?

Psychologists have expended much energy in documenting how good people are at making various kinds of intuitive judgments or decisions, whether these concern physical or abstract systems. However, before examining these findings, it is important to consider when a person's intuitive judgment is or is not liable to be considered valid.

To set the scene, imagine that an investigator is assessing the validity of someone's judgments by asking for a prediction about a physical system or, perhaps, a judgment of relative likelihood. As an example of the former, imagine that the subject is being asked about the possible trajectory that an object would take when dropped from an airplane. As an example of the latter, imagine that the question centers on whether one event is more likely to occur than another. Specific exemplars of these problems are provided in exhibit 7.

It is illuminating to consider assessments of intuitive abilities by examining the relations between three different systems or models that are depicted schematically in exhibit 8.[4]

First, there is the model or understanding that the person has of the situation with which he or she is confronted. The key issue here is, not just determining what that person's understanding is, but also determining *why* that person has developed that particular understanding. Is it based on past experiences with similar situations? If so, were those experiences such that the understanding induced was appropriate? (Was the learning environment kind or wicked?) Was the person's understanding influenced by formal training?

Second, there is the actual real-world situation about which the person is being asked to make judgments. For example, what really happens when objects are dropped from airplanes?

Third, there is the normative model of the real-world situation that

EXHIBIT 7 Two problems

---

1. Physical system problem

An object is dropped from an airplane (see below). Which trajectory is most likely?

 a) Trajectory A, falling behind the point at which it was dropped?

 b) Trajectory B, falling directly below the point at which it was dropped?

 c) Trajectory C, falling ahead of the point at which it was dropped?

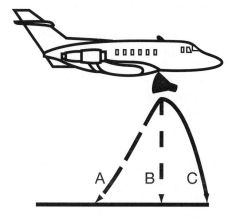

---

2. Relative likelihood problem

A certain town is served by two hospitals. In the larger hospital about forty-five babies are born each day, and in the smaller hospital about fifteen babies are born each day. As you know, about 50 percent of all babies are boys. The exact percentage of baby boys, however, varies from day to day. Sometimes it may be higher than 50 percent, sometimes lower. For a period of one year, each hospital recorded the number of days on which more (less) than 60 percent of the babies born were boys. Which hospital do you think recorded more such days? The larger hospital? The smaller hospital? About the same (i.e., within 5 percent of each other)?

Sources: Problem 1: Kaiser, Proffitt, & McCloskey (1985). Problem 2: Kahneman & Tversky (1972). The illustration used in problem 1 is reproduced, in slightly altered form, from M. K. Kaiser, D. R. Proffitt, and M. McCloskey, "The Development of Beliefs about Falling Objects," *Perception and Psychophysics* 38, no. 6 (1985): 533–539, and is used with permission from the Psychonomic Society, Inc., and Mary K. Kaiser.

EXHIBIT 8   Three models

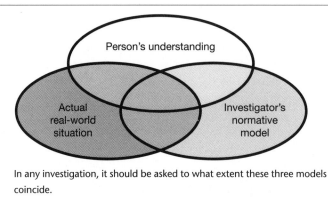

In any investigation, it should be asked to what extent these three models coincide.

the investigator is using to assess the validity of the person's response. In the case of exhibit 7 above, the physical system problem relies on Newtonian mechanics, and the relative likelihood problem relies on probability theory.

Simply stated, if all three models coincide or are the same, then intuitive responses will be assessed as accurate (provided, of course, that the person responds in accord with his or her model). However, what variables are likely to affect mismatches between the three models?

First, compare the person's model with the real world. Given the discussion in chapter 3, much will depend on the nature of the person's past experience with the phenomenon faced. Is the person able to recognize the phenomenon, and did feedback from making judgments in similar situations in the past facilitate an appropriate response? In other words, has past experience with this phenomenon taught the person the right lesson? Has the person received formal training in dealing with such a problem? And, even if the person has had experience with the phenomenon involved, he or she may not recognize this because of the misleading way in which this particular problem is posed. For example, presenting a problem in an unusual context might hide a structure with which the person is actually quite familiar.

Second, compare the real world and the normative model used by the investigator. By definition, a normative model always abstracts from reality and focuses on a few, salient variables. For example, in a question about the mechanics of motion, the investigator may instruct the person to ignore the effects of friction. Yet friction is present in everyday experience—both in the real world and in the person's experience of it. Normative models cannot capture all facets of the real world. In addition, the possibility exists that the investigator may have chosen an inappropriate normative model—a non-Newtonian model of mechanics, for example. In probabilistic reasoning problems, different assumptions about a situation can lead to different "normative" answers.[5] Moreover, as the history of science has shown repeatedly, each generation tends to believe that its normative models or paradigms are correct. Yet science is constantly changing the "enlightened" way of seeing the world.

Third, the models employed by the person and by the investigator can clearly differ if the investigator is using a method of analysis that does not match the person's experience. For example, in a problem in probabilistic reasoning, the investigator and the subject could disagree as to which data are relevant to the issue at hand.

To summarize, the three-models framework presented in exhibit 8 highlights several questions that need to be considered in examining investigations of people's intuitive knowledge and judgments. These center principally on the person's understanding of the problem faced. Critical to that understanding are the circumstances under which the person experienced the particular problem at hand as well as similar kinds of problems in the past. In other words, the person's learning history is key. As for the normative model—the standard used to judge the validity of intuitive responses—it is important to remember that it is based on specific assumptions and that what is deemed the "correct" answer depends on which scientific paradigm is currently accepted.

Intuition and the Physical World

To survive in the world, people need to take actions that have reasonable chances of success. To do this, they need to understand their environment. For example, what objects—animate and inanimate—move? What makes them move, and is it possible to predict their movements? What happens when we move and act on the environment? Which movements require the expenditure of effort, and which do not? How can we anticipate what will happen, first, in a short period of time and, then, in the longer term? What consistencies can we expect in what we experience?

Consider, for example, the effects of gravity. We all need to understand that objects fall unless supported, that a cart must be pushed or pulled up a hill but that it will roll down by itself, that missteps made when climbing trees can result in a fall and injury. But how do we come to acquire an understanding of such phenomena as gravity or motion (i.e., why objects move in ways that can be predicted)?

The process of understanding the physical world can be thought of as involving three stages. The first stage consists of direct experience. You observe, for example, that, whereas a ball will roll downhill unaided, it will not roll uphill unless someone pushes it. In the second stage, people start to formulate more general principles on the basis of observations—for example, that all objects fall to the ground unless supported. The third stage involves learning through formal instruction. Most people, for instance, have to be taught the general principle of gravity, which helps them make sense of their experience and also allows them to predict what happens in environments where gravity is not present. Thus, we can understand why astronauts seem to float when they are in space aboard the space shuttle but walk on the ground like the rest of us when they return to Earth.

Learning through observation is typically an implicit process—we do it constantly and without thinking much about it (see chap. 3). Such learning forms the basis of our intuitions about how the world works. Learning through instruction, however, requires paying explicit attention. It is not based on experience but appeals instead to logical or intellectual arguments. (It can, of course, also appeal to experience.) At any given time, it is important to realize that a person's intuitive theories—or the principles induced from experience—may or may not be "veridical"; that is, they may or may not correspond to reality. As discussed in chapter 3, experience does not necessarily teach us the correct lessons. Similarly, theories learned through instruction may not be valid. For instance, prior to Newton, generally held theories about the physics of motion were simply incorrect. (Undoubtedly, scientists will one day show that many of today's theories are incorrect.)

Consider our understanding of one implication of gravity. Studies conducted by Renée Baillargeon and her colleagues indicate that, by three months of age, children understand that an object will fall unless it is supported.[6] Presumably, children have many opportunities to observe falling objects and also notice that the upward movement of limbs is more difficult than the corresponding downward movement. However, it is one thing to notice something and quite another to extract a principle that embodies an accurate understanding of the phenomenon in question. We should not be surprised to learn, therefore, that infants' understanding of gravity is incomplete.

In the experimental paradigm in which this understanding was tested, Baillargeon showed infants the "possible" and "impossible" events illustrated in exhibit 9. The underlying assumption of this methodology is that infants will look longer at events that surprise them than they will at

EXHIBIT 9   Studying infants' appreciation of the physical world

Possible Event

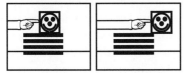

Impossible Event

This exhibit illustrates the paradigm for studying infants' understanding of support phenomena. In both events, a hand pushes a box from left to right along the top of a platform. In the possible event (top), the box is pushed until its leading edge reaches the end of the platform. In the impossible event (bottom), the box is pushed until only the left 15 percent of its bottom surface rests on the platform.

Source: Baillargeon (1994). The illustration is reproduced, in slightly altered form, from R. Baillargeon, "How Do Infants Learn about the Physical World?" *Current Directions in Psychological Science* 3, no. 5 (1994): 133–140, and is used with permission from Blackwell Publishers.

those that do not. In other words, events coded by infants as impossible will elicit surprise, whereas those coded as possible will not. Because infants are constantly trying to understand the world, it is assumed that they will look longer at events that violate their expectations.

In the possible event shown, a hand pushes a box along a platform until its leading edge reaches the end of the platform. In the impossible event, the box is pushed until only a small part of its lower surface rests on the platform. At three months of age, infants pay equal attention to the possible and the impossible events. Presumably, they are aware that contact is necessary to ensure support but do not yet appreciate the concept of how much support is needed. By six and a half months, however, infants expect the box to fall unless a significant portion of its lower surface is supported by the platform. As Baillargeon states, "These results suggest the following developmental sequence. When learning about the support relation between two objects, infants first form an initial concept centered on the distinction between contact and no contact. With further experience, this initial concept is progressively revised. Infants identify first a discrete (locus of contact) and later a continuous (amount of contact) variable and incorporate these variables into their initial concept, resulting in more successful predictions over time."[7]

The picture that emerges is that, over time, interaction with the environment leads to the development of concepts of how the world works. At different stages of development, these concepts may be more or less veridical, depending on the specific events experienced (recall the difference between kind and wicked learning environments discussed in chap. 3). Later in life, evidence suggesting alternative explanations of how the world works may be encountered and possibly integrated into our understanding.

An interesting example of the development of such concepts is found in the transition from the notion that the world is flat to the notion that it is round. As is well known, that the world is not flat was first suspected by the ancient Greeks, who noted that the position of the stars relative to the earth depended on whether observations were made in the north or the south of what was then the known world. Despite these early observations, however, it took many centuries for the concept of a spherical world to become generally accepted.

There are, of course, many reasons why we need not think of the world as being anything but flat. Almost all our experience is with a world that operates as if it were flat. When walking or driving a car, for instance, we need not take account of the curvature of the earth, nor do we need to do so when pursuing most activities that take place indoors. Indeed, there are relatively few occasions when we need to take account of the fact that the world is round—only when, for example, we are attempting to determine whether it is shorter to fly from, say, Chicago to Bangkok by going west across the Pacific or east across the Atlantic, Europe, and the Middle East.

Today, children are taught quite early that the world is round. However, since they actually experience the world as if it were flat, it is intriguing to examine how they reconcile the difference between the intuitive models that they have developed on their own and the knowledge that they are taught by trusted adults. Stella Vosniadou and William Brewer examined this question among groups of children ranging in age from six to ten years.[8] Their study reveals that, while struggling with the notion that they "should" believe that the earth is round, children hold onto a variety of inconsistent beliefs. These include such notions as the following: (*a*) the earth is really a flattened sphere; (*b*) it is a sphere that has been hollowed out so that we can live inside it (imagine a hollowed-out pumpkin); (*c*) the earth is actually flat, but it can be perceived as spherical; (*d*) the earth is shaped like a disc or a rectangle and one could, in principle, fall off the edge. Naturally, as children mature and come to understand concepts such as gravity in a more formal manner, they are able to construct models that reconcile their experience and the theories that they have been taught.

Some Problems in "Intuitive Physics"

Exhibit 10 presents six problems that have appeared in the literature on "intuitive physics." The reader is invited to solve these problems before reading what follows.

Problem 1 was posed to twenty-five undergraduate students at Stanford University who had not received any formal instruction in physics— 64 percent gave answer a, $\frac{1}{2}z$ seconds, 22 percent answer b, z seconds.[9] The question probes whether people understand the basic rationale of Galileo's experiment with free-falling bodies, and the correct answer, in accordance with the Newtonian model of mechanics, is b—the weights fall at the same speed. Answer a is compatible with an earlier or Aristotelian model of mechanics whereby heavier objects are presumed to fall at a faster rate.

Several variations of problem 2 have been used in the literature. Although many people give answer a, directly below the point of release, the correct answer is b, ahead of the point of release. The trajectory of the ball will take the form of a parabola from the moment it leaves the man's hand until it reaches the ground. There are two physical principles involved here: momentum and gravity. The object has momentum when the man releases it, but it is also subject to gravity. Together, momentum and gravity imply that it will fall forward at an increasing rate—hence the parabolic shape of its trajectory.

In a problem testing this same principle, college students were asked to walk across a room and drop a golf ball onto a target marked on the floor. Formal instruction in physics had a big effect on behavior. Of those who had had no training in physics, 80 percent dropped the ball when they were directly over the target (incorrectly), 7 percent after passing over the target (also incorrectly), and only 13 percent before reaching the target (correctly). Of those who had taken at least one course in physics, the corresponding figures were 27, 0, and 73 percent, respectively.[10]

Several different versions of problems 3 and 4 have been examined. The main result is that the majority of experimental subjects do understand that, once released, objects will continue to move in a straight line unless once again affected by outside forces. Thus, the correct response to problem 3 is to draw a straight line coming out of the tube. As for problem 4, the ball will continue to move in a straight line that is the tangent

EXHIBIT 10   How good is your intuitive knowledge of physics?

1. When dropped from a building, a four-pound ball reaches the ground in z seconds. How long would it take a two-pound ball to reach the ground?
   a) $\frac{1}{2}z$ seconds?
   b) z seconds?
   c) More than z seconds?
   d) $2z$ seconds?
   e) Cannot be determined from the data?

2. A man carrying a baseball is jogging at a speed of approximately eight minutes per mile. He releases the ball and lets it fall. Where will it first fall on the ground?
   a) Directly below the point of release?
   b) Ahead of the point of release?
   c) Behind the point of release?

3. A ball is shot into the C-shaped tube shown below. Draw the path that the ball will take as it exits the tube.

4. A ball attached to a piece of string is being spun in a circle, as illustrated in the diagram below. Imagine that the string holding the ball breaks at the point marked X. Draw the path that the ball will take after the string breaks.

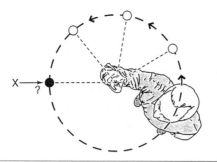

5. Imagine that you are riding a bicycle. Why is it easier to balance a bicycle when it is moving rapidly as opposed to when it is stationary or moving slowly? Suppose you hold your hands over your head and lean to the right without touching the handlebars. What will happen? Why?

6. Consider a boat with a weight on it floating in a tank of water. The water level is marked on the tank. If the weight is taken off the boat and placed in the water, what will the water level be relative to the original mark?
   a) Higher?
   b) Lower?
   c) The same?

Sources: Problem 1: Shanon (1976). Problem 2: McCloskey (1983). Problem 3: Kaiser, Proffitt, & McCloskey (1985). Problem 4: McCloskey (1983). Problem 5: Proffitt, Kaiser, & Whelan (1990). Problem 6: Proffitt & Gilden (1989). The illustration used in problem 3 is reproduced, in slightly altered form, from M. K. Kaiser, D. R. Proffitt, and M. McCloskey, "The Development of Beliefs about Falling Objects," *Perception and Psychophysics* 38, no. 6 (1985): 533–539, and is used with permission from the Psychonomic Society, Inc., and Mary K. Kaiser. The illustration (by Michael Goodman) used in problem 4 is reproduced with permission, in slightly altered form, from M. McCloskey, "Intuitive Physics," *Scientific American* 248, no. 4 (1983): 122–130.

of the circle at point X, where the string breaks. However, a substantial minority of subjects tend to believe that, in both cases, the trajectories will reflect the curvature of the paths that the objects take prior to release. Thus, in responding to problems 3 and 4, these subjects depict paths that continue to curve inward.[11]

Why do people provide such a high rate of incorrect responses to problems 1–4? Why has their experience with the world not taught them the appropriate responses? The literature provides some clues. First, it is interesting to note that most incorrect responses to problems 3 and 4 are in accord with the so-called impetus theory of physics, which holds that a body in motion must contain within it some underlying force (i.e., motion implies force). This theory is consistent with many observations and was once a standard component of the scientific thought that preceded Newton.[12]

Consider problem 1 and the prototypical experience that people have when thinking about the speed at which light and heavy bodies fall. It is easy to imagine heavy objects falling quickly and light objects—like feathers and small pieces of paper, which seem to float—falling slowly. This is because, in the real world, friction—in this case, the result of air resistance or sometimes wind—can affect small, light objects but has no discernible influence on objects with greater mass. By having subjects observe or imagine both a piece of paper and a book falling to the ground, it is easy to induce the false principle that heavy objects fall more quickly than lighter ones. (After all, a book that contains many pieces of paper is seen to fall more quickly than a single piece of paper does.) Indeed, as noted above, prior to Galileo the accepted wisdom was that heavy objects fall more quickly than lighter ones. However, when friction is not a factor (as, e.g., when sufficient mass is involved), objects of different weights do fall at the same rate.

The point that I am making is that experience can lead to false intuitions. For example, if you attempt to determine the rates at which objects of different weights fall by observing (or imagining) what happens when a single piece of paper and a book are dropped at the same time, the conclusion that you reach is likely to be false because it was acquired in a wicked environment (see chap. 3). Moreover, you are likely to retain false intuitions until they are explicitly challenged. Just consider how long humanity had to wait for Galileo to elaborate the appropriate principle. It is clear that invalid knowledge based on intuition can have a long life indeed!

The largely incorrect responses that untutored subjects give to problem 2 are surprising in the light of the number of times each of us has dropped objects or fallen and dropped objects. Why then have we not induced the correct principle from these experiences? McCloskey offers an interesting hypothesis that centers on the perceptual frame against which the falling object is seen.[13] For example, if you are walking and suddenly notice that you have dropped something, say, a coin, you will see it falling and hitting the ground only by turning around. The coin will not fall in front of you. Thus, the frame against which you see the falling coin is behind you, and, because of your own motion, it seems as if the coin has fallen straight down from the point of release. In addition, it is unlikely that you will notice the fact that the coin accelerates as it falls—this is too fine a distinction to be made perceptually. Once again, the feedback that you have received about falling objects in this kind of situation has not allowed you to infer the appropriate principle. What we have here is another example of a wicked learning environment.

An argument can, of course, be made that, with enough experience, people would be able to induce the appropriate principles underlying problems such as those presented in exhibit 10. This hypothesis was tested directly by Kaiser, Jonides, and Alexander using variations of problem 3.[14] Their argument was that people do not have much experience with balls being shot through C-shaped tubes. However, people have experienced the operative physical principle in other contexts. For example, most people know that water comes out of a garden hose in a "straight line" even when the hose itself is twisted. Kaiser, Jonides, and Alexander therefore asked people to predict the paths that both water and a ball would take on leaving a curved tube and found that significantly more people correctly predicted the path that water would take. However, little transfer of knowledge from the concrete version of the problem (involving water) to the abstract version (involving balls) seems to have occurred. In other words, just because people recognize a physical principle in one context does not necessarily mean that they will recognize it in others.

In commenting on these results, Kaiser, Jonides, and Alexander stated, "Subjects draw on specific experiences to solve the common-sense problems, and need not employ formal reasoning. The abstract problem, evoking no specific memory, requires subjects to draw upon their formal understanding of physics (which is often erroneous). First, they search for a specific solution based on relevant experiences. If this search fails, they default to a reasoning process employing formal understanding of mechanics."[15] Of interest is the fact that, because people fail to solve the problem intuitively, they attempt to reason formally—or nonintuitively—but fail to use the right principles.

Another study found an intriguing developmental trend. When presented with a curved-tube problem, preschool and kindergarten children responded as accurately as a group of college students (who, for the most part, had taken some high school or college physics courses) and more accurately than a group of third through sixth graders.[16] The implication is that very young children can form intuitive ideas about the world that are approximately correct but that further experience can cause these early ideas to be replaced by incorrect notions, notions that instruction and even further experience must correct.

Now consider the two parts of problem 5 in exhibit 10. Proffitt, Kaiser, and Whelan presented variations of this problem to undergraduate students, including members of a university bicycling club.[17] No one showed much understanding of the principle underlying the stability of the moving bicycle—that the bicycle wheels act as gyroscopes and that the bicycle's stability is proportional to the angular velocity of its wheels. Most of the twenty-five cyclists knew that the bicycle would move to the right if the rider leaned in that direction. However, only two predicted that the bicycle's front wheel would turn in the direction in which the rider leaned even if the handlebars were not touched.

How can we account for these results? Proffitt and Gilden claim that, in order to understand many dynamic phenomena, people need to attend to two or more variables. But our intuitive understanding is too simplistic. We tend to base our judgments on single variables, and this inevitably leads to errors in some circumstances.[18]

This should not, however, be interpreted as meaning that we are incapable of learning through experience to consider two or more variables. For example, in the famous conservation studies conducted by Piaget and Inhelder, young children (under age seven) are shown colored liquid in a glass container.[19] The liquid is then poured into a glass container of a different shape, and the children are asked whether the amount of liquid has changed. Most reply that it has and seem to base their judgments on a single dimension, the visible height of the liquid in the containers. The conservation principle, however, requires taking two dimensions into account, and this is something that older children (and adults) do learn from experience.

Problem 6 in exhibit 10 was presented to three famous physicists, Robert Oppenheimer (leader of the Manhattan Project), Felix Bloch (a Nobel laureate), and George Gamow (a celebrated quantum theorist). All three gave answer *c*, the water level remains the same. However, "the correct answer is that the water level goes down, because when the weight is in the boat it is displacing the volume of water equal to its mass, and when it is in the water it displaces only its own volume."[20]

I included this problem in exhibit 10 to emphasize that many problems presented by the physical world are hard to solve—and that even experts can be wrong. Our perception of the world, and our imagination of what might be, can be biased both by our experiences and by the principles that we believe are correct.

It should be noted that many of the problems discussed above were presented in a way that required explicit reasoning, that is, in written form (e.g., exhibit 10) or even verbally. However, this is not how we typically experience physical phenomena. Instead, observation is the norm. Thus, we need to know how a presentation that relies on observation affects responses.

To test this, some studies presented subjects with short films depicting physical phenomena and asked them to state whether those phenomena were anomalous. For example, in one study, films of free-falling bodies were shown in alternative presentations, one display depicting constant velocity, the other depicting constant acceleration. In another study, objects were seen to have been shot out of curved tubes in both straight and curvilinear lines.[21] In both studies, adult subjects correctly identified which motions were anomalous. Apparently, the ability to assess whether certain phenomena are consistent with known physical laws in visual displays is superior to the ability to reason abstractly about the same phenomena.[22] However, it is not perfect.[23] To the extent that the visual system is more intuitive than analytic, these results are important because they provide support for the notion that, in some cases, our intuition may be more valid than analysis, that is, explicit attempts to reason. We know more than we are able to articulate.

To summarize, people do have misconceptions about the way in which many important physical forces operate. The source of these misconceptions, however, can be traced to the conditions under which we learn about the phenomena in question. For example, our ideas about the shape of the earth and the relative speed at which bodies of different weights fall are formed by our experiences. Subsequently, these ideas are "corrected" by science, but, as pointed out before, science is not infallible. Much of what nineteenth-century physicists considered fact was overturned by discoveries made in the twentieth century. Who knows how the twenty-first century will further change the face of physics?

Most of our learning about physical phenomena occurs implicitly through observation. Thus, how we observe phenomena and our ability to discriminate affect what we feel we know. For example, we may not realize that if we drop a coin while walking, it will fall forward following a parabolic path and that it will accelerate as it gets closer to the ground—to us it simply seems as though it falls straight down. But we do know—from experience—that, if we throw a ball to a friend who is at some distance, we must aim high and that the ball will take a parabolic path through the air until it is caught. We do seem to have a good implicit understanding of some phenomena. The studies reviewed above, however, demonstrate that we often fail to abstract the appropriate physical principles from our observations and have difficulty generalizing across situations.

Intuition and Reasoning

In comparison with the literature on the intuitive understanding of physical phenomena, the literature on people's ability to reason intuitively is huge. It has also generated much controversy. At the heart of the controversy is the debate over *how*, and *how well*, people reason intuitively. In other words, are people good intuitive statisticians, logicians, economists, etc.? And, second, do people possess general "algorithms" for reasoning, or does reasoning consist of a collection of special purpose mechanisms that have developed for specific kinds of tasks?

The literature on reasoning has been heavily influenced by different normative models, for example, deductive logic, probability theory, canons of causal analysis, and economic theory. In all cases, I believe that it is important to keep in mind the three-system model outlined in exhibit 8 above. How does the *person* understand the problem faced, and why has she or he come to adopt this particular representation? What is the *real-*

world mechanism or model employed? What assumptions has the *inves-tigator* made about the situation?

The principal finding that appears again and again in this literature is that problems that have identical formal structures can elicit different responses. This can occur when problems involve different issues or contexts or simply when the format is changed in a seemingly trivial way, for example, when probabilistic information is presented in the form of frequencies as opposed to fractions or percentages. I shall first examine two well-known problems in deductive thought before considering issues of probabilistic reasoning.

Deductive Reasoning and Disconfirmation

A problem that has stimulated enormous interest is the following:[24] Imagine that you have in front of you four cards that show (from left to right) the letter *A*, the letter *B*, the number *4*, and the number *7*. You are informed that each card has a letter on one side and a number on the other. You are also informed of the rule, "If a card has a vowel on one side, it has an even number on the other side." Given the four cards in front of you, *which and only which cards* would you need to turn over to verify whether the rule is correct?

The most frequent answers to this question are the cards showing the letter *A* and the number *4* and just the card showing the letter *A*.

From a *logical* viewpoint, the rule that you are being asked to test is of the form *if p then q*, that is, if vowel then even number. In this case, therefore, you need to verify (1) that the card with the vowel, *A*, does indeed have an even number on the other side (that *p* and *q* co-occur) and (2) that the card with *the odd* number, *7*, does *not* have a vowel on the other side (that *p* and *not-q* do not co-occur). In other words, you need to verify that cards with vowels do have even numbers on the other side and that cards with odd numbers do *not* have vowels on the other side.

In testing the rule, therefore, one needs to check both the possible confirming instance and the possible disconfirming instance, yet people tend to overlook the possible disconfirmation (the fourth card). However, once the error is explained, most people understand the logic.

Now consider a variation of this problem:[25] Imagine that you work in a bar and have to enforce the rule that, in order to drink alcoholic beverages, patrons must be over twenty-one years old. You observe four "young" people in the bar: the first is drinking beer; the second is drinking Coke; the third is twenty-five years old; and the fourth is sixteen years old. Whom do you check in order to verify that the rule is being enforced?

Once again, this problem is of the form *if p then q,* that is, if drinking alcohol then over twenty-one years of age. Most people have little difficulty understanding the structure of the problem and answer correctly that one should check the first and fourth persons. (Is the former over twenty-one? What is the latter drinking? Clearly, the Coke drinker and the twenty-five-year-old are in conformity with the rule.)

Since the structure of both problems is identical from a logical viewpoint, what explains the different answers?

Several explanations have emerged in the literature. One involves the effects of familiarity of context or the simple (to state) notion that concrete problems are easier to solve than abstract ones.[26] Another is that people develop cognitive schemas (see chap. 2) that allow them to recognize various kinds of problems involving "permissions."[27] Yet another invokes the evolutionary argument that the ability to detect cheaters in social situations would have been a trait favored by the forces of natural selection. The basic rationale here is that cooperation between individuals is critical to the ability of groups of humans to survive and prosper. Thus, humans evolved the ability to check whether others have complied with the terms of agreements. The implication is that problems that involve "social contracts" (as in the bar example above) are easy to solve because we are genetically predisposed to do so.[28] Finally, it has been argued that our ability to solve such problems depends, not on evolutionary adaptation at all, but on the way in which people understand the problems with which they are presented as well as the way in which the problems themselves have been framed.[29]

The range of explanations proposed highlights the issues at the center of the debate. Do people possess general problem-solving schemas that transcend the context in which a specific problem is embedded? How does context interact with the way in which a problem is structured? To what extent do responses simply reflect format? Has evolution facilitated our ability to answer these kinds of questions and in what way? The debates on these issues have been long and not without passion.

The Visualization Hypothesis

From the viewpoint of this book, one way to consider these phenomena is to ask what role intuitive processes play both in how people understand the problems they face and in their responses. (Recall that it is not always clear whether people's responses reflect intuition, analysis, or both.) Consider again the discussion of intuitive physics presented above, especially the comparison of problems presented verbally (i.e., in either written or spoken form) and those presented visually (i.e., through films). Visual presentations often elicit a valid intuitive understanding of what are and are not anomalous phenomena. That is, people can recognize anomalous phenomena implicitly even though they may not be able to provide appropriate verbal responses.

What I am suggesting is that the content of a problem and the format in which it is presented can affect both our ability to *see* the problem and thus the solution reached. As an example, consider again the initial, abstract version of the card problem given above. When most people read this problem, it takes some time for them just to determine what is being asked. And, unless they have had some training in logic, the appropriate principles to use in solving the problem may not be apparent to them. Thus, they simply deliberate and do their best. Note well that, because they deliberate, they answer the question in an analytic, not an intuitive, manner—regardless of whether they arrive at the correct solution.

Now consider the drinking-age problem. Formally, this has the same structure as the card problem in that you are being asked to check an *if p then q* type of relation. However, in this case, it almost seems that you can *see* the problem in the sense that the scenario automatically suggests an image. Judgments about whom to check are made quickly, with little apparent effort and largely intuitively. The context and format of the problem allow you to visualize both what is happening and what you should do. The problem is also meaningful to you, and you can therefore access relevant information quickly and with minimum effort. Note that I am not claiming that no deliberation is involved. Instead, my main contention is that the drinking-age problem triggers intuitive processes, whereas the card problem does not.

To explain this and several other results in the literature, I propose what I call the *visualization hypothesis*. This states that the context and form of problems affect the ease with which people reason *visually*—and thus largely intuitively—as opposed to using a more deliberate or analytic process. Intuitive responses have a certain appeal—they are reached quickly, with little cost, and people tend to feel confident that they are correct. Indeed, we probably take the speed and ease with which we arrive at a response as evidence that it is correct. After all, many things that we do know to be correct are retrieved quite quickly from memory—for example, that $7 \times 7 = 49$. Moreover, when we first encounter problems, our initial reactions are typically intuitive. We implicitly want to see whether we can answer the question without having to expend effort.

The reader should note that I am not saying that the intuitive responses to the kind of problems being considered here will always be correct. (I provide examples of incorrect responses below.) What I am saying is that, the more people are able to reason *visually*, the more likely they are to use intuitive processes. Moreover, the form (i.e., the context and format) in which the problems are presented affects the ability to visualize.

This framing of the issues begs, of course, the question of the origin of the intuitive processes used. Clearly, one source is experience. You would expect differential familiarity with types of scenarios to affect responses, and, in fact, there is some evidence of this. Second—and I shall examine this point later (in chap. 7)—specific training can make a difference. Third, I suspect that a genetic predisposition to learn certain types of relations between variables could also be implicated (see chap. 3). However, I do not believe that there is sufficient evidence to support the evolutionary argument that we have developed special genes that enable the detection of "social cheaters." My suspicion is that survival could have been enhanced more by developing other mental abilities—for example, a greater awareness of the implications of randomness in the environment (see pp. 122–125 below) or a more systematic tendency to seek disconfirming evidence across both social and nonsocial contexts—and that these would have taken precedence over this particular social skill.

More on Confirmation and Disconfirmation

Before we take up the topic of probabilistic reasoning, consider another deductive reasoning problem, one that also tests the ability to define a rule.[30]

You are told that there is a mechanism or rule for generating groups of three numbers (e.g., "2-4-6"). Your task is to determine the rule. The way in which you are to accomplish this task is by generating sequences of three numbers. After you generate each sequence, you will be told whether it is in accord with the rule. You can continue generating sequences of three numbers until you think that you have determined the rule. To begin, you are told that the sequence "2-4-6" does conform to the rule.

Most people generate about six sequences before stating what they think the rule is. However, rather than examining their final answers, it is more illuminating to study the particular processes that they use in order to determine the rule. Typically, people extract a pattern (generate a hypothesis) from the exemplar "2-4-6"—for example, "all even numbers" or "numbers that increase by two." These initial hypotheses are then tested by offering examples—for example, "4-6-8" or "3-5-7." This kind of testing may continue for several rounds.

What is interesting to observe is that most people's strategies initially consist of trying to *confirm* their hypotheses—for example, by testing a sequence such as "4-6-8" when their hypothesis is "even numbers that increase by two." From a logical viewpoint, however, one should try to disconfirm, not confirm, hypotheses because disconfirmation is more informative.[31] Thus, in order to test the hypothesis "even numbers that increase by two," it would have been more informative to have tried, say, the sequence "8-6-4." However, people are slow to use disconfirming tests in such tasks. In general, it seems that, once they have generated a hypothesis, people want to test whether it is true and therefore frequently fail to seek disconfirmation actively.[32] (Incidentally, the rule employed by the experimenter is simply "any ascending sequence of numbers.")

I believe that there are several reasons why people do not seek disconfirmation more actively. First, observing connections or variables that co-occur is the very basis of our intuitive or tacit process of learning. We learn "naturally" from what we see, not from what we do not see. Confirmation is seeing what we expect to see, and, intuitively, the weight that we assign to our belief in a hypothesis is a function of the frequency of occurrence (see chap. 3). Second, we prefer testing whether we are right to testing whether we are wrong. After all, if we are proved wrong, we have to generate another hypothesis, and this is typically more costly (in terms of mental effort) than trying to see whether we are right. In some cases, being proved wrong may even carry emotional costs—that is, we do not like to find that our ideas are wrong.

Third, much hypothesis testing takes place in environments that are not governed by the rules of deductive logic, and we therefore do not expect that, in the normal course of events, our hypotheses will always be correct. In fact, we are typically quite happy if our beliefs are correct in a majority of cases. Moreover, strategies that involve testing whether we are right can also show us that we are wrong and that we need to revise our beliefs.

An illuminating analysis of this problem by Joshua Klayman and Young-Won Ha shows that, in many environments, a general strategy that involves seeking positive confirmation of a hypothesis can be quite effective.[33] In other words, there are—to use the vocabulary of chapter 3—kind and wicked environments in which to test hypotheses. In kind environments, seeking positive confirmation is an appropriate strategy. For example, imagine that you want to test whether a humorous or a serious advertisement is more memorable. Clearly, in this case, it is sensible to see whether people remember your advertisement better when it is humorous (i.e., a test for confirmation). But there are also wicked environments (e.g., the card and number-sequence problems) where failure to seek disconfirmation is important. Klayman and Ha emphasize that there is a distinction between realizing that disconfirmation is important and actively employing strategies that seek disconfirmation. As I shall argue later (in chap. 7), people can improve their inferential abilities by adopting more active searches for disconfirming evidence and using more imagination.

Probability and Intuition

As implied above, much of the reasoning that people are required to perform in the real world involves probabilistic outcomes. We do not know, for example, what the weather will be like on a certain day of the year. But we do know that, on average, some months (and thus days) of the year are warmer than others, some are subject to more rainfall, and so on. In other words, much of our experience is predicated on the fact that, although many events cannot be predicted exactly, we can rely on regularities that are probabilistic in the sense that they are more or less likely to occur.

The formal study of probability is similar to physics in two interesting ways. First, people and animals have coexisted and evolved in the presence of the laws of probability and physics for millions of years. Thus, to the extent that learning environments are kind, you would expect people to have good intuitions for many fundamental phenomena. Second, until fairly recently, people had difficulty formalizing their intuitive understanding of the laws of both physics and probability. As noted earlier, Newton changed the way in which educated people think about the laws of motion. More recently, Einstein changed our views about time and relativity.

Contemporary ideas about probability theory are fairly new. The outcomes of rolling dice, for example, were not well understood in ancient times, and the birth of modern probability theory is often attributed to seventeenth-century mathematicians who wanted to devise good strategies for gambling. Moreover, it was not until the mid-twentieth century that the so-called subjective view of probability was formulated.[34] This theory allows one to talk meaningfully about the probability of single events (e.g., which candidate will win a particular election) as opposed to thinking of probabilities as being defined by ratios of long-term relative frequencies—the so-called ratio of favorable to possible cases. (Think, e.g., of the probability of picking an ace at random out of a full deck of cards, i.e., 4/52, or approximately 0.08.) However, the notion of subjective probability is not accepted by all experts, and arguments about the meaning and definition of *probability* are legion.

In debates on human intuition about statistical phenomena, the point has been made that animals and insects show a remarkable ability to reason "as if" they understood many probabilistic regularities in the environment. For example, some animals have been found to exhibit "optimal foraging behavior," which seems to imply that they "know" statistical distributions of relevant variables in their environments.[35] Thus, it is asked, why are humans—with their greater cognitive capacities—so bad at reasoning with probabilities when other, "lower" species are not? The question, however, is not entirely appropriate because humans have been tested on a much wider range of tasks than animals. Indeed, it is not clear what the animal equivalents would be to some of the problems that humans have been asked to solve.

There are many ways in which people's intuitions regarding probabilistic phenomena have been tested. Moreover, it should be emphasized that the assessment of people's ability as "intuitive statisticians" has been the subject of many debates.[36] Once again, when assessing intuitive abilities, it is important to ask how people understand the problems with which they are confronted and—in particular—whether they are able to *visualize* specific situations (cf. the *visualization* hypothesis).[37]

Difficulties with Random Phenomena

There are several classes of findings that indicate how people's models of the world affect their interpretation of probabilistic phenomena. Many result from the fact that people are motivated to attribute *meaning* to what they observe.

As noted in chapter 3, we learn by observing connections. However, some connections are more important than others, and a great premium is placed in all walks of life on being able to identify precursors of success or failure. We are all motivated to identify such variables—in both the physical and the social worlds. For example, thousands of years ago, before agriculture and animal husbandry were developed, it was important for hunter-gatherers to identify signs that indicated the presence or absence of other animals (which could represent either opportunity or danger). Today, much effort is expanded, for example, in defining indicators that suggest which stocks to buy or sell and when. In interaction with others, it is important to know what certain gestures mean, and so on. In short, those who are able to identify valid indicators gain important advantages.

However, as was also pointed out in chapter 3, the environments in which we find ourselves are not always kind, and feedback can be confounded, not only by our own actions, but also by random events. In fact, the outcomes of most processes that we observe in the world reflect the influence of random events—and this is as true of the stock market as it is of such natural phenomena as the weather. Moreover, events do not come labeled *random*. Instead, this must be inferred.

Nonetheless, we are motivated to identify connections that work and to attribute cause in the presence of success and failure. However, in the real world, chance and causal factors are inevitably confounded, and this naturally leads to mistaken beliefs, such as those exhibited in "superstitious" learning (see also chap. 3). For example, a tennis player comes to believe that he should always tie his left shoe before his right because that was what he did before winning an important match; people adopt certain religious practices after observing unusual events; and so on. A key feature of these situations is the asymmetry in the costs of the two types of errors involved. Losing an important match is costly, tying the left shoe before the right is not, so why risk losing the match by tying the right shoe first?

The desire to interpret the connections that you see can also imply a failure to understand such probabilistic phenomena as *regression toward the mean*. The following example will explain this concept.

Imagine that you are a sales manager faced with the task of monitoring the performance of a salesman over time. Naturally, you would not expect his sales to be constant day in and day out. Instead, you would anticipate variation over time as a result of many different factors. These factors could include chance occurrences: the number of people that he happened to meet on particular days; different decisions made by his customers; and so on. Changes in the salesman's attitude or motivation could also affect his performance. On the whole, however, you expect him to maintain a standard or average volume of sales over time.

Now imagine that one day this salesman turns in a substandard performance. You are disappointed and let him know this. The next day, his performance improves.

A week or so later, the salesman performs well above average. You are delighted and send him a congratulatory note. The following day, his performance worsens.

What is going on here? It seems as though this salesman performs better if you express disappointment and worse if you express approval. One lesson that you could draw is to reprimand when his performance is bad and to withhold praise when his performance is good. But let us analyze the situation more carefully and ask what would have happened had you not intervened at all.

Consider again the salesman's performance over time and assume that all variation from the average or mean performance can be attributed to random factors (i.e., assume that the variation cannot be predicted). In this case, the best prediction that you can make for any given day is this mean. Thus, if you observe poor performance today, your best prediction for tomorrow is the mean, and it is more than likely that you will see performance improve tomorrow relative to today. Similarly, if you observe outstanding performance today, the best prediction for tomorrow is also the mean, and you are probably going to see performance fall tomorrow relative to today. Both the improved performance observed after a bad day and the worsened performance observed after a good day reflect simply random variation and what is termed *regression toward the mean.*

In other words, the changes in the salesman's performance could very well simply reflect random variation and have nothing at all to do with your interventions. However, as soon as we act on the world, we implicitly assume that we are making a difference, and it is difficult to separate the effects of chance and possible cause (in this case, our actions). Moreover, the situation could be much more complex than that described here. In describing a similar example, Kahneman and Tversky commented, "This true story illustrates a saddening aspect of the human condition. We normally reinforce others when their behavior is good and punish them when their behavior is bad . . . therefore, they are most likely to improve after being punished and most likely to deteriorate after being rewarded. Consequently we are exposed to a lifetime schedule in which we are most often rewarded for punishing others, and punished for rewarding."[38]

A further example of a failure to understand random variation in the presence of actions is the so-called hot-hand phenomenon in basketball. It is strongly believed by many professional basketball players and coaches that, from time to time, certain players become "hot" during a game in the sense that their performance reaches unusually high levels; for example, they achieve superior results shooting baskets. In such cases, coaches instruct their players to make sure that the "hot" player is given as many opportunities to score as is possible. However, in a statistical analysis of actual NBA games, Tom Gilovich and his colleagues showed that the hot-hand phenomenon does not exist.[39] It is a myth. Yet both players and managers continue to believe in it. Why? There are, I believe, two reasons. First, the notion of a "hot hand" makes sense to players in that they know that performance can vary from game to game. Second, players and coaches would not "see" the data, and therefore would not test the hypothesis, in the same way that Gilovich and his colleagues did. That is, nonscientists would take several successful shots in a row to be sufficient evidence that a player was on a hot streak; scientists would realize that it is necessary to take account of all the shots that a player makes in a game, according equal weight to each, before deciding that he had been on a hot streak.

Closely related to this type of situation is the phenomenon known as *illusory correlation*.[40] This refers to the tendency to believe that two variables are related when, in fact, they are not (or, alternatively, that they are more strongly correlated than is in fact the case). If, as stated in chapter 3, humans are so good at implicitly encoding frequencies and covariations accurately, why does this happen? The answer comes from considering people's models of the world. If there is an a priori belief that two variables are related, it does not take many connections between the variables to convince that this is really the case. For example, imagine a woman who has formed a certain belief about middle-aged men who wear horn-rimmed glasses. It will not take many observations for her belief to be "confirmed," and she will act as though she has observed many more instances of the connection.[41]

Finally, consider the so-called gambler's fallacy. This is the phenomenon whereby people believe that random devices such as roulette wheels or dice will exhibit the same general tendencies (or patterns of outcomes) in both short and long sequences. For example, most people know that roulette wheels are programmed so that red and black numbers will, in the long run, appear an equal number of times. Yet, if black comes up five times in a row, many people believe that red is more likely than black to come up next in order to maintain the fifty-fifty proportion. In fact, with a fair wheel, black and red are equally likely every time the wheel is spun, and the fifty-fifty proportion is maintained only in an infinite sequence. It is our desire to see the fifty-fifty proportion respected, even in short series, that overcomes our rational understanding of the phenomenon.

The examples given in this subsection are all of cases in which intuitive models of the world do not map well onto probabilistic models of random phenomena. The reason, I suggest, is that we are motivated to make sense of the world and that, by definition, random phenomena do not make sense. This is not to say that people do not have some understanding of random phenomena. For example, studies show that people do have an appreciation of such principles as the "law of large numbers" when these principles are applied to domains that are familiar to them, such as sports.[42] But, at the perceptual level, it is often problematic to distinguish the contributions of cause from those of chance. Errors are inevitable. And the costs of mistaking chance for cause, or cause for chance, are not always the same.

Specific Problems in Probabilistic Reasoning

Anyone who has taken a course in probability theory knows that the answers to many questions are far from intuitive. Consider, for example, the well-known "birthday" problem: There are twenty-three people in a room. What is the probability that two of them have the same birthday?

Most people are surprised to learn that the chances of this event occurring are just over 50 percent—given the assumption that birthdays are randomly distributed over the course of the year.[43] In many ways, this can be considered a trick question, but it does illustrate the surprising implications of certain formal analyses. Moreover, there are many phenomena—some involving large stakes—that people's intuitions do not fathom and in the consideration of which the application of analysis is important. Consider, for example, the fact that many people's naive understanding of the basic principles of financial investment causes them not to recognize the effects of compounding interest (or returns) over time. Moderate sums of money can grow to be quite substantial in relatively few years when interest rates are favorable. Indeed, economists use the term *money illusion* to indicate the failure to understand the effects of inflation on the value of money; that is, whereas $100 equals $100 today, $100 in the past is worth more than $100 today.

It is instructive to consider some problems in probabilistic reasoning that have attracted considerable attention in the psychological literature. These are presented in exhibit 11, and the reader is invited to solve them before reading further.

Problem 1 in exhibit 11 was formulated by Tversky and Kahneman.[44] It is particularly instructive because it highlights the conflict between intuition and analysis. For most people, the description of Linda clearly facilitates *visualization* and thus intuitive reasoning. In this case, the text suggests an image of Linda. This is then contrasted with the images or prototypes that people have of the different categories provided. Judgments of relative probabilities are made according to the match between the image of Linda and the different prototypes. Kahneman and Tversky call this *judgment by representativeness*.[45] Thus, for example, almost everybody considers alternative *c* more likely than alternative *f*, that is, that Linda is more likely to be "active in the feminist movement" than she is to be a "bank teller."

In addition, most people also consider that alternative *h* is more likely than alternative *f*, that is, that Linda is more likely to be a "bank teller and active in the feminist movement" than she is to be simply a "bank

EXHIBIT 11   Some problems in probabilistic reasoning: Probability format

1. Linda is thirty-one years old, single, outspoken, and very bright. She majored in philosophy. As a student, she was deeply concerned with issues of discrimination and social justice and also participated in antinuclear demonstrations. Please rank order by probability (highest to lowest) the following:

    a)   Linda is a teacher in an elementary school.
    b)   Linda works in a bookstore and takes yoga classes.
    c)   Linda is active in the feminist movement.
    d)   Linda is a psychiatric social worker.
    e)   Linda is a member of the League of Women Voters.
    f)   Linda is a bank teller.
    g)   Linda is an insurance salesperson.
    h)   Linda is a bank teller and active in the feminist movement.

2. To facilitate early detection of breast cancer, women are encouraged from a particular age on to participate at regular intervals in routine screening even if they have no obvious symptoms. Imagine that you conduct in a certain region such a breast cancer screening using mammography. For symptom-free women aged forty to fifty who participate in screening using mammography, the following information is available for this region:

    The probability that one of these women has breast cancer is 1 percent. If a woman has breast cancer, the probability is 80 percent that she will have a positive mammography test. If a woman does not have breast cancer, the probability is 10 percent that she will still have a positive mammography test. Imagine a woman (aged forty to fifty, no symptoms) who has a positive mammography test in your breast screening. What is the probability that she actually has breast cancer?

3. A cab was involved in a hit-and-run accident at night. Two cab companies, the Green and the Blue, operate in the city. Fifteen percent of all cabs in the city are Blue, and 85 percent are Green. On the night of the accident, a witness identified the cab as Blue. The court tested the reliability of the witness under similar visibility conditions with Blue and Green cabs. When the cabs were really Blue, the witness said they were Blue 80 percent of the time. When the cabs were really Green, the witness said they were Blue 20 percent of the time. What is the probability that the cab involved in the hit-and-run accident was Blue?

Sources: Problem 1: Tversky & Kahneman (1983). Problem 2: Gigerenzer (1996b). Problem 3: Tversky & Kahneman (1980).

teller." However, this judgment conflicts sharply with a basic principle of probability theory, *the conjunction rule,* which regulates the relative sizes of probabilities when one event is a component of another. In short, the conjunction rule states that the probability of a *conjunctive event* (an event consisting of two or more components or subevents) must be smaller than the probability of each of its components considered individually.

For example, the probability of meeting, say, a forty-year-old man is greater than that of meeting a forty-year-old man who is smoking a pipe. Why? It should be clear that, since not all forty-year-old men smoke pipes, the chance of meeting a man who is forty years old is greater than that of meeting a man who is forty years old *and* who smokes a pipe. More formally, let A denote the event of meeting a forty-year-old man, and let B denote smoking a pipe. Then the probability of A and B co-occurring, or $p(A \text{ and } B)$, must be less than the probabilities of A and B individually, or $p(A)$ and $p(B)$; that is, $p(A \text{ and } B) < p(A)$, and $p(A \text{ and } B) < p(B)$ (assuming that none of the probabilities is 0 or 1).

Applying this principle to problem 1 in exhibit 11 means that it is more likely that Linda is a bank teller than that she is *both* a bank teller and active in the feminist movement. (Formally, alternative *f,* "bank teller," is part of the joint event "bank teller and active in the feminist movement," alternative *h.* Since a component must by itself be more likely than a larger event of which it forms a part, *f* is more likely than *h.*)

This problem has been the subject of much controversy, and people have argued at great length about both its normative and its descriptive implications. Even after being exposed to the analytic implications of probability theory, many people still feel strongly attached to their first, more intuitive judgment and seek ways in which to justify it.

From my viewpoint, the problem is a clear example of how the speedy operation of an intuitive process—triggered by possible images of Linda—can lead people to ignore an analytic principle that they would endorse in the abstract had they been aware of it. In this respect, the problem is similar to the Müller-Lyer illusion (see chap. 1) and the puzzle posed by the "electric brae" (see chap. 2). In both cases, our senses—or our intuitive understanding—lead to one conclusion, but recourse to an explicit analytic principle leads to another. In such situations, if the basis of an analytic principle is clear, most people are able to overrule an intuitive judgment—even one to which they are strongly attached—and accept the validity of analysis. But, if the basis of that principle is not clear, intuitive judgment is likely to win out over analytic judgment. Consider, for example, that you are faced with making a complicated investment decision, that few aspects of the investment are easily quantified, and that there is no general principle (such as the law of gravity, which resolves the electric brae puzzle) to which you can appeal. Below, after we examine problem 2 in exhibit 11, I shall consider how an alternative view of the Linda problem can, by itself, overcome this particular conflict between intuition and analysis.

Problem 2—and several that are quite similar to it—has been presented to many people, including physicians and medical students.[46] Most responses—even those given by physicians—are between 70 and 80 percent. Yet the correct response (to be explained below)—according to probability theory—is 7.5 percent. Why is there such a large difference?

Once again, consider the visualization hypothesis. For most people, the format of the problem is "opaque."[47] They cannot see how to go about solving it. Moreover, not knowing explicitly how to use the data in accordance with probability theory, they simply focus on what makes sense to them. In this case, their judgments are heavily influenced by the 80 percent sensitivity rate of the test.

As mentioned above, explicit understanding of the intricacies of probability theory and, in particular, how to apply it to specific cases is a fairly new development in human thought. Still, people are remarkably efficient at tracking frequencies (see chap. 3), and frequencies bear heavily on people's judgments in probabilistic situations.[48] Gernot Kleiter has argued that people typically experience data as frequencies observed over time, a process that he calls *natural sampling*.[49] The key idea here is that people do not typically organize their experiences in the way in which the data in the breast-cancer problem are presented. Instead, over time, they encounter cases that they are able to place in different categories; for example, physicians might use the categories *patients who tested positive for cancer, patients who tested positive for cancer but were subsequently found to have/not to have the disease,* etc. Organizing—or experiencing—data in such a way makes available all the information necessary to make the appropriate probability calculations. That it does so suggests that a frequency format will be more meaningful to most people than abstract percentages (e.g., a probability of 1 percent). Is this in fact the case?

Problems 1–3 in exhibit 11 have been recast using frequencies; the revised versions are presented in exhibit 12. Consider problems 1 and 2. The formulation of problem 1 in exhibit 12 is taken from the work of Klaus Fiedler.[50] Fiedler shows that, whereas the presentation of problem 1 in exhibit 11 above leads most people to respond that alternative *h* is more likely than alternative *f,* the use of frequencies in exhibit 12 leads most people to rank alternative *f* above alternative *h.* In other words, the category *bank teller* is judged to occur more frequently than the category *bank teller and active in the feminist movement.*

EXHIBIT 12   Some problems in probabilistic reasoning: Frequency format

1. Linda is thirty-one years old, single, outspoken, and very bright. She majored in philosophy. As a student, she was deeply concerned with issues of discrimination and social justice and also participated in antinuclear demonstrations. To how many out of one hundred people who are like Linda do the following statements apply?
   a) Linda is a teacher in an elementary school.
   b) Linda works in a bookstore and takes yoga classes.
   c) Linda is active in the feminist movement.
   d) Linda is a psychiatric social worker.
   e) Linda is a member of the League of Women Voters.
   f) Linda is a bank teller.
   g) Linda is an insurance salesperson.
   h) Linda is a bank teller and active in the feminist movement.

2. To facilitate early detection of breast cancer, women are encouraged from a particular age on to participate at regular intervals in routine screening, even if they have no obvious symptoms. Imagine that you conduct in a certain region such a breast cancer screening using mammography. For symptom-free women aged forty to fifty who participate in screening using mammography, the following information is available for this region:
       Ten out of every 1,000 women have breast cancer. Of these 10 women with breast cancer, 8 will have a positive mammography test. Of the remaining 990 women without breast cancer, 99 will still have a positive mammography test. Imagine a sample of women (aged forty to fifty, no symptoms) who have positive mammography tests in your breast screening. How many of these women (i.e., ——— out of ———) do actually have breast cancer?

3. A cab was involved in a hit-and-run accident at night. Two cab companies, the Green and the Blue, operate in the city. Of every 100 cabs in the city, 15 are Blue, and 85 are Green. On the night of the accident, a witness identified the cab as Blue. The court tested the reliability of the witness under similar visibility conditions with Blue and Green cabs. When the cabs were really Blue, the witness said they were Blue in 12 out of 15 tests. When the cabs were really Green, the witness said they were Blue in 17 out of 85 tests. What are the chances (i.e., ——— out of ———) that the cab involved in the hit-and-run accident was Blue?

Sources: Problem 1: Fiedler (1988). Problem 2: Gigerenzer (1996b). Problem 3: Mellers & McGraw (1999).

Recasting problem 2 in terms of frequencies also induces a large number of people to see the structure of the problem and respond appropriately.[51] Why is this so? Consider exhibit 13.[52] As shown on the left, when information is presented in probabilistic form, you need to know how to make the appropriate calculation. On the other hand, when information is presented in terms of frequencies, the path to the answer, shown on the right, seems obvious. Basically, starting with one thousand women, you can map out the categories to which each will be assigned and thus assess how many tested positive (8 + 99) and, of those, how many had cancer (8). Having determined these two categories, all you need do is divide the number who tested positive and in fact had cancer by the total number who tested positive: 8/(8 + 99) = 7.5 percent.

These results, as well as others obtained in similar work,[53] have been interpreted as supporting the position that the human ability to reason with frequencies as opposed to probabilities is a consequence of forces of natural selection. In other words, humans have evolved to process information in the form of frequencies, not in the form of probabilities. And, indeed, much of the evidence reviewed in chapter 3 strongly emphasizes

EXHIBIT 13   Probability and frequency formats

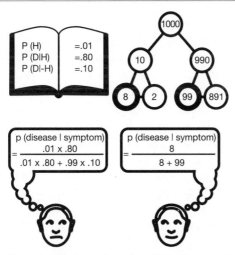

The probability format is on the left, the frequency format on the right. In this case, the frequency format obviates the need to make the formal Bayesian calculation.

Source: Gigerenzer (1996b). The illustration is reproduced, in slightly altered form, with permission.

the important role that frequency information plays in mental life, especially as it forms the basis for many of our intuitions.

However, the fact that experimental subjects are more likely to reason correctly when certain problems are framed in terms of frequencies instead of probabilities is not, in my opinion, sufficient evidence to support this genetic hypothesis. On the other hand, I do think that certain ways of formulating problems aid the visualization process and, in so doing, trigger intuitive responses. However, as noted above, just because a response is intuitive does not necessarily mean that it is correct; much depends on whether a response tendency has been learned in a kind or a wicked environment. Moreover, if we find that reframing problems in terms of frequencies instead of probabilities does not aid the reasoning process, does this mean that the evolutionary hypothesis is wrong? What if it could be shown that people sometimes make erroneous judgments when problems are framed in terms of frequencies?

We can begin to answer these questions by considering problem 3 in exhibits 11 and 12 above. As with problem 1, when problem 3 is framed in terms of probabilities (exhibit 11), people tend not to be able to respond correctly.[54] The version of problem 3 presented in exhibit 12 is framed in terms of frequencies and was developed by Barbara Mellers and Peter Mc-Graw. Like other investigators, Mellers and McGraw find that frequency formats increase the level of correct responses. However, after extensive testing of both frequency and probability formats, they also find that, in some circumstances, performance can improve irrespective of format. (In their words, whether performance improves depends "on the rareness of the events and the type of information presented.")[55] Thus, whereas presenting a problem in terms of frequencies instead of probabilities can enhance performance, so can altering (improving) formats that use probabilities. It all depends on how people *see* the information and how this triggers their mental models of the situations depicted.

A further striking example of the effects of using frequency instead of probability data is provided in a study by Paul Slovic, John Monahan, and Donald MacGregor.[56] These authors developed two versions of a problem describing the chances of a mental patient committing an act of violence within six months of being discharged from a hospital, one version framed in terms of probabilities (i.e., a 20 percent chance), the other in terms of frequencies (i.e., 20 of every 100 patients). They then presented the problem to two groups of experienced forensic psychologists and psychiatrists, asking whether they would discharge such a patient. One group was given the probability version, the other the frequency version. In the frequency condition (20 of 100 patients), 41 percent refused to discharge the patient. In the probability condition (20 percent chance), only 21 percent refused. Slovic, Monahan, and MacGregor argue that the frequency data induce more affect-laden imagery than do the probability data (see also chap. 2) and thus, in the language of this book, appeal more to the tacit system. This, in turn, suggests that presenting data in the form of vivid scenarios and anecdotes may have an even greater impact than presenting frequency data. And, indeed, there is evidence supporting this implication.[57] Once again, however, it is an open question as to which format—frequency, probability, or anecdote—induces more veridical judgments.

As a final problem in this section, consider the following. First imagine that you have been asked the following question: In four pages of a novel (about two thousand words), how many seven-letter words ending in -*ing* would you expect to find (i.e., seven-letter words of the form $----ing$)? Now consider the question, In four pages of a novel (about two thousand words), how many seven-letter words of which the sixth letter is *n* would you expect to find (i.e., seven-letter words of the form $-----n-$)?

When people are asked this question, their estimates of the number of $----ing$ words vastly exceeds their estimates of $-----n-$ words.[58] Yet, as the reader must be aware, all $-----n-$ words are also $----ing$ words. Thus, in any text, there must be more of the former than the latter (provided, of course, that there is at least one $-----n-$ word that is not a $----ing$ word). Why do people fail to see the relation between the number of $----ing$ and $-----n-$ words, particularly if they are so good at recording and remembering frequencies? The explanation, I believe, once again lies in the visualization hypothesis.[59] When answering the question, we try to visualize words with the appropriate endings.[60] For some reason, it is easier to imagine (or see) $----ing$ words than $-----n-$ words, and we use this ease of imagination as a cue in making our estimates. In some cases, however, our access to frequency information is not accurate. "Natural" or "intuitive" processes can also lead to errors.

Concluding Comments and Implications

This chapter has examined studies of intuitive abilities to make judgments in three domains: physics; deductive reasoning; and probabilistic or statistical reasoning. While the review of the literature has not been exhaustive, I believe that it is sufficient to make several key points.

First, in assessing intuitive judgments, it is not always clear whether subjects in experiments are reasoning intuitively or analytically (in the sense of using deliberation). In many cases, both modes of thought are operative.

Second, much emphasis has been placed on assessing whether intuitive skills are valid. Yet history has shown that what is considered an appropriate response can change over time. A response considered normative fifty years ago may not be considered normative today, and what about fifty years from now? In probability theory, for example, there is still considerable disagreement about the appropriate responses to specific problems.

It is critical to understand the models that subjects use to reason in the tasks that they confront. Differences in responses can often be attributed to whether subjects are able to visualize the phenomena in question. (Remember that the *visualization hypothesis* states that, to the extent that subjects can visualize phenomena, they are likely to engage in intuitive processing.) That visualization is triggered does not, however, mean that the intuitive responses generated will always be correct—at least according to current normative standards. For example, for some physical phenomena subjects were able to provide correct responses to problems that were shown to them visually (on film) but for which they could not provide correct, explicit rationales. On the other hand, in probability problems, visualization could be triggered by the context and form of questions and lead to strong beliefs in answers that violate the laws of probability theory (recall the Linda problem!).

When intuitive responses have proved to be incorrect, investigators have reacted in two different ways. Some claim that intuitive understanding is fundamentally flawed. Others suggest that, if tasks were defined "naturally," people's performance would be much closer to optimal. Underlying this latter viewpoint is the assumption that people have learned how to respond correctly in their natural environments and/or that, over time, humans have evolved response mechanisms that are appropriate to the environments that they face.

I believe that neither of these extreme views is correct and that both need to be moderated. Two issues are critical. First, we must understand how people see the problems with which they are confronted. To what extent does the "model" that the person has in mind match that of the investigator as well as the real-world phenomenon? (See also above.) Many judgment errors result from a failure to understand the demands of the problem and sometimes even to comprehend basic terms, such as the probability of a single event. On the other hand, there is considerable evidence that people do understand the implications of probabilistic phenomena with which they are familiar and that simple manipulations, such as reframing problems in terms of frequencies, can have dramatic effects on responses.

The assumptions that we learn from the natural environment and that we use evolutionarily developed traits when reasoning inferentially miss, I believe, several points. One is that, because we learn primarily from what we see, we can also learn the wrong things. (This point was considered extensively in chapter 3. Recall the concepts of kind and wicked learning environments.) In addition, as discussed in this chapter, it is difficult to identify causal agents in the presence of noise. How, for example, do you know whether your success at a task was due to something you did or to chance? In the real world, chance and cause are confounded, and we have difficulty identifying their separate contributions to what we observe.

Second, although it is intriguing, the evolutionary hypothesis fails to note that many human response tendencies represent compromises in the "human design" and therefore do not always operate optimally.[61] Consider an example drawn from human biology: the size of the female pelvis. True, its width prevents women from enjoying the same freedom of movement as men. But, if it were any narrower, women would not be able to give birth. Thus, the size of the female pelvis can be thought of as a compromise between competing demands. Similar trade-offs may have influenced the development of our innate mental abilities.

Third, if specific responses have been developed for detecting, for example, social cheaters, why were response tendencies not developed for other important inferential tasks? Why, for example, do we not have a gene that helps us better discriminate chance from cause?

Fourth, through evolution and learning, humans have developed what might be called *natural* response tendencies. However, owing largely to technological advances, the environment in which humans now operate is changing at an ever-increasing pace, and it is not clear that all our natural response tendencies are adapted to our current environments. Airplanes, nuclear power plants, and mobile telephones, for example, all present us with opportunities and dangers that our ancestors never faced. Formal education of the deliberate system is much more important for surviving in today's world than it ever was in the past.

In terms of implications for educating intuition, this chapter clearly demonstrates, first, that, while there are many situations in which analysis (deliberation) proves superior to intuition, this is not always the case. Intuition is not, therefore, always in need of education. And, when deciding whether intuition does in fact need to be educated, it is crucial that we determine the type of learning structure—kind or wicked—in which the particular type of intuition on which we are focusing was or will be acquired. Second, the visualization hypothesis emphasizes the role of observation and imagination in intuition—we seem to observe and then immediately visualize. Thus, programs to educate intuition should explicitly target people's skills of observation and imagination. Third, in most of the problems examined, people's answers seem to involve both their tacit and their deliberate systems. In the final analysis, what matters is the quality of people's judgments. This, in turn, suggests that, in improving processes that involve intuition, attention should also be paid to educating the deliberate system.

CHAPTER 5

How Good Is Intuition?

The previous chapter examined evidence concerning our ability to make intuitive judgments about characteristics of the physical world. It also examined how our intuitions fare relative to different normative reasoning schemes. This chapter examines four related issues.

The first issue is the functions that intuition performs for the organism. The related discussion presents an initial consideration of the question of whether our unconscious or intuitive selves are "smarter" than our conscious selves.

The second is the accuracy of intuitive judgments. How accurate is intuitive judgment? On what does accuracy depend, and should this or other criteria be used for judging the "goodness" of intuition?

The third is individual differences. For example, what truth is there to the notion of women's intuition? And what differences can be attributed to education, training, and intelligence? The topic of individual differences also leads to a consideration of the relation between intuition and expertise.

The fourth is the psychology of choice. Especially important here is a consideration of ways in which we intuitively evaluate alternatives in choice and issues involved in the learning of decision rules, that is, how we learn to make certain kinds of decisions.

The Functions of Intuition

By now, readers will be aware that I do not accord a mystical status to intuition. It is not an ability that is possessed by a limited number of people but rather part of everybody's normal information-processing system. True, some people do make better intuitive judgments than others. A journalist, for example, may have better intuitions than a person unaccustomed to conducting interviews as to whether someone she is interviewing is telling the truth. But we do all have thoughts or cognitive responses that *"are reached with little apparent effort, and typically without conscious awareness,"* and that also *"involve little or no conscious deliberation"* (p. 14 above). In fact, my claim is that intuitive thought is used far more extensively than deliberate or conscious processing. What varies from person to person is the domains in which intuitions are held and the characteristics of these, for example, accuracy when making predictions.

As discussed in previous chapters, intuition may be influenced by certain predispositions but is essentially the result of experience. In many ways, the organism can be thought of as a learning machine that codifies many associations and their frequencies and can access this information when newly encountered stimuli trigger connections. Moreover, it is important to emphasize that much of our intuitive knowledge is acquired in automatic or passive fashion; that is, we do not need to allocate effort to the learning process.

According to Herbert Simon, the scarcest human resource is attention.[1] I agree. If we had to control all our information processing by paying conscious attention, life would be impossible. Clearly, it is functional that so many processes operate automatically. Attention is freed for more pressing concerns.

It is not hard to generate evolutionary arguments for the existence of automatic, intuitive responses. When survival is at stake, the ability to make decisions quickly is critical. Organisms that make speedy decisions in daily activities, such as the gathering of food, also increase their chances of prospering relative to rivals who are slower. Moreover, the fact that learning occurs automatically facilitates adaptation to local conditions. In particular, even if individual members of a species are not born with specific response tendencies, the fact that they can learn these and that, in time, they become automatic has many advantages.

A case can be made that any and all information processing that is carried out automatically or without conscious awareness can be considered intuitive. However, I believe it is more meaningful to discriminate between three different levels of automatic processing: *basic, primitive,* and *sophisticated.* (The latter two terms were suggested by Arthur Reber [see below].)

By the *basic* level, I mean information processing that regulates and maintains life. This can be thought of as *instinctive behavior.* The way in which we react to hunger provides a good example. As is well-known, the feeling of hunger is precipitated by a drop in blood sugar levels. A message is sent to the brain, and the thought to seek food appears in consciousness. This happens across the life span. Babies cry when they are hungry, and children and adults typically take action to alleviate hunger. Actions can, of course, vary, and people learn which actions are more likely to be successful in different circumstances. However, the common element is an awareness of the state of hunger, and actions are initiated that are meant to overcome this. Another example is provided by thirst.

I equate *basic*-level information processing with *instincts.* People do not have to learn to notice that they are hungry or thirsty—although they do undoubtedly have to learn different ways of satisfying these needs.

It should be noted, of course, that not all changes in the body lead to instinctive behavior. Take the thyroid gland, for example. This secretes an enzyme that regulates, through the blood stream, many important functions such as the rate at which your heart beats. For different reasons, the thyroid gland may change its level of activity at a given point in a person's life and affect the metabolism. (It can become too "slow" or too "fast.") However, unlike hunger, changes in the activity of our thyroid gland do not induce thoughts that tell us to do something about it. Indeed, people usually do not even know that they have a thyroid problem until they have undergone explicit, medical tests. Whereas we do engage in instinctive behavior when the level of our blood sugar drops, we do not possess instinctive reactions to changes in the activity level of our thyroid gland.

The next two levels of automatic processing—the *primitive* and the *sophisticated*—have been suggested by Arthur Reber, who has carried out extensive research on implicit learning, that is, learning that is accomplished without conscious attempts to learn. The primitive unconscious is involved in a variety of basic information-processing functions that are "more or less devoid of meaning, affect, or interpretation."[2] Included among such functions are the automatic registration of information obtained through perception, the encoding of the frequencies of events encountered in the environment, the noting of different connections or covariations between events, and the inferring of the rules of the various systems that we encounter (e.g., the rules of grammar or weather patterns [see chap. 3]).

As Reber points out, many animals also possess the ability to encode frequency information automatically. After all, knowing the approximate statistical distributions of different aspects of the environment can be critical to survival. Where, for example, are the most likely sources of food? What locations do predators favor? And so on. Reber goes on to state that this level of automatic information processing is probably quite old in evolutionary terms. As evidence, he notes that the ability to encode frequency information is remarkably invariant across both age and states of mental health. As such, it is like many older and more primitive biological systems that are robust in the sense that their performance is not easily degraded.

As Reber sees it, the primitive unconscious functions like a machine. It simply processes information without attaching any specific meaning or affect to that information. Meaning and affect are the province of the *sophisticated* unconscious. Humans give meaning to their experience, and such meaning can both guide and affect the interpretation of subsequent perception. Our sensitivity to context when we hear stories provides a case in point.

Consider the appeal of what Bruner calls the *narrative* mode (see chap. 2). Small details of a story, for example, can immediately—and automatically—trigger connections and images that enrich our understanding. Or a few lines of a poem first read long ago can bring to mind certain memories and thus affect one's mood. However—and this is the critical point—not everyone is affected in the same way by the same things. Everything depends on the specific stocks of intuitions that people possess. Unlike the primitive unconscious, the sophisticated unconscious is quintessentially human.

As we have seen, most information processing occurs at the subconscious level. This raises the important question of whether the subconscious or "intuitive" self possesses wisdom that the conscious self lacks.[3] Sigmund Freud raised this issue a little over a century ago. His answer was a clear no. In fact, much of Freud's work consisted of uprooting subconscious influences and attempting to replace them with more rational thoughts. Seymour Epstein, however, has taken issue with this position (see chap. 2).[4] Using an evolutionary argument, he has stated that it is unlikely that subconscious processes are dysfunctional. A system that evolved by retaining effective and discarding ineffective response tendencies is unlikely to be so heavily influenced by dysfunctional tendencies.

One way in which to think about this issue is to consider the relative wisdom of the subconscious at each of the three levels under discussion. At the *basic* level, it seems hard to disagree with the wisdom of the subconscious when it comes to such phenomena as hunger and thirst. We need to know when to eat and drink because not doing so can endanger our health and even our lives. More generally, it also seems hard to disagree with the wisdom of the mating instinct since, without it, the species would not survive. Of course, if people always acted to satisfy their sexual desires, many would find life intolerable. Fortunately, humans have evolved forms of social organization that regulate sexual behavior, albeit imperfectly. Other species use the instinctive, biological mechanism of mating seasons.

At the *primitive* level, the subconscious also seems to be wise. We have mechanisms that help us learn, at little or no cost, connections and frequency data that are relevant to the environments in which we currently function. In addition, we learn much that is not of immediate relevance, and this information may prove useful in the future. The disadvantage of this form of learning is that it is based *only* on what has been observed. And, as pointed out in chapter 3, what is *not* observed can sometimes be more important for learning *valid* lessons from experience. Once again, much depends on the structure of the learning environment. Is this wicked or kind?

The wisdom of the subconscious at the *sophisticated* level is more difficult to evaluate. As far as many everyday activities are concerned, I believe that it is likely to be wise. The reason is that many such activities are rich in opportunities for good feedback, and, thus, even if initial intuitions are wrong, they can be corrected. Consider a physical example. When walking down a street, people have little difficulty making adjustments to their course in order to avoid objects or other pedestrians. Furthermore, these adjustments are effected without effort, that is, intuitively. In this case, the subconscious self is wise in that it recognizes similarities with previous experiences and automatically enacts the appropriate algorithms to reach the desired ends. (The routines used are also well practiced.) In addition, the conscious self—in the neocortex—can decide to override the unconscious when it wants. For example, there is a desire to change direction.

This situation is characterized by actions that can be immediately affected by good feedback.[5] It has also benefited from extensive learning and practice. What happens in the absence of these conditions?

Imagine, for example, that you have arrived early for a job interview and must wait for some minutes in an office until the interviewer is available. While waiting, it is impossible not to form impressions about and sense the atmosphere of the office. Indeed, strong feelings may even arise. However, are the intuitions thus generated liable to be as accurate as those that arise, for example, while you navigate a busy street?[6] Or are they more likely to mislead you? Your intuitions in the office have not been tested as thoroughly as those used to guide you in the street and are, therefore, more likely to mislead you. Moreover, unlike feelings that arise on the sidewalk to monitor your path, feelings such as those generated in the office usually must be interpreted consciously ("Why do I have this feeling of apprehension?").

At the *sophisticated* level, intuitions may act only as "weak signals." They may provide some form of notice, but it is not always clear how to interpret this. This is precisely what Antonio Damasio has referred to as the *somatic marker hypothesis* (see chap. 2).[7] Recall that, in Damasio's gambling experiments, subjects who had not suffered brain damage and thus whose explicit, rational selves could "communicate" with their underlying emotions tended to avoid the riskier choices and earned more than subjects who had suffered brain damage. Damasio argues that, in essence, people become aware that there may be problems with some options and therefore exclude these from their choice set. In this case, therefore, the wisdom of the subconscious self lies in knowing which options to avoid and would appear to be driven by a sensation of fear—that of losing money. Later in this chapter, I shall consider the more general issue of how fear of losses affects processes of choice.

Finally, is the subconscious wise in the sense of being better able to solve problems than the conscious self? This question is triggered by the so-called insight phenomenon (see also chap. 1). Many people report that, if, after struggling with a problem for some time, they put it aside and avoid consciously reflecting on it, a solution comes to mind. It seems that, while the conscious mind is otherwise engaged, the subconscious mind keeps working on the problem and, aided by chance events or new observations, suddenly produces the solution—often when we least expect it.

However, as even a little explicit thought can show, insight is not a phenomenon that occurs with great regularity. If it were, no one would ever spend time trying to solve problems. We would all just wait for solutions to appear in consciousness! So what is really happening?

I believe that arriving at solutions to difficult problems often requires one or both of the following: seeing the problem from a new perspective and making novel connections between two or more ideas. Donald Campbell has made the point that creativity in problem solving requires the generation of many "thought trials" (or novel connections) and that, holding other elements constant, the more thought trials you generate, the greater your chances of solving your problem.[8] However, as everyone knows, generating new ideas is hard work, and people tire of it quickly. Moreover, it is often the case that, the more you seem to work on a particular problem, the more you seem to be caught in particular ways of thinking (instead of exploring new ideas) and therefore fail to make progress. It is like seeking buried treasure by just digging deeper and deeper in the same hole instead of digging new holes in different locations to improve your chances of success.

To help people see problems from different angles, and to generate new ideas, many creativity techniques explicitly require people to use metaphors or analogies to stimulate connections—subconsciously—that they might not have thought of explicitly. By engaging in brainstorming or similar techniques and withholding criticism, people can give their unconscious selves a chance to play a role. In addition, by deliberately taking time away from problems,[9] there is the possibility that chance events or new observations will trigger the imagination and suggest solutions.[10] Indeed, Campbell argues that, in addition to the sheer number of thought trials, chance plays a huge—and unappreciated—role in suggesting useful associations of ideas in problem solving.

In the final analysis, it is not clear that the subconscious self is wiser than the conscious self. But it is still important to recognize that useful information that cannot necessarily be accessed at will may be stored somewhere in the subconscious. The wise strategy, therefore, is to find ways of communicating with your subconscious self. I shall return to these issues in chapter 7. And, in chapter 8, I shall consider the issue of why and when we should place more trust in our conscious or subconscious selves.

The Accuracy of Intuitive Judgment

In chapter 4, I explored the question of whether people can be considered intuitive experts in their understanding of the physical world as well as different normative schemes for decision making. Clearly, the accuracy of intuitive judgments in those areas reflects the extent to which the intuitive knowledge on which they are based is relevant. Thus, intuitive predictions of the path that an object dropped from an airplane will take will be correct if the intuitive understanding of the relevant physical principles is also correct (it will fall forward and down and increase in speed as it approaches the earth). In this section, I examine a related literature concerning people's ability to make predictions in a variety of domains. Once again, we are faced with the problem that studies do not always specify whether people's judgments rely only on intuition or whether and to what extent deliberation is also involved.

To determine the accuracy of a judgment, or, indeed, any form of prediction, you need to have a criterion for comparison. How accurate is the prediction relative to what actually happened? For example, did it rain when and where the forecaster said it would? How close were experts' predictions to the actual rate of inflation? As I shall explain below, it is not really possible to assess the accuracy of intuitive judgment in general because many intuitive judgments are made in contexts in which there are no explicit criteria. However, by carefully examining those situations in which criteria do exist, we can gain insight into the possible accuracy of intuitive judgment in general and, in particular, the factors that affect accuracy.

The Criterion of Statistical Models

Views about the accuracy of intuitive judgment have varied over time. In the first half of the twentieth century, it was generally believed that people were accurate at making judgments and that, in particular, clinicians who made judgments about different psychological conditions had excellent intuition.

But how should you assess the accuracy of judgment? What would you say if you knew that a physician was accurate in distinguishing between two diseases 80 percent of the time or that 70 percent of the hires made by a personnel manager turned out to be successes? Are these good accuracy rates for these particular tasks? Without more information, you cannot make a valid assessment. For example, the 80 percent accuracy rate of the physician would not be impressive if you knew that medical students could make the correct diagnosis 90 percent of the time. Similarly, what would happen if the personnel manager made his selections at random? It could be the case that 70 percent of applicants would be successful in the job in any case, and thus the personnel manager's expertise adds nothing to the process. In other words, to assess the adequacy of judgment, you need, not only a criterion, but also a baseline against which to measure the validity of human judgment. Clearly, a 60 percent success rate in a task where the random baseline is 20 percent is far superior to an 80 percent success rate when the random baseline is 70 percent.[11]

In 1954, Paul Meehl shocked the world of psychology by identifying a baseline against which the predictions of clinical psychologists could be compared. To assess the validity of clinical judgment, Meehl examined studies that compared human judgments with the predictions of statistical or actuarial models. In other words, he asked what would happen if the predictions of the clinicians who had examined patients were ignored and the statistical data in the patients' files used instead to predict outcomes. His comparisons demonstrated the superiority of statistical models. In other words, predictive ability would increase if statistical models took the place of clinicians. Meehl's study attracted a great deal of attention when it appeared because the domain that it examined—clinical psychology—was one in which the "human" element was deemed especially important.

The study shocked many clinicians who felt that their professional identity and competence had been threatened. However, subsequent years showed that the clinicians were not alone. Meehl's empirical results and insights have been replicated in many different domains, including, for example, predicting achievement in graduate school, the longevity of cancer patients, the prices of securities, and the outcomes of games.[12] In fact, if human judges and statistical or actuarial models are provided with *exactly the same information,* the literature has yet to report a case in which humans have made more accurate predictions than models.[13] Indeed, in some situations, humans have been given access to more information than models and still made less accurate predictions. As a case in point, consider the use of subjective impressions in interviews. In some studies, it has been found that allowing people to make use of their subjective impressions while conducting interviews degrades the accuracy of judgments relative to using only information contained in candidates' files.[14]

In the situations just described, it was possible to build statistical or actuarial models because data were available to assess the relation between cues or indicators, on the one hand, and a criterion variable, on the other. For example, the cues or indicators could be the symptoms exhibited by patients, and the criterion could be a subsequent behavior or condition. However, such statistical or actuarial models cannot be built in cases in which no criterion variable exists. Consider, for example, the task of selecting employees who will pursue a new line of work, one where success or failure will not be apparent for some years. Alternatively, the solvency of a small business could depend critically on a bank loan. Thus, if the bank manager fails to authorize a loan, he may never learn that the business could have been saved, and no subsequent criterion can be observed (see also chap. 3). How can the validity of judgment be assessed in such cases?

One intriguing method has been to build statistical models of the people making the judgments and then to investigate the circumstances under which these models are more accurate predictors than are the people from whom they are derived. This method is called *bootstrapping,* and it works like this.[15] A statistical analysis is made of the relation between the person's judgments and the information on which those judgments have been based. As an example, imagine a bank manager assessing the creditworthiness of a customer on the basis of different financial ratios. Once you have modeled the person's decision-making process, you can make predictions of future outcomes by using the model of the person, that is, by predicting what the person's predictions would be. For example, you can take data that would have been presented to the bank manager and use the model to predict the manager's judgments (i.e., the manager's assessment of the customer's creditworthiness).

Now, imagine that it is possible to compare both the manager's actual predictions and the model's predictions against a criterion. Which are likely to be more accurate, and when?

The model of the person's decision-making process is, in effect, a formula. As a consequence, it is perfectly consistent; that is, it will always make the same prediction if presented with the same information. People, on the other hand, are not perfectly consistent. Their decisions can be affected by fatigue or boredom, and their attention can wander. They will not necessarily always make the same prediction given the same information. However, unlike statistical models, people can factor into their decisions information that is not available to a model, and they can see the implications of specific combinations of cues, something that the model might not be programmed to do. A bank manager, for example, might have a sense about which businesses are likely to fail that is not captured by financial ratios. Perhaps entrepreneurial ability can be assessed by the way people talk? In other words, there is a potential trade-off between the consistency of models, on the one hand, and the ability of people to move beyond the confines of models, on the other.

The outcomes of bootstrapping models have been checked with valid criteria over a wide range of applications. The major result is that, on average, the virtues of consistency outweigh all other factors. Models generally provide more accurate predictions than the people on whom they have been based.[16]

These studies suggest inadequacies in intuition and were, in fact, often interpreted as indicating failures in human judgment. However, in assessing intuition, it is important to examine carefully the conditions under which these comparisons between human and statistical models have been made. As an example, imagine attempting to predict academic success in graduate school using an actuarial or statistical model (i.e., not bootstrapping). The information available to both humans and models is restricted to just that material from a candidate's application that can be quantified and therefore coded. Thus, each candidate's profile amounts to nothing more than a set of numbers: standardized test (e.g., GRE) scores, undergraduate grade point average, quality of undergraduate institution, and ratings of different qualitative aspects of the application (e.g., essays, letters of reference, and so on). The idea here is that, even if some of the information is qualitative, it can be captured numerically. For example, essays can be scored by rating them on the basis of, say, a seven- or ten-point scale.

Some studies allow the human judges to read all the material in the application files, and these individuals thus see profiles of candidates as more than a series of numbers. However, in the final analysis, the task involves weighting and combining a series of indicators or cues to make predictions. The comparison between humans and models is typically assessed in terms of average prediction error over a series of cases.

Clearly, at the conceptual level, humans do weight and combine the different indicators when making judgments. And, in *particular* cases, they may make better judgments than statistical models. However, as noted above, humans are not perfectly consistent. Owing to both motivational and cognitive limitations, they cannot apply the same "formula" to all cases. Yet this is precisely what statistical rules do. Moreover, provided that statistical rules have some validity, they are bound to make better predictions, *on average,* than humans.[17] The advantage of models lies in their consistency.

When faced with making judgments that will affect human lives, for example, psychological diagnoses or graduate school admission decisions, many people balk at the notion of using formulas or reducing human qualities to numbers. However, what they forget is that human judgment is still very much involved in statistical modeling. After all, someone had to decide which variables to include in the model and, in some cases, determine how those variables are related to the criterion (e.g., noting whether the relation is positive or negative).[18] Humans can do everything well except make the explicit numerical calculations, and there is no shame in admitting that a computer can do this better.

A study conducted by Hillel Einhorn—involving predicting the longevity of cancer patients—provides an interesting example of the efficacy of combining human judgment and statistical modeling.[19] Physicians made perceptual judgments of indicators in patients' biopsy slides. These judgments were then coded on rating scales and mechanically combined by a statistical model. The resulting predictions were more accurate than those produced by the physicians when they tried to combine all the information "intuitively" or "in their heads." It is true that a statistical model was used. However, no model could have been built without the use of the expert input of the physicians, albeit as "measuring devices." In this, human perceptual judgment was necessarily good because there was no alternative.

The point that I wish to stress is the following. Given the same inputs, it is always going to be the case that models will make better predictions than humans, *on average*. Indeed, this point is now well accepted in the financial services industry, where the ubiquity of "credit scoring rules" testifies to the power of the principle. But this does not mean that intuition is necessarily bad.

Ilan Yaniv and I conducted an experimental study of a case of prediction in which, we argued, intuition should have an advantage over statistical modeling.[20] We hypothesized that this would occur when people have specific expertise *and* the environment is complex and, possibly, too costly to model. To simulate these conditions, we presented university-student subjects with examples of five-letter words (taken from articles in the *New York Times*) of which only the first letter was provided (e.g., $h----$) and asked them to predict the second and fifth letters. The information supplied to subjects varied from only the words (e.g., $h----$) to the words in their full context. The only feasible statistical model available with which to work in this case is one based on counts of the frequencies of letters in the second and fifth positions of five-letter words conditional on knowing the first letter. It should also be noted that these students were experts in the sense that all were native speakers of English studying at an elite university. In their lifetimes, they must have read millions of words. How well did they perform at this task?

The standard used to evaluate performance was the statistical model of letter frequencies mentioned above: 42 percent correct for the second letter and 33 percent correct for the fifth letter. When they were given no contextual cues whatsoever, the students had success rates of 24 and 18 percent, respectively. As can be seen, although they did not perform as well as the statistical model, these experts did have some valid notions of the distribution of letter frequencies. (As noted in chap. 3, people are quite good at recording information about frequencies over time even if there is no specific motivation to do so.)[21] When, however, the students were given a few contextual cues (the title of the article and the words directly preceding and following the target word), their performance improved dramatically—to 42 and 38 percent correct, respectively (i.e., the same as or better than the model). When they were given the complete context (the title of the article and the entire sentence in which the target word was embedded), their performance reached 80 and 81 percent correct, respectively. Clearly, when an environment is complex—*complex* here being defined by the difficulty of building appropriate statistical models—humans can take account of contextual cues, and their intuitions can lead to valid judgments.

Human input is necessary to build models. In addition, there are circumstances in which people can capture information that would not be recognized by models. This naturally leads to the question of whether predictive accuracy would not be improved by using combinations of human judgment and statistical models.

Robert Blattberg and Steven Hoch noted that, in a changing environment, it is not clear that consistency is always a virtue and that one of the advantages of human judgment is the ability to detect change.[22] Thus, in changing environments, it might be advantageous to combine human judgment and statistical models. Blattberg and Hoch examined this possibility by having supermarket managers forecast demand for certain products and then creating a composite forecast by averaging these judgments with the forecasts of statistical models based on past data. The rationale was that statistical models assume stable conditions and therefore cannot account for the effects on demand of novel events such as actions taken by competitors or the introduction of new products. Humans, however, can incorporate these novel factors in their judgments. The composite—or average of human judgments and statistical models—proved to be more accurate than either the statistical models or the managers working alone.

One impression that the statistical benchmark approach can create is that human judgment is inaccurate. I think that, as a generalization, this impression is inaccurate and that much depends on the domain in which judgment is being studied. For example, as noted in chapter 4, some classic studies have demonstrated a phenomenon called *illusory correlation,* that is, the tendency to see correlations between variables when, if fact, there are none.[23] However, it is important to note that this phenomenon has been demonstrated in domains in which it is difficult to verify ideas empirically and yet people need to develop theories in order to make sense of their observations (e.g., in some areas of clinical psychology). Incidentally, this comment about illusory correlation should not be taken as an excuse for bad judgment in specific domains. But it does emphasize again the importance of understanding the learning environments in which beliefs are created and maintained and the need for people to be proactive in testing their assumptions (a topic that will be discussed in chap. 7).

To counter the impression that human judgment is inaccurate, consider the example of weather forecasting, on which a great deal of evidence exists.[24] In this case, it is important to note that the learning environment is kind. Judgments are made frequently, and feedback is immediate and unambiguous. For example, it either does or does not rain. Moreover, the public nature of predictions and of the criteria by which these can be assessed means that professional reputations are at stake. Motivation to learn and perform accurately is high.[25] Finally, because predictions do not affect outcomes (i.e., the forecaster cannot affect the weather), there is no confusion due to self-fulfilling prophecies.

Another example of good judgment is neuropsychological assessment, on which Howard Garb and his colleagues have amassed an impressive body of evidence.[26] They report levels of reliability in judgment that vary from "good" to "excellent" for several tasks. In addition, Garb has written a comprehensive book that examines many aspects of judgment in this domain and makes many suggestions for improving the quality of judgment, often involving various forms of decision aids.[27]

In summary, statistical models have provided useful benchmarks for assessing the accuracy of intuitive predictions. They have also highlighted the comparative strengths and weaknesses of both humans and computers as far as making predictions is concerned. As emphasized above, humans are not as effective as computers in weighting and aggregating information. However, they can access information that statistical models cannot. For example, humans can measure quantities that cannot be easily detected by machines (recall Einhorn's study of physicians); they can use contextual cues that would be difficult to incorporate in statistical models (recall the study asking subjects to predict the second and fifth letters of five-letter words); and they can detect changes in patterns being predicted (recall Blattberg and Hoch's study of supermarket managers).

From a practical viewpoint, we should approach the question of what tasks humans and computers can most usefully perform on a case-by-case basis.[28] In most cases, I believe we will find that human expertise should be used to identify important variables and that the task of summarizing or aggregating information should be left to computers.[29]

Confidence and Overconfidence

When making decisions, people typically consider the chances of pertinent events occurring. For example, if you are planning a holiday at a certain time of the year, you undoubtedly ask yourself what the weather is likely to be where you are going. Moreover, you may even research such relevant data as average rainfall and temperature as well as observed variations in these variables. And, in some cases, uncertainty about the weather could be a determining factor in your decision. But are you sure that the weather forecast on which you are relying is accurate, and, if so, how sure? More generally, how sure are you about the various factors (e.g., weather, exchange rate, availability of recreational facilities, etc.) that affect your decision?

Uncertainty is often assessed intuitively, and, because assessments of uncertainty constitute such important inputs to the decision-making process, the question of how good people are at assessing uncertainty has been investigated extensively. The evidence shows that, generally speaking, people are not good at expressing their level of uncertainty explicitly in probabilistic terms. On the other hand, people realize that they are uncertain in many situations, and they can be trained to assess their level of uncertainty more accurately. Let us examine the evidence.

Many studies have investigated the assessment of uncertainty using the following paradigm. Researchers ask subjects a series of questions on familiar topics, to which, however, they are unlikely to know the correct answers for sure. Subjects are instructed to answer, not precisely, but by giving a range within which they believe—with a specified degree of certainty—the correct answer falls. For example, Bob and Joe might be asked to assess the populations of cities (or the total sales of corporations or the distance between two cities) and instructed to give, not a precise number, but a range of numbers (high and low) within which they are 80 percent certain the correct answer falls. If, then, when asked about the population of London, the interval that Joe provides is smaller than Bob's, it is assumed that Joe is less uncertain about his answer than Bob. An advantage of this methodology is that, given responses to a series of questions, the researcher can determine whether Bob and Joe have assessed their uncertainty accurately. More specifically, accurate assessment occurs when 80 percent of the 80 percent confidence intervals contain the correct answer, 60 percent of the 60 percent intervals, 40 percent of the 40 percent intervals, and so on.

Many studies using this methodology find that people are consistently overconfident in that they provide intervals that are too narrow (e.g., fewer than 80 percent of their 80 percent confidence intervals contain the correct answer).[30] People also consistently express concern when confronted with the evidence of their overconfidence; while they did not necessarily expect to be good at the task of explicit probability assessment (since it is new to them), neither did they expect to be so bad! Finally, it should be noted that attempts to make this "overconfidence effect" disappear by providing warnings or offering monetary incentives have failed.[31]

Many explanations have been generated to account for these findings. Some center on issues of question difficulty, differential expertise, how questions have been asked, and so on. However, within the paradigm described, the overconfidence effect is real. Moreover, other studies show important inconsistencies in people's ability to assess uncertainty when sets of uncertain events are described in different ways.[32]

For example, imagine a garage mechanic who examines a car that cannot be started and is asked to assess the chances of different factors (e.g., electrical fault in the starter mechanism, dirt in the carburetor, and so on) being *the* cause. The mechanic is provided with a list of several possible causes, including a catchall category *all other causes.* To be consistent with probability theory, the assessments made by the mechanic of the probability that each of the various causes, including the catchall category, is *the* cause should add up to 100 percent. However, the general finding is that assessments are sensitive to the number of separate, possible causes listed and that there is an "out of sight, out of mind" effect. That is, when fewer causes are listed, they tend to be weighted disproportionately, with the result that causes covered by the catch-all category are implicitly underweighted.

From the viewpoint of this book, these studies illustrate that people have difficulty translating feelings of uncertainty into *explicit* judgments of probability. However, three additional sets of findings need to be considered before concluding whether intuitive assessments of uncertainty are or are not good.

The first set of studies presents a more optimistic view of the ability to express uncertainty. In the task used, people expressed their degree of confidence when answering questions that had only two possible responses (e.g., "Which German city has the greater population? Heidelberg or Bonn?"). The task required indicating one of the alternatives and stating (in terms of a scale ranging from 50 to 100 percent) the probability that the correct answer had been chosen. If people are "well calibrated," there should be a correspondence between their probability assessments and the relative frequencies with which their answers are correct. Thus, questions that are given assessments of, say, 70 percent should, on average, be answered correctly 70 percent of the time. (This involves exactly the same rationale as the paradigm assessing uncertainty described above.)

But what happens if people are asked, not only to provide a probability assessment for each response, but also to estimate (at the end of the session) how many of those probability assessments were correct? For example, how many assessments that fell within the range 60–69 percent were actually correct?

Gerd Gigerenzer and his colleagues asked just these kinds of questions.[33] They found that the probability assessments that people assigned their answers indicated overconfidence. However, people's final estimates of how many of their probability assessments were correct were actually lower than their original assessments. That is, whereas people might have assigned, say, a probability assessment of 70 percent to several questions, they would have gone on to estimate that only 60 percent of those assessments were correct. What is interesting here is that, if the second estimates are substituted for the original estimates, people's judgments become well calibrated (see above).

The implication is that, when considering accuracy in prediction over a series of cases, people are more realistic. One interpretation of this phenomenon is that adopting a broader perspective brings the reality of everyday experience to mind. We all know, for example, that "sure things" do not always happen. Thus, it seems reasonable to discount individual estimates. Another, related interpretation is that frequencies are more meaningful to people than probability estimates (see also chap. 4).[34]

In a second set of studies, Ilan Yaniv and Dean Foster nicely demonstrated that people do have intuitive notions of the uncertainty inherent in specific estimates.[35] The starting point of their investigation was the observation that the manner in which estimates are stated verbally often implies a level of uncertainty. Consider, for example, the difference in implied meaning when someone tells you that 100 people—as opposed to, say, 103—attended a meeting. When you hear 100, the immediate reaction is to assume, not that exactly 100 people, but that approximately 100 people attended the meeting. Most people imagine that the figure 100 was obtained by counting in groups of 10. On the other hand, when you hear 103, the implication is that this is a more precise estimate because it has been expressed in units. You may not expect 103 to be exactly correct, but you would be surprised if the true number differed by more than a few units.

Yaniv and Foster analyzed many such situations and showed that the metric, or standard of measurement, that people use to express an estimate reflects their inherent level of uncertainty as well as their desire to communicate this uncertainty to others. Thus, the issue is not that people lack an intuitive appreciation of the uncertainty of specific events or quantities. The problem is that they do not usually express their uncertainty in an explicitly and rigorously probabilistic form.

The third set of studies addresses the question of whether it is possible to train people to assess probabilities more accurately and, if so, under what conditions? Weather forecasters have received particular attention since they are now often required to provide explicit probability estimates (e.g., the chance of rain at a specific time in a specific place). Evidence shows that, with training, practice, and feedback, weather forecasters can assess their uncertainty about the weather accurately (i.e., it does rain 70 percent of the times that they predict a 70 percent chance of rain).[36] In other words, people can learn to assess probabilities that match reality. (It should be noted, however, that the environments in which weather forecasters are learning are kind [see above], which undoubtedly affects their ability to learn appropriately. I shall return to this issue in chap. 7.)

More on Factors Affecting Accuracy

There are two ways of looking at accuracy in judgment. One involves errors relative to a criterion, as considered above (see pp. 144–150). The other asks what factors do or do not lead to making accurate judgments. Clearly, people can and do make errors, but they are also capable of remarkable accuracy. We need to examine both situations.

One domain in which intuitive judgments play a critical role is social life. Each of us learns automatic ways of reacting in social situations, and this can lead, over time, to patterns of behavior that have both functional and dysfunctional consequences. For example, an important dimension of what has become known as *emotional intelligence* involves the ability to understand the dynamics of social situations.[37] People who can "read" others accurately and know how to initiate contact possess an enormous advantage.

Given the importance of this skill, it should be no surprise that the topic of judging social situations and personalities has attracted a great deal of attention.[38] Moreover, much work has documented the kinds of errors that are often made. For example, many papers have described what is known as the *fundamental attribution error*—an asymmetry in the attribution of cause when people are considering the behavior of others as opposed to their own.[39]

The key idea here is that, in trying to understand the behavior of others, people tend to attribute observed behavior to personality factors as opposed to characteristics of situations. After all, it is easy to explain other people's behavior in terms of personality, especially when the concepts and correlates of our intuitive "personality theories" are not well defined (e.g., "I knew he would do that because he is an angry kind of person"). On the other hand, when making sense of our own actions, we tend to explain them in terms of the situations in which we find ourselves (e.g., "I snapped like that because I found myself in an intolerable situation"). In other words, personality drives the behavior of others, but situation drives our own.[40]

One explanation for this asymmetry is perceptual. In trying to make sense of what others do, we perceive personalities as salient against a background of different situations. In explaining our own actions, we perceive changes in situations as salient against the stable background of our own personality.

David Funder has made a useful contribution to the attempt to understand the conditions under which judgments of personality are or are not liable to be accurate.[41] Building on ideas elaborated in the 1950s by Egon Brunswik, Funder asks what conditions have to hold for people's judgments of the personalities of others to be accurate.[42] His conclusion is that four factors determine accuracy: *relevance, availability, detection,* and *use.*

To illustrate, imagine that you are judging whether someone is generous. First, there should be behavioral cues that are *relevant* to the trait. (People who are generous go out of their way to help others.) Second, these cues must be *available* for observation. (Is it possible to see the person engaging in acts of generosity? Perhaps he donates a good deal of money to charitable causes but does so anonymously.) Third, to what extent can you *detect* the cues? (Were you yourself in a position to observe his generous acts?) And, fourth, are the cues denoting the trait *used* in an appropriate manner in the act of judgment? (Are the cues indicating generosity weighted and combined correctly? For example, are the more valid cues given more weight than those that are only marginally relevant?)

Funder argues that each of his four factors can be thought of as having a multiplicative effect on the accuracy of personality judgment. Thus, if even one of the four factors does not hold, the resulting judgment cannot be accurate. (Imagine, e.g., that each factor is rated on a separate 0–1 scale where 0 indicates that a factor does not hold. Clearly, if even only one of the factors is rated 0, judgment cannot be accurate.) Funder's model thus clearly shows why accurate personality assessment is so difficult. Not only must the concept (in this case, what a generous person is) be valid, but the behavioral cues on which the assessment is based must be relevant, available, detected, and used appropriately. The accuracy of personality judgment is a joint function of the characteristics of the situation (relevance and availability) and the actions of the person making the judgment (detection and use).

Seen from this perspective, it is clear that few personality judgments will be accurate. I do not, of course, mean to suggest that people should not be held accountable for making, and especially for acting on, erroneous judgments. On the contrary, when attempting to assess personality, we should be aware that the process is difficult and act accordingly— that is to say, cautiously. And, in that cautious spirit, before judging whether people are good judges of personality, we should consider the factors that contribute to personality judgments.

"How Good" Does Intuition Need to Be?

One problem in evaluating the quality of intuition (e.g., when making personality judgments) is that its outputs are often vague (a feeling that something is strange or a sense of mistrust when conversing with a stranger). Thus, assessing accuracy per se can be problematic—there is no precise criterion that can be applied. In many cases, therefore, it is more important to ask how good intuition needs to be. For example, a general feeling or an intuition that a stranger is not trustworthy may be sufficient to guide behavior until more information is available, even though the hypothesis has not been sharply formulated in behavioral terms. (As a case in point, consider Damasio's experiments [discussed above], in which people acted as though they had been warned against making certain risky choices.)

In many cases, *speed* is a valuable dimension of intuitive thought. A situation immediately sets in motion an intuitive reaction—which is functional provided that the resulting action is not mistaken. Simple examples are provided by situations to which we respond (essentially automatically) with physical movement (e.g., hitting the brakes when the brake lights of the car in front of us are activated). In most cases, an approximate judgment is all that is needed in the short term because this can be corrected quickly as the situation evolves. However, a speedy judgment (intuition) that is wrong may also prove costly. For example, imagine a football player on defense who misreads the actions of the players on offense and, instead of intercepting the pass that he was sure was coming his way, can only watch helplessly as his opponents score.

As these examples show, it is difficult to talk about the quality of many intuitions unless one explicitly specifies the characteristics of the task environment. For example, how quickly must a response be made? What are the costs of errors and the benefits of being correct? How accurate need judgment be? Can errors be corrected by feedback?[43] Unfortunately, the literature is silent about the quality of most intuitions that people use to navigate the vagaries of everyday life, and it is therefore impossible at present to reach a conclusion as to the *overall quality* of human intuitions. The point that I wish to emphasize, however, is that the value of intuition should not be assessed simply in terms of predictive accuracy in well-defined situations.

Individual Differences

The popular imagination has it that some people—women especially—are more intuitive than others. But is there in fact any basis for such systematic individual differences?

The view taken here is that intuition is like expertise in the sense that it is specific to particular domains. Someone who has good intuitions when playing tennis may have bad intuitions when playing bridge. Someone who has good intuitions when attempting to solve mathematical problems may have bad intuitions when attempting to solve personal problems. Now, this does not mean that people cannot have good intuitions in more than one domain because clearly many do. What I am claiming is that, because intuition in general is largely a function of experience, and because no two people have exactly the same experiences, the domains in which intuitions are good are bound to differ from person to person. Thus, in posing the question of individual differences, we need to specify the domain in which we would expect to find these as well as the classes of people among whom such differences would be observed.

Expertise

The viewpoint just expressed is consistent with the analysis of learning presented in chapter 3. It is also consistent with a growing literature on expertise. Studies in this area have examined experts in many different domains, for example, chess, medicine, music, physics, literature, and various sports.[44] Several findings emerge from these studies.

First and foremost, expertise is limited to domains. The master chess player, for example, may have little ability to understand problems in physics.

Second, expertise is acquired only by exposure to and activity within domains. Thus, to achieve expertise in, say, chess or physics, you must devote a great deal of time to these activities.

Third, to achieve outstanding performance in any domain takes years of dedication. Moreover, high performers are those who have followed demanding regimes of deliberate practice and have typically benefited from the guidance of good teachers or coaches.

Fourth, and perhaps surprisingly, experts are not necessarily more accurate than novices when making certain types of predictions.[45]

This fourth finding was hinted at above (see pp. 144–150). One possible explanation is the fact that certain phenomena (e.g., daily changes in stock market prices) are inherently unpredictable. In addition, I believe there is a social phenomenon at work. People seek certainties in life, and it is the task of experts to provide these. Thus, people expect experts' predictions to be accurate. This, in turn, encourages both the experts and their public to explain away inaccurate predictions and thereby maintain the illusion that the experts are always correct. As an example, consider the large number of people who subscribe to investment newsletters. In many ways, these newsletters are like fortune-tellers. People crave certainty, and someone is always happy to oblige.

What exactly differentiates experts from novices? Basically, experts process information differently.

First, experts acquire habits that help them process more information. They learn to counteract limitations in short-term or working memory and are able to "chunk" information more effectively. In other words, despite facing normal limitations on memory, experts find ways of restructuring information so that they can take more into account. (See also chap. 3.) For example, whereas a medical student might see a patient's symptoms as several different items of information, the experienced physician may recognize the same information as an instance of a pattern of symptoms, that is, a specific disease.

Second, experts and novices use different problem-solving strategies. Novices tend first to identify a specific goal and then work backward through the details of the problem to find a way to reach that goal. Experts, however, tend first to take in the details of the problem they face, then determine (through a process of recognizing similarities) the general framework that best fits the data, and, finally, work forward from that framework to explore possible solutions (goals). The process that novices follow (working backward) is more deliberate; the process that experts follow (working forward) is more intuitive. Not surprisingly, experts solve problems faster than novices.[46]

Gary Klein and his collaborators have made extensive studies of the decision-making processes of experts—including firefighters, nurses, military commanders, and chess players.[47] In many of the situations examined, decisions were made speedily under conditions that most would consider stressful. Klein calls the descriptive model that he derives from his observations *recognition-primed decision making*. According to this theory, experts are able to act speedily because they are quick to recognize the kind of situation they face and, in particular, whether the situation differs from what they expected to find.

For example, Klein describes the case of a firefighter who suddenly ordered his entire crew to evacuate a building in which they were fighting a fire. Immediately after the building was evacuated, the floor on which they had all been standing collapsed. Had the crew not evacuated the building, all would have been killed. The intriguing feature of this incident was that the firefighter was puzzled by the specific nature of the fire he was facing. Specifically, he sensed something out of the ordinary, something that he did not expect given the situation as first assessed, and, like Antonio Damasio's "normal" subjects (see chap. 2), took action to avoid possible danger. In other words, his intuition warned him of danger even though he did not know exactly what the danger was.

Experience and perception play a huge role in Klein's model of decision making. The key notion is that, on the basis of past experience, people develop intuitive expectations that can be either confirmed or disconfirmed. Confirmation will suggest certain actions; disconfirmation (deviation) will suggest others. That expertise is domain specific is also quite clear in Klein's model.

It should be noted that intuitive expectations are not necessarily limited to experts. Recall, for example, the earlier discussion of infants' intuitive understanding of such physical phenomena as gravity. In brief, infants are shown pictures of possible and impossible phenomena. If they register surprise, the assumption is that their "recognition-primed" expectations have been violated (see pp. 106–107). The surprise experienced on seeing balls roll (seemingly) uphill instead of downhill at the electric brae is also the result of a violation of recognition-primed expectations (see p. 28).

Klein's studies have focused on the specific kinds of intuitive abilities that experts develop. They have also focused on situations in which the stakes are high. The underlying principle, however, appears to be generally applicable. People can be trained to develop their intuitive skills within specific domains.

What does it take to become an expert and to attain the highest level of proficiency within a particular domain? Anders Ericsson and Neil Charness have analyzed many cases in different domains and reject explanations that invoke innate talent.[48] Instead, they describe a process whereby early interest (in, e.g., music) is first nurtured in a supportive environment and subsequently encouraged to develop through extensive practice. The difference, they argue, between people who perform at the highest levels and those who do not can be attributed to amount and quality of practice—and, in particular, to what they term *deliberate practice*, practice that is conducted in ideal learning conditions (typically involving high-level tutoring). Motivation must also be sustained over many years.

Contrary to the Ericsson-Charness view, there are researchers who take the view that some portion of the aptitude to perform at the highest levels is innate. One such researcher is Howard Gardner, who has conducted extensive work on the nature of intelligence, the different forms that intelligence can take, and the lives of highly creative people.[49]

Clearly, the debate is hard to resolve. It may be that we are all born with only minuscule differences in aptitude and that, with a supportive environment, deliberate practice, and sustained motivation, those differences grow greater and greater over the years.

If you talk to experts in different walks of life, you will find that their intuitions have been acquired through many hours of experience and in what often seems like an unstructured manner. Physicians, for example, start as medical students and learn clinical skills "on the job," mainly by observing and doing. Most of the experts studied by Gary Klein (see above) obtained their skills in the same way. Diana the antiquarian and Kevin the trader—to whom I introduced you in chapter 1—have never received formal instruction in their areas of expertise.

When issues of individual differences are raised in the context of intuition, it is clear that the ability to learn from experience is key, and I shall return to this topic in subsequent chapters. For now, it will suffice to quote a summary statement from Ericsson and Charness: "Individuals do not achieve expert performance by gradually refining and extrapolating the performance they exhibited before starting to practice but instead by restructuring the performance and acquiring new methods and skills."[50] In our terms, if you want to improve your intuitive performance in a given domain, you must question the way in which you learn from experience and acquire new skills. You must also maintain the motivation to improve.

This subsection has several implications for educating intuition. These involve gaining experience in the domain in which you wish to develop intuition; obtaining expert instruction and accurate feedback; learning to counteract the limitations of working memory by "chunking" or processing information more effectively; allowing yourself to see in problems similarities to what you already know instead of forcing a deliberative framework to find a solution; being willing to restructure how you do things and to acquire new skills; and, finally, being motivated to keep practicing your skills. I shall return to these points in chapter 7.

Female-Male Differences

It is difficult to have a conversation about the subject of intuition without someone raising the issue of women's intuition. Loosely speaking, most people think of this in the domain of interpersonal relations and perceptions. In short, there is a widely held cultural stereotype that women make more accurate interpersonal judgments than men. Women, on the other hand, are not generally thought to be more intuitive than men in male-dominated activities such as engineering. While we should be encouraged that the stereotype at least acknowledges the domain-specific nature of intuition, the question remains: Do women in fact make more accurate intuitive judgments about interpersonal matters?[51]

Earlier, I discussed David Funder's analysis of accuracy in judgments of personality (see pp. 155–156). One lesson to be learned from Funder and applied to the present discussion is the need to define carefully what is meant by *accuracy in interpersonal perception*. Fortunately, Tiffany Graham and William Ickes have examined the evidence on this issue and have nicely distinguished between what they call the *different empathic abilities* of men and women. They have identified three types of abilities: (1) *vicarious emotional responding,* or "the tendency for subjects to exhibit or report the same emotion as that experienced by a target person when they view the target in an emotion-evoking situation";[52] (2) *nonverbal decoding ability,* which involves identifying (as opposed to matching) the emotional state of a target individual; and (3) *empathic accuracy,* which involves specific inferences being made about the content of another person's thoughts or feelings.

Graham and Ickes's summary shows that women do possess greater intuitive ability than men as far as vicarious emotional responding and nonverbal decoding ability are concerned. In other words, women are better than men at relating to and understanding the emotions being experienced by another person. They are also better than men at understanding nonverbal signals or, as Judith Hall puts it, at "decoding nonverbal cues, at recognizing faces, and at expressing emotions via nonverbal communication." Indeed, in an extensive review of the relevant literature, Hall makes the point that differences between the sexes are much greater in nonverbal than in verbal skills and behaviors.[53]

The evidence on empathic accuracy, or the ability to infer the content of another person's thoughts or feelings, is mixed. Graham and Ickes maintain that, if women do in fact show greater empathic accuracy than men, it is because of differences in motivation, not differences in ability.

Graham and Ickes report two further interesting findings. First, when decoding nonverbal behavior, women's advantage over men diminishes in the presence of what Graham and Ickes call *leaky cues,* that is, cues that are extraneous or misleading. Second—and more important for our concerns—*men can learn to reach the same skill levels as women.* In other words, this form of intuition, like others, is a behavioral skill that can be improved.

Incidentally, one disadvantage of many of the studies on which these results are based is that, although age differences are examined among children, adolescents, and adults, there is not much variation in the ages of the adult populations. Subjects tend to be young adults, often college students. It would be interesting to know whether and how these differences vary across the life span.

In speculating about why women possess greater intuitive ability (as defined here) than men, Graham and Ickes review two possible explanations, both advanced by Hall. The first is evolutionary; it holds that, as primary caregivers for the young, women would be differentially selected, relative to men, for their ability to decipher nonverbal communications. (Men, it is assumed, would have been selected for their hunting-and-gathering skills.) The second is environmental: it holds that girls and boys are socialized into culturally defined gender roles that encourage different ways of interacting and dealing with people. More specifically, girls behave in ways that are more respectful of the feelings of others and are less dependent on aspects of physical power which play such an important role in the socialization of boys.

Graham and Ickes suggest that both explanations could be correct. They hypothesize that there might once have been very small, selective evolutionary pressures that gave advantages to women in decoding nonverbal communication. Moreover, once these differences were noticed, they became established in public consciousness, and both men and women have been socialized into believing that they exist and that they are quite large. The result is a kind of self-fulfilling prophecy at the societal level that has greatly magnified the size of any real genetic differences.

My own interpretation is that, as children, females learn to make more accurate observations of others engaged in social interaction than do males and that this accounts, in large part, for the enhanced intuitive ability that they later exhibit as adults. My hypothesis is that the pressure to learn is social and cultural in origin and that this pressure has its roots in the fact that, in many societies, females are not socialized to play leadership roles. As a consequence, they act like minority groups and are treated as such by males. This means that, in order to be successful, females need to observe how others act before taking action themselves and learn to be adaptable. Members of majority groups, on the other hand, do not feel the same obligation to observe the reactions of others. They just take action but, in so doing, lose the opportunity for developing their observational skills.[54]

Once again, this suggests that, with appropriate training, men's intuitions in this domain can be as accurate as those of women (see chap. 7).

That women are better than men at decoding nonverbal messages suggests that they know better than men what signs to examine. But this also raises another question. Do women use different strategies for processing information, or does their advantage arise simply from using their mental strategies more consistently?

Joan Meyers-Levy has provided some clues to the answer to this question in developing what she calls the *selectivity hypothesis*.[55] The essence of this idea lies in the distinction between information-processing strategies that alternatively eliminate or integrate information. According to Meyers-Levy, men tend to use highly selective information-processing strategies, strategies that focus speedily on relevant information, and attempt to reach quick conclusions. Women, on the other hand, use strategies that are more comprehensive and that pay more attention to detail than do those employed by men. Men's strategies are better adapted to making quick decisions. Women are more willing to take seemingly irrelevant information into account. Meyers-Levy argues that advertisers are aware of and capitalize on these differences. For example, advertisements directed toward men tend to have simple messages that go straight to the point. Advertisements that target women, on the other hand, do not shy away from providing detailed descriptions that invite readers to engage more fully with the text. As with differences in the ability to decode nonverbal messages, it is unclear whether these differences reflect genetic or environmental influences, or both.

Education, Training, and Intelligence

Given the importance of learning in acquiring expertise, we should expect to find differences that can be attributed to both education and professional training. Differences that result from education should involve the extent to which educated people have internalized certain ways of thinking so that these have become intuitive to them. In chapter 7, I shall discuss, for example, how different types of graduate education affect how people reason about everyday problems. Professional training, of course, should have a big effect on how people reason intuitively in their domain of expertise and requires no further comment here.

A particularly interesting phenomenon—one documented by a variety of studies—is the ability demonstrated by certain "uneducated" people to perform what seem like complicated algebraic calculations in the course of different occupations. Given our particular interest in intuition, the crucial point to note about these studies is that all show how well people can learn when the environments in which they are doing so are kind. For example, a study of workers in a milk-processing plant shows that they fill orders by learning to use what seem to the uninitiated like complicated mathematics.[56] Similarly, Stephen Ceci and Jeffrey Liker have documented the remarkable ability of certain racetrack gamblers to estimate odds at the beginning of a race.[57] What is particularly fascinating, and relevant to our concerns, is that, when gamblers were divided into groups by level of expertise, there was no significant difference in IQ between groups. In other words, level of expertise was unrelated to what in our society is the conventional measure of intelligence.

In subsequent chapters, I shall return to the issues of both training and intelligence. In particular, I shall examine different concepts of intelligence and whether and how these affect the ability to learn from experience, and thus to acquire appropriate intuitions.

Cognitive Styles

There is a large questionnaire-based literature describing respondents' self-reported preferences for styles of thinking and, in particular, for using so-called intuitive versus more rational modes of thought.[58] As noted in chapter 1, much of this work was inspired by Carl Jung's psychoanalytic theory of personality. Some questionnaires also measure differences in so-called learning styles.[59] Such instruments are often used in applied settings such as management and business training seminars, and participants report that they find them valuable in thinking about how they and others think and learn. If nothing else, they highlight the fact that people have different preferences for how they like to think and learn about the world. Moreover, these preferences can change over time. I shall address this issue again briefly in chapter 8.

Intuition and Choice

There is a huge and fascinating literature on how people make choices. Typically, this is thought of in the following way. A person faces two or more alternatives each of which is characterized by a number of dimensions that are potentially relevant to the choice. For example, imagine choosing between several job offers. These are the alternatives. The dimensions are characteristics of the jobs, for example, remuneration, location, prospects, benefits, and so on. Thus, choosing one job offer over another boils down to choosing one profile of dimensions over another. In many cases, uncertainty is an important dimension, and choices are often conceptualized in the form of gambles, for example, an 80 percent chance of gaining $1,000 versus a 40 percent chance of gaining $2,000.

The issues investigated in this literature center on *which alternative* people choose and *how* they make the choice. The mental strategies or rules that people use for choice can be described as either confronting or avoiding two types of conflict: *emotional* and *computational*. As an example, imagine that you are offered two jobs, one in Paris and one in Rome. Assume that you prefer to live in Paris but that the job in Rome pays more. Are you prepared to trade off a preferred location for a higher salary? This conflict is *emotional* in the sense that it involves giving up something you like (choosing either a preferred location over a higher salary or vice versa). It is *computational* in the sense that you must estimate how much pay you are prepared to forgo in order to live in Paris as opposed to Rome (see also pp. 171–173).

Conflict-confronting strategies explicitly face both conflicts and usually lead to well-reasoned choices because all factors are carefully considered and weighted. But they require effort and are difficult to execute even when few dimensions are involved (as in choosing between the jobs in Paris and Rome). Going beyond this simple example, imagine employing a conflict-confronting strategy when faced with different investment opportunities for your business. Elaborating the advantages and disadvantages of each, and facing the relevant trade-offs, is a much more complicated and costly process. Choosing in this way is very difficult.

Conflict-avoiding strategies typically reduce the mental effort (the computational conflict) involved in choice. However, many also provide rationales for choice that are acceptable to the individual and thus also reduce potential emotional conflict. For example, a conflict-avoiding strategy for the job-selection problem could be to identify location as critical and thereby exclude the job that is not in Paris.[60]

Conflict-confronting strategies are deliberative. Conflict-avoiding strategies, on the other hand, may use deliberative inputs but are subject to intuitive influences. One of the most interesting findings in the choice literature is that changes in the way in which problems are presented can affect people's decisions and that most people are unaware of the importance of these presentation effects. To discuss these findings, I distinguish between two types of situations. In the first, different presentations of the same alternatives lead to different choices. In the second, the addition or deletion of alternatives from a specific set of alternatives leads to a change in apparent preferences.

Presentation Effects: Alternatives Specified

It is well-known that the way a question is asked can affect the response.[61] In many choice problems, the way alternatives are presented can influence the values or weights given to them and, on occasion, even cause a reversal in apparent preferences. Underlying this phenomenon are two aspects of the way in which we intuitively process information.

The first is that evaluative judgments are not absolute but relative. Consider the fact that making evaluative judgments is a constant feature of everyday life. Is it warm or cold? Is it early or late? Did the company perform well or poorly? A factor common to all evaluative judgments is that they are made relative to a *reference point*, which is sometimes stated but usually implicit.[62] Temperatures that are considered to be warm for Chicago in January are considered to be cold for Chicago in July. An hour that is considered to be early for dinner in Madrid is considered to be late for dinner in Frankfurt. A company's performance could be considered good compared to that of a competitor but bad compared to its own expectations.

The second is the tendency to pay differential attention to factors on the different sides of the reference point. In particular, if one side can be classified as "good" and the other as "bad," then more weight is typically given to the bad side. While I do not claim to know why this is the case, it is easy to generate an evolutionary argument that paying more attention to dangerous ("bad") as opposed to safe ("good") situations is likely to enhance survival.

Making comparative as opposed to absolute judgments is both easy and effective. This response mechanism, however, does not operate independently of the bias in evaluation. To observe the effects of both mechanisms operating together, consider the two versions of the same problem presented in exhibit 14.[63]

The two versions of the problem are identical except that the proposed solutions to the first are formulated in terms of gains, those to the second in terms of losses. In other words, plans A and C are identical, as are plans B and D. However, people do not respond to the two versions of the problem in the same way. There is a strong tendency to choose plan A when presented with problem 1 and plan D when presented with problem 2. In other words, the safe option is chosen when the problem is couched in terms of gains, the risky option when it is couched in terms of losses. The implication is that "losses loom larger than gains" or that people are more motivated to avoid losses than they are to achieve equivalent gains.

EXHIBIT 14 Two choice problems

---

1. Imagine that you have just heard that the sole supplier of a crucial component is going to raise prices. The price increase is expected to cost your company $6,000,000. Two alternative plans have been formulated to counter the effect of the price increase. The anticipated consequences of these plans are as follows.

   a) If plan A is adopted, your company will save $2,000,000.

   b) If plan B is adopted, there is a one in three probability that $6,000,000 will be saved and a two in three probability that nothing will be saved.

Question: Do you favor plan A or plan B?

---

2. Imagine that you have just heard that the sole supplier of a crucial component is going to raise prices. The price increase is expected to cost your company $6,000,000. Two alternative plans have been formulated to counter the effect of the price increase. The anticipated consequences of these plans are as follows.

   a) If plan C is adopted, your company will lose $4,000,000.

   b) If plan D is adopted, there is a one in three probability that there will be no loss and a two in three probability that your company will lose $6,000,000.

Question: Do you favor plan C or plan D?

Source: Hogarth (1987), following Tversky & Kahneman (1981). Both problems are reproduced, in slightly altered form, from *Judgement and Choice: The Psychology of Decision* (2d ed.), by Robin M. Hogarth, © 1987 John Wiley & Sons Limited, with permission.

This phenomenon is called *loss aversion*, but, as has been demonstrated, what is perceived as a loss or a gain is subject to semantic manipulation.

In the psychological literature, these types of results are often referred to as *framing effects*.[64] The key notion is that the perspective, or frame, that we adopt in looking at a problem greatly affects our response. Moreover, that it does so is the result of intuitive processes in the sense that we lack an awareness of how framing affects our choices.

Presentation can affect more than just choices between specific alternatives. Consider, for example, a campaign that is trying to persuade people to use less energy in their homes. It is more effective to tell people that the goal is "to avoid waste" than it is to tell them that it is "to save money." Somehow, we are more attracted to taking action to avoid waste than to save money—losses do loom larger than gains.

Related to loss aversion are such phenomena as *sunk costs,* the *sta-*

tus quo bias, and the *endowment effect.*[65] All can trace their origin to the fact that, once we have spent money on something or have something in our possession, we are reluctant to cede our rights to it. We do not want to incur a loss.

In the case of sunk costs, people are reluctant to admit that a project in which they have invested may not be worthwhile. They therefore spend more money in an attempt to recoup their initial investment. (Banks in many countries have lost fortunes doing precisely this!) The status quo bias and the endowment effect both involve a reluctance to change what one already possesses for something that may or may not be of equal value. That is, people are reluctant to incur a loss. For example, assume that you have given half the people in a room a pen and the other half a coffee mug. Now assume that you let them know that the pens and the mugs are of the same economic value and that, if they wish, they may exchange them (pens for mugs, mugs for pens). One would expect that half the people would wish to engage in an exchange. But, once people have one or the other in their possession, they tend to be unwilling to do so.[66]

Presentation Effects: Adding or Deleting Alternatives

At one level, people are aware that adding or deleting alternatives can affect people's preferences. For example, consider an election with three candidates, R, D, and I. Assume that D and I have taken similar positions on the issues (both are, say, liberal Democrats), positions that are quite different from that taken by R (who is, say, a conservative Republican). Assume further that the pool of potential voters is roughly equally divided between those with liberal and those with conservative inclinations. Given such a situation, most people realize that, unless either D or I withdraws from the race, neither has much of a chance of winning the election since the liberal vote will most likely be split between D and I, leaving R with the majority of votes.

Now consider the following scenario: Suppose that you want to buy a compact disc (CD) player but that you have not yet settled on a model. You pass by a store that is having a one-day clearance sale. It is offering a popular SONY player for just $99 and a top-of-the line AIWA player for just $169, both well below list price. Do you buy the SONY, buy the AIWA, or wait until you learn more about the various other models available?

Next, consider a variation of that scenario: Suppose that you want to buy a CD player but that you have not yet settled on a model. You pass by a store that is having a one-day clearance sale. It is offering a popular

SONY player for just $99, well below the list price. Do you buy the SONY or wait until you learn more about the various other models available?

When presented with the first scenario, 27 percent of subjects chose to buy the SONY, 27 percent chose to buy the AIWA, and 46 percent chose to wait. When presented with the second scenario, 66 percent chose to buy the SONY, and 34 percent chose to wait.[67]

An interesting feature of this problem is that its structure is similar to that of the election problem but that the choice involved affects individuals *as individuals,* not as members of a larger group. Of further interest, of course, is the fact that the decision to buy the SONY player is so strongly affected by the availability of the AIWA player. In the first scenario, it seems as though the availability of the AIWA adds an element of uncertainty to the decision-making process—something that is missing from the second scenario—thereby giving people a reason to delay making a choice.

More generally, if people were always to use deliberative, conflict-confronting strategies that evaluate each alternative independently, presentation effects would have no effect on choice. However, in making comparisons between alternatives, it is difficult not to notice similarities and differences, which can often drive choices.

Consider yet another variation of the type of problem just described: Imagine that you have to choose between three job candidates, Arthur, Bill, and Claude. Arthur and Bill are similar in several important ways. They have had similar educations and job experiences, and they even come from the same part of the country. Claude is different in terms of education, experience, and even nationality. Now imagine further that the fact that all three candidates are equally well qualified can be objectively established.

Ideally, each candidate should have an equal chance of being selected. However, on reflection, I believe that we all know that the similarity between Arthur and Bill will affect Claude's chances. In some scenarios, Claude would be eliminated immediately, and the choice would then be between Arthur and Bill. In others, an initial choice would be made between Arthur and Bill, and the "winner" would then face Claude. In either case, approaching the decision-making process sequentially mitigates the inherent conflict, sometimes helping, and sometimes hurting, Claude.

Learning Rules for Choice

In chapter 3, I mentioned that part of our learning consists of observing regularities in the environment (e.g., grammar or weather patterns) and deriving rules from those observations. However, we can also learn rules when making choices, and, over time, this process become automatic and essentially inaccessible to introspection.

Consider the following scenario:[68]

> Imagine you are in a supermarket deciding which can of peas to buy. You are conscious of the need to consider price and quality in your choice and do so by adopting the following decision rule: if the price difference between brands is less than or equal to 5 cents, choose the higher quality product; otherwise, choose the cheaper brand. Whereas one could quibble about the amount of the 5 cents limit, this heuristic rule is easy to apply. Moreover, to most people it seems sensible in that two important attributes of price and quality are explicitly considered. Indeed, many people openly acknowledge using rules of this type when shopping. However, consider the implications of the rule if you were faced with the following alternatives:

Brand	Price	Quality
X	60 cents	High
Y	55 cents	Medium
Z	50 cents	Low

> Specifically, consider what would happen if you were to choose between pairs of the alternative brands. In a comparison between X and Y, you would prefer X; between Y and Z, you would choose Y; however a comparison between X and Z leads to the choice of Z. In other words, the apparently sensible heuristic that considers both price and quality implies an inconsistent ordering of your preferences over the three brands of peas. (That is X is preferred to Y; Y is preferred to Z; but Z is preferred to X.)

There are several points to make about this example. First, the rule being used seems like a sensible, intuitive one. After all, it takes into account the important variables price and quality. Second, whereas many people will readily admit that they employ similar rules when making different kinds of decisions, they are unaware that such rules can embody inherent contradictions.[69] Third, when we use rules of this kind in making decisions, we receive feedback (in the sense that we buy one of the three cans of peas), but rarely negative feedback, feedback that alerts us to the logical inconsistency inherent in the rule that we used. In this case, the only feedback that we receive is whether we are satisfied with the can of peas that we purchased. If we are, our use of that rule is reinforced, and, over time, it becomes part of our stock of intuitions.

Once again, the structure of the learning environment is important in determining how we learn to make decisions and thus our future intuitive choice processes.

How Good Are Intuitive Rules of Choice?

It is clear that people make extensive use of decision rules that fall short of the comprehensive nature of conflict-confronting choice strategies. But just how good are these rules? Do they result in satisfactory outcomes or in unsatisfactory outcomes?

In a famous 1955 essay, Herbert Simon discussed the fact that, when making decisions, people cannot possibly make all the computations that are required by full economic analyses—or, more specifically, that are assumed by economic theory. Thus, people cannot be *rational* decision makers in the strict economic sense. Instead, they are subject to what Simon called *bounded rationality*. Humans do not "maximize," as is assumed in economics; rather, their decisions involve "satisficing." The key idea here is that, in evaluating alternatives, people set goals in the form of *levels of aspiration* (e.g., I need a job in Paris that pays at least $x per year). Alternatives are then accepted or rejected depending on whether they meet these aspirations. In other words, are they satisfactory?

In this process, much clearly depends on how the levels of aspiration are set as well as on the particular alternatives that people encounter in the environment. For example, what would happen if you could not find a job in Paris that pays at least $x? You might then lower your aspiration level. But that might mean that you have already passed up a job that would have paid more than your new aspiration level.

This example shows that boundedly rational decision strategies do have limitations. However, whereas rational decision making in the strict economic sense is beyond our abilities, boundedly rational decision strategies are not and in many cases lead to satisfactory, if not optimal, outcomes. Since Simon's pioneering paper, many researchers have investigated the kinds of decision rules that people use. The general consensus is that, even in situations where computational demands are not high, people still use "simplifying" decision strategies. Consider the example given above of the choice between three cans of peas. Even when faced with only two variables—in this case, price and quality—people still seek ways of avoiding the conflict inherent in choice.

The "goodness" of decision rules clearly depends on both the characteristics of those rules and the structure of the tasks in which those rules are used. To take a simple example, if you were operating in a random environment where it is impossible to predict outcomes of actions, your best strategy would be to choose at random. Doing so is almost costless, and you would perform no better even if you expended a great deal of effort trying to understand possible cause-and-effect relations. (Imagine, for example, trying to guess the daily ups and downs in the stock market.) As the environment becomes more structured, however, the quality of your decision rules becomes more important.[70]

Making such generalizations can be problematic because it is difficult to characterize the types of environments in which decision rules are used. Nonetheless, several interesting findings have emerged, mainly when the decision alternatives being examined (e.g., which stereo system to purchase) can be characterized on a number of different dimensions (e.g., price, sound quality, aesthetic appeal, ease of use). Studies have shown that, under not too restrictive conditions, simple models that involve taking what essentially amounts to an average across all relevant attributes can result in good decisions.[71] Detlof von Winterfeldt and Ward Edwards describe many of these problems as having *flat maxima*.[72] This means that the final evaluations are not sensitive to variations in weights given to individual attributes. The effect tends to be more marked as the number of relevant attributes increases. With only two attributes, weighting does make a difference.[73]

John Payne, James Bettman, and Eric Johnson have conducted numerous simulations in order to assess how well different strategies perform across different environments.[74] They have also conducted meticulous studies of how people make choices. They characterize strategies in terms of accuracy (relative to a normative model), effort (in terms of mental operations required to employ a strategy), and speed. Their environments vary in complexity, as characterized, for example, by different numbers of alternatives and attributes as well as different degrees of conflict between alternatives.

The simulation results show, first, that simple strategies often perform quite well compared to "optimal" methods of choice. However, the relative performance of strategies is sensitive to changes in task characteristics. In examining how humans handle the same tasks, Payne, Bettman, and Johnson find that people are sensitive to the demands of different types of tasks or environments and that they adapt their strategies accordingly. From the viewpoint of this book, a key finding of this work is that, when confronted with different tasks, people seem to have an intuitive sense of how to "decide how to decide." It is as if they make intuitive assessments of the costs and benefits of different mental strategies when faced with different types of choices. This, in turn, suggests that people have repertoires of implicit decision rules on which they can call.

Gerd Gigerenzer and his colleagues have recently launched a vigorous examination of the way in which simple decision rules can—depending on characteristics of both rules and tasks—lead to good decisions. Adopting an evolutionary perspective, they argue that, over time, humans have acquired an "adaptive toolbox" containing decision rules that are designed to meet the demands of specific tasks. Their starting point is to ask what kinds of tasks humans would have needed to handle in their natural environments and thus what kinds of tools would have evolved to meet those demands. For example, one feature of many environments is the fact that many variables are correlated. Thus, there are many ways—that is, many different combinations of variables or cues—that could be used to reach the right decisions. In other cases, the manner in which alternatives are distributed in the environment (i.e., the way in which the environment is organized) can affect the success of specific, heuristic strategies. In several examples, they show that simple decision rules, such as basing your choice only on what you think is the most important variable or choosing an alternative that seems more familiar (or "recognizable"), can lead to excellent, if not optimal, choices. Gigerenzer and his colleagues argue that these kinds of decision rules are fast, frugal, and computationally cheap.[75]

Once again, this research points to the importance of the environment and, since people must clearly learn when these rules do or do not seem to work, the extent to which learning structures are kind or wicked. However, as with the work of Payne, Bettman, and Johnston, it also highlights the need to educate people as to when they should or should not use simplifying rules of choice. People may develop an intuitive sense of when and what rules to use. But how can they educate this "meta" choice process? I return to this question in chapter 7.

Some Concluding Comments on Goodness

It is difficult to determine *how good* intuition is in terms of some overall measure. This chapter has discussed the functions of intuition and stressed that intuitive processing is more the rule than the exception. Some comments were also addressed to the issue of whether the intuitive self is "wiser" than the conscious self and under what circumstances. This issue will be considered again in chapter 8.

The current chapter argued that the "goodness" of intuition can be characterized on many dimensions (e.g., speed, accuracy, and effort). It also argued that the judgment of accuracy is not necessarily straightforward since, in order to determine whether a particular strategy is successful, the corresponding base rate (the rate at which random choice leads to success in the same situation) must also be determined. It provided an overview of the literature on intuitive predictions, noting that, in many situations, human predictive ability is inferior to simple statistical models (largely because the latter are perfectly consistent). Nonetheless, human—and often intuitive—inputs are essential to creating statistical models, and, in some cases, combinations of human judgment and statistical models are superior to both.

Intuition is used extensively in social judgment and interactions. The experimental evidence suggests that people are not good judges of personality. However, it is important to stress that judgments of concepts such as personality involve many components. For example, people have to be able to observe the traits that indicate that a person has a specific personality. (How would you know that someone was generous if you had no access to evidence of relevant behavior?) Moreover, such traits may not be easily detectable in social interactions. Thus, in many situations, it is not possible for people to make accurate judgments.

The notion of women's intuition was discussed in relation to the more general topic of individual differences. What is typically referred to as *women's intuition* was seen to be a form of expertise in interpersonal relations. The relation between expertise and intuition was also explored. It was shown that expertise is domain specific and that the various ways in which it is acquired and developed can have important implications for both understanding and educating intuition. These implications will be examined further in chapter 7.

Finally, I discussed the literature on choice. Choice involves conflict, and people typically choose to avoid conflict. Doing so can, however, lead to inconsistencies. In addition, the intuitive tendency to evaluate possible outcomes of choices relative to implicit reference points, coupled with what seems like an inherent desire to avoid loss, automatically triggers different responses to problems that are presented or "framed" in different ways. People learn decision rules through experience, and these rules become part of the stock of intuitions on which they draw to resolve the conflicts of choice. Moreover, people seem to possess an intuitive sense that different, simplifying choice strategies are more or less effective in different task environments. This knowledge, however, is not perfect and thus raises the issue of how this skill might also be educated.

CHAPTER 6

A Framework for
Understanding Intuition

The five previous chapters have explored different aspects of the nature of intuition. This chapter interprets the evidence and develops a theoretical framework for understanding intuition. The goal is to provide a foundation on which suggestions to educate intuition can be based.

The chapter is organized along the lines of the five key ideas previewed in chapter 1, except that the framework itself is presented only after discussing the first three, namely: (1) one organism but many information-processing systems, (2) learning shaped by experience, and (3) two systems for learning and doing. The purpose of these discussions is to summarize and amplify issues treated in the five preceding chapters. I do this prior to outlining the framework because I believe that it is important to think of intuition within the broader context of the different mechanisms that people use in processing information. This also permits a more concise presentation of the framework itself.

Next, I discuss the fourth key idea—intuition as expertise—prior to defining seven guidelines for educating intuition that are suggested by the framework and the accompanying evidence presented in this book. These culminate in the fifth key idea—making scientific method intuitive—which is further elaborated in chapter 7.

One Organism but Many Information-Processing Systems

As noted in chapter 2, it is difficult to think about complex phenomena unless we use some kind of analogy. For example, in trying to understand why Wanda, a normally levelheaded person, responds to a coworker's request with an angry outburst, we might appeal to the analogy of pressure building up slowly and silently behind a dam until the dam finally breaks and the floodwaters burst forth. (Alternatively, we could think of how pressure needs to be released from steam boilers or pressure cookers.) When considered at face value, as a normal, reasonable, and not unexpected part of the workday, the coworker's request seems insufficient to cause Wanda's outburst. When, however, considered in terms of floodwaters building behind a dam, it becomes that last drop that caused the dam to break, the proverbial straw that broke the camel's back. Analogies aid the reasoning process; they help us make sense of the world. The power of analogical thinking lies in the fact that it is inherently intuitive. We do not need to explain our analogies because, if they are apt, others *see* them and, thus, understand them.

Analogy plays an important role in science. Many analogies have become part of the late twentieth-, early twenty-first-century zeitgeist and have, as a result, become highly influential. The two that are most important to our concerns here are to the computer as an information-processing device and to Darwin's theory of evolution.

The computer analogy is important because it highlights the fact that actions that people take are the result of processing information—whether explicitly or implicitly, and often both. The analogy to evolutionary theory is important because it highlights the fact that the overall goal of the species is survival (specifically, the survival of one's gene pool) and that behaviors persist if they are adaptive. The two analogies are linked by the question, Why have humans come to possess their particular configuration of information-processing systems?

The answer suggested by evolutionary theory is that our current systems have met what could be called the *survival test*—that is, the systems that we possess today have ensured survival to this point in time. However, this answer should be tempered by several observations.

First, whereas one particular configuration has evolved, it is not the only configuration that could have emerged to handle the same set of environmental challenges. The environment to which we have adapted is quite complex, and several different solutions could have evolved to deal with the same set of tasks. Evolution works by building on existing structures rather than rejecting old ones and building anew.

Second, even though our systems may seem "good enough" to handle tasks encountered in the past, we have no assurance that they are or ever were optimal. Just as learning works by observing connections (remember that we cannot learn from something that we cannot see), evolution works by adapting to *what is there*. As was pointed out in chapter 3, adaptations that work are retained, as are connections that have been reinforced. However, since neither system is capable of utilizing what has not been observed, we cannot tell whether the best design has been achieved or the optimal action taken.

Third, the configuration of systems that we possess today was not necessarily "designed" to handle the tasks we currently face. Thus, whenever a particular feature is considered in isolation, it must be kept in mind that it may have evolved to handle different tasks and that it therefore functions inefficiently in today's environment. Of course, this inefficiency may be the result of a necessary trade-off. For example, modern humans would undoubtedly like to have more short-term or working memory capacity. Current capacity, however, may well represent a compromise in "design" that allowed our ancestors to survive.[1]

Fourth, evolutionary processes possess no insight into the future. They adapt only to present needs and may leave an organism ill prepared for the future. Environments change—often in quite unpredictable ways—and, unless the process of adaptation works quickly enough, species can disappear. Indeed, the fossil record shows that most species eventually disappear (whether they die out or evolve). Why should the fate of humans be any different?

Finally, by making and using tools, we humans have in essence changed the rules of the evolutionary game, obviating in some instances the need to adapt in order to overcome certain dysfunctional characteristics that would otherwise have been "selected out." Consider, for example, how advances in medicine, hygiene, and agriculture have reduced infant mortality as well as prolonged the lives of many people. Today, many who would not have survived in preceding generations are able to pass on their genes to future generations. Moreover, the new generations can live with handicaps that would have been fatal in the past, for example, different forms of diabetes.

The point of these observations is not to dismiss the analogies to the computer and evolutionary theory but to suggest caution. Despite the fact that analogies are often critical to understanding, they are *not* the phenomena of interest. (As the general semanticists remind us, "The map is not the territory.")

Nevertheless, analogies are undoubtedly useful. As suggested above, when faced with the question of why we possess our particular configuration of information-processing systems, the evolutionary perspective suggests where to look for an answer—in the demands of the environment. Indeed, it is illuminating to rephrase the question of what we do in terms of what we *need* to do, in other words, in terms of the demands imposed on us by the tasks that we face.

In doing so, it is important to recognize that our human systems are less complex than the environments in which they operate. We cannot possibly have unique responses to all possible situations (see also below). Thus, because we are constrained by what we can do, much behavior reflects adaptation to situations.

Although the computer analogy helps psychologists think about how the mind works, it does not go far enough. True, it does raise issues such as how information is brought into a working space, how subroutines are signaled to perform calculations, and how information is stored and output. But it is inadequate to cover the full range of intuitive phenomena. A computer, for example, is essentially serial in its operations, and this does not capture all the kinds of behavior that we have considered.

In this book, I take the view that the human organism consists of many information-processing systems working together toward common goals. Moreover, the richness of many of the phenomena considered lies in the fact that there are *multiple* systems. Given this fact, perhaps a better analogy would be to a modern jet airplane (an airliner or a fighter jet). Here we have something that is supported by several separate but interrelated information-processing systems, that depends on many different computers.

Let us explore this analogy briefly, extending it slightly to consider the airplane *and* its pilot as together constituting the organism.

The pilot represents the airplane's short-term or working memory and *part* of the perceptual system, that is, upper-level cognitive processes that are deliberate in nature and that consume the airplane's (or organism's) attention. In addition, the pilot will also have acquired a certain number of automatic reactions in the course of her past flight experience, and these intuitions are part of those available to the whole organism or system.

Since the pilot cannot possibly continuously and consciously monitor all the airplane's systems, the other information-processing systems in the aircraft are automated. And, at any given point in time, they will all be functioning, both to regulate processes inside the aircraft and to monitor conditions outside.

Some of the automatic systems are *innate*—they are "hardwired" or built into the aircraft. Others may be programmed to meet specific tasks, such as developing flight plans. The "innate" systems regulate the aircraft's internal operations and send messages to the conscious processor (the pilot) in emergency situations. For example, if part of an engine ceases to function appropriately, a message will be relayed to the pilot so that she can attend to the problem. Similarly, information about levels in the fuel tanks ("degree of hunger") is also relayed to the pilot. (Since modern aircraft come equipped both to signal and to counter "overheating" and other dangerous situations, the analogy can even be extended to encompass the emotions.)

Of course, the aircraft's systems also routinely—and automatically—monitor data about the flight in the same way humans record data on frequencies and covariations. Even if these data are not used in the course of a particular flight, they do provide a record of the airplane's experience, that is, they become part of its memory. The important point is that recording this information does not consume the attention of the pilot.

The pilot can choose to operate in different modes. At times, she will take complete control of the aircraft. At others, she may allow various automatic systems to take over.

The point that I wish to emphasize here is that humans have a variety of different information-processing systems that vary from the innate to the fully conscious, that most of these systems operate continuously, and that these features are not adequately represented by the computer analogy. For that matter, many of the phenomena considered so far in this book do not necessarily fit comfortably in the airplane analogy. For example, it does not illuminate how affect and meaning may be attributed to certain experiences. It does not seem enough simply to say that the pilot represents the human element.

What the airplane analogy accentuates is the distinction between, on the one hand, the limited, deliberate, and attention-consuming activities of the pilot and, on the other hand, the large number of automatic information-processing systems that contribute to the functioning of the aircraft. It also emphasizes that both need to function as one supersystem.

The analogy further highlights differences between the ways in which the pilot and the automatic processes learn. The automatic processes learn by noting what happens and keeping records; that is, learning is based on *what occurs*. The pilot, however, does not learn only from what she sees. She is able to pose counterfactual questions and use her imagination in order to facilitate the learning process. Indeed, one of the main differences between conscious and automatic processes is that conscious processes are able to use imagination. This does not mean, of course, that imagination cannot be triggered automatically, as, for example, when a counterfactual response to a situation comes immediately to mind. (For instance, an accident occurs, and you immediately ask yourself, "What would have happened if . . . ?") But responding to the counterfactual question consumes attention.

Finally, the airplane analogy focuses attention on the differences in levels of automatic processes discussed in chapter 5. There—building on ideas suggested by Arthur Reber—I suggested the existence of three levels of automatic processes: *basic, primitive,* and *sophisticated.*

Basic processes are innate. In terms of the airplane analogy, these are reactions that are built into the airplane's systems from the start. Thus, different types of aircraft are equipped with different capacities depending on the environments in which they are intended to function. Fighter planes, for example, are designed to effect maneuvers (avoiding enemy planes or antiaircraft fire) that would be impossible for passenger airliners.

Primitive processes are those that help the aircraft keep track of what is happening by tallying data (frequencies of potentially relevant aspects of the environment and so on). Since such tasks would differ little from aircraft to aircraft, one could expect the mechanisms used to accomplish these tasks to be quite similar among all types of aircraft.

Sophisticated processes are the automatic, intuitive mechanisms that the pilot uses for flying. The distinction between the *primitive* and the *sophisticated* processes is that the former is free of affect and meaning. This means therefore that aircraft will differ because each has a different pilot and those pilots bring different sets of experiences to bear on the task at hand. Consider, for example, the way in which the automatic reactions of a fighter pilot are likely to differ from those of the pilot of a passenger aircraft on first noticing an unidentified aircraft on the radar screen. Or, to take another example, two pilots' responses to a given weather pattern are likely to depend on the type of aircraft that they are flying and their own previous experience.

The answer as to *why* our information-processing systems exist in their present form is complex. Clearly, they evolved to deal with problems our ancestors faced in the past, but this may bring little comfort to us as we think about the kinds of environments we face now and what might lie ahead in the future. It is not clear, for example, that natural selection has prepared humans for the important tasks of monitoring instruments that control large technological systems such as nuclear power plants, manned space flights, or air-traffic control systems. Compared to other species, however, humans have the enormous advantage of having evolved powers of imagination that enable us to think beyond what we have seen or experienced. It is important to understand that much of our behavior is automatic and programmed in much the same ways as the systems aboard an airplane. But we also have the ability to act in ways that are not programmed and that allow us to fly—that is, think—in areas of space where no one has ventured previously. Moreover, whereas this imaginary knowledge is not perfectly reliable, it can have many advantages.

Learning Shaped by Experience

To explore the notion of how we learn, it is useful to ask what features an information-processing system needs in order to learn efficiently. In other words, if we were able to design from scratch an optimal system for learning, what would its features be? When the question is posed in this way, answers are undoubtedly influenced by hindsight. We already know a lot about how human and other organisms actually do learn. Still, the exercise usefully highlights several key issues.

Assuming that the goal of learning is to ensure the survival of the species (see above), the logical starting place is an analysis of the nature of the environment in which learning takes place. There are two important considerations. First, the environment contains many different types of objects, interaction with which affects the organism in ways that can be considered "good" or "bad." (By *objects,* I mean all things—animate or inanimate, material or otherwise—in the environment.) Second, as noted above, it must be the case that the environment is more complicated than the organism. In other words, we must accept the constraint that the variability in responses that the organism can produce can never match the variability of objects in the environment. From the viewpoint of the organism, uncertainty will always be an important feature of the environment. There will, therefore, always be a need to simplify.

Assume for the moment that the mind of the newborn is a tabula rasa. In this case, learning must clearly center on determining, first, whether objects are good or bad for the organism and, second, how to elicit good outcomes and avoid bad ones. The amount of learning that the organism can be expected to achieve therefore depends on both the relative distributions of good and bad objects in its environment and the extent to which these can be differentiated.

At the limit, consider an organism that inhabits a world in which all objects are good and indistinguishable one from the other. In this case, there would be no need for learning. The organism would simply survive—in paradise, as it were—and, unless its environment changed, it would never need to evolve. But no real-world environments are like this. Organisms do, therefore, need to learn.

Now consider an organism that is incapable of learning but that is genetically programmed to recognize and respond to certain features in the environment. In environments in which life-threatening objects occur frequently, natural selection clearly favors those species that take immediate action to avoid danger. However, in environments in which dangerous objects are rare, preprogrammed reactions could be dysfunctional. The organism would overreact to some stimuli. There are, therefore, trade-offs to consider (the cost of failing to save a life vs. the cost of a false alarm) that are affected by the frequency with which danger is encountered in the environment.

More generally, in an uncertain environment in which the two kinds of error are not the same—for example, failing to save a life is more costly than raising a false alarm—you would expect to observe bias in learning. That is, the organisms that survive will have learned to favor one response over the other; for example, certain stimuli will trigger the reaction to flee a potential danger rather than waiting to investigate what it might be.

A key element of learning is noting connections or covariations— that is, what happens when something else happens. But what holds these ideas together in the mind? Clearly, the mechanism of learning must contain something that cements mental connections. Presumably, this is provided by observed regularities in the environment (e.g., sugar typically tastes sweet) or is part of a mental image that has its origin in past experience (e.g., that a sofa is likely to be heavier than a chair because past experience has shown that large objects are heavier than smaller ones).

A further consideration is that maintaining many instances of covariation in the mind is costly and that other ways of remembering and accessing experience may be more effective. This, in turn, suggests that learning might involve shortcuts or generalizations—in other words, rules. For example, in learning how to throw a ball a certain distance, it is not necessary to have observed many past attempts. You can generalize from a few observations and test the generalization in practice.

Experience with "objects" will involve classifying them as good or bad (and how good or how bad) with particular attention being paid to those you want to approach or avoid. Once again, this raises the issue of whether organisms would be better off if rules for classification were genetically endowed or learned anew by each individual member of the species. And, once again, the answer probably depends on circumstances. However, what does seem advantageous is to have innate mechanisms that aid the classification process.

Finally, whereas having a process to learn is undoubtedly effective, the ability to develop new processes for learning would also be very advantageous. Consider, for example, an organism that learns how to learn appropriate lessons from experience better than others.

Bearing in mind the warning given above about hindsight, what do we know about the processes of learning that is relevant to this discussion? First, note that—despite the assumption of the preceding exercise—the human organism is *not* a tabula rasa, that it is, in fact, "hardwired" to make certain distinctions. Several investigators postulate that our human genetic inheritance includes the ability to determine distinct objects as well as the ability to discriminate between the animate and the inanimate.[2] In looking at a chair, for example, small infants do not categorize it as four legs with something on top. Instead, there seems to be an inherent understanding of what are and are not whole or distinct objects. This understanding is clearly critical to learning. It is also critical to the ability to count.

The literature also emphasizes several of the other points made above. For example, uncertainty and biased responses have been the subject of many studies, as have the mechanisms involved in the acquisition of superstitious beliefs. In addition, categorization and judgments of similarity and causation are all implicated in learning. Finally, the advantages that humans have over other species in being able to learn, not just from what they see, but also from what they do not see (i.e., the ability to utilize imagination in the learning process [see chap. 3]) illustrate the advances that can be made by an organism that possesses the ability to invent new ways of learning.

The purpose of this discussion is not to repeat material covered in earlier chapters (particularly chap. 3) but to reemphasize several points about learning. These concern multiple levels of learning, learning traps, the learning of tastes and preferences, and intellectual achievement that goes beyond experiential learning. I now briefly consider these issues.

Multiple Levels of Learning

As noted previously, much learning happens automatically, and we are powerless to prevent it. At an almost instinctual level, we are "prepared" to learn some reactions after minimal experience. Consider, for example, the fear of heights or snakes, fears that can be triggered by just one exposure and that, for many, are quite difficult to overcome.

On the other hand, it may take many trials and different forms of explanation for us to learn connections between variables that we are predisposed to see as unrelated. For example, in the nineteenth century, it seemed quite improbable that tiny organisms called *bacteria*—which could not be detected by the unaided human eye—were capable of causing disease. How could such tiny bacteria have such large effects? Moreover, contiguity of cause and effect was not obvious in that the impact of bacteria in creating disease was not always immediate.

Another phenomenon is the vast amount of learning that takes place implicitly across a wide range of experience and that requires only minimal attention. This takes two forms. First, there is the well-established ability of humans to accumulate a great deal of information concerning the frequency of objects encountered in the environment. Second is our ability to make generalizations or extract rules from what we observe even though we may not be able to articulate such rules.

The learning of language provides a simple example of the latter. As children, we all learn to speak and, typically, handle grammatical regularities and exceptions with some skill. Later in life, we are astounded when we analyze our native language in school and discover notions of grammar which we comply with in practice but are unable to articulate in theory. In a series of experiments, Donald Broadbent and his colleagues have demonstrated the existence of this phenomenon experimentally by examining adults interacting with economic simulation games.[3] When playing these games, people can become quite adept at making appropriate decisions and yet show little understanding of the underlying principles of the game as measured by their attempts to articulate what they are doing.[4]

Clearly, when we pay attention to what is happening around us, we see and can learn in a conscious sense. What is fascinating, and critical to many of the arguments in this book, is that we also learn when we are paying little (or in essence no) attention. Moreover, in some cases, these automatic learning processes are more effective in the sense of creating and maintaining connections than when conscious attention is allocated to the process. Conscious attention is a two-edged sword. In some cases, overt knowledge of context can induce valid learning quickly by directing attention to the appropriate variables. In other cases, contextual knowledge can blind the learner to the implications of what he or she is seeing. In short, valid cues help conscious learning; invalid cues hinder conscious attempts to learn.

Learning Traps

Although automatic learning is effective, its very nature implies that its validity depends on the *learning structure* in which it takes place (see chap. 3). If the learning structure is *kind*—that is, if feedback is accurate—valid learning can result. If, however, the learning structure is *wicked*—that is, if feedback is misleading—no learning or invalid learning can take place. Superstitions, for example, are often learned in wicked environments. People notice a connection, form a belief, and then are loath to test that belief for fear of destroying the connection. Recall the tennis player who always ties the right shoe before the left (see chap. 3). He dare not change this routine lest doing so will change his luck.

Of course, holding to superstitious beliefs is not always harmful. In some cases, superstitious behavior is functional. Consider again our tennis player. Tying the right shoe before the left may be part of a routine that helps him prepare himself mentally for matches. Consider also an example made famous by anthropologists, that of the Cree Indians in Canada.[5] Before going on hunting expeditions, these people burn a stag's antlers and then interpret the remains to determine the direction that the hunt should take. The fact that there is no likely validity to these interpretations is in one important sense immaterial. The Cree have developed what is essentially a randomizing device, a means of ensuring that their prey cannot predict where they will hunt. Thus, the superstitious behavior is functional. Note well, however, that the functionality of the behavior in question depends entirely on the environmental circumstances. In certain cases, holding superstitious beliefs can be costly. Consider, for example, the now-defunct medical practice of bleeding that was thought to cure fevers.

The learning environment can also trap people in stereotypic response modes. Consider the so-called water-jug experiments, in which people are asked to solve a series of problems that involve obtaining a specific volume of water given three empty jars for measures.[6] In the first of the series, the measures of jugs A, B, and C are 21, 127, and 3, respectively, and the problem is to obtain a volume of 100. People see that this can be achieved by first filling jug B, then using jugs A and C to reduce the amount of water in B by one measure of A and two of C. In formal terms, this rule can be expressed as $B - A - 2C$. Moreover, subjects soon discover that the same rule can be used to solve the remaining problems in the series. However, what they fail to notice is that the latter problems in the series can be solved by different and much simpler rules. For instance, consider the measures 23 (A), 49 (B), and 3 (C) with a request to obtain a volume of 20 as well as the measures 15 (A), 39 (B), and 3 (C) with a request to obtain a volume of 18. The rule $B - A - 2C$ clearly works for both problems. However, far simpler rules that solve these problems are $A - C$ and $A + C$, respectively. The point is that, once people have learned a response tendency or rule and this has been reinforced, the learned behavior becomes an impediment to finding other, possibly better ways of handling the task at hand.

This tendency was also demonstrated in the experiments conducted by Barry Schwartz that were described in chapter 3, experiments in which subjects were rewarded for discovering the proper sequences of responses (switching on lights in a display). Subjects whose reward varied with performance were less successful at the task than were those who received fixed rewards. Assuming that the effect of incentives is to direct people's attention in specific ways, these results imply that explicit attempts to learn can be less effective than more implicit modes.[7]

Of course, I am not advocating that people should pay less attention when engaged in problem solving or learning. What I am saying is that the environment in which a task takes place can have important effects on people's actions and what they come to believe. Our automatic learning processes function well. However, it is typically—and implicitly—assumed that learning takes place in a kind environment and is, therefore, valid. To use a scientific metaphor, these automatic processes are not guided by a scientist, schooled in the principles of experimental design, and who only collects data in a way that allows the drawing of valid conclusions. Instead, automatic processes can entice people into learning traps.[8]

Learning Tastes and Preferences

Over the last fifty years or so, descriptions of how people make decisions have been much influenced by so-called normative models derived from economics and statistical decision theory. This is not to say that psychologists believe that people make decisions using the processes described by these models. In fact, the contrary is true.[9] However, the models point to two important classes of variables that influence decision making. One is information about "states of the world" that can affect decisions, information that is expressed in terms of probabilities. For example, in considering whether to hold a picnic on a certain day, you would undoubtedly be concerned about the chances of bad weather (whether you expressed this in precise probabilistic terms or simply characterized the chances as being, say, high or low). The other is information about what in economics is called *utility*—that is, how much you like the consequences of different outcomes. For example, the utility of the picnic on a good day is undoubtedly larger than (preferred to) that of the picnic on a bad day.

In statistical decision theory, probabilities are allowed to be "subjective" (i.e., people can hold their own idiosyncratic beliefs about events, such as the chances of rain), but those beliefs are still supposed to conform to the known laws of probability. So, for example, if you assign a 60 percent probability to the event that it will rain at the picnic site on the day of the picnic, you must also assign a 40 percent probability to the event that it will not rain. That is, the sum of probabilities of so-called complementary events must always be 100 percent. Moreover, even if people's individual estimates (of the chances of rain) differ at the outset, these should converge over time to similar values when they see the same evidence (storm clouds gathering in the sky).[10] In other words, the theory implies that the differences among people's beliefs will disappear as those beliefs are revised in the light of new evidence. (Some beliefs, of course, will need more revision than others.) In this sense, the theory can be thought of as providing a benchmark model for the way in which people should learn from experience, that is, by revising their beliefs.

The situation concerning utility is quite different. First, utility is conceptualized as being "exogenous." This means that its unspecified origins are not part of the model but accepted as externally determined or "given." Indeed, when faced with puzzling and even self-destructive behavior such as drug addiction, economists assume that people are "rational" and then explore what set of utilities (tastes or preferences) would optimize the observed behavior.[11] There is no benchmark model that explains where utilities come from or how they do or should change with experience.

In psychology, there is an awareness that utilities or values are learned and can change over time, but it is difficult to identify a well-articulated theory that distinguishes the learning of values from the learning of beliefs. Generally speaking, the hedonic principle—that people seek pleasure and avoid pain—is invoked. However, I agree with Jerome Kagan that psychologists overuse the hedonic principle in explaining how considerations of value (or utility) affect people's behavior.[12] There are many phenomena that indicate that people do not always take actions that maximize hedonic returns (i.e., that maximize pleasure obtained and minimize pain avoided). Consider, for example, help given to strangers and other unselfish, altruistic deeds, actions that occur daily. Of course, one might argue that people find satisfaction in such altruistic activity, and, thus, in this sense, they are still maximizing their hedonic returns. But this is just the same intellectual game that is played by economists (as when they assume, e.g., that drug addicts are rational actors [see above]) and avoids the issue of how people acquire utilities in the first place and why utilities might differ among people.

In humans, tastes and preferences are both innate and learned. It is clear that we are born with certain innate preferences—we prefer sweet to bitter-tasting foods, for example. And the evolutionary explanation of why this is so should be obvious. Also, certain preferences are a function of maturation—the desire to participate in sexual activity, for example. However, many of the preferences that guide daily behavior are clearly learned. Why, for example, do you prefer one kind of music to another? Why does one style of writing appeal to you but not another?

In chapter 2, I discussed the work of Robert Zajonc on the mere-exposure effect—the creation of positive affect merely through frequency of exposure. Zajonc's work is critical because he demonstrated—in a controlled, laboratory setting—that even minimal exposure can create positive affect. How strong, then, will the mere-exposure effect be in our everyday lives, where exposure is often far greater?

Start with music. It is clear that preference for music is a function of the type of music to which an individual is exposed. Consider, for instance, the difficulty that Westerners have appreciating Eastern music, and vice versa. Consider as well the fact that, as a Scot who has lived his adult life outside Scotland, I am always moved when I hear bagpipe music. Yet I never explicitly decided to acquire a taste for hearing this musical instrument.

It is clear that the simple fact of living exposes us to a culture (or cultures) in all its various aspects, thereby forming our tastes—the food we eat, the types of sports we participate in or follow, the way we dress, and so on. And, most often, such exposure is not a matter of choice—although some people do consciously seek and study different cultures or are influenced by others (e.g., parents often direct their children's choice of schools and professions).

It is important to emphasize that some preferences formed outside our conscious awareness could be contrary to our conscious intentions. In addition, our preferences for the familiar can induce prejudices. For example, if your mental image of the CEO of a large corporation is a man, you may not be able to view a woman in that position in an unbiased manner. Note well, however, that this does not imply conscious prejudice on your part. It is just that, over time, all the CEOs that you have encountered have been men and that you have grown comfortable with males in these roles. As noted previously, our subconscious selves record many frequencies. Deviations from the norm attract attention and are not examined in the same way as exemplars of the norm.

In many cases, people are faced with choices that involve guessing how they will like outcomes that will be experienced in the future. For example, imagine a person who decides to enroll in a health club even though she does not know for sure whether she will like exercising. In cases like this, the person has to predict her future preferences. However, if preferences are mainly a function of past interactions with the environment, it is not clear that people will be accurate in predicting their own future preferences. Yet it is knowledge of precisely these future preferences that should be used to make decisions in the present.[13]

The point that I wish to make is simple and important. Many tastes and preferences are learned subconsciously by exposure to different cultures and experiences. This means that the values—or tastes and preferences—that guide intuitive choices have not always been consciously acquired. Thus, we may feel quite comfortable with many choices even though we lack awareness of why we exhibit certain underlying preferences. Our intuitions reflect our cultural capital.

Beyond Experiential Learning

To this point, I have mainly discussed learning that takes place through experience (interaction) with the environment. However, humans also learn in other ways. For example, a large fraction of time spent in school is devoted to acquiring knowledge that is codified. That is, we learn what others have learned and distilled in the form of facts and theories. Among that distilled knowledge are explicit rules or procedures for information processing—mathematics, statistical theory and methodology, the canons of scientific reasoning, and so on. As we gain familiarity and facility with such modes of reasoning, they become part of our intuitive stock and, as such, can be invoked with minimal effort.

The main difference between learning through explicit instruction, on the one hand, and learning through experience, on the other, lies in the fact that the former requires greater effort.[14] (Learning through experience depends heavily on automatic processes and is therefore much easier.) The level of relevant cultural capital already acquired can, however, mitigate the amount of effort involved in explicit instruction. To take an example, consider a fourteen-year-old boy who has a great deal of difficulty learning facts about geography and history in school but who loves baseball and can assimilate an enormous number of facts about the sport just by reading a newspaper or watching television. This is not to say that the boy learns these sports facts subconsciously: clearly, he must absorb them consciously and just as consciously exclude other, irrelevant stimuli. But, unlike the facts about geography and history, the sports facts stick with little effort. Why? Because, thanks to an interest in baseball, he has a preexisting stock of relevant cultural capital that facilitates the acquisition of further knowledge about the sport.

What makes codified knowledge and explicit instruction so important is the fact that it obviates the need for direct experience and thus facilitates advances in human society. (I do not, of course, mean to denigrate the role that experiential learning plays in our lives. Both forms of knowledge—codified and experiential—affect the quality of human thought substantially.) It takes only one Leibniz or one Newton, for example, to discover the calculus and distill that knowledge, and it is available to all. As long as records of it exist, it does not need to be rediscovered by successive generations. Codified knowledge, however, typically has a short "shelf life." If we do not review it or use it on a regular basis, it is often lost to us. (Use it, or lose it!) How many of us, for example, can recall the calculus that we learned in college if we have not used it in ten, twenty, thirty years?

Finally, as noted previously, the validity of experiential knowledge depends on the environment in which it is acquired. Codified knowledge can help people understand this important point and augment tacit ways of learning with appropriate methodological tools. I discuss this further in chapter 7.

Two Systems for Learning and Doing

As noted above, the human organism has many different types of systems for processing information. Depending on the perspective taken, the successful completion of a particular set of actions could involve several systems or just one (perhaps one composed of a number of subsystems). Consider perception. At one level, this is the system that translates images of what is in a person's visual field onto the brain. Yet it also consists of several subsystems that are involved in extracting relevant features of the environment, matching what is experienced to past images, and so on. In other words, what we call a *system* depends on both the function that we are studying and the level at which we are conducting the analysis. What is a system at one level of analysis could be a subsystem at another level.

In chapter 2, I reviewed the notion adopted by many investigators of a dichotomy between two *modes of thought,* often referred to simply as *intuition* and *analysis.* For the purposes of this book, and despite my recognition of multiple systems of information processing, I am going to maintain a dichotomy. In particular, I am going to distinguish between processes that do and do not occur automatically, that is, without and with conscious attention or effort. I recognize, however, that this dichotomy is simplistic in that the automatic/nonautomatic distinction is really more of a continuum. And this, in itself, is probably a function of the fact that many different systems are involved in processing information simultaneously. For example, even when automatic processes are being executed, some low levels of conscious attention may be engaged in monitoring activity. In addition, many responses that people make reflect both types of processes; that is, they are combinations of automatic and nonautomatic processes or, in other words, subconscious and conscious processing.

A disadvantage of the automatic/nonautomatic distinction is that it obscures possible differences between types of subconscious processes. For example, it does not distinguish between two important types of automatic responses: those that are genetically preprogrammed and those that were initially learned and only gradually became automatic. Nor does it discriminate between, say, emotional and nonemotional response systems. For example, our intuitions about what is a potentially dangerous situation would seem to be quite different from our intuitions concerning appropriate grammar in language. On the other hand, it has a practical simplicity and allows us to consider different sources of reactions as contributing to what we call *intuition*. Moreover, the distinction between conscious (or nonautomatic) and subconscious (or automatic) is critical because it draws attention to what is under human control.

The two-system framework proposed here is similar to the dichotomous models suggested by both Seymour Epstein and Kenneth Hammond (see chap. 2). For simplicity, I call the systems the *tacit* and the *deliberate*.

The deliberate system involves the processing of information through *deliberate, conscious mechanisms*. This system is effortful and relatively slow and can involve both content (i.e., what is being processed) and rules (i.e., how the content is being processed). A simple example of deliberate-system thought would be adding a column of figures: one is aware both of what is being added to what and of the explicit rules of addition.[15] As a further example, imagine considering the various advantages and disadvantages of an action that you are thinking about taking. Note that I have avoided using the words *logical* or *analytic* to describe the deliberate system because there is no reason why deliberate, conscious thought should follow the dictates of logic or even what many people would call *analysis*. On the other hand, the deliberate system is analytic in the sense that a conscious attempt is typically made to break down tasks into components.

The tacit system therefore covers *all thought processes that are neither deliberate nor conscious*. Even though I have chosen to call this a single system, it should be clear that—as stated above—it receives inputs from many of the organism's different information-processing systems, including the neural, sensorimotor, affective, and even cognitive systems. We can therefore also think of the tacit system as being influenced by the deliberate system.[16]

As noted above, the output of thought is not limited to either the tacit or the deliberate system. Instead, mental activity typically involves both systems and, on occasion, may involve compromise or conflict between them. Indeed, it is difficult to imagine any sequence of thoughts that does not involve some input from the tacit system. Consider, for example, being presented with problems in physics, logic, or probabilistic reasoning such as those described in chapter 4. When you read the problems and try to understand them, it is clear that you (automatically) invoke the tacit system first, to see whether you recognize the problem, before using the more effortful mechanisms of the deliberate system. In other words, deliberate-system thought requires that people have already applied some structure to a problem. However, structure is not given but must be inferred from context, and reactions to context are very much in the domain of the tacit system.[17]

Whereas the tacit system involves processes that are or have become automatic, it should be made clear that it is *generally* goal directed. In other words, its actions further the goals of the organism. As a physical example, imagine walking from one side of a room to the other in order to pick up an object. The goal of picking up the object is formulated explicitly, but the actions necessary to walk are executed automatically (i.e., without conscious awareness), in service of the goal.

There are, however, exceptions to goal-oriented behavior. In these cases, patterns of behavior have been learned, have become automatic, and are then enacted in specific circumstances. Moreover, many of these types of behavior are "bad" for the organism (e.g., such "bad habits" as addictions or inappropriate angry outbursts), and some of these bad behaviors would be rejected as inappropriate if the people who exhibit them took more time to think through the consequences of their actions. However, they do happen, and, in retrospect, people often regret what they have done, expressing that regret in such terms as "If only I had thought about what I was doing." By *thought*, of course, they mean the explicit, effortful process of the deliberate system, not the effortless, merely reactive response of the tacit system. In effect, these situations involve a conflict between the tacit and the deliberate systems, a conflict in which explicit knowledge about what should be done (as formulated in the deliberate system) is not strong enough to overcome what have become automatic behaviors.

The tacit system accounts for the lion's share of mental life. It is heavily involved in processes of perception and understanding and depends on multiple contextual cues that trigger memory. For example, studies show that subjects learn the appropriate statistical relations between variables far more quickly when the variables are explicitly (concretely) labeled and identified as being something within subjects' experience. (In other words, it is easier to see that two variables are correlated if you are told that they represent height and weight than if you are told simply they are X and Y).[18] Of course, the tacit system is not always perfectly reliable. It can, for example, mislead people into thinking that two variables are correlated when, in fact, they are not (or, alternatively, that they are more strongly correlated than is in fact the case)—a phenomenon known as *illusory correlation* (see pp. 125, 149).

The tacit system requires little or no effort. It is the system that allows us to understand immediately the implications of stories and scripts. The power of metaphor, for instance, lies in the fact that—through recognition of similarities—people immediately see images that can make powerful arguments. The tacit system is also the basis of those reactions in social settings where, for example, people have a sense of indebtedness and a desire to reciprocate when a stranger unexpectedly does something for them. We have learned from past experience that it is uncomfortable to feel that we owe somebody something, especially a stranger. The reaction to reciprocate is "unthought" (the tacit system) and immediate and often enacted before we realize the consequences (in deliberate thought).

One of the most important features of the tacit system is the effortless way in which people learn from experience. The critical point, of course, is *what* they learn. As noted previously, people accurately note and remember connections, covariations, frequencies, and emotional experiences—often without an awareness that they are doing so. However, as noted before, such learning is based on what is seen, not on what is *not* seen, and thus the validity of learning depends on whether learning structures are kind or wicked (see chap. 3).

The deliberate system operates when people are processing information in short-term working memory. It involves both effort and awareness but is not necessarily logical or rational in the sense that people may explicitly enumerate reasons for actions that defy the dictates of logic or rationality (however these are defined). Learning can also be a deliberate system activity (e.g., explicit instruction). But this typically requires much effort (see also above).

Three characteristics of the way the tacit system operates can lead to important, cumulative effects.

First, habits acquired in the course of making minor, everyday decisions can adversely affect the way major, extraordinary decisions are made. That is, in the course of everyday living, people acquire decision-making habits that allow them to handle minor problems automatically, and, while these habits may lead to an incorrect decision here and there, the cost is usually not great. Such habits are hard to suppress,[19] however, and are therefore often invoked in the face of major decisions, regardless of whether they are appropriate.

Second, the effect of many minor decisions, each in itself relatively unimportant, can be cumulative and therefore consequential. For example, wasting money by not choosing wisely in the supermarket may not be important on a single day. However, the same behavior repeated over several years can become quite costly. Similarly, whereas one bad investment decision will not necessarily force a corporation out of business, many bad investment decisions can.

Third, small actions or decisions are frequently elements of sequences of behavior that can interact with actions taken by others. In social interactions, for example, initial judgments and actions can trigger the reactions of others and have long-term consequences. For instance, a person who starts, as a child, to learn how to "read" the emotions of others—and thereby encourages positive reactions—could develop relationships throughout life that will not be experienced by the person who is slower to acquire such skills. Once again, small differences can have large cumulative effects.

Intuition: A Framework

The goal of this book is to understand the phenomenon of intuition in order to recommend ways in which it can be educated. From the discussions in the previous chapters, it is clear that intuition operates within a complex system for processing information that has evolved over millions of years. We thus need to think of intuition within the context of this complex system. It cannot be treated in isolation.

Because intuitive processes operate beyond conscious awareness, intuitions can essentially be considered faits accomplis, things that must be dealt with *after* the fact. It is therefore critically important to recognize that, in order to understand and improve intuitions, you must understand *the process by which they were acquired.* If, for some reason, that process has been biased, the outcomes of the process (i.e., intuitions) are also likely to be biased.

By way of analogy, consider what happens when astronauts walk on the moon. The act of walking under normal conditions can be likened to the process of achieving an intuition in that both occur automatically, without conscious awareness of the way the end result is achieved. The moon, however, represents far from normal conditions. Its gravity is a fraction of that of the earth. Consequently, since our astronauts have learned to walk on the earth and are accustomed to dealing only with the effects of its gravity, their walking habits will be less useful in other environments. Specific, conscious adjustments (e.g., adding weights to their boots) must be made if they are to overcome their learned "bias" and succeed in walking on the moon.

In other words, if the conditions in which a particular intuitive process was acquired are the same as those triggering later recourse to that process, the resulting intuitive response is likely to be functional. If they are not, bias or error may result.

In addition, we have seen that the environment (or learning structure) in which intuitions are acquired can be classified as kind or wicked and that tasks can be more or less exacting (i.e., the costs of mistakes can differ). What is important for educating intuition is knowing that intuitions that have been acquired in kind environments are likely to be functional and those acquired in wicked environments are likely to be dysfunctional.

But behavior (including learning) does not depend only on the structure of the environment. It also depends on the characteristics of the organism and how these interact with the environment. For this reason, our theoretical framework also needs to state the critical features of the information-processing system that learns and takes actions in different types of environments.

As noted above, the view taken here is that it is possible to simplify the variety of information-processing systems of which we are composed by making a division between what I have called the *tacit* and the *deliberate* systems. The main difference between these systems is that the deliberate system operates in conscious mode and consumes attention and that the tacit system operates in preconscious and subconscious modes and consumes little or no attention. (I exclude the possibility that some attention may be engaged in monitoring the activities of the tacit system.)

The diagram presented as exhibit 15 schematizes the interconnections between the tacit and the deliberate systems. In this diagram, solid-line boxes indicate the functions of the deliberate system, dotted-line boxes those of the tacit system. The two right-hand boxes (boxes 5 and 6), labeled

EXHIBIT 15 The deliberate and tacit systems

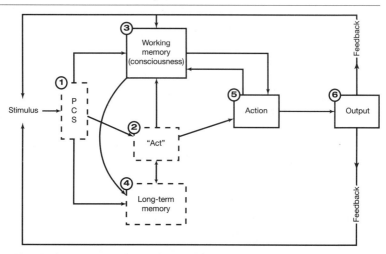

The stimulus is an "object" or a "thought." PCS = preconscious screen. The dotted lines indicate functions of the tacit system.

action and *output*, denote events that can be observed in the environment by (in principle) both the organism producing them and third parties.

The diagram illustrates how the tacit and the deliberate systems interact in the processing of a stimulus (shown on the left of the diagram). The stimulus can take several forms: it can be external to the organism (i.e., something that is seen, heard, or felt); it can also be internal (e.g., a thought may trigger other thoughts). Underlying the framework are two assumptions that will be elaborated below. The first is that each stimulus encountered is initially processed by a *preconscious screen,* an automatic mechanism that decides whether the stimulus will or will not enter consciousness. This intuitive decision process reflects both innate and learned tendencies. The second assumption is that of a *scarce resource* principle. The key idea is that the deliberate system is a limited resource and must therefore be used sparingly.

An explanation of the framework will be aided by a consideration of three distinct types of cases: (1) that of *recording without conscious awareness,* in which information about stimuli is recorded unconsciously and stored for possible future use; (2) that of *taking action automatically,* in which a stimulus automatically triggers an action, with the result that the person is aware of the action only after it has been taken; and (3) that of *taking action deliberately,* in which consciousness plays an important role in determining the action taken.

Recording without Conscious Awareness

This first case is simple to explain. A stimulus is encountered by the preconscious screen (box 1) and deemed to require neither attention nor action (box 2). It is simply recorded tacitly in long-term memory (box 4). This very basic process is at the heart of tacit learning and the accumulation of facts and frequencies that has now been so well documented in the literature. It requires neither effort nor intention, yet the information stored can be subsequently recalled when needed, even for tasks that we could never have imagined. Thus, whereas no effort is ever made to record how many times we have undertaken a certain action or seen something, we are still able to estimate the approximate frequency with relative ease and accuracy.

(A good example of stored frequencies put to an unimagined use is the study [reviewed in chap. 5] in which subjects were asked to predict the second and fifth letters of five-letter words but where they saw only the first letters. Clearly, no one ever sets out to try and learn this kind of information explicitly. However, through tacit experience, we acquire a good sense for different frequencies in our environment.)

The utility of this system cannot be overestimated. We can keep track of much experience without having to pay attention. Moreover, there is good evidence that this ability is shared by many animals and is quite robust in the sense that it is not affected adversely by age or bad health. Nonetheless, the system does have costs. One is that tacit knowledge is necessarily a function of the particular environment that each individual faces. However, as noted above, if the learning structure is wicked, such learning may not be functional. Second, much tacit exposure to certain types of experience is likely to induce confidence. However, since we do not know explicitly how we acquired such knowledge, it is difficult to assess whether our confidence is justified. We may experience a feeling of confidence—or lack of confidence—but be unable to articulate why we have such feelings.

Taking Action Automatically

The framework also illustrates how automatic actions occur outside consciousness. A classic example is the case of reactions to fear-inducing stimuli. Consider, for instance, what happens when, unexpectedly, you hear a dog barking very close behind you. Typically, before you realize what is happening, an involuntary action on your part moves you away from the source of the noise. In terms of exhibit 15, the stimulus of the dog barking is transferred from the preconscious screen (box 1) to the "act" function (box 2), which, in turn, sets in motion the action (box 5) of moving away from the source of the noise. In short, what Joseph LeDoux calls a *learned trigger* sets in motion an action that requires no conscious control. This does not mean, of course, that consciousness is not involved. Indeed, you do become aware of what is happening, and information also goes from the preconscious screen (box 1) to consciousness or working memory (box 3). However, information travels this route more slowly, and awareness of what has happened (i.e., awareness that the "act" function [box 3] has been triggered) occurs only after the action (box 5) has already taken place.

It is not difficult to accept the notion that we should be equipped with or learn automatic reactions for handling potentially dangerous situations. In fact, even if we are mistaken on occasion, the advantages of being able to act without deliberation are clear. However, such automatic reactions are not limited to fear-invoking stimuli. The same basic process underlies all automatic behaviors. Consider, for example, your reactions when driving an automobile or walking along a crowded street. You are constantly making small adjustments to your path even though you are paying little, if any, conscious attention to the process.

The same processes that guide actions in the physical domain (e.g., driving and walking) also operate in the social. When you engage in social interaction, many forms of automatic behavior are triggered by subtle and sometimes not so subtle cues. For example, studies demonstrate that the way in which people sit and the physical gestures that they make are often automatically—and unconsciously—triggered by the behavior of others. In interaction, people unwittingly mimic the behaviors of others.[20]

Moreover, specific behaviors can also be triggered subconsciously by peripheral and seemingly unrelated stimuli. For example, in a study conducted by John Bargh, Mark Chen, and Lara Burrows, two groups of subjects were required to complete a so-called scrambled-sentence task in what was ostensibly stated to be a test of language proficiency. In this task, the materials supplied to one of the groups contained many stereotypical references to the elderly, whereas the materials supplied to the other did not. After the subjects completed the task, the experimenters surreptitiously measured how long it took them to walk down the corridor away from the room in which the experiment was conducted. Results showed that subjects who had worked with the texts containing stereotypical references to the elderly took longer to walk down the corridor. Yet the material made no explicit reference to the fact that the elderly walk more slowly. Subjects also subsequently reported that they had no knowledge of the presence of the elderly stereotype in the materials they received. Moreover, no subjects believed that these words had any effect on their subsequent behavior.[21]

An interesting implication of this and similar studies is how people interpret their behavior or the actions that they have just taken. Typically, we like to think that our actions are the result of our own goals and wishes. However, if actions precede conscious awareness, this must mean that, on occasion, we interpret or make sense of our behavior by assuming that we had actually intended to do what we did. In other words, actions determine intentions. Clearly, this implication follows from a simple interpretation of the automatic nature of behavior. However, as I shall indicate below, it fails to take account of the role that the deliberate system can also play in determining what we do.

In his best-selling book *Emotional Intelligence,* Daniel Goleman describes a phenomenon that he labels *emotional hijacking* whereby people become victims of their own emotional outbursts.[22] For example, imagine a situation in which a person becomes annoyed because he has been made to wait longer than he expected for assistance from a salesclerk. When, at last, someone is able to assist him, he cannot contain his anger. However, the more he complains, and the more the salesclerk fails to seem sufficiently apologetic, the angrier he becomes. His behavior rapidly escalates into a torrent of angry words that he cannot control.

The framework depicted in exhibit 15 can also clarify this phenomenon. In essence, people have learned to respond automatically to certain emotional stimuli and are unable to control these reactions. In addition, each response becomes itself a stimulus to further reaction, and a vicious cycle is set in motion. In other words, people's behavior has been "hijacked" by their own emotions and is no longer under their conscious control. That does not mean, of course, that people cannot learn to control their emotional outbursts. But doing so requires intervention by the deliberate system.

Within the present framework, the origin of emotional hijacking can be explained by the person's idiosyncratic learning history. Essentially, learned, automatic responses to certain stimuli—responses that have been acquired in wicked learning environments—produce strong behaviors that are not easily suppressed. Once again, we observe that tacit learning can produce both functional and dysfunctional behavior.

Taking Action Deliberately

But not all behaviors are automatic. People can use the deliberate system to concentrate on stimuli and to produce specific actions. Imagine, for example, what happens when you solve a puzzle or make up your mind to do something. Moreover, the deliberate system can overrule outputs of the tacit system provided that action has not already taken place. An example of this (already cited in chap. 2) is the way we overcome prejudices. Clearly, we all learn prejudices through the operation of the tacit system. But this does not mean that we *must* act in accordance with the prejudicial thoughts that suddenly appear in consciousness. On the contrary, we can train the deliberate system to censor these kinds of thoughts and to suppress the kinds of behaviors they suggest. In addition, as noted above, we can learn to control actions suggested by our emotions.

People can also consciously form intentions and decide when and when not to let automatic processes take control. Consider driving a car. Typically, we decide where we want to go and then delegate many of the functions to automatic processing. However, we continue to focus just enough attention on the task of driving to allow us to assume full control if necessary. It is true, as indicated above, that sometimes actions precede intentions and that the latter are therefore interpreted in the light of the former. But this need not be the case if people devote sufficient attention to the task or situation at hand.

Conscious attention is a limited commodity and therefore a costly one. As stated above, the framework assumes a *scarce resource* principle. The deliberate system is used sparingly. It is allocated to tasks that are deemed important at given moments in time but can be reallocated to other tasks as the situation demands. It is rarely shut down completely and often performs a monitoring function. In most cases, the tacit system is our "default" system, and the deliberate system is invoked either when the tacit system cannot solve the problem at hand or when the organism is making some conscious decision (e.g., planning what to do). At any given time, however, both the tacit and the deliberate systems will be operating simultaneously.

Consider two examples of how the systems work together. First, recall the discussion presented above of what happens when you face a type of problem in reasoning with which you are unfamiliar (see chap. 4). The tacit system quickly seeks to identify aspects of the problem to which it can relate, and the deliberate system tries to work through the problem in a more effortful, step-by-step manner. Second, contrast this situation with handling a type of problem with which you are already quite familiar. In this case, the tacit system quickly "sees" an answer, and the deliberate system is used, if at all, only to check it.

It should be noted that these two examples show that it is difficult to know whether people have answered problems intuitively. In particular, the extent and manner of using the tacit and deliberate systems depend on how familiar subjects already are with specific types of problems as well as how those problems are presented. For example, an expert in probability theory will easily identify the structure of, for example, problem 1 in exhibit 11 above (p. 127) and will therefore not violate the rules of probability theory in her answer. In other words, she (i.e., her tacit system) instantly recognizes the way in which the problem is structured, an initial answer suggests itself, and then the deliberate system is invoked to check and possibly revise that initial answer. A novice, on the other hand, may well not understand the problem (tacitly or deliberatively) and, unable to answer the problem analytically (i.e., using the deliberate system), is happy to embrace whatever intuitive answer suggests itself. (Indeed, the fact that an answer appears rapidly in consciousness with little effort may be taken as a clue that it is right.) In short, experts and novices both use the tacit and the deliberate systems in answering this question, but in different ways. Moreover, one can imagine how different questions can trigger differential use of the two systems. In this particular case, both the expert and the novice made heavy use of the tacit system, but, whereas the expert's intuitive knowledge is appropriate, the novice's intuition is invalid.

A further example is provided by the comparison (first offered in chap. 4) of the results of studies that presented reasoning problems in written form with those of studies that presented problems visually (using film). A typical problem asked subjects to describe the trajectory of a ball emerging from a curved tube. Although many subjects were unable to identify the trajectory correctly when presented with word problems, more succeeded when they were shown films of possible trajectories and asked to identify which was correct. The two versions of the task clearly required the use of both the tacit and the deliberate systems. However, whereas subjects had difficulty understanding the word problem using both systems, it seems that they were able to identify the correct film sequence using only the tacit system.

In chapter 4, I formulated the visualization hypothesis, which states that people are more likely to engage in intuitive processing when they can see (i.e., visualize) the phenomena in question. In the case of the physical phenomena discussed above, it seems that the tacit system knew more (i.e., was more accurate) than the deliberate (or both combined). However, using the tacit system to visualize Linda (described in problem 1 of exhibit 11 above) induces many subjects to violate the laws of probability theory. As illustrated by, for example, the Müller-Lyer illusion (see exhibit 1, p. 11) and the electric brae (see chap. 2), the fact that we see something in a particular way and have confidence in what our tacit systems are telling us does not mean that intuitive judgments are always well founded.

The fact that people process information primarily in the tacit mode means that many behaviors are enacted automatically. However, people still have considerable latitude in deciding when and how often to engage in deliberate processing, and this suggests the existence of important individual differences. Indeed, Ellen Langer has written persuasively about states that she calls *mindlessness* and *mindfulness*. These correspond roughly to what I have characterized as the use of the tacit and the deliberate systems, respectively. Langer argues that too often people have a tendency to let their thoughts run on "mindlessly" or "automatically" and that they fail to realize how much they can improve the quality of their lives if they become more "mindful," that is, take more direct control of their mental activity. She goes on to provide impressive experimental evidence showing the beneficial effects on physical health and even longevity of engaging in more mindful activity. In many cases, all that is required is a modest increase in the challenges posed by the everyday environment.[23] In chapter 8, I shall discuss several aspects of Langer's ideas and experimental results.

Feedback

Discussion of the framework presented in exhibit 15 would be incomplete without considering the effects of feedback and understanding how this interacts with characteristics of the environment. As noted previously, whereas cognitive processes occur inside the head and cannot be observed, actions and outputs (boxes 5 and 6) occur, for the most part, in the environment and can be observed by both the person producing them and others. Indeed, as noted above, the interpretation of automatic actions often takes place after the fact. This is indicated in exhibit 15 by the arrow that leads from action (box 5) to consciousness or working memory (box 3).

Feedback from the environment occurs because actions (box 5) lead to outcomes (box 6). For example, if you turn on the switch controlling a lamp, electric current will cause the lightbulb in that lamp to become illuminated. The feedback obtained from most minor actions is immediate and affects both consciousness or working memory (box 3) and long-term memory (box 4). However, it is important to note that observed feedback also becomes a stimulus that is subsequently processed by the preconscious screen (box 1). Thus, whereas its effect on working memory (box 3) can be direct (when the person is paying specific attention to the feedback), its effect on long-term memory is mediated by the preconscious screen. (Note the links from box 6 back to the stimulus at the left of exhibit 15.)

Moreover, as previously explained in chapter 3, your actions can set in motion a series of action-outcome feedback loops that can become self-reinforcing. That is, the feedback from your own action (box 6) becomes the next stimulus to be processed by the preconscious screen (box 1), which leads to further action, further feedback, and so on. For instance, that you smiled at your acquaintance and that the smile was reciprocated can affect your sense that the person really likes you. However, had you not smiled in the first place, your acquaintance might not have smiled back, and your automatic reaction would have been to infer a lesser attraction.

The situation just described involves immediate feedback, yet we should note that this can be subject to distortion. Feedback can also be delayed, subject to extraneous random factors, or biased in other ways. Imagine, for instance, the task of personnel selection. The result of a decision made today—whether we hired the appropriate person for the job—may not be apparent for several months or even several years, by which time other factors may have arisen obfuscating the outcome (making it difficult to tell, e.g., whether we hired the wrong person or whether we made the right choice given the situation but that this then changed).

Feedback is the link between the person's information-processing system and the environment. As stated previously, the validity of automatic learning within the tacit system depends on the quality of feedback, which, in turn, is determined by the structure—kind or wicked—of the learning environment.

Summary

The framework presented in exhibit 15 depicts two information-processing systems, the tacit and the deliberate. The tacit system operates automatically and consumes little or no attention. In contrast, the deliberate system operates consciously and requires effort. Although the point is not made explicitly in the diagram, many different systems can be thought of as contributing to the tacit system, particularly the emotions.

The framework assumes that all stimuli—including feedback—are first processed by the preconscious screen. This allows us to react quickly to certain stimuli before the slower conscious processing takes place. After screening, the organism decides whether information will be relayed to consciousness, but this decision can also be affected explicitly by a decision to allocate conscious attention (as when a person is concentrating on something). Thus, deliberate processing always follows tacit processing in time, although, on occasion, the lag may be quite brief.

The framework further assumes a *scarce resource* principle. The tacit system is the default information-processing mode, and, given the cost of attention, the deliberate system is used sparingly. Individuals, however, can differ in the extent to which they make more or less use of the deliberate system for information processing.

The tacit system learns from what it observes in the environment, and this, in part, is a result of the feedback engendered by its own actions. The validity of the knowledge acquired by the tacit system is conditioned by the environment in which the learning takes place. Learning can also occur within the deliberate system. However, this is effortful, and what is acquired can dissipate unless reinforced.

Finally, the framework presented in exhibit 15 is static in the sense that it shows only what is happening at one given point in time. Many processes or reactions to stimuli that once relied heavily on the deliberate system can over time become automatic and thus bypass consciousness. This migration from the deliberate system to the tacit is an important characteristic of the phenomenon of expertise.

Intuition as Expertise

In previous chapters, I have discussed the relations between expertise and intuition. I have also suggested that intuition can be thought of as a form of expertise. This is a useful way of considering intuition, but it is a mistake to equate the two concepts. I therefore now elaborate on these ideas by considering similarities and differences between expertise and intuition.

Similarities

Expertise and intuition are similar in that both are acquired largely through experience and, as a consequence, are domain specific. That is, expertise in, say, physics does not necessarily imply expertise in sociology. Similarly, a large stock of intuitive knowledge about classical music will have no application to tennis.

Like expertise, intuition can be acquired in two distinct ways—explicit instruction and tacit or experiential learning. And it is often hard to distinguish one from the other. For example, an economist can acquire economic intuitions by attending classes on economic modeling (explicit learning) or by taking a job that gives him hands-on experience at economic modeling (experiential learning). But he can also acquire economic intuitions by attending an academic seminar, an experience that falls somewhere in between. The point of an academic seminar—like that of, say, a master class for musicians—is, not specific instruction on particular points, but simply ("merely") exposure to scholarly debate, exposure that adds implicitly to one's stock of intuitive capital. By listening to or watching or working with the best in a particular field, both high standards and ways of reaching those standards can be assimilated.

In practice, both intuition and expertise depend heavily on many of the same key psychological mechanisms, for example, judgments of similarity and the use of constraints in memory that facilitate recognition. Expertise and intuition also tend to be highly perceptual processes. In short, the concepts are quite similar.

Differences

It is a mistake, however, to equate intuition and expertise. For one thing, expertise often requires the explicit use of conscious analytic thinking, that is, deliberate-system thought. Imagine, for example, a mathematician. She may have an intuitive idea of how to solve a particular problem. But her expertise does not lie only in her intuitive ability. It also involves knowing which analytic tools should be used to elaborate a proof (tools that must be explicitly manipulated). Similarly, a physician's expertise resides, not only in being able to diagnose a disease intuitively, but also in knowing which tests to order (a conscious process involving selection among alternatives) and in being able to interpret the results of those tests. In short, expertise makes use of both intuitive and deliberative processes.

A second difference between intuition and expertise is that, whereas it makes sense to talk about different levels of expertise, this type of distinction makes less sense when we speak about intuition. Experts can differ in how much they know and thus in relative levels of expertise—but this applies to both tacit and deliberate knowledge.

On the other hand, some people can be said to be more intuitive than others when dealing with certain kinds of issues. For example, an expert chess player is undoubtedly able to assess certain moves intuitively (or with minimal effort), whereas a less-experienced player would need to deliberate at some length to reach the same kinds of conclusions.

As this example shows, levels of expertise in a domain may be correlated with the use of intuition in the same domain, but this is not the same as saying that there are different *levels* of intuition. Similarly, some people describe others or even themselves as being more intuitive than others. However, what this means is that people differ in the extent to which they rely on intuition as opposed to more deliberate thinking when facing different kinds of problems. In other words, this reflects preference for styles of dealing with problems and does not imply that some styles are necessarily better than others.[24] In short, one cannot simply equate levels of intuition with levels of expertise.

Third, intuition and expertise are validated in quite different ways. For the most part, intuition is validated informally and implicitly. People use intuition constantly, and, unless they become aware that it has led them astray, they will continue to rely on it. The lack of direct disconfirmation ("no news is good news") is sufficient validation.

The validation of expertise, however, is more objective, involving explicit social recognition (of both simple expertise and levels of expertise) and measurement against certain established criteria. Physicians, for example, have undergone training and passed examinations. College and university professors are recognized on the basis of similar criteria; they are also judged on the basis of their publications (both quality and quantity). Chess masters have achieved their status by winning a certain number of tournaments. Stock market analysts are recognized as expert on the basis of the accuracy of their predictions.[25]

A fourth distinction between intuition and expertise lies in the fact that, whereas people develop intuitions to handle problems in many different domains, expertise is usually more concentrated in specific domains. Thus, you may have developed intuitions that guide your reactions in a variety of social situations as well as intuitions that guide you in interactions with the physical world (e.g., while driving an automobile), but you are not necessarily an expert in any of these domains. We make use of intuition in almost all our activities, yet few of us are experts in more than a limited number of areas.

Intuition as a Form of Expertise

Despite the differences outlined above, thinking of intuition as a form of expertise can be useful. It directs attention to the domain specificity of intuition and its reliance on the environmental conditions under which it is acquired. It also relates intuition to that aspect of expertise that is acquired passively through mere exposure to the domain. It differs, of course, in that it is not socially recognized in the way expertise is and is less dependent on the prior acquisition of codified knowledge through a deliberate learning process. Unlike some forms of expertise, intuition is not certified. No one need pass an examination in order to practice intuitive judgment.

Seven Guidelines for Educating Intuition

The framework presented in exhibit 15 provides, in simplified form, a way of organizing much of the evidence presented in this book. What implications does this suggest for the task of educating intuition? How can we take advantage of the strengths and weaknesses of *both* the tacit and the deliberate systems in order to help people make better judgments and decisions? There are three considerations to keep in mind.

First, the framework clearly illustrates the important role played by the environment and, in particular, the quality of feedback in determining whether people acquire valid intuitions.

Second, whereas automatic responses are often functional, the framework also implies that dysfunctional aspects of automatic behavior must be curbed. The deliberate system must be trained to guide and control, as necessary, the activities of the tacit system.

Third, by implying that the dysfunctional aspects of automatic behavior must be curbed, the framework points to a gap in our knowledge. If the deliberate system is to provide a more active role in guiding the tacit system, what principles or rules should it use in doing so?

In what follows, I suggest different strategies for educating intuition that take account of these three considerations. The following seven guidelines represent a distillation of these strategies: (1) Select and/or create your environments. (2) Seek feedback. (3) Impose circuit breakers. (4) Acknowledge emotions. (5) Explore connections. (6) Accept conflict in choice. (7) Make scientific method intuitive.

Underlying these guidelines are the assumptions that people recognize the differences between the tacit and the deliberate systems and that they are motivated to gain greater control over their thought processes. In Ellen Langer's terms (see above), people want to be more "mindful" and less "mindless."[26]

The first two guidelines recognize the importance of the environment and feedback. The next four recognize the need to guide and control the tacit system. The last provides the set of principles that the deliberate system should use to guide the activities of the tacit system. I now briefly consider each guideline, elaborating further in chapter 7.

Select and/or Create Your Environments

As noted many times in this book, much of what we learn—as well as the validity of what we learn—depends on the characteristics of the environments in which we find ourselves. Tacit learning is reactive. The organism adapts to the environment. *What* we learn is a function of the opportunities offered by the environments in which we live and act. Whether learning is veridical depends on other characteristics of the environment. Is it kind or wicked?

People, however, need not be passive and simply accept the environments with which they are confronted. Instead, they can take a proactive approach to learning, exposing themselves to environments that foster opportunities in areas that they wish to develop, and even finding ways to create kind environments. In short, environments can be deliberately chosen to develop cultural capital in the desired directions.

Seek Feedback

Feedback is an important element of the framework presented in exhibit 15. It affects both the tacit and the deliberate systems. When environments are kind, the automatic processing of feedback is both critical and functional. However, wicked environments are characterized by faulty feedback that can be misleading as a result of, among other things, delays, random disturbances, absence, and other confounding factors.

When functioning in wicked environments, it is important to search for feedback actively and systematically. In social interactions, for example, we have little difficulty forming impressions of the people we meet. And these impressions are important in that they direct our behavior. We are friendly, for instance, toward those who appear to be friendly toward us. We should, however, consider such impressions to be at best preliminary hypotheses and, before placing much reliance on them, test their validity lest they lead us to take actions that are not in our own interests. This principle is understood (implicitly if not explicitly) by con men, whose art consists of creating the impression that they can be trusted and never allowing that impression to be challenged. In other words, they engineer false feedback.

More generally, the deliberate system can greatly enhance the tacit system by developing the habit of seeking feedback in order to test connections, ideas, or hypotheses that the latter forms so quickly and readily. This point will be further emphasized in chapter 7.

Impose Circuit Breakers

An important feature of the framework presented in exhibit 15 is that many acts (i.e., thoughts or behaviors) are triggered automatically and that we become aware of them only after the fact. And we are grateful that we can act without thinking (i.e., using deliberate-system thought) when doing so means that we have avoided danger (by, e.g., stepping out of the way of a falling object). However, there are also many occasions when we would have been better served had we been able to screen our automatic actions before taking them.

Earlier, I discussed the fact that we cannot avoid acquiring stereotypes. But this does not mean that we are necessarily compelled to take the actions that are prompted (unconsciously) by these stereotypes. Indeed, through deliberate effort and instruction, we can learn to censor such automatic reactions. That is, we can use our deliberate systems to create explicitly what I call *circuit breakers,* processes that allow us to interrupt automatic, tacit system processes, thereby guiding our behavior if not actually changing underlying attitudes. In Langer's terms, we can learn to become more "mindful."

To take a specific example, imagine dealing with a con man—or, to be more precise, imagine learning to recognize that you are being conned. In order to do this, you must learn to install circuit breakers in your mental routines; that is, you must train yourself not to rely on first impressions (in this case good) but to stop and think twice about whether someone is in fact as reliable as he seems. Just as we cannot avoid tacitly forming prejudices, we cannot avoid forming a good first impression of con men. But we can learn not to act uncritically on the basis of that first impression.

Another example can be found in the introduction and use of nonsexist language, in both speech and written communication. While in many circles today it is considered inconsiderate at best to use sexist language, such was not always the case. My generation, for example, had to unlearn old habits, not always an easy task. But those of us who made the effort learned that, with practice, nonsexist language eventually became second nature. In short, a deliberately learned circuit breaker ("think before you utter a pronoun") became automatic.

As this example illustrates, circuit breakers must typically be tailored to different types of behavior. However, in chapter 7, I shall discuss circuit breakers that are more generally applicable.

Acknowledge Emotions

Although the framework in exhibit 15 distinguishes between two kinds of systems, the tacit and the deliberate, it should be clear that this schematization is simplistic. In particular, the tacit system contains many subsystems that could be treated as separate systems. Our emotions could be said to constitute one such system. And, within that one system, we could distinguish the (sub)systems that control different emotions (fear, joy, etc.).

As noted in previous chapters, emotions involve—for the most part—learned reactions. Moreover, these reactions are accompanied by physical correlates, for example, increased heart rate, changes in facial expression, and so on. People, however, are not necessarily aware of their own emotional reactions and, when they experience emotion consciously, may not be able to identify the particular emotion that has been triggered.

Nonetheless, as has been made clear by the work of Antonio Damasio and Joseph LeDoux (see chaps. 2 and 3), taking account of emotional reactions is often a functional, even necessary, part of taking action. People need to be open to their emotions as well as to the emotions of others. Indeed, there is now considerable awareness of the importance of *emotional intelligence* in guiding behavior in appropriate ways.[27] This does not mean, of course, that emotion should always be the driving force behind decision making. There are times, for example, when restraining emotional reactions such as anger is more intelligent than giving way to such feelings.

The principle that emerges is that we should acknowledge that our emotions are part of our intuitive apparatus and treat them as data.[28] Of course, treating our emotions as data does not mean becoming cold and calculating, emotionless. It means listening to our emotions, getting in touch with them, being aware of what we are feeling—because those feelings provide information that must be taken into account, even when they are vague and we are not completely certain what we are feeling.

Explore Connections

As noted on several occasions, the tacit system is particularly sensitive to the use of the narrative mode, which persuades in ways that differ from more direct, deliberative approaches. Narrative (analogies, stories) has an immediate appeal. We understand by *seeing*.[29] And what we see is often a connection that would not otherwise have been made. The implication for educating intuition is that we should consciously use narrative to make connections that would not be suggested by more logical modes of thought. Instead of accepting the terms in which problems are explicitly stated, we should give our imagination free rein and see where it takes us.[30]

For example, imagine that you have to deal with the practical, but difficult, problem of providing career guidance to a younger colleague. Instead of planning what you will say logically, why not plan it imaginatively?

Why not imagine what parents would be likely to say to their children, grandparents to their grandchildren, members of the clergy to their congregants, sports stars to rookies, movie stars to Hollywood newcomers, and so on? Of course, there is no guarantee that such imaginative simulation—such *seeing*—will trigger new and unusual connections, but it is much more likely to do so than a more logical analysis of alternatives. And you have little to lose. At the worst, the process will have been essentially effortless and possibly even fun.

More generally, narrative provides a way of accessing aspects of your knowledge that you may not at first realize are relevant to your current concerns. Such playful exploration can also be more fruitful than logical analysis in that each connection implies further connections, which imply further connections, and so on.

Accept Conflict in Choice

The scarce resource principle is an underlying assumption of the framework presented in exhibit 15. That attention is limited—and costly—means that typically we initially seek to resolve problems using the tacit system. However, as we have seen, choice involves conflict, and, if we decide to face the conflict, it consumes effort. We have also seen that conflict in choice can take two forms—computational and emotional—both involving trade-offs. Assessing trade-offs requires deliberate effort. How much are you willing to give on one variable to gain on another? (This is computational conflict.) Are you even willing to consider a trade-off in the first place? For example, are you willing to contemplate the choice between saving the cost of an insurance premium and benefiting from accident insurance for your children? (This is emotional conflict.)

As illustrated in chapter 5, it is possible to avoid conflict when making choices. However, avoiding conflict comes at the cost of inconsistencies that can be dysfunctional. For example, our choices may simply reflect the manner in which problems have been presented. Moreover, this can become quite pernicious when we experience and come to prefer the alternative selected in this manner (the mere-exposure effect). In other words, our preferences are formed by the way in which other people have framed choices for us.[31]

One way to avoid these problems is to develop a specific circuit breaker when you are faced with a choice problem, one that stops the choice process and asks, "What are the trade-offs?" By doing so, you are reminded to accept the conflict in choice. Clearly, having such a circuit breaker does not guarantee that you will always make the right choice.

However, it does mean that you will be able to make choices in a more conscious manner and to confront differences that you may experience between deliberate and tacit preferences (i.e., the classic conflict between analysis and intuition). I shall return to this important issue in chapter 8.

Make Scientific Method Intuitive

As noted previously, the strength and weakness of tacit learning is the fact that it is tied to what has been experienced. It is necessarily limited. On the other hand, deliberate processes can produce impressive intellectual achievements.

One such achievement—known generally as *scientific method* (i.e., the methods or rules of scientific reasoning)—allows us to learn more effectively from experience. An important element of my proposal for educating intuition essentially consists of instruction and practice in different aspects of scientific reasoning. The goal is that these rules will become automatic and move from the deliberate to the tacit system. In other words, I propose to make scientific method intuitive.

For example, it is important to realize that observing simple connections between variables does not necessarily imply the existence of a valid relation. It is critical to ask whether other connections could have produced the same effects and to imagine the data that we cannot see. Alternatively, and if possible, we should adopt a more experimental attitude toward our experiential learning. Clearly, it would be absurd to expect that scientific method would ever dominate our tacit system processes. But I believe that the quality of thinking in many situations would be greatly improved if it were invoked automatically. This notion is explored in depth in chapter 7.

Concluding Comments

This chapter had three goals:

The first was to outline three key ideas about human information processing—one organism but many information-processing systems, learning shaped by experience, and two systems for learning and doing—so that the topic of intuition could be seen in the context of what it achieves for the organism.

The second was to develop a simple two-system framework of human information processing in order to summarize concisely much of the information presented in this book and to derive guidelines for the goal of educating intuition. Critical to this framework were the notion of the preconscious screen, which filters all information encountered by the organism, and the scarce resource principle, which implies the default status of the tacit system (i.e., problems will be handled tacitly whenever possible).

The third was to present seven guidelines for educating intuition, guidelines motivated by the framework presented previously. These took account of the effects of the environment (and particularly the quality of feedback) on learning, the need to help the deliberate system know when to curb automatic behavior enacted by the tacit system, and principles that the deliberate system should use in helping the tacit system acquire more functional responses. Underlying the guidelines is the assumption that people need to learn to manage their thought processes actively. There is much to gain by playing to the different strengths of the tacit and deliberate systems and avoiding their respective pitfalls. In chapter 7, I rely on these guidelines when developing a framework for educating intuition. In chapter 8, I recognize that work on this topic is incomplete. I therefore explore several conceptual issues and provide suggestions for future investigations.

CHAPTER 7

A Framework for Developing Intuition

The title of this book is *Educating Intuition*. In the six preceding chapters, I have explored what scientific psychology can tell us about intuition at the beginning of the twenty-first century. And, in chapter 6, I also presented seven guidelines for educating intuition that were motivated by the framework summarizing the relations between the tacit and the deliberate systems of information processing. In the present chapter, I suggest a framework for educating intuition that builds on those seven guidelines. I do not claim that I have found a unique and valid way of teaching people how to acquire good intuitions. However, my suggestions are consistent with one of the most thorough examinations of the concept of intuition to date.

I begin the chapter by emphasizing the first of the seven guidelines: *Select and/or create your environments.* I emphasize that intuition is largely the fruit of experience. Thus, in order to educate intuition, it is important to emphasize *what* you learn from experience and *how* you learn. This means making sure, not only that you acquire appropriate (i.e., correct) intuitions, but also that the environments (the learning structures) in which you acquire those intuitions are appropriate. Central to my thesis is the notion that, although we all learn from experience, it is not clear that we always learn the right lessons. Since learning structures affect what is learned, it is important to understand this and seek—or even create—the kinds of experiences that will lead to good intuitions.

A related point is that intuitions are primarily domain specific. A person who has good intuitions about physical phenomena, for example, may lack intuition when dealing with cultural or social phenomena. Learning, however, involves both content and rules. By *content,* I mean *what* people learn; by *rules,* I mean *how* they learn what they learn.

To illustrate, imagine George, the dermatologist introduced in chapter 1, as he examines a patient. During the examination, George encounters a certain skin condition for the first time and thus augments his knowledge base. But there are different strategies—or rules—that he could implement in this particular situation. For example, does he immediately relate what he is observing in this particular situation to previous observations? Does he verify his initial assumptions? In many cases, there will be an interaction between content and rules because what people see undoubtedly affects how they learn about it. Consider, for example, the different ways in which expert and novice dermatologists are likely to examine the same symptoms.

Relative familiarity with a domain affects both the content acquired and the rules used for learning within that domain. Moreover, some rules for learning are more effective than others. It is therefore important to determine whether people can acquire good rules for learning that can be employed *across* domains. For example, can the rules used to diagnose a skin condition also be used to determine whether a job applicant is likely to perform satisfactorily if hired, or are they domain specific? I shall argue, in fact, that, while intuitions themselves are domain specific, people can learn to learn from experience in a manner that can be applied across domains.

Next, I present the three components of a framework for developing intuition: awareness, the acquisition of specific skills, and practice.

First, paradoxically, even though intuitive learning takes place largely tacitly, only by being aware of the process can we manage it (by being aware, e.g., of whether an environment is kind or wicked). Otherwise, we leave what we learn to chance.

Second, we must acquire specific learning skills. Specifically, we must learn to observe better, learn to speculate more intelligently about what we see, always be willing to test our ideas, and learn to think carefully about how we can generalize from experience. In other words, we must follow guideline 7: *Make scientific method intuitive.* And, in the process, we must also follow guidelines 2 (*Seek feedback*), 4 (*Acknowledge emotions*), 5 (*Explore connections*), and 6 (*Accept conflict in choice*).

Third, we must practice, and practice, and practice.

Finally, I discuss the relation between intuition and intelligence.

The Importance of Experience—*Select and/or Create Your Environments*

The model elaborated in the preceding chapters emphasizes that intuition is largely acquired automatically through experience in specific domains. We adapt to the environments to which we are exposed. Consider, for example, culture. In general, we do not set out to learn about our own cultures. Instead, we all learn about—or adapt to—our cultures over time *without thinking* about the process. Through experience, we develop a sense of what is and is not normal, what people do and do not say in specific circumstances, and so on. Indeed, not until we are confronted with another culture do we realize the kinds of assumptions made in our own. It has been said, for instance, that, in order to learn what is truly distinctive about their own culture, Americans must live abroad.[1]

Culture, it should be noted, is not just a variable that differs among nations. Different regions within nations, even different cities within regions, can develop different cultures. Different cultures can even be found within the same organization. The "culture" of professors of English literature, for example, differs in important ways from that of professors of theoretical physics. And, although these cultural differences often cannot be observed by third parties, they can make communication very difficult.

In the business world, too, financial managers have quite different perspectives than, say, marketing managers and may not see problems in the same way. Companies that merge to form a single corporation provide another striking example. Mergers naturally make people think in terms of economies of scale and cost and expected financial benefits. What they tend to overlook are the difficulties that arise from the fact that each business has, over the years, developed its own principles of doing business, principles that are usually tacit (and that were therefore learned intuitively), that are rarely made explicit, and that can therefore lead to misunderstanding and conflict.

Precisely because so much of intuition is acquired tacitly through interaction with the environment, you need to expose yourself to the domain in which you wish to develop your intuition. This principle is recognized, at least implicitly, by professions that require their members to serve periods of apprenticeship. Apprentices learn by working alongside their masters and observing what they do.

Consider, for example, a study conducted by the late Hillel Einhorn that examined the cognitive processes of physicians studying biopsy slides of cancer patients. Einhorn built statistical models of three physicians in order to assess how they combined and weighted their observations in the process of judging the severity of the disease. Among medical professionals, this task is held to require expertise and to be highly intuitive, relying heavily as it does on visual perception. Interestingly, one of the physicians that Einhorn studied was the student of one of the others, and both weighted and combined the different pieces of information in similar ways. Their strategies, however, differed from that of the third physician.[2]

Even if formal apprenticeships of some sort are not required by a profession, it is clear that experience makes a huge difference. Recall Diana the antiquarian from chapter 1. Diana has spent all her working life in the business of antiques, and she was also brought up in a household that knew a great deal about antiques. She received little formal instruction but, judging by her skills, clearly obtained superb training in evaluating antiques.

Thus, without wishing to belabor the obvious, exposure to a domain is a necessary condition for acquiring intuitions about that domain. Simple exposure, however, does not necessarily guarantee that *valid* intuitions will be acquired. The validity of intuitions depends on the conditions under which those intuitions were acquired.

As explicated in chapter 3, the main process of learning through experience involves noticing connections, connections that are subsequently strengthened. The major advantage of this process is that it allows the organism to adapt to its environment. In other words, what is learned is relevant to the environment. The disadvantages are, first, that the organism cannot learn from what it cannot see and, second, that feedback can be misleading. In other words, the wrong lessons can be learned from experience.

The conditions under which people learn—what I have called *learning structures*—can be characterized along a continuum running from *kind* to *wicked*. Whether an environment is kind or wicked depends both on whether feedback is relevant or irrelevant and on whether the task involved is lenient or exacting (see exhibit 6, on p. 88 above). If intuitions have been acquired in kind environments, they are likely to be good—at least in that particular environment. If they have been acquired in wicked environments, they are likely to be bad.

To illustrate, consider the conditions under which a professional tennis player learns to sharpen her intuitions for the game. She trains almost every day for many years, and she often plays matches that pit her against a variety of opponents. The feedback that she receives is immediate and unambiguous (a bad serve, a ball that lands out of bounds), and the task is exacting (small errors—e.g., the ball failing to clear the net—can be costly). And, even if she does not at first associate a bad outcome with the particular actions that caused it, she will have many opportunities to relearn the lesson. It should be clear that the environment within which she is working is kind, that the conditions are good for acquiring valid intuitions.

Short-term weather forecasting also takes place in a kind environment. Feedback is excellent, forecasters soon learn whether their predictions were accurate, and those predictions have absolutely no effect on actual weather conditions. Intuitive judgment in this domain is therefore very likely to be good—as good, that is, as the random nature of the phenomenon being forecast will allow.[3]

Now consider physicians working in a hospital emergency room—a classic case of a wicked learning environment. Rarely do emergency room staff see the outcome of treatment. In cases of minor injury or illness, follow-up care is provided by the patient's own physician after discharge. In cases of more serious injury or illness, patients are transferred to a different ward for further evaluation and follow-up care. Emergency room staff therefore cannot rely on long-term feedback; they can observe only what happens in the short term. They also have few opportunities to experiment and often no way of knowing whether the task at hand is lenient (many conditions can be treated with antibiotics) or exacting (shortness of breath is symptomatic of many conditions, some minor, some potentially life threatening).

Another task that takes place in a wicked learning environment is predicting which of several job candidates is the most likely to succeed. The criteria by which success is judged are often vague, feedback concerning success or failure is delayed (often for long periods), the subsequent job performance of rejected candidates in similar positions cannot be observed, and performance can be affected by the simple fact of having been judged suitable for the job (the act of choice sets in motion a self-fulfilling prophecy). The conditions under which intuitions are acquired are therefore poor, which is unfortunate given that impressions (i.e., intuitions) play such a large role in the selection process.

In exhibit 16, I provide a list of questions—or circuit breakers—that can help determine whether intuitions (yours or those of others) were acquired in kind or wicked environments. Given the process of connections and reinforcement by which we learn, the kind of analysis prompted by such a set of questions is important for three reasons.

First, it enables us to assess the probable quality of intuitions. Those acquired in kind environments are likely to be valid. Those acquired in wicked environments should be regarded with suspicion.

EXHIBIT 16 Questions about learning structures

In assessing the validity of your intuitions, it is important to ask about the learning structure in which these were acquired. Was this wicked or kind? The following questions should help you assess this. To provide a context for the questions, imagine that you want to make a decision, perhaps, to hire a colleague on the basis of your intuitive feeling about the person.

1. *Compare* your learning structure with *known examples.* Is it, for example, like that of the professional tennis player (kind) or the emergency room physician (wicked)? (See pp. 217–218.) In what ways?

2. *How many times* have you made this kind of judgment or decision in the past? Do you really know what your track record is? Remember that confidence in intuition can be a two-edged sword. Unless something makes us explicitly aware of past errors, having done things many times in the past can make us quite confident. But this confidence may not be justified.

3. What kind of *feedback* have you received in the past?

   ♦ Has this been *clear,* that is, unambiguous? A criterion such as relative success in a job, for instance, could be quite vague.

   ♦ How *immediate* was the feedback? In other words, did you receive feedback on your judgment or action soon afterward?

   ♦ Was feedback *compromised* in any way? For example, could it have been biased by self-fulfilling prophecies or other actions?

   ♦ What role has *luck* played in past situations of this type?

4. Is this *important*? If it is, it will be worthwhile trying to analyze it in some detail. Do not rely on intuition alone.

Second, it enables us to select environments more actively. Because we do have some control over the kinds of environments to which we are exposed, we should proactively seek those that favor the acquisition of valid intuitions.

Third, it enables us to see how we can change environments in such a way that valid learning is facilitated. Because we often have some measure of control over our environments, we can often restructure them in ways that improve the feedback obtained.

Can Good Rules for Learning Apply across Domains?

I distinguished above between the substantive *content* that people acquire when they gain intuitive knowledge and the *rules* that they use for acquiring that intuitive knowledge. I also emphasized that the degree of interaction between content and rules depends on just how expert an individual is in a particular domain. In terms of educating intuition, it is important to determine whether rules that people use for learning within one domain can also be used in other domains. In addition, can people learn to apply abstract rules across domains? That is, can good abstract rules for learning be generalized?

Whereas these questions have not been examined explicitly in the context of acquiring and improving intuition, a research program conducted by Richard Nisbett and his colleagues has investigated a series of related issues. These studies have examined rules for reasoning and asked to what extent people can learn abstract principles and then apply these principles across different domains.

For example, if in the course of studying logical reasoning people learn a particular principle, will they be able to apply that principle to other types of problems? Through the nineteenth century, most educators thought that, yes, they would be able to and used this notion to justify formal discipline-based educational programs that stressed the teaching of mathematics, logic, and the classical languages. The underlying rationale was that these disciplines would teach people *how* to think in ways that could be applied across many areas. However, at the beginning of the twentieth century, Robert Thorndike challenged this belief, his experiments having led him to believe that most inferential processes are highly task or domain specific and that the human mind is ill suited to learning and applying abstract rules for reasoning. Jean Piaget later suggested that the acquisition and use of abstract inferential rules was more a function of self-discovery and could not be helped much by instruction.[4]

The extensive program of research conducted by Nisbett and his colleagues covered rules in deductive logic, probability theory, methodological reasoning, and economic cost-benefit analysis.[5] Their methodology involved different types of studies. In some, subjects were formally trained and tested (immediately after training as well as after some delay) in the use of particular rules, such as principles of statistics or economics. In others, comparisons were made between the reasoning skills of university students from different disciplines. The researchers also examined whether professors from diverse academic specializations used principles of economic cost-benefit analysis in making everyday choices and whether those who did were more successful in their jobs (as measured by salary increases).

While subjects probably did not respond intuitively to all the problems posed, the results are nevertheless most revealing. For one thing, people can learn certain formal rules and then apply these rules across different domains. Also, training in a discipline does make a difference.

For example, graduate training in psychology and medicine has a positive effect on statistical and methodological reasoning, and students of law learn to use the logic of the conditional. On the other hand, graduate students in chemistry, who receive little exposure to these topics in their studies, do not perform as well as the other students when tested on these principles. Looking at even greater exposure to certain principles, Nisbett and his colleagues showed that, even when professors of economics are faced with problems that are not economic in nature, their reasoning processes are likely to reflect economic principles.

On the other hand, there seems to be a limit to what can be taught and then generalized across domains. For example, people have great difficulty applying certain formal rules of logic outside the domain in which they have been taught unless a specific context is provided. This phenomenon was discussed in chapter 4 in relation to Wason's well-known four-card problem. In certain contexts, people have difficulty knowing what information to seek when testing a logical relation of the type "if p then q." However, if the same kind of problem is formulated in the context of checking whether someone is cheating, people are quick to sense what kind of information to seek. For example, if you know that, in a bar, only those over twenty-one are allowed to drink alcoholic beverages, it seems trivial to know what you should ask, and of whom, if you know either only people's ages or only what they are drinking.

Nisbett and his colleagues propose what might be called an *analogue hypothesis*. This states that, if people already possess intuitive reasoning schemes that are similar (but not identical) to normative rules, it is possible to help them adapt the former so that they operate like the latter. For example, Nisbett argues that adults generally possess intuitive notions concerning the law of large numbers in statistical reasoning. Thus, if they receive formal instruction about the law and some of its implications, they will be able to recognize situations in which it is applicable in different domains.

For example, the law of large numbers implies that the characteristics of random samples are more likely to mirror those of the parent population when those samples are large than when they are small. Thus, if people are able to recognize that problems involve samples that are drawn from larger populations, they will be able to apply this principle no matter what the domain involved. Moreover, when asked for explanations of certain events, they will be more likely to provide appropriate statistical responses. For instance, when considering how well a professional golfer is playing, people know that it is more meaningful to base judgments of form on the results of several rounds as opposed to just one or two. In addition, a person with good statistical intuitions will not overinterpret form when judgment is based on just one round but will recognize the effects of random variability in a sport where outcomes are not wholly controlled by skill. ("Aces" or holes in one, e.g., are largely a matter of luck but nevertheless affect players' scores.)

The use of arithmetic reasoning provides another example. Several studies have shown that the basic ability to count objects is present in humans from early infancy.[6] In other words, humans possess abstract rules that enable them to distinguish and enumerate objects across quite different domains. On the other hand, we also know that people must be taught the rules of arithmetic (addition, subtraction, multiplication, and division) before they can apply them across a wide range of topics. But people do learn to relate abstract principles of arithmetic and intuitive notions of counting and, with practice, can become quite proficient in reasoning abstractly with numbers. Indeed, in some societies where primary education is lacking, people learn to perform what seems like quite complicated arithmetic when trading commodities. In other words, there is an intuitive base that can be educated—formally or through experience, or both.

The work of Nisbett and his colleagues is a cause for optimism because it suggests that it is possible to train people in inferential techniques that generalize across different domains. As stated above, what seems to be critical is, first, that the techniques taught correspond to approximate, abstract rules that people already use and, second, that people are able to interpret experience in terms of the categories that are needed in order to apply the rules appropriately. The example given previously of thinking in terms of samples, populations, and even sampling schemes provides a case in point. Consider, too, the use of arithmetic principles. However, it is not clear for which normative rules we already have abstract representations, even if these are imperfect. On the other hand, the studies show that, when abstract principles are emphasized through disciplinary training over a period of time (as in graduate school), they definitely mark the way in which people think.

From personal experience, many of us know that discipline-based training can really affect how people both reason and see the world. In some cases, this is particularly striking. For example, although I am not an economist, I have interacted with economists during most of my professional career. What strikes me about their discourse—particularly when they speak to each other—is how the terminology and reasoning processes of economics work their way into almost all topics. Whether the topic is sports, economic phenomena, politics, or even academic curricula and appointments, the discussion is framed in terms, for example, of "sunk costs," "transaction costs," "positive (negative) externalities," "opportunity costs," "demand characteristics," "competitive forces," "substitution effects," and so on. Indeed, when faced with issues that they find hard to conceptualize, such as problems involving personal relationships, they seem to have a strong desire to translate the discussion into economic terms as well as a great sense of relief when they can tag the unfamiliar with familiar labels ("Oh yes, I think we have an agency problem here").

My economist colleagues gain a lot by translating what they see into terms that they manipulate with such ease. And their ability to do so is reinforced through daily experience. Moreover, to the extent that the economic principles that they use are appropriate to the circumstances considered, we can observe the good application of abstract principles of reasoning applied across a variety of domains. (In many instances, this is in fact the case!) It is also true to say that a lot of the thinking in these circumstances involves intuition as I have defined it—much represents common cultural capital. The danger—or "costs," as my economist colleagues would say—is that the intuitive transformation of a discussion into economic terms is sometimes too readily resorted to (or too hard to resist) and, as a result, problems are defined and treated in inappropriate ways.[7]

A Framework for Developing Intuition

Intuition is largely acquired in automatic fashion through experience. Thus, to educate intuition it is necessary to improve the ability to learn accurately from experience. How can this be achieved?

As noted above, controlling the type of experience is critical. But more can be done. The framework that I suggest has three components: (1) creating awareness; (2) a framework for acquiring specific learning skills; and (3) practice.

Creating Awareness

The *scarce resource* assumption of the model presented in chapter 6 is important because it drives the notion that the tacit system is the default mode of information processing. Moreover, people can choose to avoid expending the effort required to use the deliberate system. Indeed, given that the tacit system requires so little effort, why—it can be asked—should people take the trouble to use the deliberate system? I shall address this question more fully in chapter 8. In the meantime, I simply note that failure to engage the deliberate system implies an essentially passive attitude toward life. Such a life is one in which you learn from experience but in which you play no role in choosing your experiences. You become simply the product of what happens to you.

What is clearly required is a proactive attitude whereby people become more active managers of their information-processing resources. As noted in earlier chapters, both the tacit and the deliberate systems have their advantages and disadvantages. But they must be managed, and, for most people, this implies more active use of the deliberate system. Paradoxically, one result of educating your intuition will be that you allocate more time to directing your deliberate thought processes.

Creating an awareness of the potential deficiencies of experiential learning is, I believe, a two-step process. First, people need to be exposed to personal experiences that allow them to discover, for themselves, why taking greater control of their thought processes is in their best interest.[8] Second, they must understand at an intellectual level why learning from experience has limitations. Thus, it is important that they understand, for example, the effects of different types of learning structures (see above).

The importance of experience suggests that people should participate in behavioral simulations or activities in which they are confronted with the negative consequences of their usual ways of behaving (including thinking, making decisions, reacting to others, and so on). Moreover, the effect of these exercises is likely to be greater the more the emotions are involved. For instance, simulations could include life-and-death situations in which people tend to make the wrong decisions. Following such exercises, however, it is critical that people also gain an intellectual understanding of the implications of their behavior, be introduced to tools that can develop their decision-making skills, and be given opportunities to practice these new skills (see also below).

Chris Argyris of the Harvard Business School has developed an intriguing technique for helping people understand the kinds of implicit assumptions that they make in interpersonal interactions. The essence of Argyris's technique consists of analyzing dialogues and examining the differences between what was said and what was really meant. To achieve this, he has two parties engage in a dialogue that is recorded and transcribed. Subsequently, each person examines the transcription. Argyris instructs each individual to write next to the written record what he or she was really thinking when speaking and listening to the other person as well as what he or she thought the other meant but did not say.[9] After both parties have examined their own record of the conversation, they are asked to exchange records (and observations).

This exercise highlights several things. One is the discrepancy between what is said and what is thought. Communication is not always honest. A second is the implicit assumptions that people are making. (You might assume, e.g., that the other person might be offended by—or at least not agree with—what you really think and therefore tailor what you say accordingly.) Another is how untested assumptions can not only impede honest communication but also engender dysfunctional, self-fulfilling prophecies (by highlighting, e.g., the fact that you were willing to act on the basis of untested assumptions).

More generally, Argyris makes the point that many people—and particularly those who succeed in graduating from our better academic institutions—do not necessarily have good skills for learning from experience.[10] Many successful people who have gained positions in today's leading corporations owe their success to the fact that they have completed rigorous programs of education that have stressed intellectual skills and formal learning. Prestigious consulting companies and financial firms on Wall Street, for example, recruit largely from the best universities and business schools, and their recruiting practices favor graduates with high test scores and grade-point averages. These people's success, therefore, is intimately related to academic learning, not experiential learning. Moreover, their very success can reduce their willingness to examine their own assumptions. Argyris argues that many people, and particularly those with impressive academic backgrounds, engage only in what he calls *single-loop learning*, or learning that tends to confirm what they already know or think that they know. He also argues—persuasively—that the most significant form of learning is what he calls *double-loop learning*, or learning in which people question what they (think they) know and thus are able to progress more effectively.

I do not believe that there is a single approach to making people aware of the way in which we learn from experience and of the need to be concerned about this process. However, if you are to educate your intuition, you clearly must have such an awareness as well as the motivation to take appropriate steps.

A Framework for Acquiring Specific Learning Skills

If all learning structures in the world were kind, our tacit systems would ensure that we always learn the right lessons from experience (and I would not be writing this book). To educate your intuition in a particular domain, therefore, you would need only to expose yourself to specific sets of experiences. But not all learning structures are kind. And humans have evolved capacities for learning in wicked structures. These include the powers of imagination and communication through language.

Imagination allows us to learn from what we do not see. We often establish cause, for instance, by appealing to alternative, counterfactual scenarios in our imagination. As an example, consider thought experiments of the type, "Would the accident have occurred if the driver knew that the brakes didn't work?" It is by asking questions like this that we come to understand the way in which the world works. Such questions depend critically on our ability to see the world differently from how it really is. In other words, they enable us to learn from what we do not see.

Language allows us to communicate what we have learned and to make hard-won knowledge available to all. For example, it took many years for the double-helix structure of DNA to be discovered. However, once discovered, this knowledge was quickly codified and preserved and can now be handed down from generation to generation. Language makes one person's discovery available to millions. Moreover, through technology—a product of human imagination—we have vastly increased both the speed and the scale of communication.

As the history of science and ideas has constantly shown, many "truths" about the world have a short shelf life. We now know that many of our ancestors' ideas were just plain wrong, and it is likely that our descendants will find many of our ideas quite mistaken. An issue that has plagued humans for centuries is the question, How do we know when our knowledge is correct? For example, should we trust what is today considered to be a physical law just because it always seems to have held in the past?

Although there is no precise formula for justifying our knowledge, many agree that the canons of scientific reasoning, first outlined by Francis Bacon in the seventeenth century, provide a good set of guidelines.[11] In essence, the canons—sometimes also known as *scientific method*—suggest a set of principles for learning about the world. They are well accepted in the sense that most scientists use them in assessing the validity of hypotheses or theories. I therefore propose to rest the framework for educating intuition on this basis. My belief is that, if people develop mental habits that are based on the principles of scientific method, then the quality of their intuitive thoughts and inferences should improve. This hypothesis is similar to that investigated by Richard Nisbett and his colleagues when they found that people who have assimilated economic principles of cost-benefit analysis are able, on average, to make better economic decisions than those who have not.

In essence, I want people to learn to apply scientific reasoning intuitively—that is, I want them to develop mental habits such that responses *"reached with little apparent effort, and typically without conscious awareness"* (p. 14) incorporate principles of scientific reasoning. I call this *making scientific reasoning intuitive* (guideline 7 from chap. 6). Also, keeping in mind the hypothesis advanced by Nisbett and his colleagues (see above), I am conscious of two things. First, a successful set of abstract rules is likely to be one that *modifies*—as opposed to one that *replaces*—processes that people already use. Second, it is also likely to be one that allows people to assign experiences from different domains to categories that are consistent with this more normative way of learning.

Exhibit 17 presents a framework inspired by scientific method. It breaks the process of learning from experience down into four stages: *observation, speculation, testing*, and *generalization*.[12] The key idea here is that each stage requires different skills to counteract and cooperate with our normal, tacit, automatic way of learning. As noted in earlier chapters, learning involves the observation of connections, which lead to hypotheses, which are then reinforced. However, there are important questions that need to be asked about the connections observed. Are these significant or due to chance? How can we test ideas suggested by the connections? What do they mean relative to what we already know? In wicked learning structures, we cannot rely on our tacit learning system to produce valid knowledge.

In the scheme illustrated in exhibit 17, a clear distinction is made at the outset between what is observed and what this might mean. There is no rush from observation, the first stage, to conclusion, the final stage. Instead, the second stage of the process involves speculating as to different meanings or ideas that could explain what has been seen. This is typically a creative task and requires imagination. The third stage involves testing the earlier notions and requires a different mind-set from speculation. Finally, the fourth stage involves relating tested and partially tested ideas to the rest of your knowledge and assessing its significance.

I now consider each stage. My contention is that the probability of learning the right lessons from experience can be improved if you are able to improve your skills at each of these four stages.

OBSERVATION The fictional detective Sherlock Holmes once said, "It is a capital mistake to theorise before one has data. Insensibly one begins to twist facts to suit theories, instead of theories to suit facts."[13] This is excellent advice. It also emphasizes that we should separate facts from opinions and avoid rushing to premature conclusions. But, in order to gather data, you need to know how to see. And, when we see, we typically resort to theories to guide our perceptions. Indeed, the Italian playwright Luigi Pirandello once remarked that a fact is like a sack—it won't stand up unless you put something inside it (i.e., you need a theory).

EXHIBIT 17 Four stages of learning

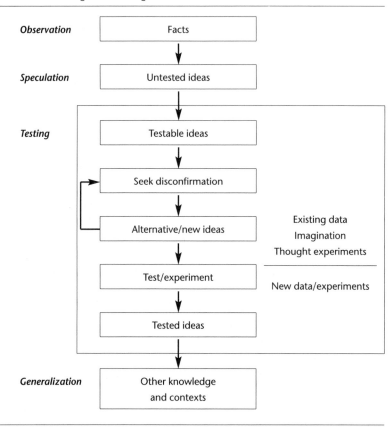

The statements by Holmes and Pirandello suggest that two types of observational skills are important. One depends on knowledge of a domain to know what to look for (Pirandello). The other is general and tries to examine issues without being influenced by prior, theoretical ideas (Holmes). Both are important, but they rely on different, even opposite, processes. I begin by considering the former and find, once again, that relating expertise to intuition provides an excellent starting point.

Professional wine tasters learn to perceive differences in wine through experience as well as explicit instruction about both the physiology of the tongue and the processes by which wines are produced. Aircraft pilots learn how to recognize different types of cloud formations and how these relate to weather patterns. George, the dermatologist introduced in chapter 1, learned to recognize different types of skin conditions by understanding the etiology of certain diseases and observing many different cases. In short, theory plays a large role in observation. It guides what you look for and what you see.

The analogy with expertise emphasizes the need for *good* theory in any domain in which you wish to develop intuition. It should be understood, however, that I am using the term *theory* broadly, to refer, not just to *scientific* theories, but, more important, to *all* the theories—explicit or implicit—that guide our daily actions. In this broader sense, we all have theories about what others might do in certain circumstances, how social conventions work, what motivates people, and so on. This does not mean that these theories are well articulated. They may also be imprecise. But they form the basis of many of our expectations and anticipations. They guide our actions.

The notion that theory plays a role in perception, or that theory guides observation, is not new. Consider the following experiment conducted over fifty years ago by Jerome Bruner and Leo Postman.[14] Subjects were shown playing cards in conditions that allowed seeing them only briefly. They were subsequently asked to identify the cards shown. Several of the cards, however, had incongruous colors and suits—for example, a red ace of spades or a black ace of hearts. Results showed that subjects both took longer to identify incongruous cards and made more mistakes in doing so. On one occasion, twenty-seven of the twenty-eight subjects evinced what the experimenters called a *dominance reaction:* for example, red spades were reported as black or simply as hearts. Several subjects also reported compromise colors: for example, red spades were reported as brown. In other words, the expectation that hearts will be red and spades will be black affects what you see.

Now consider how this phenomenon might occur in a setting that is more typical of everyday life. Imagine, for example, that you are in charge of a small sales force. Your implicit model—or theory—of how your salespeople relate to each other is based on your past experience. In fact, you probably have many implicit theories—about what motivates salespeople, how they react to competitors' actions, and so on. Moreover, without your realizing it, these theories guide what you observe in their behavior. However, unless your theories are approximately correct, you may fail to see the significance of some important behaviors. You may notice, for example, that one salesman never talks about one of your company's competitors. What you may not realize, however, is that this is not because he knows nothing about that company. On the contrary, it is because he is considering taking a position with it.

My main point is that your theories or ideas affect what you see. This therefore highlights the need to develop both good theories and good observation skills, that is, observation skills that are sensitive to whether your theories are, in fact, appropriate. Your observation skills should enable you to question your own theories—in a manner akin to the way in which Argyris's notion of double-loop learning operates. For example, consider again the Postman and Bruner card experiment. People report seeing the red cards as brown because what they see is, in effect, a compromise between what they expect to see and what they actually see. In other words, they allow their implicit assumptions to interfere with their actual, physical perceptions. Their observations are conducted in too routine a manner. As a consequence, they miss important information.

Now translate this card experiment to situations outside the psychological laboratory. Imagine again the scenario in which you are in charge of a small sales force. Your theory is that customers are generally satisfied with your products. You therefore fail to notice small signs of discontent that should be a warning to you. Because this possibility is not part of your current theory, you do not see evidence that could challenge your beliefs.

Perceptions can also be biased by the context in which you find yourself. Social pressures, for example, can influence what you see. Solomon Asch illustrated this in a classic experiment.[15] A subject enters a room in which there are already several people. The experimenter shows the people two lines on a screen and then asks each person, in turn, which line is longer, A or B? The subject is the last person to be asked and is therefore able to hear the others' responses. Although line A looks longer than line B, the subject hears each person say that B is longer. Of course, the other people in the room all colluded with the experimenter in saying that B was longer. What is significant in this case is the reaction of the subject. A significant number of people allow themselves to be influenced by social pressure and say that B is longer.

Of course it can be argued that, even though subjects *say* that B is longer, they still recognize that A is in fact longer. However, this is a situation in which the perceptual task is not difficult. There is little ambiguity. People do not need the opinions of others to guide their inferences. But now imagine that people are judging a more ambiguous stimulus, such as the relative merits of two job candidates. In this case, social pressure becomes a much more powerful influence. If everyone else thinks that candidate B is better than candidate A, you may well be led to revise your own opinion.

The literature also contains numerous examples of perception being biased by subtle effects such as states of relative hunger. For example, in one experiment, two groups of subjects saw words that were flashed briefly on a screen. The two groups differed in that one had not eaten for some time before the experiment. Results showed that members of this group reported seeing many more food-related words.[16] In other words, physical state affected what people saw.

I stated above that there are two types of observational skills. The first skill is heavily dependent on theory or knowledge of context (Pirandello). It helps you identify what others might not see. Consider, for example, the difference between experienced and inexperienced physicians when diagnosing disease. Domain-specific knowledge enables the former to see what the latter might miss. More generally, knowledge allows the speedy interpretation of contextually rich information. Can you see the important information and filter out the irrelevant? The second skill is more general and tries to avoid imposing your knowledge on what you see (Sherlock Holmes). Can you really see the facts as they are instead of through a filter of preconceived notions or theories? Recall the experiment utilizing incongruous playing cards.

Making observations in specific domains leads to focusing attention in particular ways. Improving your general observational skills, however, implies the reverse. It means seeing the world from different perspectives and noticing what might normally be missed. How can this skill be developed?

First, it is important to accept the fact that all your observations must, to some extent, be affected by your theories. Such awareness is by itself an important first step. Second, different activities can develop observational skills. These include the following:

Learn to draw or make sketches. The advantage is that this will oblige you to look at details in your perceptual field that you had previously overlooked. Some people avoid drawing because they lack the relevant technical skills. They are embarrassed by the quality of their sketches. There are several antidotes: do not show your sketches to others (or, at least, wait until you have gained more skill); take lessons; or perhaps try photography, which does not require the technical skills that drawing does but can still develop observational skills.

Make time to observe what is around you. Explicitly examine things in the street that you usually take for granted. For example, on your way to work, ask yourself how the architecture differs from one block to the next. Can you describe the differences in detail? Alternatively, ask yourself how things may have changed (or been moved) in a room since the last time you were in it.

Keep a pad at hand in which to write down observations that attract your attention or details of situations. One useful technique for training observational skills is what I call *blank page fun.* It works like this. Take a pad of paper with you to meetings. (Doing so is perfectly legitimate since most people take notes during meetings.) Paper is two sided, and most people typically write on just one side. Instead of (or along with) taking notes, however, use the blank side of the page to write comments to yourself during the meeting about what you notice happening. (No one will pay any attention to what you are doing; if someone sees you writing, it will be assumed that you are taking notes.) For example, perhaps someone looks like she does not understand; someone else is wearing an unusual tie; most of the people look bored. You can also use the page to write other notes to yourself—perhaps thinking about what you will do after the meeting. I call this *blank page fun* because it helps you get through boring (although often necessary) meetings. I also predict that this activity will make you more sensitive to what is happening—you will see more—and you may also find it amusing.

In short, I am suggesting that, if you are to develop your general observational skills, you must find activities that force you to look at things from new perspectives. It is clear that our theories will always structure what we see to some extent. However, it is surprising just what you can learn to see if you cultivate an attitude of curiosity. For example, when taking a walk, how many different exemplars can you see of a given type? When walking in the woods, for instance, how many different types of small animals or birds are you able to observe? When walking down a city street, in what ways are doorways the same, and in what ways are they different? Alternatively, try to look at things as though you were a different person. Imagine, for example, that you are a six-year-old child. What would you see then? What would the world look like to you if you had been transported in time from the sixteenth century to the twenty-first?

EMOTIONS AS DATA   From the perspective of intuition, it is important to remember that your emotions are an important source of data—this follows from guideline 4 from chapter 6, *Acknowledge emotions.* At one level, it might be thought that my insistence on improving your theories as well as separating facts from opinions suggests that the decision-making process should be free of emotional influences. This is not the case. My belief is that our emotions are like our theories. They are there, and we cannot ignore them. Instead, it is healthier simply to accept that *emotions are data* that need to be explained.

For example, imagine that, every time you see John, a colleague at work, you feel anger. One way of dealing with this is to ignore it. The feeling is ridiculous. Adults should not become angry just because they see someone. However, this is not a wise reaction. Instead, I believe that you should accept your emotion as data—that is, accept the fact "I become angry when I see John"—and then deal with it as something that needs to be explained. Indeed, the apparently inexplicable emotion provides an opportunity for communication between the deliberate and the tacit systems.

SOME COMMENTS ON CHOICE   As noted in chapter 5, choice problems are heavily influenced by how people see problems or how problems are framed. Moreover, people often subconsciously reframe problems in order to avoid the conflicts in choice. In choice problems, however, it pays to confront the conflict and explicitly deal with trade-offs. If you do not, your choices may simply reflect how they are seen.

The antidote is to establish a circuit breaker that reminds you to confront the conflict. Learn to *accept conflict in choice* (guideline 6 from chap. 6). For example, imagine that you are buying a new television. Instead of just choosing whichever one seems best, ask yourself, "What are the critical trade-offs?" This question could, in turn, lead to discovering information that would not typically be seen, for example, data on repair costs.

Finally, in exhibit 18, I summarize a number of suggestions meant to help people improve their skills of observation.

SPECULATION   The literature on problem solving and creativity suggests that people do not speculate enough when dealing with inferential problems.[17] There are two reasons. First, speculation takes effort. It can be hard work to generate alternative explanations—or "thought trials"—to account for what you see. Once you have arrived at an explanation, it is difficult to engage in other thought trials. Second, emotionally, people resist changing the mental path on which they have already embarked. People like their ideas and are reluctant to change them. Moreover, additional explanations reached through other thought trials may make you uncertain. You thought that you had an explanation. Other explanations confuse the issue.

The literature on creativity documents the tendency that we have to censor our own ideas as well as those of others. This cuts down on considering other, speculative ideas or hypotheses. It can also lead to jumping prematurely to conclusions. Once again, imposing automatic reactions or circuit breakers (guideline 3 from chap. 6) not to close down particular av-

EXHIBIT 18 Improving skills of observation

1. Distinguish observations (facts) from speculations. Some rules of thumb:
   - Facts are data that involve a minimum of inference (or guessing) to understand or record.
   - Facts are events that independent observers would describe in the same way.
   - Facts are not opinions.
   - Your own emotions are facts (for you).
2. When observing behavior, ask yourself what assumptions the people you are observing are making about the situations they confront. Put yourself in their shoes. How do they see the world?
3. What are your assumptions about what you are seeing? Adopt another role for observing; for example, assume that you are from a different country, work for a different company, perform a different job function, are a different age, or are a different gender.
4. What regularities or patterns do you see? Over time? Among different people?
5. What deviations from the norm, exceptions, or irregularities do you notice? What is the norm from which these deviate? Is this the appropriate norm?
6. Is what you observe similar to a situation with which you are familiar? Why, and how?
7. What don't you see? What's missing?
8. What details are you ignoring because they are, you assume, not important?
9. What is your unit of analysis? (For example, a person, a group, a company?) How would changing this affect what you see?
10. Be attentive to your emotions as well as to the emotions of others.
11. Concentrate on *seeing* as opposed to just *looking*.

enues of thought may counteract this. In addition, the use of analogy to increase the contextual richness within which issues are considered may, in turn, increase the chance of connecting fertile links at conscious and subconscious levels (guideline 5 from chap. 6).

In general, speculation can be helped by trying to view issues from different perspectives. As with perceptual skills, it may sometimes pay to imagine the solutions or ideas that might be adopted by other people, those from different cultures or other times and with different life circumstances. What explanation would someone in another department of your company, or even a competitor, give? How would you explain your idea to an elderly relative who has little idea of what you do for a living?

The act of speculation itself cannot be intuitive, at least according to the definition used in this book. It requires explicit effort. However, what can be learned is the intuitive reaction to engage in thought trials (once again, impose a circuit breaker). With practice, speculation can become less effortful and, in some cases, a source of satisfaction. In addition, the use of acquired mechanisms—which have become intuitive over time—can guide and manage the speculative process. For example, there is a need to know when to keep developing thoughts and when to rest. Experienced problem solvers develop intuitions as to when to use techniques, such as analogical thinking, to increase the odds of finding useful connections or alternative considerations.

As implied above, the quality of thought can be improved by practicing speculation. Exhibit 19 contains several ideas for improving your skills of speculation.

EXHIBIT 19   Improving skills of speculation

1. Use the word *because* to link observations and explanations. For example, imagine that your boss arrives late at a meeting and fails to apologize. Why? To generate ideas, imagine different ways of completing the sentence "My boss was late for the meeting and didn't apologize *because . . .*" Keep asking why.

2. Adopt another role. Imagine someone quite different from yourself, someone whom you might know or invent. Ask how that person would interpret the events. What ideas would she or he develop?

3. Try looking at the world from a different temporal perspective. Imagine that you are already in the future and are using hindsight to explain what happened in the past. Consider two or three different outcomes—perhaps "excellent," "bad," and "average"—and explain how they would have come about.

4. Ask yourself why your first idea might be wrong.

5. Don't hesitate to generate alternatives that seem silly or outlandish. Have fun! Be creative! Trying drawing or doodling. Don't feel constrained. Playing with alternatives—even crazy ones—can trigger useful ideas.

6. Don't expect your first ideas to be correct and ready to be acted on. New ideas are like newborn babies; you have to take care of them and help them mature.

7. Play with analogies and stories. Make connections freely.

8. Make the effort to generate different ideas. Quantity typically precedes quality.

9. Practice!

TESTING A major benefit—and a potential danger—of intuitive thought is the speed with which conclusions are reached. Moreover, in many cases, there is an accompanying sense of confidence. In kind learning structures, this is not a problem. However, when learning structures are wicked, you may learn the wrong lessons from experience, act on false beliefs, engage in self-fulfilling prophecies, and so on.

The fact that we learn so easily from what we see has its downside. We do not always think to learn from what we do not see, and, even if such information is available, we may still ignore it. This was brilliantly demonstrated by the psychologist Peter Wason in his experiment involving the number-sequence problem (see chap. 4). The point of Wason's experiment—as well as of many other related tasks—is that, once people have acquired a belief in a hypothesis (i.e., an idea), there is a strong tendency to seek information that *confirms* the hypothesis. However, if we are truly to verify the hypothesis, we need to consider evidence that could *disconfirm* it.

To illustrate, reconsider exhibit 3 above (see p. 81), which looked at the possible relation between the word *spoon* and the object spoon. Recall that, in order to assess whether there is a valid relation between two variables, you must compare two ratios, $a/(a + b)$ and $c/(c + d)$. If the difference between these two ratios is large, then this is good evidence for the existence of a valid relation.

You might also think of this relation as being that between a hypothesis that takes two states (true and not true) and data that also take two states (consistent with the hypothesis and inconsistent with the hypothesis). Now imagine that you have a belief in the hypothesis. To validate this belief, you need to observe data in all four cells of exhibit 3. People tend, however, to assume the truth of the hypothesis and look only for data consistent with this—in other words, data in cell *a*. Furthermore, if they take action based on their hypothesis, data from cells *a* and *b* may be all that they are ever able to observe. This is because they cannot observe outcomes of actions that they have not taken, that is, cells *c* and *d*. (When, e.g., you have two candidates for a job and can hire only one, you clearly cannot see how the candidate you did not hire would have performed in the job.)

Numerous studies have shown that people fail to test their ideas by seeking the kind of information contained in cell *c*—data representing possible disconfirmation. Although it is true that strategies that involve seeking confirming evidence can be quite effective in some environments,[18] you cannot count on always being in kind learning structures.

The key advice for testing can be summarized as follows: *When you have what you think is a good hypothesis (or belief or idea), ask yourself what could change your mind. What evidence would you need to see to be convinced that you are mistaken?* Clearly, you cannot expect to be able to answer this question intuitively. However, what you can acquire is an intuitive reaction—or circuit breaker—that sets in motion this line of questioning. Consider a couple of examples.

Imagine that you are interviewing a candidate for a job. After a while, you sense intuitively that the candidate will be successful in the job. In other words, you have implicitly formed a hypothesis that this is a good candidate. In this case, the typical reaction is to seek information that is consistent with the hypothesis. For example, you examine the candidate's record in the light of what a successful candidate would have done, and so on. What I am suggesting that you do instead, however, is that, once you are aware that you have formed an opinion, you should develop an immediate, intuitive reaction or circuit breaker that says, *Test this by looking for possible negative evidence.* That is, you should now start a line of questioning that is meant to determine whether the candidate is weak. For example, what did the candidate fail to do in his previous job?

As another example, imagine that you are thinking of buying a house. You have seen one house several times and feel intuitively that it is just right. At one level, you could say that you have "fallen in love" with the house. In these circumstances, it is normal to want to maintain a good feeling toward the house and to consider only factors about it that preserve the good impression. However, once again, it is important to invoke the intuitive counterreaction: Can I find information that will change my opinion? For example, have I really considered the implications of paying higher taxes? What about possible repairs? Is the neighborhood as desirable as I think?

Now, in many cases—such as those offered above—it may not be possible to see negative evidence. Instead, this must be imagined. In this sense, it is important to note that imagination may often be as important in testing your beliefs as in speculating or generating hypotheses in the first place. The key point is that, by asking questions that can potentially disconfirm your beliefs, you stand a better chance of making good decisions.

At a practical level, how do you acquire the intuitive reaction of starting the search for possible disconfirming evidence? After all, many times you may not even be aware that you have already formed an opinion. My suggestion is to start by analyzing your own thoughts about small, everyday matters. Consider, for example, the reactions that you have to colleagues' behavior. Why did one colleague come late to a meeting? Was it that he really did not respect the time or that he really did receive an important, unexpected telephone call? Take time to write down some of your hypotheses so that you become aware of the fact that you are constantly having opinions (see the blank page technique suggested above). One reason that we may fail to test our opinions by searching for disconfirmation may be precisely because we are unaware of the opinions that we are forming.

Guideline 2, *Seek feedback,* summarizes the point of many of the observations made above. In some cases, feedback will be easy to find. In others, it may be missing or misleading. And, in cases where it is missing, it may have to be imagined. The key is to ask yourself how you would know whether you were right or wrong. What evidence or feedback would you have to see?

The discussion presented above has been at the individual level. However, much feedback and learning is social in nature, and it is important to take advantage of this fact. For example, in some medical specialties, physicians hold regular meetings in which they discuss aspects of cases that are difficult to diagnose. In these situations, the criteria are often vague (so no one can know for sure what is correct), but the exchange of views can be most instructive. One of the attractions of a good academic environment is the chance to attend seminars and discussions where scholars debate their ongoing work. Apart from the intellectual stimulation that these meetings provide, there is a chance to test your ideas against the critical minds of others. In many ways, those minds act like different conditions and can be used to see how strong your ideas really are. Both medical conferences and academic seminars provide fertile ground for testing and generalization because the people who attend them are typically motivated to critique new ideas by identifying circumstances in which they do not apply. For example, a researcher may think that she has found a new way to solve a particular kind of problem. Her colleagues, however, will delight in finding exceptions to what she thought was a general rule.

These kinds of meetings can also be organized in the business world. For example, one very successful company, a world leader in certain kinds of consumer products, regularly organizes "confrontations" when new products or strategies are being considered. These meetings, many of which take place in the "confrontation room" at world headquarters, are designed to engender spirited debate about the advantages and disadvantages of different strategies.

As these kinds of meeting show, people can learn a lot in an environment in which specific ideas are put forward, together with evidence, and then critiqued. Not only, however, do people learn about the substance being discussed; they also acquire—often tacitly—mental agility to reason in this way so that the mechanisms of scientific reasoning become internalized or, in other words, more *intuitive*. An important implication is that the rules of debate adopted within groups can have a great effect on the types of reasoning skills that people acquire. To educate and improve your intuition, therefore, it is important to test your ideas against the arguments and opinions of others. An organized group setting that allows you to do that represents an excellent environment for learning as well as an invaluable source of feedback (*Select and/or create your environments* [guideline 1]; *Seek feedback* [guideline 2]).

Of course, not all groups provide good feedback. Indeed, too many are dysfunctional. In selecting or managing groups, a useful rule of thumb is to seek or organize groups in such a way that *what* is said is more important than *who* says it.

Finally, in exhibit 20, I offer a number of tips for improving your ability to test your own beliefs.

EXHIBIT 20   Improving skills of testing

1. Get into the habit of searching for possible disconfirming evidence.
2. Continue to generate alternative ideas—understanding is rarely complete. Ask yourself what you would expect to see if different ideas were true. How could you check these predictions?
3. Be aware that taking action may prevent you from ever being able to check your idea or hypothesis. That is, taking action may prevent you from seeing the outcome of the action that you didn't take. Act, or don't act, but don't fool yourself.
4. When possible, check your ideas with other people.
5. Don't expect to find "smoking guns"—except in well-defined situations.
6. To what extent are your beliefs in ideas dependent on particular pieces of evidence? How valid is that evidence? How would your beliefs change if the evidence were less reliable or even missing?
7. What evidence would lead you to change your beliefs?
8. Could what you see be due to chance? In whole, or in part? (Recall regression toward the mean and the gambler's fallacy [see pp. 123–125].)
9. To what extent do you want your specific idea to be true? Does this color your understanding?
10. Remember that, in dealing with people, it is usually possible to check ideas or hypotheses only at the level of actual, observed behavior. We rarely, if ever, have access to underlying motivations.
11. Seek feedback!

GENERALIZATION   How do people know that they have learned from experience? How do they know that the experience gained in a particular domain can be generalized to others? These are important issues.

The practice of writing down what you think you have learned in a journal has many advocates. At one level, it is a way of generating feedback in that reading what you have written is similar to looking at yourself in a mirror (*Seek feedback*). You can externalize or "see" what you have learned. In keeping a journal, however, several points should be heeded.

First, you should recognize the specific circumstances in which your knowledge was gained. What leads you to believe that a lesson can be generalized to a wider range of phenomena? Under what conditions do you think it might not be true? In other words, what are its limits?

For example, you may have learned something about how you are perceived at work. But are you necessarily seen in the same way in other settings (by, e.g., fellow members of a social club)? To what extent are the situations similar or different? For example, do you behave differently in the two settings, and, if so, how?

Second, does what you have learned suggest specific applications? For example, imagine that you believe that you have learned how to judge job applicants' responses to your questions. In other words, you have evidence that your intuitions in this domain are quite accurate. Do you think that this skill also applies to evaluating employees who already work for your company? Does it apply to selecting which painter to choose when redecorating your house? The tasks are similar, and perhaps your new skill can be generalized.

Third, does what you have learned remind you of anything? What is this? Were you right or wrong on previous occasions, and, if so, why? For example, in watching a movie, you feel that you understand why the central character takes a specific action. It reminds you of something you once did yourself. But, once again, how do the situations differ? Did the character in the movie really experience the same kinds of pressures as you did, or are you seeing more into the situation than is there? As in all these situations, what is key is the extent to which the situation in which you learned your lesson has structural similarities with other circumstances.

In short, posing the question of generalization is important. Intuition is the result of experience in a particular domain. When facing new tasks, we need to ask why past experience is relevant and, if it is, to what extent.

Practice

Skills—both physical and mental—are improved through practice. For example, recent studies of the acquisition of skills by expert performers explicitly highlight the role of practice and good instruction.[19] Learning to do things correctly (and seeking good feedback) and practicing the correct way makes good sense. This, in turn, suggests the need to help people practice learning from experience on a daily basis.

The framework provided above indicates many different skills—involving aspects of observation, speculation, testing, and generalization—that can be practiced to improve the quality of learning. It is unlikely, however, that all these dimensions can be improved at one time. Instead, an incremental strategy seems advisable. Start by working on only one or two skills until they become easier and eventually automatic. Ideally, the first step would be to assess skill levels across the different stages of learning outlined in exhibit 17 above. However, this is difficult to do. Thus, it may be more effective to isolate those skills that have been shown in the literature to have the greatest potential payoffs for improving the quality of learning.

Given the speed with which people are able to move from observations to conclusions in everyday inference, the first skill that I emphasize is systematically questioning your own ideas. In other words, *impose circuit breakers* that force you to *seek feedback*. To do this, I suggest starting with simple, everyday events and keeping in mind just a couple of key questions: specifically, "Why do I think that?" and "How would I know if my idea was wrong?"

To illustrate, imagine that you have tried to reach a professional colleague by telephone, leaving messages, yet have not received a call in return. In situations like this, it is easy to jump to conclusions in an intuitive manner—for example, to think that your colleague wants to avoid you. The danger, of course, is that you leave this belief unchecked and start to act as though it were true. However, stopping to ask yourself why you reached the belief and what evidence you would need to disprove it can be illuminating. First, you can realize that there are many reasons why your colleague did not return your call; second, if you wait, you could well find out *the* reason; and, third, by waiting, you may avoid taking an inappropriate action.

It should be evident that life would be impossible if you questioned all your implicit conclusions in the manner suggested here. My advice, therefore, is to start to practice this kind of activity a certain number of times each day so that, as circumstances demand, this line of questioning becomes part of your natural way of thinking. To reach this stage, however, will take deliberate effort. The reason that I believe that these particular questions are important is that they help the individual improve two dimensions of thought. First, asking "Why?" can trigger alternative explanations and thereby improve speculation (*Explore connections*). Second, both "Why?" and "How would I know if I were wrong?" can motivate the search for possible disconfirming evidence that is so important to the quality of thinking (*Seek feedback*).

The second activity that I advocate is improving your powers of observation. Above, I provided several suggestions, such as drawing or taking notes during meetings. I also believe that systematically trying to observe the world from perspectives other than your own can both improve your observational skills and be a lot of fun. For example, when walking through your place of work, imagine that you are six years old, and ask yourself what you see. We need to realize that, whereas everyone can *look at* the world, not everyone *sees* what is there. Seeing requires practice.

The points made above outline general ways of improving your ability to learn from experience and thus acquire better intuitions. However, intuition is largely domain specific, and this raises the issue of how to improve your learning skills in specific domains.

Charles Abernathy and Robert Hamm have made an interesting suggestion in the context of teaching surgeons to acquire better intuition.[20] Abernathy and Hamm argue that much of the intuitive expertise of surgeons lies in the mental scripts that they have developed for dealing with cases. In other words, when confronted with a patient, experienced surgeons are able to construct stories about how certain kinds of actions are likely to lead to specific outcomes, what to do depending on how events unfold, and so on. As experts, these surgeons reason by assessing the present states of their patients and imagining future sequences of actions and events.

Abernathy and Hamm suggest supplementing the formal training of medical students and younger surgeons with surgical scripts taken from real cases involving experienced surgeons. The scripts themselves take the form of recordings (presented in written format) of the verbalized thoughts of experienced surgeons who are asked to think aloud as they examine and contemplate different cases. Abernathy and Hamm argue that such scripts allow novices to walk through cases with experienced professionals, benefiting from their experience and tacitly acquiring their intuitions.

The concept of professional scripts is intriguing. If generalized, it suggests a way of providing the benefits of apprenticeship but in a much more condensed form. In other words, if scripts were collected from many "masters," "apprentices" could learn much more than they would in the course of a standard apprenticeship.

It should be emphasized that professional scripts are quite different from the case studies that are so popular in business schools. The case-study method has students discuss and debate situations taken from the business world, for example, a company considering making an investment or launching a new product. They are asked to recommend a decision and elaborate a rationale, and the professor uses the discussion to emphasize different conceptual points. In many cases, there is no right answer.

A script version of the business case study would be quite different. Students would engage in little debate. Instead, they would study expert analyses made by experienced members of the business community—possibly guided by a professor.

As it is typically used by business schools, the case study is not a way to build good intuitions for solving business problems. There is no clear criterion that distinguishes good from bad decisions. The experience is superficial, and it offers little chance to learn from expert practitioners. It does, however, socialize students to think about problems in certain ways and to use a specific vocabulary. In other words, it does add to the students' general cultural capital. In addition, it undoubtedly develops skills in some forms of public speaking and debate.

In addition to case studies, simulation games have become popular in many areas of professional training, from business to the military. In aviation, for example, the use of flight simulators is common and quite successful. What role do these simulations play in developing intuition? Once again, there can be no doubt that such simulations and games—and there are many different types—engage tacit learning and thus develop participants' intuitions.[21] Whether they teach the right intuitions, however, depends on whether the characteristics of the simulated environments match those of their real-world counterparts. It also depends on whether the simulations have been designed to be kind or wicked learning environments.

To conclude, practicing the skills of intuition is important. My recommendation is to start slowly by isolating a few skills, work on these, and then gradually incorporate them into your way of thinking through repeated practice. Over time, these skills will become less effortful and even automatic. At that point, more skills can be developed and added to your repertoire.

Intuition and Intelligence

What is the relation between intuition and intelligence? This is not a simple question to answer because, on the one hand, intuition is largely domain specific and, on the other, many people now argue that there are multiple forms of intelligence.

Three lines of ideas and psychological research are relevant to these issues.

The first is the work of Howard Gardner, who has challenged the notion that intelligence is a unique construct that can be measured by so-called IQ tests.[22] Instead, Gardner argues, there are seven distinct and relatively independent forms of intelligence: linguistic; logical-mathematical; spatial; musical; kinesthetic (i.e., physical coordination); interpersonal (the ability to understand others); and intrapersonal (the ability to understand ourselves). These forms of intelligence can be thought of as separate units or modules of cognitive ability and cover quite different dimensions. Gardner's work has been influential in educational circles and has been refreshing in the sense that it has drawn attention away from thinking that IQ in the narrow, academic sense is the only form of intelligence. Different goals require different skills.

How do Gardner's ideas relate to the notions of intuition explored in this book? First, both recognize the importance of domain. The main difference is that, whereas I claim only that intuition is determined by exposure to specific domains, Gardner also posits domain-specific components that are genetic in origin. Consider musical intelligence. In Gardner's model, people have different genetic endowments for musical intelligence, and these differences influence their later intuitions as musicians. In other words, their intuitive musical ability is not a function simply of education and experience. To avoid misunderstanding, I emphasize that Gardner is not saying that you need to be born with good, innate musical intelligence to become a good musician. But it certainly helps.

The second set of ideas is the notion of *emotional intelligence*, which has been popularized by Daniel Goleman.[23] Emotional intelligence is also domain specific and is similar to the interpersonal and intrapersonal forms of intelligence defined by Gardner. Goleman's thesis is that people are much more effective in life if they are able to combine academic intelligence and professional experience with an emotional "intelligence" or maturity that allows them to understand, relate to, and empathize with others. As such, we can think of part of Goleman's emotional intelligence as being intuitive in the sense that people may not know why they are acting appropriately in specific circumstances. In this sense, it is reminiscent of Antonio Damasio's concept of "somatic markers" (discussed in chap. 2), whereby, as a result of past emotional experiences, people sense indicators that suggest appropriate ways of behaving even though they cannot necessarily identify the underlying reasons. Like Damasio, Goleman points out the dysfunctional consequences of people lacking emotional intelligence. They may act emotionally when they should not (by, e.g., becoming too easily enraged), and they may fail to attend to emotions when they should (by, e.g., failing to notice signs of emotions in others). The emotionally intelligent person tends not to make these kinds of mistakes.

The third line of research—conducted by Robert Sternberg and his colleagues—is on *practical intelligence*.[24] Practical intelligence is what most people think of as common sense and is based on what the researchers have described as "tacit knowledge." It is interesting to compare its features with those of intuition. According to Sternberg, tacit knowledge has three characteristics. First, it is procedural in nature. In other words, it is knowledge about *how* to do things as opposed to knowledge of facts. (This is what other psychologists have called *procedural* as opposed to *declarative* knowledge.) Second, it is relevant to goals that people value; that is, it is used to help people achieve what they want. Third, it is acquired through experience and without help from others.

The tacit knowledge that underlies practical intelligence is thus similar to intuition in that it is acquired tacitly through experience. Indeed, Sternberg provides data that practical intelligence increases as people get older even though other mental skills, as measured by IQ tests, decline. (Apparently, people become "wiser" but not "smarter.") On the other hand, the proponents of practical intelligence claim that it can apply across several domains and is not limited to specific aspects of, say, a person's professional expertise. It refers to a general, everyday problem solving skill—or common sense—and, as such, does not have the kind of domain specificity that I claim characterizes intuition.

On the other hand, it would be absurd to assume that practical intelligence can be applied to all domains. For example, people with much practical intelligence would not automatically be experts in antiques, as is Diana the antiquarian, whom we met in chapter 1. But they would also probably have enough common sense to know this and not act as though they were experts. Thus, the domain of practical intelligence is common, everyday problem solving and, as such, is quite compatible with the notions of intuition developed in this book.

Finally, Sternberg and his colleagues emphasize that practical intelligence differs from conventional notions of intelligence as measured by

IQ tests. First, as noted above, whereas scores on IQ tests decrease as people become older, scores on measures of practical intelligence increase. Experience becomes more important relative to academic, intellectual ability. Second, several studies have shown that people are capable of impressive mental feats in practical situations and that such performance is unrelated to IQ scores. These studies include, for example, the order-filling ability of workers in milk-processing plants and the ability of race-track handicappers to employ complex and effective algorithms in making judgments.[25] (See also chap. 5.) Note, however, that, although these two demonstrations of superior cognitive performance are unrelated to IQ score, they are quite domain specific. In this sense, they are consistent with the notions expressed in this book as to how people acquire intuitive expertise.[26]

Summary Comments

This chapter has explored the possibilities for educating intuition. By its very nature, intuition tends to be acquired tacitly, in an incremental manner. We are typically not aware that we have acquired intuition in a domain until something brings this to our attention. For example, when faced with a decision, we sense that we should take a particular course of action without fully understanding why.

If we wish to acquire intuition in a specific domain, there is no substitute for good experience. The "goodness" of experience lies in the extent to which feedback helps people acquire the right lessons from experience. Is the learning structure kind or wicked? It is important that people understand this point because, in many cases, we can identify, select, and even create the kinds of experiences to which we are subject. In addition, we need to recognize when our experience could be misleading.

The quality of intuition depends, not just on gaining exposure to appropriate experiences, but also on the mechanisms that people use for learning from experience. I have argued in this chapter that it is possible to improve the quality of what we learn by improving the rules that we use for learning. Instead of just learning automatically from what we see, we also need to learn from what we do not see.

I have suggested a framework for improving the quality of what we learn that is based on the canons of scientific method. This framework emphasizes the need to develop different skills at different stages: observation, speculation, testing, and generalization. In short, I recommend identifying and practicing key skills so that, in effect, scientific method becomes intuitive. In particular, I stress developing reactions (circuit breakers) that allow people to questions their beliefs, to generate alternative understandings of what they observe, and to seek evidence that could be critical for determining the validity of their beliefs. I also strongly encourage people to observe the world with greater interest and curiosity. We need to *see* and not just *look*.

Whereas most intuition is domain specific, the rules for learning that I recommend can be thought of as general. Does this imply a contradiction? I do not think so. The rules that people naturally use for learning from experience are based on noticing connections and reinforcements and, as such, are quite general. My recommendations do not run counter to these "natural" rules but simply suggest certain modifications. Moreover, several studies have shown that it is possible to modify people's natural way of reasoning by teaching them normative principles and that this can lead to more effective decision making.

Finally, I conclude that it is possible to educate and improve our intuition. However, this requires much practice and, as a consequence, the motivation to practice.

CHAPTER 8

Further Issues and Challenges

One of the goals of science is to explain mysteries. When mysteries are explained, however, it is easy to lose our sense of wonder. We are no longer challenged because we understand. Nonetheless, it is important to remember that the phenomena underlying mysteries still exist. Recall, for example, the electric brae (see chap. 2), where objects are seen to roll *uphill*. How is this possible? The scientific explanation is an optical illusion. Once explained, the phenomenon loses its mystery. We can understand what we see at the electric brae in terms that are intelligible to us and that no longer violate our belief systems. There is no more surprise. Yet it is important to emphasize that the phenomenon of seeing objects roll uphill still persists.

Like the electric brae, intuition has a mysterious fascination. In this book, I have explored the phenomenon as a prelude to suggesting ways in which it might be educated. Whereas many people attribute mysterious qualities to intuition, my explanations of it are expressed in terms that are quite ordinary. Intuition is seen to be an important and normal element in the way in which we all process information. There is no magic about it— although I should add that, to me, all our information-processing systems are remarkable and that the fact that we can explain some of them makes them no less remarkable. Even after the phenomenon is explained, it still exists and should continue to command respect.

My exploration has covered a wide range of psychological research that is not typically treated within the same framework. The starting point involved feelings of unease concerning the whole topic of intuition (see pp. ix–x). Some of these feelings reflected practical concerns (how to help people make better decisions), others curiosity, and still others confusion as to what people really mean when they invoke the concept of intuition. J. Sterling Livingstone's description of how some managers are purportedly able to select the right employees triggers many of these feelings: "When pressed to explain how they 'know' whether a person will be successful, superior managers usually end up by saying something like, 'The qualities are intangible, but I know them when I see them.' They have difficulty being explicit because their selection process is intuitive and is based on interpersonal intelligence that is difficult to describe. The key seems to be that they are able to identify subordinates with whom they can probably work effectively—people with whom they are compatible and whose body chemistry agrees with their own."[1]

This quotation is taken from a well-known article that appeared in the *Harvard Business Review*. The main point of the article is to explain what is called *the Pygmalion effect* or what I described in chapter 3 as the process of self-fulfilling prophecies. From my viewpoint, the most interesting feature of the quotation is how useless it is to anyone who wants to improve his or her ability to select capable subordinates. Readers are told only that "superior managers" somehow manage to do this in a way they cannot describe. This clearly emphasizes both the need to elucidate intuition and the need to find ways of educating it.

In chapter 1, I described four different people (Kevin, George, Anna, and Diana) who clearly use intuition in their daily lives and who, in varying degrees, might be as successful as Livingstone's "superior managers." I next proposed a working definition of the concept of intuition: "The essence of intuition or intuitive responses is that *they are reached with little apparent effort, and typically without conscious awareness. They involve little or no conscious deliberation*" (p. 14). I then proceeded to examine five major issues: how psychology can illuminate the nature of intuition (chap. 2); how people acquire intuitions (chap. 3); how good people's intuitions in fact are (chaps. 4–5); how intuition fits into the larger picture of human information processing and what this implies for its education (chap. 6); and how we can educate intuition (chap. 7).

In this final chapter, I revisit some of the issues raised in earlier chapters and also raise others. In particular, I first reconsider my definition of *intuition* by contrasting it with the concepts *instinct* and *insight*. Second, I elaborate on the question of whether and when people should trust their intuition or resort to a more deliberate style of reasoning. Third, I briefly discuss individual differences. Fourth, I consider issues related to making educational programs operational and, especially, the question of why people should expend effort to educate their intuition. Fifth, I raise a number of open questions that suggest avenues for further research on both the underlying psychology of intuition and how we can educate our intuition more effectively. Finally, I provide some concluding comments.

The Three *In*-s: Instinct, Intuition, and Insight

In everyday speech, people seem to have little difficulty manipulating three difficult concepts that all begin with the prefix *in*-. These concepts are instinct, intuition, and insight. For example, consider such expressions as "he is an instinctive politician," or "she shows a lot of intuition in approaching difficult problems," or "what an insightful solution." Clearly, we all understand what is meant by each of these expressions. However, defining each of the concepts is difficult. Moreover, when we observe a behavior or response, we may not be able to decide whether what we have witnessed is the result of instinct, intuition, or insight. I now consider each of the *in*-s by contrasting, first, instinct and intuition and, then, insight and intuition.

Of the three *in*-s, *instinct* is probably the easiest to define. An instinct is an inherent response tendency that occurs automatically. For example, when you suddenly see a bright light, your immediate, automatic reaction is to shut your eyes, to shield them, or to do both. You do not think about this; you just do it. This response is an example of the inherited tendency to take automatic and protective action in the face of potentially dangerous stimuli. It is easy to understand why natural selection endowed us with such a protective mechanism. Eyesight can be critical to survival.

On the other hand, consider expressions such as "he is an instinctive politician." At one level, this represents a metaphoric use of the term *instinct*. It is unlikely that the person making the statement really believes that the person concerned has inherited the genes that make for good politicians (if these exist!). Instead, the expression implies that the person acts *as though* his genetic inheritance is such that he does not need to think through his actions—they come naturally to him. At another level, the expression also denotes a failure to explain why the politician is so able— hence an appeal to metaphor and the tacit admission that his aptitude cannot be explained.[2]

However, there are many kinds of behavior that lie between the extremes of truly instinctive behavior, on the one hand, and behavior that may be seen as instinctive but is in fact intuitive, on the other. For example, consider a professional tennis player. She may be genetically predisposed to excel at sports—like tennis—that require good hand-eye coordination. And, even if her skill is due to practice, feedback, and expert instruction, some of her actions can still be attributed to her natural athletic ability. It would therefore not be inappropriate to describe some of her shots as *instinctive.*

While it would be illuminating if we were able scientifically to determine the relative contributions of nature (our genetic inheritance) and nurture (what we learn) to automatic behavior, doing so would be extremely difficult, if not impossible. Fortunately, it is not important that we do so. The reason is that we can be confident that a significantly large proportion of intuitive behavior is learned and that we already possess the ability to influence the conditions under which such learning takes place.

Conceptually, I suggest adopting the convention that the term *instinct* be reserved for the automatic behavior to which I referred in chapters 5 and 6 as *basic*-level information processing, that is, information processing that regulates and maintains life. Thus, thoughts that recognize feelings of hunger would be classified as instinctive. On the other hand, thoughts that automatically recognize feelings of anger or fear in the presence of certain stimuli would be classified as intuitive. The critical distinction lies in the fact that the latter reflect learning and the former do not. In other words, whereas all humans experience the same reaction (hunger) when their blood sugar levels drop, not all respond in the same way to stimuli triggering anger or fear.

Now consider intuition and insight. In chapter 1, I illustrated the concept of insight by recounting the apocryphal story of Archimedes in his bath suddenly recognizing the principle of the displacement of water. Archimedes experienced what we might call a *flash of insight,* a sudden, unexpected thought that solves a problem. At one moment he was puzzled by the phenomenon he was investigating but not consciously working on the problem. The next moment he knew the answer. The explanation for this phenomenon provided in chapter 1 was that noting the change in the water level of his bath allowed Archimedes to see the problem from a new perspective.[3] Critical to this experience were the facts that, first, he was not actively—or consciously—seeking the solution when he found it and, second, he already possessed the knowledge necessary to solve the problem. What he had previously failed to do was access the relevant knowledge in his long-term memory.

Reports of experiences similar to that of Archimedes are frequent in the history of science. For example, the famous French mathematician Henri Poincaré wrote about one of his own experiences in the following way:

For fifteen days I strove to prove that there could not be any functions like those that I have since called Fuchsian functions. I was then very ignorant; everyday I seated myself at my work table, stayed an hour or two, tried a great number of combinations and reached no results. One evening, contrary to my custom, I drank black coffee and could not sleep. Ideas rose in crowds; I felt them collide until pairs interlocked, so to speak, making a stable combination. By the next morning I had established the existence of a class of Fuchsian functions, those which come from the hypergeometric series; I only had to write out the results, which took but a few hours.[4]

From the viewpoint of this book, it is important to note that this phenomenon reflects the operation of subconscious processes that, for whatever reason, people are able to access at particular moments. The general process seems to involve three stages. First, the person deliberately works on the problem and thinks hard about it. Typically, it is a problem of some importance to the individual concerned. Second, the person puts the problem aside for a while. Third, when the person is apparently otherwise occupied, some event triggers the appearance of a solution in consciousness. For Poincaré, this was the sleeplessness caused by coffee; for Archimedes, it was seeing what happened to the water level in his bath. What is not clear is how much relevant mental activity occurs at a subconscious level during the time that the problem has been put aside.

Such flashes of insight are most commonly associated in the public imagination with significant breakthroughs—for example, Archimedes' bath or Newton's formulation of the law of gravity after observing an apple falling from a tree. However, they are not limited to such discoveries. Most of us, in fact, have experienced moments of sudden illumination— about both important and trivial matters.

In an important paper, Kenneth Bowers and his colleagues argued that intuition can be thought of as occurring in contexts of justification, on the one hand, and discovery, on the other.[5]

By *context of justification* is meant the kind of cognitive task in which people are expected to produce a final answer to a specific question. For example, many of the tasks discussed in chapter 4 involving physics and deductive and probabilistic reasoning are of this type. The subject is presented with a specific problem involving, say, probabilistic reasoning and is asked to respond (see, e.g., the problems presented in exhibit 11, on p. 127 above).

By *context of discovery* is meant the kind of cognitive task that involves guesses or hunches about possible hypotheses. In other words, once a problem has been described or seen, a hypothesis appears in consciousness with no awareness of the underlying process that generated it. For example, imagine that you are working on a crossword puzzle. At first sight, a clue may not mean much to you. Yet, after a while, certain words (i.e., hypotheses) just seem to suggest themselves. You are not aware of how the underlying process works, but you can quickly test whether the words generated meet the constraints of the puzzle. Moreover, you probably feel more confident about some possible solutions than others.

According to Bowers et al., "Intuition involves *informed* judgment in the context of discovery."[6] They propose that, when people are confronted with a problem, their memories are engaged and search is initiated by so-called clues to coherence. The Bowers model depicts human memory as consisting of mnemonic networks that can be activated by a process of spreading activation (see chap. 2).[7] The process involves two stages.

In the first, or *guiding,* stage of intuition, there is an implicit sense of coherence that guides the process of spreading activation, thereby determining which aspects of memory become salient, that is, activated. Bowers et al. stress that this subconscious notion of coherence need bear little resemblance to what would be considered coherent in conscious thought.

The second, or *integrative,* stage of intuition occurs when a certain idea or hypothesis has received sufficient activation to rise above the threshold of awareness. In this way, it appears to the person as if the idea has just presented itself, whereas, in fact, the subconscious has been working on it for some time. The output of this process (in discovery) is typically a hunch or hypothesis that is attractive to the person who has generated it but that may still need to be validated. And, indeed, in a series of experiments involving word associations and the recognition of incompletely drawn figures, Bowers and his colleagues were able to provide evidence supporting this conception of intuition.

At first sight, this view of intuition seems different from the kinds of insight experiences reported apocryphally of Archimedes or by Poincaré. However, I believe that it is a question of degree. In the cases of Archimedes and Poincaré, both men had already spent considerable time thinking about their problems and exploring mental paths that had proved unfruitful. Thus, when they became aware of the appropriate structure of their problems, they were able to recognize immediately that they had found *the* answers. Moreover, had they not possessed the knowledge necessary to evaluate the validity of their solutions, they would not have recognized them as such.

On the other hand, the subjects in Bowers's experiments were dealing with novel problems, that is, problems on which they had not previously expended effort. In addition, it is not clear that, if they had found *the* answers, these would have been obvious to them.[8] Thus, responses that appeared in consciousness were not accompanied by feelings of great certainty. I believe—although we have no way of knowing—that it is highly likely that both Archimedes and Poincaré went through similar experiences while generating *incorrect* hypotheses in the early stages of their problem-solving activities. However, because none of these early efforts allowed them to see the appropriate structure of their problems, they were quickly forgotten. In short, there is considerable bias with respect to which insight stories are remembered and passed on.

The scientific insight stories do differ from the paradigm studied by Bowers et al. in that, in the latter, the subjects had intuitions when they were consciously attempting to solve problems. However, once again, I do not think that this changes the basic process. It is a question of degree. Stories told to illustrate the insight phenomenon are simply more dramatic.

To conclude, I believe that insight is a form of intuition. However, the term *insight* is typically reserved for those moments when people suddenly realize that they can "see into" the structure of problems. Moreover, the phenomenon typically occurs when people are not consciously engaged in problem solving and is accompanied by a strong conviction of certainty, that is, of having discovered "the truth." At the same time, there are many situations in the context of discovery where people become aware of possible solutions and yet do not experience certainty.[9] However, as noted in earlier chapters, the degree of confidence that we have in our intuitions depends on our learning history. In addition, the validity of our intuitions depends on the nature of the learning environment in which they were acquired. Was this kind or wicked? There are clearly many cases where people experience insights that turn out to be quite wrong. And quite tentative hunches are sometimes correct.

What to Trust? The Conflict between Intuition and Analysis

Even when making a decision or judgment in as deliberate a manner as possible, it is difficult—if not impossible—to avoid the intrusion of the tacit system. Whatever the outcome of the deliberate system, the tacit system always seems to be present and can be thought of as a permanent circuit breaker for its deliberate counterpart. Do you, for example, feel comfortable with your analysis? How does the outcome of your deliberations compare to your initial intuitions? Do you understand why your intuition might have been mistaken? And so on.

When intuition and analysis agree, there is no conflict. But what if you cannot reconcile divergent recommendations? What should you do? Trust your intuitions? Trust your analysis? At an anecdotal level, many people readily admit to placing greater trust in their intuitions. Is this really a smart strategy? Or do people misrepresent what they actually do?

In chapters 4 and 5, I provided some evidence relevant to this debate. The studies reviewed in chapter 4 compared the outcomes of people's judgments with those of analytic models of physics and deductive and probabilistic reasoning. It is difficult, however, to generalize from these studies to our current question. One reason is that analytic models were used as the standard of accurate judgment. Thus, intuition could be only as good as—never better than—analysis.

A second reason is that we do not know the extent to which people actually used deliberate and tacit processes in making their responses in the studies reviewed. For example, we do not know whether subjects' incorrect responses reflected input from their tacit systems, on the one hand, or recourse to deliberate processes that did not use the same analytic model as the investigators, on the other. What we do know is that, in cases where problems were presented in more natural formats, responses tended to be more accurate.

A possible interpretation of these results is that natural formats—for example, video clips when judging physical laws and frequency formats when engaged in probabilistic reasoning—facilitated the use of the tacit system. However, on this basis alone, it would be foolish to suggest that people should put more trust in their tacit systems. For example, the famous Linda problem (see exhibit 11 above) could be taken as an example of how problems that invoke tacit processes (by appealing to imagination) have the opposite effect—inducing error.

The studies reported in chapter 5 provide more direct evidence. In many predictive tasks, people's judgments have been contrasted with statistical rules. The results are unequivocal. When people and models have access to the same information, the models make more accurate predictions. Thus, if people deliberately choose to use a model instead of relying on their judgment, we can say that deliberate thought is superior in these kinds of tasks. Once again, we do not know how much the tacit and the deliberate systems are involved in unaided judgment, but the decision to use a statistical rule for prediction clearly implies deliberate thought. Interestingly, in at least two studies, subjects were given the option of making predictions using a statistical rule or trusting their own judgments. In addition, subjects were paid according to the accuracy of predictions. In both studies, subjects lost money by trusting themselves as opposed to the rule.[10]

A possible reason for this result is that people sense a loss of control if they base the decision-making process on a rule. Moreover, because people know that rules cannot be perfect predictors in uncertain environments, there is a feeling that their use implies condoning errors that could have been avoided. Yet what people often fail to realize is that unaided judgment also leads to errors, typically more errors than would have been made had rules been relied on. In other words, people find it hard to understand that you need to accept error to make less error.[11]

On the other hand, the value of following certain kinds of rules is appreciated in the financial industry. Here, extensive use is made of so-called scoring rules to assess credit risk.[12] At one level, you can think of these rules as being institutionally enforced circuit breakers. Instead of relying on their own judgment, credit officers are required to use analytically based rules.

There is a considerable literature that advocates the use of different decision aids to foster deliberate thought. These vary from simple-to-use checklists to quite sophisticated methods of decision analysis.[13] They are all predicated on the assumption that the quality of decisions is improved when deliberate processes are substituted for intuitive. Moreover, some studies have provided support for this claim.[14] Bucking this trend, a few studies have directly addressed the issue as to whether people should simply trust their initial judgments—that is, intuitions—or decide only after some deliberation. The results of these studies favor intuition. Below, I shall discuss these contradictory findings. However, I first propose to consider theoretical reasons why and when people should have more trust in the outcomes of their tacit or deliberate systems.

To do this, I consider three questions. First, under what conditions is intuition likely to be valid? Second, when is deliberate thought likely to be valid? Third, how is performance affected by the match between type of task and mode of thought (tacit or deliberate) used? Finally, after considering the evidence, I shall raise two further questions. What is the cumulative effect of relying on the tacit system as opposed to the deliberate, and vice versa? And what happens when the debate is raised to the societal level from the individual?

The Validity of Intuition

The answer to the first question has already been discussed in this book on several occasions and centers on how intuitions have been acquired. *People should trust intuitions acquired in kind environments but not those acquired in wicked environments.* This important point can be amplified by elaborating on the discussion presented in chapter 5 that raised the issue as to whether the conscious self is "smarter" than its subconscious counterpart. Once again, I consider this at different levels of the subconscious: basic, primitive, and sophisticated.

As stated above, basic-level processes can be considered instincts. As such, they are the result of evolutionary forces and would not have come into existence unless they served some useful purpose. For example, it is unwise to ignore feelings of hunger and thirst when they denote the need to eat and drink. However, precisely because the evolutionary process involves adaptation to *past* environments, we should consider how the environments that we face today compare with those faced by our ancestors. Our instincts may not all be functional in today's world.

For example, consider the way in which the environment has changed over millennia in terms of the abundance and availability of different types of food and drink. For thousands of years, humans survived on the food that they were able to find. There was little choice, and people had to seize the opportunities presented to them. However, this is no longer the situation today, at least in the richer nations of the world, and the inability of the deliberate system to regulate the intake of food and drink has become a major problem. Too many people eat and drink too much and do not discriminate between what is and what is not healthy. In short, the environment has changed so much that always following the urges of the tacit system can be dysfunctional. The deliberate system must actively intervene—in the form of explicit self-control mechanisms (e.g., diet plans)—if we are to overcome the manner in which the environment has changed.[15]

In short, in considering whether instincts are smarter than the conscious self, it is probably reasonable to expect that they are functional. Nonetheless, there will be exceptions in cases where the environment has changed. Moreover, as civilization advances and continues to change the environment, the need for active intervention by the deliberate system will become even greater.

Primitive-level processes, it will be recalled, are involved in many of the automatic record-keeping mechanisms of the tacit system, for example, the recording of information on frequencies and covariations. For this, we would normally expect the tacit system to be quite reliable. And it is. However, once again, all depends on the extent to which the environment in which frequencies were experienced matches the task at hand. In earlier chapters, we considered the formation of prejudices and stereotypes. We have little experience, for instance, of women in senior posts in the business world, and, thus, those in top jobs tend to attract undue attention. This, in turn, can lead to attributing their actions to the fact that they are women even though gender may be irrelevant.[16] Therefore, to avoid acting on the basis of prejudices or stereotypes that simply reflect how our tacit system captures statistical features of the environment (e.g., the rarity of women in top jobs), there is a need for active intervention by the deliberate system. In other words, precisely because the tacit system so faithfully records what we experience, we need deliberate circuit breakers to overcome the automatic tendency to make inferences on the basis of statistical abnormalities.[17]

In chapter 5, I also discussed the sophisticated subconscious and pointed out that, in many cases, it could be wiser than the conscious self. However, once again, a person's learning history is crucial.

The Validity of Analysis or Deliberate Thought

In thinking about the validity of deliberate thought, much depends on the complexity of the task faced and the extent to which deliberate thought can capture salient features of that task.

At one extreme, consider situations where there is a well-defined and accepted model of the task at hand. Here, there seems little doubt that the deliberate mode should be preferred. One example is determining the sum of several numbers. In this situation, deliberate thought will typically produce a more accurate answer than an intuitive guess. Moreover, most people will prefer to trust deliberate methods (i.e., the rules of arithmetic), although they will inevitably make an intuitive guess as to how large the sum is likely to be. Indeed, as noted above, this can be thought of as an automatic circuit breaker that is generated by the tacit system to guard against possible errors by the deliberate system.

At the other extreme, imagine complex decisions such as launching new products, making large investments, selecting new medical treatments, and so on. In all these cases, people typically use significant amounts of deliberate thought. But, at the same time, there is an acute awareness that analytic models cannot capture all aspects of the situations faced and that small errors in analysis can have important consequences. Thus, decisions are rarely made on the basis of deliberate thought alone but are backed up by intuitive appreciations that are more holistic in nature. In really complex situations, this mode of thought is probably appropriate, and, when they are faced with major decisions, it is important that people feel comfortable with what they are doing. Comfort is best achieved through understanding, and, in this, both deliberate thought and tacit thought have important roles to play.[18]

Now consider decisions that are intermediate in complexity. These could include, for example, evaluating candidates for a job, selecting a product such as a personal computer or video recorder, and so on. The difficulty of discussing the validity of deliberate thought in these cases lies in the variety of different types of deliberate thought that can be applied. For example, one type is simply enumerating reasons important to the choice process. Another is constructing a formal model that specifies the attributes of the choice task and their relative importance, evaluates each of the alternatives in terms of each of the attributes, and employs a mathematical model to calculate the overall values of the alternatives. A great advantage of constructing a formal model is that it ensures consistency over a series of decisions that, in turn, can have a positive effect on validity.[19] The disadvantage of simply enumerating reasons is the lack of control over reasons invoked. I shall return to this point below.

To conclude, there is little doubt that deliberate thought should be preferred to intuition when the use of a simple formal model is appropriate (such as when adding a series of numbers). As situations become more complex, however, it becomes problematic to know whether the appropriate type of deliberate thought is being applied. Admittedly, it seems trivial to say that, if the appropriate mode of deliberation is used, people should trust deliberate thought. Perhaps it is more constructive to note that one of the goals of education is to teach people *when* they should use *specific* forms of deliberate thought. Consider the following two examples.

Imagine that you have joined a health club, paying a nonrefundable membership fee. Subsequently, you find that you do not like the club. Moreover, you have found another club that you *do* like. This is a classic "sunk cost" situation, and the appropriate economic model for deciding to join the second club involves ignoring the nonrefundable membership fee already paid to the first club. However, uneducated deliberation might lead to a "waste not, want not" argument that recommends postponing joining the second club until your membership at the first expires. Clearly, deliberation can take many forms, and education can help make the appropriate distinctions between good and bad arguments or rationales.

Second, imagine that you are making an economic forecast and have available the opinions of several experts. Which opinion should you rely on? If you rely on more than one, how should you combine their forecasts? Whereas your intuition may lead you to trust one or two particular forecasters, there is much evidence that your best strategy would be simply to take the average of the forecasts made by *all* the experts.[20] Indeed, explicitly using this "take the average" rule is an example of exploiting the power of deliberate thought. My contention is that there are many situations like this in which people want to follow their intuitions but are more likely to be successful knowing *when* to apply an *appropriate* rule. Once again, this highlights the role of education (see also pp. 272–276 below).

The Match between Task and System

In a seminal paper, Kenneth Hammond and his colleagues have offered a useful theoretical framework for thinking through whether we should place more trust in intuition or in analysis.[21] Hammond et al. build a theoretical framework around two important constructs or systems and their interaction. First, they postulate that people can process information in a variety of ways along a cognitive continuum that runs from *intuition* to *analysis* (see also chap. 2). Between these two extremes are various mixes of intuition and analysis that are characterized as *quasi-rational*. Second, they postulate that tasks can also be ordered along a continuum that differs with respect to their capacity to induce intuition, quasi rationality, or analytical cognition. Moreover, they lay out in some detail different properties of what they call *intuition* and *analysis* as well as the characteristics that lead tasks to be intuition inducing, on the one hand, and analysis inducing, on the other.

As a simple example, consider two tasks. One involves paying for your groceries at the supermarket. The other asks you to choose between different color bedspreads. In Hammond's scheme, the first task clearly requires and induces analytic thought. Whereas you may guess roughly how much you should be paying, most people engage in deliberate thought; that is, they follow the rules of arithmetic. (See also the example of adding given above.) For the second task, it possible that you could construct some kind of analytic principle involving the color spectrum. However, the task clearly calls for an intuitive, aesthetic judgment.[22]

Hammond suggests that the validity of people's judgments will be affected by the extent to which there is a match between the demands of the task, on the one hand, and the type of cognition used, on the other, that is, intuition or analysis. In other words, someone could find analysis superior to intuition on one task but intuition superior to analysis on another. For instance, in the example given above, intuition is likely to be inferior to analysis in assessing your grocery bill but superior in assessing colors of bedspreads. And, indeed, in a study involving highway engineers, Hammond et al. found empirical support for this theoretical framework.[23] Moreover, as will be seen below, this result has been replicated in a different context by John McMackin and Paul Slovic.[24]

My amendment to the Hammond model would be to stress the role of learning. The fact that a task induces intuitive (i.e., tacit) processing does not mean that this will necessarily be more effective than deliberate thought. For example, many stimuli or tasks can induce stereotypic reactions. But it takes active thought to question whether stereotypes are justified and to correct initial impressions if these are misguided.

On Studies Contrasting Intuition and Deliberative Thought

Timothy Wilson and Jonathan Schooler conducted an interesting investigation (described below) of the effect of introspection—in the form of providing explicit reasons—on the quality of choice. In reflecting on the question of whether people are better off trusting their initial feelings or taking the time to reason deliberately, Wilson and Schooler first make the point that many of our preferences are acquired unconsciously, through interaction with our environment, and that we cannot explain them because we do not know what caused them. (This is consistent with what Zajonc calls the *mere-exposure effect* [see chaps. 2 and 6].) They go on to suggest that, in many choice situations, there are also salient and plausible reasons for and against alternatives that people will recognize as being relevant. Moreover, if people think explicitly about the choice, these reasons are likely to come to mind. Further, "reflecting about reasons will change people's attitudes when their initial attitude is relatively inaccessible and the reasons that are salient and plausible happen to have a different valence than people's initial attitude."[25] Wilson and Schooler therefore argue that, if they are unable to justify their initial preferences, people will change them in the face of salient arguments. If we accept this conclusion, we must next ask whether such change is for the good.

Wilson and Schooler studied college students' preferences for different courses and different brands of strawberry jam. Subjects were divided into two groups: an experimental group, which was required to list reasons for choices made, and a control group, which was not. And, since, in studies involving preferences, establishing what is and is not "good" is always problematic, the opinions of experts were used as the criterion of "goodness." Results showed that, whether deciding between courses or between brands of jam, making reasons for choices explicit led to inferior decision making.

According to Wilson and Schooler, what happened was that thinking about the choice led the subjects in the experimental group to consider reasons that were nonoptimal. Thus, had they not spent time thinking, their responses would have been similar to those of the subjects in the control group, whose initial preferences were closer to the attitudes of the experts.

In a further, related study, two groups of students evaluated several posters and were allowed to choose one to take home. Subjects in one group were asked to engage in explicit introspection as they evaluated the posters; those in the other were not. About three weeks later, subjects in the second group were found to be more satisfied with their choices.[26]

Although studies such as these have been cited as examples of how intuition may be superior to analysis, care should be taken in generalizing.[27]

First, while some studies do show that deliberation can affect preferences if subjects are unaware of the origins of those preferences,[28] other studies have obtained the opposite results: that subjects who are aware of the origins of their preferences are less likely to change those preferences after deliberation.[29]

Second, in studies in which subjects did in fact change their preferences, the quality of their final choices declined (from "good" to "less good"). However, had the initial judgments been "less good," it is not clear whether, with deliberation, they would have improved (become "good") or declined (become "bad"). What seems clear is that, when explicitly asked about the rationale behind their choices, people will change their choices if those choices are not consistent with the reasons that they are able to produce. Thus, if deliberation were structured to highlight "good" reasons, outcomes might well be better than initial intuitions.

Third, subjects provided with decision aids that force them to make the reasons for their decisions explicit have been shown to be more satisfied with their decisions than are subjects who were not provided with such aids.[30] Similarly, in the area of judgmental forecasting, several studies have examined the validity of so-called decomposition methods. It has been shown that, when people are required to split ("decompose") the prediction task into subtasks, make judgments about the parts, and then use a rule to aggregate the different judgments, their forecasts are more accurate than when they are asked to estimate the outcome directly.[31]

Fourth, John McMackin and Paul Slovic have recently both replicated Wilson and Schooler's results and reinforced the importance of understanding the joint effects of types of task and cognition emphasized by

Hammond.[32] Specifically, McMackin and Slovic asked subjects to make judgments in two tasks. One involved assessing how much people would like advertisements (an "intuitive" task), the other estimating uncertain facts, such as the length of the Amazon River (an "analytic" task). There were two groups of subjects. One was just asked to answer the questions; the other was explicitly instructed to provide reasons for their answers. Results showed that, for the intuitive task (advertisements), providing reasons had a negative effect on performance, thereby replicating Wilson and Schooler. On the other hand, generating reasons had a positive effect on performance in the uncertain facts task. Thus, McMackin and Slovic also replicated Hammond's results involving the interaction of type of cognition with type of task; that is, intuition was seen to be more valid in an intuitive task, analysis in an analytic task.

Fifth, there is much evidence that, when requested to verbalize their thoughts, people shift to a more deliberate mode of information processing. What needs to be made clearer, however, is whether and when this leads to better outcomes.[33] For example, there is evidence that the performance of subjects engaged in problem solving is negatively affected when they are instructed to verbalize their thoughts, but this effect is seen only with problems that require "insightful" solutions, not with more analytic problems. Verbalization, it seems, forces people to act in deliberate mode and cuts off access to tacit processes.[34] Yet, as discussed previously, in certain types of problem solving it is important for people to access their subconscious. Similarly, recognition memory is highly dependent on the tacit system and can be less accurate if people are asked to make explicit use of the deliberate system through verbalization.[35]

Cumulative Effects

In chapter 6, I referred to the work of Ellen Langer, which is also relevant to the questions being considered here. Recall that Langer distinguishes between two types of mental activity: "mindless" and "mindful." In mindless mode, people act as though they are on automatic pilot. Thus, they simply let their automatic thoughts and reactions control situations and do not think through what they are doing. They rarely question situations in which they find themselves and automatically enact behaviors inherited from the past. Responding to stereotypes is a good example of this behavior. Another is the unquestioning acceptance of expert advice just because it comes from experts. In mindful mode, on the other hand, people are more aware of what they are doing and take control of their actions instead of simply enacting overlearned behaviors.

Langer attributes mindless behavior to three sources. First, she points out how we allow the categories or concepts that we use to classify the world to entrap our perceptions and understandings of objects, people, and situations. Thus, when we think of, say, a pencil, we immediately classify it as something that can be used for writing. But a pencil is a piece of wood and might also be used, on occasion, for other purposes (e.g., to help light a fire, as a book mark, as a chopstick, as a lever, and so on). Second, Langer talks of the dangers of automatic behavior that we have also discussed. Third, she emphasizes the danger of always basing actions on a single perspective. In her empirical work, Langer has demonstrated many examples of the power of mindful thinking and how, if applied on a regular basis, it can have important, positive effects on people's lives, for example, improving health and increasing longevity. Mindful people, it would seem, gain a greater sense of control over their lives, something that is particularly important for the well-being of the elderly.[36]

Finally, it may seem odd to include a discussion of Langer's work under the general topic of whether to trust intuition or analysis. Typically, this topic is examined by considering a limited number of specific decision problems. However, an interesting feature of Langer's work is that it relates to patterns of mental activity *over time* as opposed to just one or two isolated decisions. In other words, adopting a more mindful attitude toward life can induce important *cumulative* effects even though the differences between tacit and deliberate thought might be quite small in specific cases.[37]

From Individual to Social Choices

So far in this book, I have discussed how differences between the tacit and the deliberative systems affect *individuals*. However, groups of people—and society in general—are also involved in learning and making decisions. What happens when the debate over intuition versus analysis is raised to the societal level?

Above, I discussed the work of Kenneth Hammond and his concepts of task and cognitive continua. Hammond has applied the cognitive continuum concept, not just to an analysis of individual decision making, but to an analysis of issues in public policy. In particular, he asks how policy makers acquire the knowledge that leads them to take different positions. The key ideas are laid out in schematic form in exhibit 21, which depicts the consequences of different ways of learning, or—as Hammond refers to them—*modes of inquiry* (see also chap. 2). It shows how different variables interact with different modes of cognition, sometimes helping

EXHIBIT 21 Modes of inquiry

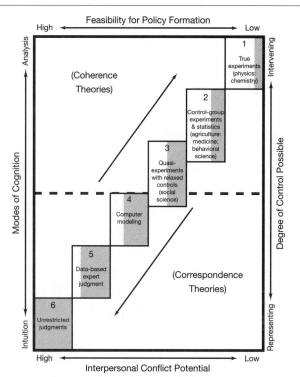

Modes of inquiry are located with relation to the extent to which it is feasible to base policy formation on them, the extent to which they involve intervention or representation of circumstances, the extent to which they induce interpersonal conflict, and the extent to which they induce degrees of intuition and analysis. The shaded area in each box indicates the degree to which the cognitive activity induced is covert. The closer a mode of inquiry lies to the upper-right-hand corner, the more likely it is to be associated with a coherence theory; the closer a mode of inquiry lies to the lower-left-hand corner, the more likely it is to be associated with a correspondences theory.

Source: Hammond (1996). The illustration is reproduced, in slightly altered form, from K. R. Hammond, *Human Judgment and Social Policy: Irreducible Uncertainty, Inevitable Error, Unavoidable Injustice,* © 1996 by the Oxford University Press, and is used with permission.

policy makers learn from experience, sometimes hindering them from doing so. This, in turn, can explain why policy makers who share the same goals often favor different means (policies) of reaching those goals.

The diagram in exhibit 21 illustrates the interactions between six variables and how they affect the different modes of inquiry that are represented by the six boxes that lie on the diagonal. The six variables are the following:[38]

1. *Modes of cognition.* These extend from intuition to analysis. See the left-hand vertical axis of exhibit 21.

2. *Degree of control possible.* This refers to the extent to which policy makers can or cannot intervene in a situation (see the right-hand vertical axis). In some situations, for example, it may be possible to intervene by running experiments (as when dealing with well-defined scientific issues—see the upper-right-hand side of diagram). In other cases, policy makers may not be able to intervene but only observe what happens, for example, by monitoring certain indicators.

3. *Feasibility.* This refers to whether the different modes of cognition can be feasibly used (see above the horizontal axis).

4. *Interpersonal conflict.* This refers to the extent to which different modes of inquiry have the potential to increase or reduce interpersonal conflict (see below the horizontal axis). The assumption made here is that, the more open and explicit the process, the less chance there is of interpersonal conflict based on differing interpretations of situations.

5. *Covert nature.* This refers to the extent to which the cognitive processes involved are covert (indicated by the shading in the boxes representing the six modes presented).

6. *Coherence/correspondence theories.* The different modes of inquiry differ in the extent to which they rely on coherence and correspondence theories, by which Hammond means the criteria that people use to establish what is or is not correct. The distinction here is similar to Bruner's distinction (see pp. 29–30) between "arguments" that are used to establish "truth" within logicoscientific reasoning and the "lifelikeness" to which people appeal when in the narrative mode. For Hammond, coherence theories meet the canons of rationality and thus imply agreement with abstract principles; correspondence theories, on the other hand, are empirically based and imply agreement with what is observed.

The diagram clearly illustrates the difficulty of acquiring valid knowledge about the world. It is hard to acquire knowledge that can be validated in some objective or, at least, replicable manner. The top-right-hand corner (box 1) indicates that this usually occurs only in true experimental situations in the natural sciences. Instead, as you move away from the ideal situation in the top-right-hand corner (box 1) toward the lower-left-hand corner (box 6), the ability to distinguish valid from invalid knowledge becomes harder. However, box 6 is the situation in which most human knowledge is acquired.

As the diagram further notes, the mode of inquiry in box 6 is that of unrestricted judgments, which depend heavily on intuition, are covert, can be easily implemented, have great potential for interpersonal conflict, cannot benefit from intervention, and rely on correspondence with observation for validation. On the other hand, the true experiments in the upper-right-hand corner for the most part involve analytic cognition, require intervention, are not really feasible in most real-world settings, have little potential for interpersonal conflict, and depend heavily on rational principles for validation. Between the extremes are different methods that vary on all the variables.

Hammond's diagram, as well as much of his empirical work, clearly illustrates the difficulty of acquiring valid knowledge about the world. In addition, it highlights the difficulty of getting people to agree with each other about what is in fact valid knowledge. If judgments depend heavily on intuition and people cannot provide explicit rationales for the policies that they favor, it is unlikely that people with different backgrounds will reach similar conclusions. This, in turn, argues strongly for the use of the deliberate system in the social decision-making process. At one level, it is impossible to avoid using intuition in reaching conclusions. However, it is unreasonable to expect others to follow your intuitions unless they have blind faith in your opinions.[39]

Individual Differences

As noted in previous chapters, there is considerable interest in the extent to which some people are more intuitive than others. Much of this interest is, I believe, fueled by everyday amateur psychology. We like to be able to describe and classify people and to explain behavior. In most people's minds, there is little difference between personality traits, on the one hand, and what might be called *styles of thinking*, on the other. Thus, when we describe someone as *intuitive*, we often mean both a style of thinking and a personality trait.

Psychologists have, of course, expended much effort attempting to elucidate the concepts of both personality and styles of thinking.[40] Moreover, both fields of research have been subject to cyclic waves of interest. Many appealing ideas have been suggested. Empirical studies, however, typically demonstrate that human behavior cannot be well explained by appealing to a few concepts of personality or thinking styles.

From the evidence reviewed in this book, it is clear that people's responses reflect two systems, the tacit and the deliberate. What is not so clear is when they prefer to use one or the other system. From a theoretical viewpoint, I believe that three broad statements can be made.

First, different types of task induce different types of information processing. Thus, for example, tasks that have a strong visual component tend to induce tacit processing.

Second, a person's individual learning history (including formal education) plays a huge role in determining whether that person will process a specific task in tacit or in deliberate mode. One of the key points made in the book is the similarity between expertise and intuition and the fact that intuition is domain specific. Thus, whereas for one person a task may invoke immediate tacit processing, for another deliberation may be the only alternative.

Third, ways of thinking have cumulative effects across time. Thus, we would expect people who are, to use Langer's term, more "mindful" to process information in a more deliberate manner than others. However, once again, this tendency is likely to be strongly affected by the context in which people find themselves.

As noted above, attempts have been made in the literature to develop questionnaires that determine just how intuitive people are. For example, in chapters 1 and 5, I mentioned the popularity of the Myers-Briggs Type Indicator, which builds on Jung's classification of personality types.[41] More recently, in an attempt to validate his theory of two independent modes of thinking, the *intuitive-experiential* and the *analytical-rational* (a distinction that is quite similar to that made in this book between the tacit and the deliberate systems), Seymour Epstein and his colleagues developed a questionnaire meant to measure individual differences in thinking styles.[42] Their Rational-Experiential Inventory (REI) consists of two parts, a modified Need for Cognition (NFC) scale[43] and a Faith in Intuition (FI) scale, that they believed would capture the two types of thinking.

If we accept that these instruments measure what they are meant to, then their psychometric properties provide clear support for two independent modes of thinking. However, the items in the FI scale refer mainly to intuition in the domain of interpersonal relationships, and this is particularly the case for the subset of the scale that was administered to the larger population in Epstein et al.'s studies.[44] Thus, from my viewpoint, I find it difficult to say that the investigators really captured tendencies toward tacit or intuitive processing at a *general* level.

In the light of the evidence reviewed in this book, I believe that it is possible to measure individual differences in the tendency and willingness to engage in deliberate processing, for example, to measure how much more "mindful" some people are than others. On the other hand, precisely because the tacit system is so dependent on specific types of experience, it seems more reasonable to assume that people's propensity to engage in tacit processing varies as a function of the type of task or domain with which they are confronted. Thus, whereas one person might be highly intuitive when dealing with interpersonal relationships yet have little or no intuitive ability when dealing with mathematical problems, another person might have the opposite profile, that is, be quite intuitive in mathematics but not in interpersonal relationships. This suggests, therefore, that a series of scales should be constructed to measure intuitive thinking in different domains or types of activity. Indeed, it may be appropriate to think of intuitive ability in the same way that people are now starting to consider intelligence, that is, not as one central construct but as several independent constructs (see the discussion in chap. 7).[45]

Making Programs Operational

One implication of this book is that, if people want to improve and educate their intuition, they must take positive steps that involve effort. Indeed, a paradoxical outcome of educating your intuition is that you will become more "mindful" in Langer's sense; that is, you will make more use of the deliberate system. In particular, you will become more aware of which type of thought—deliberate or tacit—you are using.

In chapter 7, I made several proposals that can help people educate their intuition. At one level, these can be thought of as proposals for self-improvement and, seen in this light, are similar to thousands of self-help programs that are available in areas such as healthy eating, exercise, language learning, and other domains. However, the vast majority of these programs fail. People begin them enthusiastically and may even make progress for a while. Nonetheless, maintaining commitment is difficult. Why should a program for educating your intuition be any different?

It would be foolish to pretend that educating your intuition will take no effort. However, it is important to realize that it is possible to take account of the way in which the tacit system works and make the educational process less difficult. Consider, in particular, the first two guidelines for educating intuition suggested in chapter 6: *Select and/or create your environments* and *Seek feedback.*

Once you have decided on the domain in which you wish to educate your intuition, it takes effort to define the appropriate environment and, in some cases, more to create it. However, once you are exposed to such an environment, the process of acquiring good intuitions is automatic—your tacit system does the work for you. Note that this is quite different from, say, an exercise program, each session of which requires effort even if you are in the right environment. Just being present regularly in a gymnasium does not mean that you will become fit. You must also exercise! On the other hand, being in the right learning environment can help you acquire good intuitions—even if you are not always explicitly paying attention. For example, in the apprentice system, students learn much simply by working alongside masters even though the latter may rarely explain what they do. True, as stated above, it does take effort and sometimes creativity to select the appropriate environment. But, once that environment has been chosen, the magic of intuition is that you can rely on the tacit system to do much of the work for you.

There is an important corollary to what I have just stated: because your tacit system is always operative, you are already learning in the environment to which you are currently exposed. Even if the environment is wicked, your intuition is still being "educated"—but in an inappropriate manner. There is therefore a huge opportunity cost in not selecting or creating the right environment.

The second guideline, *Seek feedback,* does not have the inherent advantages of the first. Many of the environments in which we live are characterized by poor and even misleading feedback. This is particularly the case in interpersonal relationships and in the workplace, where people do not always say what they mean and where we tend to rely on nonverbal cues that may or may not be valid. In addition, many actions that we take can be self-fulfilling; for example, we judge people to be friendly because they reciprocate our smile. On the other hand, there are many ways of engineering feedback. One is to ask for it! This may not be easy, but we can make it easier for ourselves by also providing feedback to others. Another is to pay someone to provide feedback. Clearly, this cannot be done in all domains, but there are many experts in different skills who can be hired. For example, consider consultants who specialize in small-group processes and other kinds of organizational issues. Various forms of psychotherapy may also be thought of as providing feedback (even if the therapy is nondirective). In short, seeking feedback does take effort. But the burden of the work can be shared with the source of the feedback.

Whereas the means by which we can implement the first two guidelines enumerated in chapter 6 are similar in that we can choose or create the environments in which our intuitions are educated, this feature is not shared by the other guidelines. Instead, these require individual actions and the effort to develop the appropriate frames of mind. For example, consider the guidelines *Impose circuit breakers* and *Acknowledge emotions*. Both require sustained individual effort before they can become automatic, and this raises the issue of how to maintain the necessary effort. One way may be to institutionalize a "time-out" procedure for yourself. The idea here is to associate an image—taking time out—with occasions on which you need to interpret your next "play" or "move," as in professional sports. Making—or imagining—the physical sign that indicates that a time out has been called may also help establish this routine.[46]

As a general strategy, I suggest first identifying which skills you wish to develop and then prioritizing them. To do this, start by assessing your strengths and weaknesses using the guidelines for educating intuition outlined in chapter 6 as well as the skills of learning detailed in chapter 7 (i.e., observation, speculation, testing, and generalization). Next, list those skills that you would most like to acquire, for example, to test systematically for disconfirming information, to seek relevant trade-offs in choice, to listen to emotions before reacting, and so on.

The next step is to limit attention to two or at most three skills. Then, over a period of weeks, find a way that forces you to remember what these skills are on a *daily basis*. You should be concentrating on reinforcing two components: knowing what the skill is and identifying moments when you could have used or did in fact use the skill.

To illustrate, imagine that you wish to develop the skill of testing beliefs or hypotheses by searching for possible disconfirming information. The first step is to develop mechanisms that bring the existence of this principle to your attention on a daily basis. Fortunately, there are many devices that can be used to do this automatically. One possibility is to make use of your personal computer. For example, you could use as the password for your email account the name of the skill or an easily recognized abbreviation of it, for example, *disfirm1*. Thus, each time you access your email account, you will be forced to remember the name of the skill. While waiting for your mail, or at other idle moments at your computer, you could then ask yourself whether and when you have actually tried to disconfirm a hypothesis.

The idea here is that the existence of the principle underlying the skill is brought regularly and forcibly to mind by a variety of processes that are instrumental parts of your everyday life. Other ways of doing this include having your computer interrupt you with messages bearing the name of the skill, having the name of the skill appear as part of a screen saver, and so on.

In all these cases, the idea is the same. You arrange to be automatically reminded of the specific skill that you wish to acquire. Of course, you could also use nonautomated means; for example, the name of the skill could be written on a ruler or some other device that you handle every day. However, in general, this method is probably more effective when actual effort is required on your part, for example, typing a password.

Once you have done this for some time, the existence of the concept should be well reinforced, and you will also notice that you pay less attention to the concept when, for example, you access your email. At this time, you should move on to another skill, and so on, and so on—until you feel that you have developed the appropriate automatic reactions.

It would be foolish to suggest that the ideas outlined will be sufficient to help you educate your intuition at zero cost. In fact, you should assume that, the greater effort you put into the process of education, the more you will get out of it. My major point, however, is to emphasize that there are important, qualitative differences between embarking on a program to educate your intuition, on the one hand, and starting, say, a fitness program, on the other. The main difference is that the tacit system is already constantly educating our intuitions whether we want it to or not. It is therefore critical to ensure that our intuitions are being educated in the appropriate manner. Perhaps the most important message of this book is to make people aware of this fact.

Some Open Questions

As noted in chapter 1, intuition has not been a major topic of scientific investigation. Nonetheless, psychology does have much to say that illuminates the concept, and, even though our understanding is incomplete, we can still help people in the important practical task of educating their intuition. In this section, I discuss six open questions, the answers to which would significantly advance our knowledge.

The first question is how to specify further the framework for considering the joint operation of the tacit and the deliberate systems that I presented in chapter 6 (see exhibit 15, on p. 196 above) and to test possible implications. This framework was inspired by many findings in the literature and was useful as a conceptualization of how, given the current state of our knowledge, we should go about educating intuition. However, in its current state, it is not a model or theory in the scientific sense. For example, it makes no predictions as to *when* people will use the tacit or the deliberate system and is silent about many processes.

One useful direction to take would be to provide greater specification of the tacit system in terms of subsystems and processes. In the present framework, this covers many possible candidates, for example, the different emotional systems, tacit memory processes, and so on. It would also be desirable to link observable intuitive phenomena more closely to specific biological processes. For example, both Antonio Damasio and Joseph LeDoux link their biological evidence to hypotheses about the way people react automatically to certain types of stimuli, that is, Damasio's somatic marker hypothesis and LeDoux's learned triggers. Matthew Lieberman has made a link between functions performed by the basal ganglia and processes of implicit learning and intuition. And Alice Isen and her colleagues have argued that increased levels of dopamine in the brain are associated with feelings of positive affect that have consequences for how people process information.[47] However, intriguing as they may be, these hypotheses and findings still leave much that is not understood.

The second question is what effects different types of tasks (or different environments) have on intuition. Three issues at least are involved here.

First, there is a need to investigate and elaborate the pioneering work of Kenneth Hammond on the concept of a task continuum. To what extent do tasks induce different forms of cognition? Is Hammond's conceptualization correct? In what way should it be refined? Curiously, although several papers reviewed above have investigated whether—loosely speaking—intuition or analysis provides more valid responses, only one (apart from the work of Hammond et al.) explicitly uses the task continuum concept to illuminate the issues.[48]

Second, there is a need to determine how task characteristics interact with learning. For example, we know that, for some tasks, increasing familiarity leads to more automatic or tacit processing. However, does this happen for all kinds of task? Casual empiricism suggests, for instance, that we learn to recognize faces faster than we might learn patterns in numbers. Are there connections between this type of phenomenon and the visualization hypothesis proposed in chapter 4?

Third—and central to the main thesis of this book—there is a need to characterize learning structures better. Whereas the evidence that I have reviewed suggests that the concept of learning structures makes sense and that learning structures do indeed affect the validity of the intuitions that we acquire, what are the limits of this concept? Moreover, is it possible to find better ways of defining kind and wicked structures a priori? How does prior knowledge interact with different learning structures? Do the effects of learning environments change depending on whether prior beliefs are valid or invalid?

The third question is the whole topic of implicit learning. Whereas there is already a sizable literature on this topic,[49] several issues need to be addressed in the context of the current work.

First, we need to develop a better understanding of the environmental conditions that favor implicit learning. This is important for educating intuition because a better understanding would provide ways of thinking about the kinds of learning environments that we should seek, create, or avoid.

Second, more work needs to be done on individual differences. In particular, it would be helpful if we were able to identify in advance who is and who is not liable to learn well in a given environment.

Third, the concept of cultural capital and the notion that preferences (or utilities) are acquired passively through exposure to different environments require further investigation. This particular issue has, of course, huge social consequences given the power of the media to determine many of the experiences to which we are all exposed. How can individuals learn to deal with these forces?[50] In addition to elucidating the concept of intuition, a better understanding of tacit learning could have important consequences for clarifying such practical issues as how to engineer different corporate cultures or how to facilitate on-the-job training in many applied settings.

The fourth question is the extent to which intuitive skills are domain specific. In this book, I have taken the view that, because intuition is dependent on experience, it is necessarily limited to the domains in which it is acquired. On the other hand, it is clear that some intuitive skills apply across domains. (For instance, the ability to classify phenomena in terms of relevant statistical models, such as the law of large numbers, is appropriate to understanding both opinion polls and golf scores.) Is this a paradox, and can it be explained?

One possible explanation is a distinction between intuitions that are acquired with the aid of explicit instruction and intuitions that are acquired entirely through experience. Consider the law of large numbers. This is typically learned explicitly as a statistical principle that applies when considering the characteristics of samples and populations. Thus, whenever a phenomenon can be interpreted as involving samples and populations, people can immediately recognize the application of the principle—and, if they do this often enough, the process becomes automatic, that is, intuitive. Now contrast the process of tacit learning, for example, learning to read body language. Typically, tacit learning is acquired through direct experience and without explicit instruction in abstract concepts. It would be illuminating to investigate differences between intuitions that are acquired explicitly and implicitly.

The fifth question is understanding different aspects of intuition and identifying the best ways of classifying these from an educational viewpoint. The assumption is that specifying and classifying the functions of different types of intuition will help identify their strengths and weaknesses. This, in turn, should facilitate the development of educational programs.

For example, in the work of Bowers et al., reviewed earlier in this chapter, a distinction was made between intuition in the context of *discovery* and intuition in the context of *verification*. Within the latter category, we could also distinguish between the role that intuition plays in judgment or inference and the role that it plays in choice. Moreover, in chapter 7, I suggested that intuition plays different roles at different stages of learning (i.e., observation, speculation, testing, and generalization), and suggestions for educating intuition were made using this classification. On the other hand, because intuition is so domain specific, it is legitimate to question whether classifying intuition by, say, functions of general learning processes is appropriate. For example, it could be that a more modular approach to developing intuition by domains will prove more fruitful.

The sixth question is defining, implementing, and evaluating programs for educating intuition. This is clearly a huge task, and there are many different ways in which it can be accomplished. It is illuminating, however, to distinguish between programs that intervene by changing the environments in which people act and those that actively teach people certain skills. As an example of the potential power of the former, it is instructive to consider the programs that Ellen Langer and her collaborators have run with residents of homes for the elderly. By changing those environments so that the residents became more responsible for certain material aspects of their everyday lives, Langer found that the residents also became more "mindful" and that this, in turn, had positive benefits in terms of health.[51]

As noted above, the theoretical framework developed in this book certainly supports the idea of educating intuition by engineering the environment. Of particular interest, therefore, is determining which aspects of people's environments have the most potential for educating their intuition in the appropriate manner. For example, to what extent and when are different types of incentives functional or dysfunctional? What are the effects of providing explicit instructions?

In addition to changing environments, studies can also evaluate specific tools for educating intuition. For example, in chapter 7, I mentioned the technique of surgical scripts advocated by Charles Abernathy and Robert Hamm.[52] As will be recalled, the idea behind this technique is that medical students can gain access to the intuitions of successful surgeons by reading think-aloud protocols of the experts recorded while analyzing real cases. I further suggested that this technique might be extended to other professions. For example, business students could study the protocols of leading consultants analyzing markets and companies. Once again, it would be illuminating to test this technique formally and see whether it could be applied across different domains.

Finally, within the context of specific tools or intellectual concepts, many studies could examine different aspects of the framework presented in chapter 7 in ways similar to the studies conducted by Richard Nisbett and his colleagues on the learning and generalization of principles of economic and statistical reasoning.

Concluding Comments

In the course of researching and writing this book, I have had the good fortune to discuss the topic of intuition with people with different levels of knowledge of the psychological literature. For those with little or no knowledge, the idea that intuition can be educated seems strange. Their beliefs about intuition tend to be categorical: people either do or do not have good intuition. There is, however, a sense that intuition does come from experience (recall Kevin the trader) but genuine surprise at the notion that it can be explicitly educated. All, however, seem fascinated by the mysterious ways in which intuition seems to function, and many have told me stories about intuition that, on occasion, were even mystical in nature. Intuition is very much a part of lay psychology.

As noted previously, I consider intuition—as I have defined it—to be a normal part of the way in which we process information. As such, it deserves to be studied in the same way as other topics in psychology. Moreover, precisely because the basic processes by which intuition operates cut across the way in which psychologists typically partition behavior (e.g., cognitive, emotional, social, and so on), I believe that it provides an illuminating perspective. Indeed, within the two-system model of tacit and deliberate processes, it is difficult to think about intuition without considering a fairly broad framework and the interrelations between different aspects of behavior.

A personal outcome of working on this book is a deeper appreciation for what I consider three important characteristics of how we currently interact with our environment. First, there is the speed at which the human race is changing the nature of the world in which we live. Human skills have a short shelf life. Second, so much of our learning is based on the tacit observation of connections or covariations that we just happen to meet in our environments. Yet we also know that, although this form of learning is adaptive in many situations, it is limited. In particular, it is anchored in the past, and it does not allow us to learn from what we do not see. Third, as stated by Herbert Simon, attention is the most scarce of human resources.[53] Managing our attention is therefore of critical importance.

My objective in writing this book has been to understand the phenomenon of intuition so that we can find ways to educate it. Clearly, there is much that is not known, and we can all look forward to the discoveries that will be made in the future. At the same time, it is also clear that psychology already has much to tell us about the nature of intuition and that this knowledge can and should be used in the educational process. As noted previously, if we do not take an active role in educating our intuition, our tacit processes will do this for us—the cost, however, is that our intuitions, or cultural capital, may reflect, not our goals, but simply our chance interactions with the environment. Finally, educating our intuition involves learning to manage our thinking. This, in turn, can help us make the best use of our most precious resource—attention.

APPENDIX TO CHAPTER 1 —
SOME BOOKS ON INTUITION

In this appendix, I briefly review four books that have been devoted to the psychology of intuition. These are works by Malcolm Westcott, Frances Vaughan, Tony Bastick, and Charles Abernathy and Robert Hamm.[1] I cannot claim that these books exhaust what is known. However, they do provide an overview of the quite different ways in which the topic has been examined.

Malcolm Westcott's *Toward a Contemporary Psychology of Intuition* is a scholarly work that provides excellent reviews of both the philosophical and the psychological work on intuition prior to 1968 (the year in which it was published). The book also reviews and reports Westcott's own experiments on intuition.

Westcott's experimental work is guided by his definition of intuition, namely, "intuition can be said to occur when an individual reaches a conclusion on the basis of less explicit information than is ordinarily required to reach that conclusion."[2] To test this conceptualization, Westcott investigated the extent to which subjects were able to solve problems in the form of verbal and numerical series and analogies. The problems were constructed in a manner that allowed access to an increasing number of cues over time, and subjects were asked to solve the problems using as few cues as possible. In addition, the problems were constructed in a manner that required no particular domain-specific knowledge.

In analyzing his results, Westcott crossed two measures of performance, relative success in the task and amount of information used, in order to identify four extreme groups. *Intuitive thinkers* were successful and used little information. *Wild guessers* were unsuccessful and used little information. *Careful, cautious successes* were successful and used a lot of information. *Careful, cautious failures* were unsuccessful and used a lot of information. This kind of analysis is, of course, post hoc and should be treated cautiously. Westcott found that he could not explain the differences between the four groups in terms of levels of academic achievement, and thus intelligence, but he did claim to find stable personality differences between the groups.

In a further set of studies using a similar research design and methodology, Westcott created a test of what he called *perceptual inference* in which he asked subjects to identify an object on the basis of an increasing number of perceptual cues.

The advantage of Westcott's definition of *intuition* was that it allowed him to develop a methodology that could test whether people differ reliably in their ability to solve problems or identify objects with less information than others. And, indeed, he found this to be the case. However, I question Westcott's interpretation of his results. First, it seems tautological to assume that subjects who solved the problems successfully were using intuition and that those who did not were not. *Wild guessers,* for example, could have been using bad intuitions. Second, in Westcott's first set of experiments, the stimuli were constructed so that they would, as much as possible, not require domain-specific knowledge (or in Westcott's terms "not require any particular subject-matter knowledge").[3] However, as I argue throughout this book, there is considerable evidence that supports the notion that intuitive thought operates largely on knowledge that is domain specific. In other words, a person can be quite intuitive in one domain of activity and not so intuitive in another. It all depends on specific, individual experience.

Frances Vaughan's *Awakening Intuition* was published in 1979 and is quite different from Westcott's book. As her title suggests, Vaughan's goal is to help people become more aware of their intuition, to realize what it can achieve for them, and to be able to use it more effectively in their lives. Indeed, much of the book is devoted to suggesting ways in which readers can become more in touch with themselves and, as a consequence, their intuition.

For Vaughan, "Intuition is true by definition. If a seemingly intuitive insight turns out to be wrong, it did not spring from intuition, but from self-deception or wishful-thinking." Vaughan also claims that people can "get information and know things intuitively by means other than the usual sensory channels." For Vaughan, intuition can be experienced at four different levels: physical, emotional, mental, and spiritual. As an example of the physical, she notes the "kind of jungle awareness which enables primitive people to sense danger when there are no sensory cues of its presence."[4] Thus, she argues, learning to trust your bodily responses is part of learning to trust your intuition. Awareness of intuition at the emotional level typically involves knowing how to react to one's emotions in interpersonal situations and is supposed to be at the heart of what is known as *women's intuition*. Intuition at the mental level involves the ability to reach conclusions or insights on the basis of limited information (a conception similar to Westcott's). This, combined with emotional awareness, may be what underlies the gut feelings or hunches described by people in the business world. Finally, spiritual intuition is associated with mystical experiences.

Psychologists working within the scientific tradition would not accept many of Vaughan's statements about intuition. For example, we see in chapter 5 that it is not always clear whether intuitions—or, indeed, other statements—are true. (It also seems odd to say that something is not intuition unless it is true!) In addition, most psychologists are skeptical of claims of extrasensory phenomena. Nonetheless, much of the advice offered by Vaughan seems sensible. She advocates, for example, opening oneself to experience, increasing the ability to observe, and exploring, questioning, and possibly changing one's assumptions about the world. As is shown in chapter 7, similar recommendations can also be advanced from a less mystical point of view.

Tony Bastick's *Intuition: How We Think and Act* is based on a Ph.D. dissertation and was published in 1982. For the student of intuition, it contains many interesting comments on the psychological literature, often quite wide-ranging. At the heart of Bastick's theory of intuition is the notion that people encode information emotionally. As he states, "Our thoughts and behaviours are the decoded versions of this information which, associated by their contiguous common feelings, tend to be recalled when we experience these emotions."[5]

Bastick develops an explanatory concept that he calls an *emotional set*. This is a grouping of feelings, emotions, thoughts, and behaviors that have come to be associated in a person's mind with a particular stimulus such that, when one element is aroused, for example, the emotions, the set becomes salient to the person and influences behavior. People can therefore be thought of as having learned many different emotional sets over their lifetimes, and it is these that govern behavior. Intuition, for Bastick, occurs when people combine several redundant or overlapping emotional sets, in a directed way, to resolve the conflict caused by the fact that emotional sets may be suggesting alternative responses. He calls this *directed primary process thinking*.

Bastick's theory sounds complicated. It is! However, I believe that its value lies in highlighting the role that emotion, and cues that elicit emotion, can play in intuitive thought. In chapter 2, I consider the subject of intuition and emotion further.

Charles Abernathy and Robert Hamm's *Surgical Intuition* (1995) is more recent than the other books considered here and quite different. The goal of the authors is to improve the decision-making ability of surgeons, and the emphasis on intuition is interesting in and of itself. The book derives from the previous lack of success teaching surgeons the analytic principles of statistical decision theory. In other words, it seems as though surgeons have difficulty improving their decision-making skills in their domain of expertise by studying formal, analytic methods that transcend domains. Perhaps, then, they can learn better from studying more domain-specific material?

For the general reader, the early chapters of the book are interesting in that they discuss various ways in which intuition has been defined and treated in the psychological literature. Indeed, the treatment can be described as encyclopedic. The book also covers much general literature in cognitive psychology, with a particular emphasis on examples that would appeal to medical experts.

The model of intuition that evolves is domain specific. Surgical intuition is largely a function of expertise and experience with surgical problems. To acquire surgical intuition, therefore, there is little substitute for surgical experience. In a companion volume, Abernathy and Hamm offer access to a set of surgical scripts that can be used to augment the training of surgeons.[6] Surgical scripts are transcripts of the thoughts verbalized by experienced surgeons that are obtained by asking surgeons to think aloud while dealing with specific cases. The idea here is that, in the absence of real experience, medical students and younger surgeons can gain much from studying, and eventually internalizing, the kinds of thoughts that come to the minds of experienced practitioners. In others words, since most surgical intuition is gained through experience, surgical scripts provide a way of artificially increasing the range of experience from which people can learn. Surgical scripts are discussed more specifically in chapter 7.

CHAPTER 1

1. See, e.g., Rowan (1986). See also Agor (1986), a report on the use of intuition by top executives.

2. There is, of course, also an extensive literature that discusses the kinds of errors that people can make when using intuitive judgment. However, these books have typically failed to define *intuition* per se. See, e.g., Hogarth (1987), Sutherland (1994), and Bazerman (1997).

3. For an excellent discussion of the contributions of philosophers to the concept of intuition, see Westcott (1968, chap. 1). See also the work of Piaget (e.g., Piaget, 1971).

4. For a review, see Westcott (1968, chap. 2).

5. Jung (1926).

6. Briggs and Myers (1976).

7. *Merriam-Webster's Collegiate Dictionary* (1996, 615).

8. Hammond (1996, 60).

9. See Brunswik (1952, 1956) and Hammond (1955).

10. See also Einhorn and Hogarth (1982).

11. Hammond (1996) provides an interesting discussion of the relation between intuitive and formal thought processes in the context of discoveries made by Charles Darwin and Richard Feynman.

12. The term *cultural capital* has been used in a somewhat different context by DiMaggio (1982). (I thank Mitchell Koza for pointing this out to me.)

13. Shirley and Langan-Fox (1996, 564).

14. See Sloman (1996).

15. See also Hammond (1996) and Lopes and Oden (1991).

16. *Merriam-Webster's Collegiate Dictionary* (1996, 605).

17. See Maier (1931) and Wertheimer (1959).

18. In other words, if two monks must cross at a single point on the same day, there must be a point that the same monk will cross on different days.

19. See Ohlsson (1992).

20. Many references support statements made in this section. Additional readable accounts are provided by Damasio (1994) and Pinker (1997).

21. For a more complete discussion of the meaning of *consciousness,* see Damasio (1999).

22. Miller (1956) is the classic reference to such limitations and still one of the most readable.

23. Whitehead (1911).

24. Tversky and Kahneman (1973).

25. People also learn by being told that there is an association between two variables, and this subsequently guides what they "notice."

26. In chap. 3, where learning is discussed in greater detail, I prefer to use the expression *connections* rather than *associations* or *contingencies.*

27. See, e.g., Ericsson and Charness (1994).

28. See Rogers (1961). This point is amplified in chap. 7 below.

CHAPTER 2

1. *Brae* is a Scottish word meaning "hillside" or "slope."

2. See Hammond (1996).

3. See Bruner (1986, 11).

4. Holbrook and Schindler (1994) specifically note the importance of implicit culture in reaching potential customers in advertising. They provide evidence that different cohorts are likely to be sensitive to the cultural figures who were salient at particular formative times in their lives.

5. Schank and Abelson (1977); Abelson (1981).

6. Epstein (1994) also points to a number of other theorists who have postulated two (or more) modes of processing. These include Freud's (1900/1953) distinction between the primary process and the secondary process (but Epstein rejects Freud's depiction of the primary process as maladaptive); Bruner's (1986) paradigmatic and narrative modes (see above); several classifications of phenomena in cognitive psychology; and proposals from developmental psychology positing a distinction between *logos* and *mythos,* or between rational, analytic and intuitive, holistic modes of information processing (Labouvie-Vief, 1989, 1990); as well as distinctions made by Tversky and Kahneman (1983). In short, Epstein claims much support for the notion that two distinct systems are responsible for people's judgments.

7. Epstein (1994, 715).

8. In chap. 1, I defined the terms *conscious* and *subconscious* by reference to information in working memory. Specifically, a subconscious process does not consume attention within working memory. My understanding of a *preconscious* process is that this also represents processing that takes place subconsciously or outside working memory. However, the output of a preconscious process may find its way into working memory and thus can subsequently consume attention. This means that people are not aware of how they arrived at the outputs of their

preconscious thoughts. I elaborate further on the role of the preconscious in chap. 6.

9. Tversky and Kahneman (1974, 1983).

10. In chap. 5, I consider the thorny issue of whether heuristic processes or analytic approaches provide "correct" answers.

11. Epstein, Lipson, Holstein, and Huh (1992).

12. Kirkpatrick and Epstein (1992); Denes-Raj and Epstein (1994). The importance of frequency in both automatic processes and probabilistic choices is discussed further in chaps. 3 and 4.

13. Rips (1989).

14. Brunswik (1952); Hammond (1955).

15. Slovic and Lichtenstein (1971). But see also Reilly and Doherty (1992).

16. In the 1960s and 1970s, an operational definition was given to the term *intuition* within the multiple regression formulation of the lens model (Hursch, Hammond, & Hursch, 1964). Imagine subjects who are asked, over a series of cases, to predict a criterion variable on the basis of several informational cues. Subjects' judgments are then regressed on the cues to define their implicit strategies. In addition, a test is made of the correlation between the residuals from those regressions and the criterion. If this correlation is significant, it indicates that people are either using cues that were not specified in the regression model or combining cues in ways that were not captured by the linear regression models of their judgments. This correlation (or at least a function of it) is said to measure *intuition*.

At one level, this was a brave, early attempt to define operationally a difficult concept. However, with hindsight, it is now clear that (*a*) subjects may not have been aware of how they were using the cues that did prove to be significant in their linear models and thus that even this part of their processing could be described as intuitive (indeed, there was evidence of this [see Slovic & Lichtenstein, 1971]) and/or (*b*) subjects could have been consciously using valid cues that the experimenter had failed to supply. In both cases, it is hard to see how one can justify the residual-criterion correlation as the measure of intuition when this is defined as involving little or no conscious deliberation.

17. There is an apocryphal story about a college at Oxford University where the dons used to guess aloud (in a kind of competition) the height of guest speakers. Over time, the person who performed best in this task was a mathematics professor. His strategy was simply to report the average of the judgments made by his colleagues. See also Hogarth (1978).

18. See Peters, Hammond, and Summers (1974) and also Hammond et al. (1987).

19. See, e.g., Dunbar (2000).

20. Hammond (1996, 147).

21. Hammond et al. (1987).

22. See, e.g., Skinner (1984a, 1984b).

23. Newell and Simon (1973).

24. See, e.g., Kleinmuntz (1968).

25. See Schneider and Shiffrin (1977) and Shiffrin and Schneider (1977).

26. I shall examine this point in greater detail in chap. 3.

27. Anderson (1983).

28. See Rumelhart and McClelland (1986). Mention should also be made of the so-called spreading-activation models developed in the 1960s and 1970s. These can be thought of as the forerunners of the PDP models. See, e.g., Collins and Loftus (1975).

29. Smolensky (1988).

30. Smolensky (1988, 5).

31. For a discussion of related empirical phenomena, see Greenwald (1992).

32. For work describing rules in decision making, see Hammond (1955) as well as Anderson (1981).

33. See, e.g., Tversky (1977), Mervis and Rosch (1981), Medin and Smith (1984), Medin (1989), and Medin, Goldstone, and Gentner (1993).

34. See, e.g., Schütze (1996).

35. The essays in Gernsbacher (1994) discuss many of these kinds of phenomena.

36. See esp. Anderson (1981).

37. Zajonc (1968, 5).

38. The frequencies were taken from the so-called L count of Thorndike and Lorge (1944).

39. Kunst-Wilson and Zajonc (1980).

40. Holbrook and Schindler (1994) maintain that, at certain times in life, cultural preferences are especially sensitive to the mere-exposure effect. For example, we may tacitly encode much more information about popular music and films in the teen years and early twenties than at any other time.

41. Greenwald (1992).

42. One need only look at cigarette advertisements. The central message of the manufacturers is usually conveyed by way of pleasant images, e.g., of attractive personalities and surroundings. Health warnings are presented factually but in such a way as to attract little notice.

43. Bargh (1996, 169).

44. Bargh and Chartrand (1999, 462).

45. Chartrand and Bargh (1999).

46. Cialdini (1993).

47. As will be seen in chap. 6, it is not clear that modern theorists can really escape postulating the existence of some form of organizing system even if the homunculus theory is now avoided. For a sophisticated discussion of this issue, see Damasio (1999).

48. What one chooses to call a *system* or a *subsystem* is to some extent arbitrary. Usually, a system is defined in terms of the function that it serves. However, some systems serve multiple functions or perform functions on behalf of other systems.

49. See Buss et al. (1998).

50. See the discussion of Paul MacLean in LeDoux (1996).

51. LeDoux (1996, 98).

52. Lewontin (1979).

53. See, e.g., LeDoux (1996, 32–33).

54. LeDoux (1996).

55. LeDoux (1996, 127).

56. Lieberman (2000, 125).

57. Damasio (1994).

58. Damasio (1994, 173).

59. See Damasio (1994) and Bechara et al. (1997).

60. See, e.g., Pinker (1997, 369).

61. See Lazarus (1984) and Zajonc (1984).

62. See, e.g., Isen (1987, 1993).

63. In a fascinating paper, Gregory Ashby, Alice Isen, and And Turken (1999) have proposed a neuropsychological theory that links the presence of the chemical dopamine in certain parts of the brain to positive mood states. Whereas they do not claim that increased dopamine levels cause positive affect, they do note an important correlation. This work is important because it begins to link knowledge of psychological states with physical measures of brain activity.

64. See, e.g., Mellers et al. (1997).

65. See, e.g., Luce, Bettman, and Payne (1997) and Luce, Payne, and Bettman (1999).

66. Within the framework adopted by the researchers, this means that people engage in more in-depth processing but that they try to avoid direct confrontation with the negative emotion by looking at the alternatives *within* attributes. For example, how do the alternatives vary on attribute X, on attribute Y, and so on? Note that this mode of processing can avoid facing the trade-off *between* attributes on each alternative.

67. Forgas (1995).

68. Pacini, Muir, and Epstein (1998).

69. See, e.g., Hänze (1997) and Hänze and Meyer (1998).

70. Slovic, Finucane, et al. (in press).

71. George Loewenstein and his colleagues have recently proposed that many puzzling findings in risk perception can be attributed to "risk as feelings." In other words, stated judgments of risk are heavily influenced—often in a preconscious manner—by such feelings as fear. For example, many people judge (or "feel") that travel by air is more risky than travel by road even though they know (i.e., have given deliberate thought to the issue) that this is not the case (Loewenstein et al., 2001).

72. This is not to say that you cannot put yourself in a situation that is likely to induce emotions, e.g., listening to music or watching a movie or play.

73. See, e.g., Pinker (1997, 414–416).

74. I am grateful to Harry L. Davis for this insight.

75. Goleman (1995).

CHAPTER 3

1. These are committees established by universities to verify that experimental procedures do not violate ethical standards. A similar experiment was reportedly also conducted by Emperor Frederick, the thirteenth-century ruler of the Holy Roman Empire.

2. Herrnstein and Miller (1996).

3. Hogarth (1974).

4. Watson and Rayner (1920).

5. Bregman (1934).

6. Seligman (1970, 1971).

7. Garcia (1981); Garcia et al. (1968); Garcia, McGowan, and Green (1972).

8. Maurer (1965).

9. Pinker (1994).

10. Marcus et al. (1999).

11. Spelke (1994, 1998).

12. Spelke (1994, 439).

13. Baillargeon (1994, 133).

14. Shultz (1982).

15. This argument is also made by Arthur Reber (1993).

16. I prefer to use the word *connections* to refer to what most psychologists call *contingencies*.

17. It could also be said that a complex association is a rule.

18. See Seligman (1970, 1971).

19. LeDoux (1996).

20. See White (1959).

21. See also Tarabulsy, Tessier, and Kappas (1996).

22. Hasher and Zacks (1979, 1984).

23. Hasher and Zacks (1984, 1379).

24. Berry and Broadbent (1984); Broadbent and Aston (1978); Broadbent, FitzGerald, and Broadbent (1986).

25. Reber (1989a, 219).

26. See Reber (1993).

27. Lewicki, Hill, and Czyzewska (1992, 801).

28. In a recent article, Matthew Lieberman (2000) summarizes much literature in support of the notion that implicit learning processes are "the cognitive substrate of social intuition" (p. 109) and, in particular, of several aspects of nonverbal communication. He further argues that, at a physiological level, specific parts of the basal ganglia (in the brain) are heavily implicated in both intuition and implicit learning.

29. See, e.g., Allan (1993).

30. See, e.g., Staddon (1988).

31. See Einhorn and Hogarth (1978).

32. Under some circumstances, strategies that rely almost exclusively on cell *a* can be quite effective (see, e.g., McKenzie, 1994). Below, however, I show that the circumstances depend on whether the learning structure is what I call *kind* or *wicked*.

33. To simplify matters, the two variables have been dichotomized. However, the general point can still be made.

34. See Merton (1936).

35. Thomas (1983, 22).

36. Schwartz (1982).

37. On outcome-irrelevant learning structures, see Einhorn (1980).

38. See Hogarth (1981).

39. Compare the concept of exactingness developed by Hogarth et al. (1991).

40. See Roese (1997).

41. The differences between *short-term* or *working* memory and *long-term* memory were explained in chap. 1.

42. Bartlett (1932) conducted the classic studies on this topic.

43. Loftus (1979).

44. Vicente and Wang (1998).

45. For a similar phenomenon involving memorizing situations in chess, see Chase and Simon (1973a, 1973b).

46. See, e.g., Tversky (1977).

47. See Chase and Simon (1973a, 1973b).

48. Ericsson and Lehmann (1996, 294).

49. Ericsson and Lehmann (1996, 290).

50. LeDoux (1996, 180). See also Claparède (1951).

CHAPTER 4

1. Kahneman and Tversky (1982, 124).

2. Tversky and Kahneman (1983, 313–314).

3. Detlof von Winterfeldt and Ward Edwards (1986, chap. 13) provide an interesting discussion of what is and what is not an intuition. They also propose a classification of different types of intuition that is similar to Kahneman and Tversky's.

4. Compare Einhorn and Hogarth (1981).

5. See, e.g., Birnbaum (1983).

6. Baillargeon (1994).

7. Baillargeon (1994, 134).

8. Vosniadou and Brewer (1992).

9. Shanon (1976).

10. McCloskey (1983).

11. McCloskey, Caramazza, and Green (1980); McCloskey (1983); Kaiser, Proffitt, and McCloskey (1985); Kaiser, Jonides, and Alexander (1986).

12. For discussions of impetus theory and the hold that this had in the Middle Ages as well as among students who are starting to learn physics, see, e.g., Shanon (1976), Clement (1982), and McCloskey (1983).

13. McCloskey (1983).

14. Kaiser, Jonides, and Alexander (1986).

15. Kaiser, Jonides, and Alexander (1986, 311).

16. Kaiser, McCloskey, and Proffitt (1986).

17. Proffitt, Kaiser, and Whelan (1990).

18. Proffitt and Gilden (1989).

19. Piaget and Inhelder (1958).

20. Proffitt and Gilden (1989, 389).

21. See Shanon (1976) and Kaiser, Proffitt, and Anderson (1985), respectively.

22. See also Kaiser, Proffitt, and McCloskey (1985).

23. Proffitt, Kaiser, and Whelan (1990).

24. Wason (1966).

25. See, e.g., Gigerenzer and Hug (1992).

26. Wason and Johnson-Laird (1972).

27. Cheng and Holyoak (1985); Cheng et al. (1986).

28. Cosmides (1989); Gigerenzer and Hug (1992)

29. Liberman and Klar (1996)

30. Wason (1960).

31. This point is nicely illustrated by the game Mastermind.

32. See also Bruner, Goodnow, and Austin (1956).

33. Klayman and Ha (1987).

34. de Finetti (1937); Savage (1954).

35. Einhorn and Hogarth (1981); Cosmides and Tooby (1996); Staddon (1988).

36. See, e.g., Kahneman and Tversky (1996) and Gigerenzer (1996a).

37. Michael Doherty (personal communication, 2000) has made the interesting observation that people can differ considerably in the extent to which they visualize phenomena and/or make use of imagery in thought. This therefore suggests a possible individual difference variable that could explain variations in the types of responses that people give to some of the problems discussed in this chapter. Presumably, more highly visual people make greater use of their tacit systems.

38. Kahneman and Tversky (1973).

39. Gilovich, Vallone, and Tversky (1985).

40. Chapman (1967); Chapman and Chapman (1969).

41. Kareev (1995) has shown that the sampling distributions of correlations tend to be quite skewed. The consequence is that people may overestimate the strength of connections between variables when samples are small (Kareev, Lieberman, & Lev, 1997). At one level, this may be functional in that possible connections are brought to attention. However, it can also lead to overestimating the strength of relations between variables.

42. Nisbett et al. (1983).

43. People tend to reason analytically when faced with this problem, but their analysis is typically incomplete. They know that, if you choose two people at random, the probability of their both having the same birthday is 1/365 (assuming that each day of the year is equally likely and excluding leap years). However, they fail to imagine how this will translate into the probability of any two out of twenty-three having the same birthday. An illuminating way to examine this problem is to note that the probability of at least two people having the same birthday is the same as one minus the probability that no two persons have the same birthday (i.e., one minus the complementary event). To calculate this, ask yourself first how many possible distributions of birthdays (over the year or 365 days) twenty-three people could have. This is 365^{23}. Now ask yourself how many ways no two people (out of twenty-three) could have the same birthday. This is $365 \times 364 \times 363 \times \ldots \times 343$. Thus, the probability that at least two people have the same birthday is $1 - [(365 \times 364 \times 363 \times \ldots \times 343)/365^{23}]$, or 0.5073. More generally, letting n be the number of people in the group, the probability that at least

two have the same birthday is given by the formula $1 - \{[365 \times 364 \times 363 \times \ldots \times 365(-n + 1)]/365^n\}$. (I thank Michael Greenacre for providing me with the explicit rationale.)

44. Tversky and Kahneman (1983).

45. Kahneman and Tversky (1972).

46. This particular problem was first introduced in the literature by Eddy (1982). The wording, however, has been taken from Gigerenzer (1996b). See also Casscells, Schoenberger, and Grayboys (1978), Gigerenzer and Hoffrage (1995), and Hammerton (1973).

47. For an illuminating discussion on the difference between "transparent" and "opaque" problems, see Tversky and Kahneman (1986).

48. See, e.g., Estes (1976).

49. Kleiter (1994).

50. Fiedler (1988).

51. Gigerenzer and Hoffrage (1995); Gigerenzer (1996b).

52. From Gigerenzer (1996b).

53. See Cosmides and Tooby (1996) and Christensen-Szalanski and Beach (1982).

54. Tversky and Kahneman (1980). By using a straightforward application of probabilistic reasoning, "the" answer to this question is 0.41 (however, see also Birnbaum, 1983).

55. Mellers and McGraw (1999, 417). See also Fiedler et al. (2000).

56. Slovic, Monahan, and MacGregor (2000).

57. Hendrickx, Vlek, and Oppewal (1989).

58. Tversky and Kahneman (1983).

59. Tversky and Kahneman (1983) refer to this as being an instance of their availability heuristic (Tversky & Kahneman, 1973).

60. The word *visualize* is used here broadly, as meaning "bringing to mind in a concrete kind of way." Thus, for some people, visualization could involve imagining words in written form; for others, it could involve saying words to themselves.

61. See Campbell (1959) and Hogarth (1981, 1987).

CHAPTER 5

1. Simon (1996).

2. Reber (1989a, 231).

3. Greenwald (1992); Loftus and Klinger (1992).

4. See, e.g., Epstein (1994, 1998).

5. See also Hogarth (1981).

6. Michael Doherty (personal communication, 2000) has remarked that it

seems odd to compare intuitions in the form of inferences (e.g., forming impressions about the office atmosphere) and actions (e.g., swerving to avoid other pedestrians when walking down the street). I believe, however, that both situations involve intuitive inferences; it is just that in the latter the responses that are triggered are immediate and in the former they are not. Note also that the intuitive inferences formed while waiting in the office could influence subsequent actions, e.g., how you interact with the people there.

7. See Damasio (1994). See also LeDoux (1996) on *learned triggers*.

8. Campbell (1960). See also Hogarth (1987).

9. See Hogarth (1987, chap. 8). Selwyn Becker (personal communication, 2000) also makes the point that time away from a problem can alleviate fatigue that could inhibit responses.

10. As illustrated in Maier's (1931) famous "hat-rack" problem, attention can be drawn subtly to cues that trigger solutions even though people are unaware of the influence of such cues. Campbell (1960) also stresses the role of chance in solving problems.

11. I assume here that costs and benefits are comparable in the two situations.

12. See Dawes (1979), Einhorn (1972), Keren and Wagenaar (1987), Kleinmuntz (1990), and Sawyer (1966).

13. Dawes, Faust, and Meehl (1989).

14. Sawyer (1966).

15. Goldberg (1970).

16. Camerer (1981); Camerer and Johnson (1991).

17. The only condition that needs to hold here is that the models assign the right "signs" to the variables. For example, if test scores are positively correlated with the criterion, then models predict that, holding everything else constant, candidates with higher test scores will perform better. Recall, too, that both models and humans are basing their predictions on the same variables.

18. See Dawes and Corrigan (1974) and Einhorn and Hogarth (1975).

19. Einhorn (1972).

20. Yaniv and Hogarth (1993).

21. For example, it is highly unlikely that our subjects had ever approached their prior reading with the notion that, one day, they would be asked to guess the second and fifth letters of five-letter words of which only the first letter was provided. Yet they did have good notions about the relevant statistical distributions!

22. Blattberg and Hoch (1990).

23. See, e.g., Chapman (1967), Chapman and Chapman (1969), and Crocker (1981).

24. See, e.g., Murphy and Winkler (1984).

25. These conditions also apply, of course, to financial markets. However, note that the prices of financial instruments (e.g., stocks, bonds, etc.) are affected by judgments made by many people.

26. Garb and Schramke (1996).

27. Garb (1998).

28. See also Kleinmuntz (1990).

29. This idea was nicely captured in a paper by Robyn Dawes and Bernard Corrigan, who stated, "The whole trick is to decide what variables to look at and then to know how to add" (1974, 105).

30. For a review, see Russo and Schoemaker (1989). For an update on these studies and specification of the conditions under which overconfidence effects vary in size, see Klayman et al. (1999).

31. See, e.g., Fischhoff (1982).

32. Fischhoff, Slovic, and Lichtenstein (1978).

33. Gigerenzer, Hoffrage, and Kleinbölting (1991).

34. Gigerenzer, Hoffrage, and Kleinbölting (1991) also demonstrate that calibration is affected by the extent to which the questions that subjects are asked are representative of the subjects' knowledge base. Representative questions lead to better calibration.

35. Yaniv and Foster (1995).

36. Murphy and Winkler (1984).

37. Salovey and Mayer (1990) and Goleman (1995).

38. See, e.g., McArthur and Baron (1983), Swann (1984), and Kruglanski (1989).

39. Ross (1977).

40. These statements should be taken as simplifications of more complex phenomena.

41. Funder (1995).

42. Brunswik (1956).

43. See, e.g., Hogarth (1981).

44. See, e.g., Simon and Chase (1973), Ericsson and Smith (1991), Ericsson, Krampe, and Tesch-Römer (1993), Ericsson and Charness (1994), and Ericsson and Lehmann (1996).

45. See, e.g., Camerer and Johnson (1991).

46. This also suggests why experts sometimes fail to solve problems in simple ways. The frameworks at their disposal are general-purpose algorithms that may obscure the simple structure of some problems.

47. Klein (1998).

48. Ericsson and Charness (1994).

49. Gardner (1995).

50. Ericsson and Charness (1994, 731).

51. In a recent review of the literature on intuition, Shirley and Langan-Fox (1996) have stated, "The notion of women being more intuitive than men has not been supported by research" (p. 566). I believe that, as formulated, this assertion has little meaning because it is important to state in which specific domains women are supposed to be more intuitive than men.

52. Graham and Ickes (1997, 118).

53. Hall (1984, 143 [quotation], 144). In a more recent study, Kari Edwards (1998) has shown that both men and women are well attuned to temporal cues in facial expressions of emotion (i.e., cues that indicate the onset of an emotional expression in another person, e.g., someone beginning to be angry). However, in tests of this skill, women performed significantly better than men.

54. For evidence that people with minority status have better observational skills than those with majority status, see Frabble, Blackstone, and Scherbaum (1990).

55. Meyers-Levy and Maheswaran (1991); Meyers-Levy (1998).

56. Scribner (1984).

57. Ceci and Liker (1986, 1988).

58. See, e.g., Briggs and Myers (1976).

59. See, e.g., Kolb (1984) and Boyatzis and Kolb (1991).

60. For more discussion of conflict in choice, see Hogarth (1987, chap. 4). For extensive experimental evidence and detailed discussion of the effects of different strategies, see Payne, Bettman, and Johnson (1993).

61. See, e.g., Hogarth (1982).

62. Much of this section is inspired by the work of Amos Tversky and Daniel Kahneman. See, in particular, Kahneman and Tversky (1979) and Tversky and Kahneman (1981).

63. See Hogarth (1987, 94–95) as well as Tversky and Kahneman (1981).

64. Tversky and Kahneman (1981); Hogarth (1982).

65. See, e.g., Thaler (1991).

66. There is not a large conceptual difference between the *status quo bias* and the *endowment effect*. The former typically refers to the reluctance to change something that you already own or do in favor of an alternative; that is, you are fixated in the status quo. For example, imagine someone who allocates savings to a pension fund by investing equal amounts in risky and safer investments (stocks and bonds). The status quo bias involves persisting in this pattern of behavior even if aware of other, possibly more attractive options (e.g., that, historically, stocks have provided greater returns over time than bonds). The endowment effect, on the other hand, refers to the psychological value that people attach to what they own, or have been given, and their unwillingness to part with this as demonstrated in the experiment involving mugs and pens.

67. See Shafir, Simonson, and Tversky (1993).

68. From Hogarth (1987, 5–6), which is adapted from Einhorn (1980).

69. I have verified this statement with literally hundreds of managers attending seminars that I have conducted.

70. Even in situations that are not random, costless strategies can be surprisingly effective (see Hogarth & Makridakis, 1981).

71. See, e.g., Dawes and Corrigan (1974), Einhorn and Hogarth (1975), and Einhorn and McCoach (1977).

72. See von Winterfeldt and Edwards (1986).

73. To see why, think of a two-attribute (say, price and delivery time) problem. If price and delivery time are positively correlated, you will have no conflict because one alternative will probably be better than the other on both dimensions (low price and short delivery time as opposed to high price and long delivery time). Thus, you have a choice problem only when the attributes are negatively correlated (e.g., low price and long delivery time as opposed to high price and short delivery time). In order to make a choice in this case, you will have to decide which variable is the more important (price or delivery time and by how much). If you simply decide to ignore one of the two attributes, then choice can be determined by a single variable (price or delivery time).

74. See Payne, Bettman, and Johnson (1993).

75. See Gigerenzer, Todd, and ABC Research Group (1999).

CHAPTER 6

1. For a fascinating discussion of this point, see Campbell (1959). Note, too, that experts seem to find ways in which to increase the effective capacity of their short-term or working memory (see, e.g., Ericsson & Kintsch, 1995; Ericsson & Lehmann, 1996).

2. See, e.g., the excellent review of these and related issues in Pinker (1997). See also Brase, Cosmides, and Tooby (1998).

3. See, e.g., Broadbent and Aston (1978) and Broadbent, FitzGerald, and Broadbent (1986).

4. See also the excellent book by Arthur Reber (1993).

5. See Moore (1957) and a further example in Dove (1993).

6. See Luchins (1942).

7. See also Reber (1993).

8. Fiedler (2000) presents a fascinating analysis of how the nonrandom sampling of experience can induce invalid learning.

9. See Simon (1955) and, more recently, Gigerenzer, Todd, and ABC Research Group (1999).

10. This involves the repeated application of Bayes's theorem and assumes

that no individual starts out "dogmatically," i.e., by assigning a probability of 0 or 1 to a hypothesis.

11. For an example of this kind of work in the field of drug addiction, see Murphy and Becker (1988).

12. Kagan (1996).

13. Daniel Kahneman and his colleagues have conducted studies identifying some of the difficulties that people encounter predicting their own preferences (see, e.g., Kahneman & Snell, 1992; and Schkade & Kahneman, 1998).

14. It is, of course, not true to say that *all* learning through experience is easy. (Consider the motivation and time that it takes to acquire expertise in any area of activity.) Indeed, developing expertise through direct experience can be as onerous as acquiring knowledge through academic instruction. However, a major difference between the two processes is that experiential learning results in the acquisition of much tangential knowledge (without effort), whereas academic learning is more specific and goal oriented.

15. Note that people who spend a great deal of time performing such calculations (e.g., accountants) can develop automatic mental algorithms for performing algebraic operations that would be more accurately classified as involving tacit processes. In essence, they recognize patterns of data and can simply read off responses as opposed to having to expend effort.

16. This notion that the tacit system is influenced by the deliberate system is similar to Izard's (1993) model of motivation activation.

17. For further discussion, see Einhorn and Hogarth (1981).

18. See, e.g., Miller (1971) and Sniezek (1986).

19. For experimental evidence, see, e.g., the literature on problem framing (Hogarth, 1982).

20. Chartrand and Bargh (1999).

21. Bargh, Chen, and Burrows (1996).

22. Goleman (1995).

23. Langer (1989, 1997).

24. A small "questionnaire industry" exists that allows people to assess the effects of their own preferred styles (e.g., Briggs & Myers, 1976).

25. It should be noted, however, that the relation between expertise and the ability to predict events within the domain of expertise is not simple (see Camerer & Johnson, 1991).

26. Joshua Klayman (personal communication, 2000) has remarked that many people would prefer to go through life "effectively" but mindlessly. I do not believe that this is possible.

27. Goleman (1995).

28. I am grateful to Harry L. Davis for suggesting this term.

29. Michael Doherty makes the point that many people do not make

heavy use of visualization and thus may not understand *by seeing*. I agree that some people are better able to visualize than are others. However, this does not preclude understanding *by seeing* when it means "perceiving connections automatically," e.g., when an analogy links two previously unrelated phenomena.

30. One possible danger with analogies is that, even though they provide models, we sometimes take them too seriously. One antidote is use several different analogies, thus introducing different perspectives. (See Einhorn & Hogarth, 1987.)

31. On presentation effects, see Hogarth (1982).

CHAPTER 7

1. As people grow older, it becomes increasingly difficult to adapt to new environments. This may of course be the result of the physiological process of aging. But it may also be the result of having grown so accustomed to a culture over the years that it has become ingrained.

2. Einhorn (1972).

3. The notion here is that phenomena that we predict can be described as a function of both systematic and random factors. We can understand and, therefore, predict the systematic factors. Phenomena vary, however, in the sizes of both the systematic and the random factors.

4. Cheng et al. (1986); Nisbett et al. (1983); Nisbett et al. (1987); Fong and Nisbett (1991); Fong, Krantz, and Nisbett (1986). See also Ploger and Wilson (1991) and Reeves and Weisberg (1993).

5. Larrick, Morgan, and Nisbett (1990); Larrick, Nisbett, and Morgan (1993); Lehman, Lempert, and Nisbett (1988); Lehman and Nisbett (1990). See also Kosonen and Winne (1995).

6. See, e.g., Starkey, Spelke, and Gelman (1990).

7. These comments are not meant to disparage economists in particular. Similar statements can probably be made about members of any profession governed by such a strong paradigm, one to which practically all subscribe. I discuss economics rather than psychology because psychologists tend to work with a wider range of models and the discipline therefore lacks the unity provided by the economic paradigm.

8. I have always been impressed by the force of the following words by the psychologist Carl Rogers: "I have come to feel that the only learning which significantly influences behavior is self-discovered, self-appropriated learning" (1961, 276).

9. For examples of this technique, see Argyris (1989) and Senge (1990).

10. Argyris (1991).

11. See, e.g., Bacon (1620/1994).

12. Much of the detail of this framework was influenced by my work with

Harry Davis and Joshua Klayman developing ways to help MBA students learn from their experiences in consulting projects.

13. Conan Doyle (1981, 17).

14. Bruner and Postman (1949).

15. Asch (1951).

16. Buckhout (1974).

17. Campbell (1960); Hogarth (1987).

18. Klayman (1995); Klayman and Ha (1987).

19. Ericsson and Charness (1994); Krampe and Ericsson (1996).

20. Abernathy and Hamm (1994, 1995).

21. Gary Klein (1998) advocates several of these kinds of simulations to help people acquire the intuitive ability to recognize key features of real-world decision-making situations.

22. Gardner (1983).

23. Goleman (1995, 1998).

24. Sternberg (1995, 1997a, 1997b); Sternberg and Lubart (1996); Sternberg et al. (1995).

25. On workers in milk-processing plants, see Scribner (1984). On racetrack handicappers, see Ceci and Liker (1986, 1988).

26. It is not clear to me why Sternberg et al. (1995) cite these studies to show that practical intelligence is independent of IQ because the skills observed are very domain specific and there is no evidence as to whether the subjects exhibited practical intelligence in other domains.

CHAPTER 8

1. Livingston (1988, 129).

2. In fact, I believe that it would be more accurate to describe such an individual as an *intuitive* politician. However, in ordinary discourse, people tend to confuse the words *intuitive* and *instinctive.*

3. Ohlsson (1992).

4. Poincaré (1913, 387).

5. Bowers et al. (1990).

6. Bowers et al. (1990, 73).

7. See also Yaniv and Meyer (1987).

8. To recognize creative solutions to problems, it is important that people have good causal models of the context in which the problems are embedded. Thus, it is often relatively easy to recognize good solutions to physical problems because people tend to have good ideas about how physical systems work. On the other hand, recognizing good solutions for social problems is more problematic because, in this domain, it is more difficult to understand causes and effects. Con-

trast, for example, evaluating whether a new type of corkscrew will work and evaluating whether a new idea to motivate employees will work. It is relatively easy to determine—to understand or see—whether a simple mechanical device will work but more difficult to know how people will react.

9. See, e.g., the excellent review of this literature in Dorfman, Shames, and Kihlstrom (1996).

10. Arkes, Dawes, and Christensen (1986); Yaniv and Hogarth (1993).

11. Einhorn (1986).

12. See, e.g., Showers and Chakrin (1981).

13. For approaches differing in complexity, see Raiffa (1968), Keeney and Raiffa (1976), Russo and Schoemaker (1989), Edwards (1977), and Hammond, Keeney, and Raiffa (1999).

14. See, e.g., Einhorn and McCoach (1977) and Yntema and Torgerson (1961).

15. See also the recent analysis of this issue by Pinel, Assanand, and Lehman (2000).

16. See the excellent analysis of this phenomenon in Kanter (1993, chap. 8).

17. See also Fiedler (2000).

18. When faced with making important decisions, many people prefer to "sleep on it." This suggests that they want to see whether the tacit system will discover some new aspects of the problem that the deliberate system has overlooked or, alternatively, whether the tacit system will give more (or less) weight to key factors.

19. As a further example, I can testify to having found the use of explicit models such as these very useful when evaluating student papers. Although the evaluation process is necessarily subjective and I often find it difficult to express all that I like and dislike about the papers, the discipline of scoring them according to the same set of criteria clearly improves consistency and ensures greater fairness. The process, however, never totally eliminates my intuitive likes or dislikes.

20. See, e.g., Hogarth (1978).

21. Hammond et al. (1987).

22. The tasks also differ in that the analytic task has a clear and unambiguous answer. For the intuitive task, however, appeal could be made to judgments by experts.

23. Hammond et al. (1987).

24. McMackin and Slovic (2000).

25. Wilson and Schooler (1991, 182).

26. Wilson et al. (1993).

27. See, e.g., Gigerenzer, Todd, and ABC Research Group (1999).

28. See also Wilson et al. (1993).

29. Wilson, Kraft, and Dunn (1989).

30. Kmett, Arkes, and Jones (1999). This study also concerned decisions by college students concerning courses.

31. MacGregor (in press).

32. McMackin and Slovic (2000).

33. For an excellent discussion of this and related issues, see Schooler and Dougal (1999).

34. Schooler, Ohlsson, and Brooks (1993).

35. Schooler and Engster-Schooler (1990).

36. Langer (1989, 1997).

37. In similar fashion, we should also note the cumulative importance of deliberate thought in mental simulations that allow people to plan future activities and regulate their emotions. It is hard to see how these functions could be achieved by the tacit system alone, and, indeed, the capacity to plan for the future by imagining the unknown is probably one of the quintessential human abilities (Taylor et al., 1998).

38. See Hammond (1996, 233–238).

39. For an excellent review of this work, see Hammond (1996).

40. See, e.g., the review by Sternberg and Grigorenko (1997).

41. Briggs and Myers (1976).

42. See Epstein et al. (1996).

43. The original NFC is a well-known scale that, among others things, captures differential receptivity to different types of information (Cacioppo & Petty, 1982).

44. See Epstein et al. (1996, table 2, p. 394, and table 5, p. 399). Recently, Pacini and Epstein (1999) have developed a new version of the REI that includes a broader set of questions in the intuitive scale. Whether this resolves the issues raised here, however, remains an open question.

45. This paragraph was stimulated by a conversation with Chris Hsee.

46. The notion of a time out will be familiar only to those who have some familiarity with popular American sports. I apologize to those for whom it is not part of their cultural capital.

47. Damasio (1994); LeDoux (1996); Lieberman (2000); Ashby, Isen, and Turken (1999).

48. I refer in particular to the papers by Wilson, Schooler, and their colleagues, all of which were published after Hammond's work. The exception is the work of McMackin and Slovic (2000).

49. See, e.g., the review by Seger (1994).

50. In the past, this problem was usually considered to affect only totalitarian states. However, it has today spread worldwide, as witnessed by the fact that

more and more of our media sources are controlled by multinational corporations that want to shape our preferences.

51. Langer (1989) reviews several studies with similar results.

52. Abernathy and Hamm (1994, 1995).

53. See Simon (1996).

APPENDIX

1. Westcott (1968); Vaughan (1979); Bastick (1982); and Abernathy and Hamm (1995).

2. Westcott (1968, 97).

3. Westcott (1968, 102).

4. Vaughan (1979, 45, 46, 66).

5. Bastick (1982, 354).

6. Abernathy and Hamm (1994).

Abelson, R. P. (1981). Psychological status of the script concept. *American Psychologist, 36,* 715–729.

Abernathy, C. M., & Hamm, R. M. (1994). *Surgical scripts: Master surgeons think aloud about 43 common surgical problems.* Philadelphia: Hanley & Belfus.

Abernathy, C. M., & Hamm, R. M. (1995). *Surgical intuition: What it is and how to get it.* Philadelphia: Hanley & Belfus.

Agor, W. H. (1986). The logic of intuition: How top executives make important decisions. *Organizational Dynamics, 14,* 5–18.

Allan, L. G. (1993). Human contingency judgments: Rule based or associative? *Psychological Bulletin, 114,* 435–448.

Anderson, J. R. (1983). *The architecture of cognition.* Cambridge, MA: Harvard University Press.

Anderson, N. H. (1981). *Foundations of information integration theory.* New York: Academic.

Argyris, C. (1989). *Reasoning, learning, and action.* San Francisco: Jossey-Bass.

Argyris, C. (1991, May–June). Teaching smart people how to learn. *Harvard Business Review,* 44–54.

Arkes, H., Dawes, R. M., & Christensen, C. (1986). Factors influencing the use of a decision rule in a probabilistic task. *Organizational Behavior and Human Decision Processes, 37,* 93–110.

Asch, S. E. (1951). Effects of group pressure on the modification and distortion of judgments. In H. Guetzkow (Ed.), *Groups, leadership, and men.* Pittsburgh: Carnegie Institute of Technology Press.

Ashby, F. G., Isen, A. M., & Turken, A. U. (1999). A neuropsychological theory of positive affect and its influence on cognition. *Psychological Review, 106,* 529–550.

Bacon, F. (1994). *Novum organum: With other parts of the Great Instauration* (P. Urbach & J. Gibson, Eds. & Trans.; Paul Carus Student Editions, Vol. 3). Chicago: Open Court. (Original work published 1620)

Baillargeon, R. (1994). How do infants learn about the physical world? *Current Directions in Psychological Science, 3,* 133–140.

Balzer, W. K., Doherty, M. E., & O'Connor, R. (1989). Effects of cognitive feedback on performance. *Psychological Bulletin, 106,* 410–433.

Bargh, J. A. (1996). Automaticity in social psychology. In E. T. Higgins & A. W. Kruglanski (Eds.), *Social psychology: Handbook of basic principles*. New York: Guilford.

Bargh, J. A. (1997). The automaticity of everyday life. In R. S. Wyer Jr. (Ed.), *The automaticity of everyday life* (Advances in Social Cognition, Vol. 10). Mahwah, NJ: Erlbaum.

Bargh, J. A., & Chartrand, T. L. (1999). The unbearable automaticity of being. *American Psychologist, 54*, 462–479.

Bargh, J. A., Chen, M., & Burrows, L. (1996). Automaticity of social behavior: Direct effects of trait construct and stereotype activation on action. *Journal of Personality and Social Psychology, 71*, 230–244.

Bar-Hillel, M. (1980). The base-rate fallacy in probability judgments. *Acta Psychologica, 44*, 211–233.

Bartlett, F. C. (1932). *Remembering: A study in experimental and social psychology*. New York: Macmillan.

Bastick, T. (1982). *Intuition: How we think and act*. New York: Wiley.

Bazerman, M. (1997). *Judgment in managerial decision making* (4th ed.). New York: Wiley.

Bechara, A., Damasio, H., Tranel, D., & Damasio, A. (1997). Deciding advantageously before knowing the advantageous strategy. *Science, 275*, 1293–1295.

Berry, D. C. (1996). How implicit is implicit learning? In J. Underwood (Ed.), *Implicit cognition*. Oxford: Oxford University Press.

Berry, D. C., & Broadbent, D. E. (1984). On the relationship between task performance and associated verbalisable knowledge. *Quarterly Journal of Experimental Psychology, 36*, 209–231.

Birnbaum, M. H. (1983). Base rates in Bayesian inference: Signal detection analysis of the cab problem. *American Journal of Psychology, 96*, 85–94.

Blattberg, R. C., & Hoch, S. J. (1990). Database models and managerial intuition: 50% model + 50% manager. *Management Science, 36*, 887–899.

Bowers, K. S., Regehr, G., Balthazard, C., & Parker, K. (1990). Intuition in the context of discovery. *Cognitive Psychology, 22*, 72–110.

Boyatzis, R. E., & Kolb, D. A. (1991). Assessing individuality in learning. *Educational Psychology, 11*, 279–295.

Brase, G. L., Cosmides, L., & Tooby, J. (1998). Individuation, counting, and statistical inference: The role of frequency and whole-object representations in judgment under uncertainty. *Journal of Experimental Psychology: General, 127*, 3–21.

Bregman, E. (1934). An attempt to modify the emotional attitude of infants by the conditioned response technique. *Journal of Genetic Psychology, 45*, 169–198.

Briggs, K. C., & Myers, I. B. (1976). *Myers-Briggs type indicator.* Palo Alto, CA: Consulting Psychologists Press.

Broadbent, D. E., & Aston, B. (1978). Human control of a simulated economic system. *Ergonomics, 21,* 1035–1043.

Broadbent, D. E., FitzGerald, P., & Broadbent, M. H. P. (1986). Implicit and explicit knowledge in the control of complex systems. *British Journal of Psychology, 77,* 33–50.

Bruner, J. (1957). Going beyond the information given. In H. E. Gruber, K. R. Hammond, & R. Jessor (Eds.), *Contemporary approaches to cognition.* Cambridge, MA: Harvard University Press.

Bruner, J. (1986). *Actual minds, possible worlds.* Cambridge, MA: Harvard University Press.

Bruner, J., Goodnow, J. J., & Austin, G. A. (1956). *A study of thinking.* New York: Wiley.

Bruner, J., & Postman, L. J. (1949). On the perception of incongruity: A paradigm. *Journal of Personality, 18,* 206–223.

Brunswik, E. (1952). *Conceptual framework of psychology.* Chicago: University of Chicago Press.

Brunswik, E. (1956). *Perception and the representative design of experiments* (2d ed.). Berkeley: University of California Press.

Buckhout, R. (1974). Eyewitness testimony. *Scientific American, 231,* 23–31.

Buss, D. M., Haselton, M. G., Shackelford, T. K., Bleske, A. L., & Wakefield, J. C. (1998). Adaptations, exaptations, and spandrels. *American Psychologist, 53,* 533–548.

Cacioppo, J. T., & Petty, R. E. (1982). The need for cognition. *Journal of Personality and Social Psychology, 42,* 116–131.

Camerer, C. F. (1981). General conditions for the success of bootstrapping models. *Organizational Behavior and Human Performance, 27,* 411–422.

Camerer, C. F., & Johnson, E. J. (1991). The process-performance paradox in expert judgment: How can the experts know so much and predict so badly? In K. A. Ericsson & J. Smith (Eds.), *Toward a general theory of expertise: Prospects and limits.* Cambridge: Cambridge University Press.

Campbell, D. T. (1959). Systematic error on the part of human links in communication systems. *Information and Control, 1,* 334–369.

Campbell, D. T. (1960). Blind variation and selective retention in creative thought as in other knowledge processes. *Psychological Review, 67,* 380–400.

Caramazza, A., McCloskey, M., & Green, B. (1981). Naive beliefs in "sophisticated" subjects: Misconceptions about trajectories of objects. *Cognition, 9,* 117–123.

Casscells, W., Schoenberger, A., & Grayboys, T. B. (1978). Interpretation by physicians of clinical laboratory results. *New England Journal of Medicine, 299,* 999–1001.

Ceci, S. J., & Liker, J. (1986). Academic and nonacademic intelligence: An experimental separation. In R. J. Sternberg & R. K. Wagner (Eds.), *Practical intelligence: Nature and origins of competence in the everyday world.* New York: Cambridge University Press.

Ceci, S. J., & Liker, J. (1988). Stalking the IQ-expertise relationship: When the critics go fishing. *Journal of Experimental Psychology: General, 117,* 96–100.

Champagne, A. B., Klopfer, L. E., & Anderson, J. H. (1980). Factors influencing the learning of classical mechanics. *American Journal of Physics, 48,* 1074–1079.

Chapman, L. J. (1967). Illusory correlation in observational report. *Journal of Verbal Learning and Verbal Behavior, 6,* 151–155.

Chapman, L. J., & Chapman, J. P. (1969). Illusory correlation as an obstacle to the use of valid psychodiagnostic signs. *Journal of Abnormal Psychology, 74,* 271–280.

Chartrand, T. L., & Bargh, J. A. (1999). The chameleon effect: The perception-behavior link and social interaction. *Journal of Personality and Social Psychology, 76,* 893–910.

Chase, W. G., & Simon, H. A. (1973a). The mind's eye in chess. In W. G. Chase (Ed.), *Visual information processing.* New York: Academic.

Chase, W. G., & Simon, H. A. (1973b). Perception in chess. *Cognitive Psychology, 4,* 55–81.

Cheng, P. W., & Holyoak, K. J. (1985). Pragmatic reasoning schemes. *Cognitive Psychology, 17,* 391–416.

Cheng, P. W., Holyoak, K. J., Nisbett, R. E., & Oliver, L. M. (1986). Pragmatic versus syntactic approaches to training deductive reasoning. *Cognitive Psychology, 18,* 293–328.

Chi, M. T. H., Glaser, R., & Farr, M. (1988). *The nature of expertise.* Hillsdale, NJ: Erlbaum.

Christensen-Szalanski, J. J. J., & Beach, L. R. (1982). Experience and the base-rate fallacy. *Organizational Behavior and Human Performance, 29,* 270–278.

Cialdini, R. B. (1993). *Influence: Science and practice* (3d ed.). New York: Harper-Collins.

Claparède, E. (1951). Recognition and "me-ness." In D. Rapoport (Ed. & Trans.), *Organization and pathology of thought: Selected sources.* New York: Columbia University Press.

Clement, J. (1982). Students' perceptions in introductory mechanics. *American Journal of Physics, 50,* 66–71.

Collins, A. M., & Loftus, E. F. (1975). A spreading-activation theory of semantic processing. *Psychological Review, 82,* 407–428.

Conan Doyle, A. (1981). *The celebrated cases of Sherlock Holmes.* London: Octopus.

Cosmides, L. (1989). The logic of social exchange: Has natural selection shaped how humans reason? Studies with the Wason selection task. *Cognition, 31,* 187–276.

Cosmides, L., & Tooby, J. (1996). Are humans good intuitive statisticians after all? Rethinking some conclusions from the literature on judgment under uncertainty. *Cognition, 58,* 1–73.

Crocker, J. (1981). Judgment of covariation by social perceivers. *Psychological Bulletin, 90,* 272–292.

Damasio, A. R. (1994). *Descartes' error: Emotion, reason, and the human brain.* New York: Avon.

Damasio, A. R. (1999). *The feeling of what happens: Body and motion in the making of consciousness.* New York: Harcourt Brace.

Dawes, R. M. (1979). The robust beauty of improper linear models. *American Psychologist, 34,* 571–582.

Dawes, R. M., & Corrigan, B. (1974). Linear models in decision making. *Psychological Bulletin, 81,* 95–106.

Dawes, R. M., Faust, D., & Meehl, P. E. (1989). Clinical versus actuarial judgment. *Science, 243,* 1668–1674.

de Finetti, B. (1937). La prévision: Ses lois logiques, ses sources subjectives. *Annales de l'Institut Henri Poincaré, 7,* 1–68. (Reprinted in English as "Foresight: Its logical laws, its subjective sources," in H. E. Kyburg Jr. & H. E. Smokler [Eds.], *Studies in subjective probability* [New York: Wiley, 1964].)

Denes-Raj, V., & Epstein, S. (1994). Conflict between experiential and rational processing: When people behave against their better judgment. *Journal of Personality and Social Psychology, 66,* 819–829.

Denes-Raj, V., Epstein, S., & Cole, J. (1995). The generality of the ratio-bias phenomenon. *Personality and Social Psychology Bulletin, 21,* 1083–1092.

DiMaggio, P. (1982). Cultural capital and school success: The impact of status culture participation on the grades of USD high school students. *American Sociological Review, 47,* 189–201.

Dorfman, J., Shames, V. A., & Kihlstrom, J. F. (1996). Intuition, incubation, and insight: Implicit cognition in problem solving. In J. Underwood (Ed.), *Implicit cognition.* Oxford: Oxford University Press.

Dove, M. R. (1993). Uncertainty, humility, and adaptation in the tropical forest: The agricultural augury of the Kantu. *Ethnology, 32,* 145–167.

Dunbar, N. (2000). *Inventing money: The story of Long Term Capital Management and the legends behind it.* New York: Wiley.

Eddy, D. M. (1982). Probabilistic reasoning in clinical medicine: Problems and opportunities. In D. Kahneman, P. Slovic, & A. Tversky (Eds.), *Judgment under uncertainty: Heuristics and biases.* New York: Cambridge University Press.

Edwards, K. (1998). The face of time: Temporal cues in the facial expressions of emotion. *Psychological Science, 9,* 270–276.

Edwards, W. (1977). Use of multiattribute utility measurement for social decision making. In D. E. Bell, R. L. Keeney, & H. Raiffa (Eds.), *Conflicting objectives in decisions.* Chichester: Wiley.

Einhorn, H. J. (1972). Expert measurement and mechanical combination. *Organizational Behavior and Human Performance, 7,* 86–106.

Einhorn, H. J. (1980). Learning from experience and suboptimal rules in decision making. In T. Wallsten (Ed.), *Cognitive processes in choice and decision behavior.* Hillsdale, NJ: Erlbaum.

Einhorn, H. J. (1986). Accepting error to make less error. *Journal of Personality Assessment, 50,* 387–395.

Einhorn, H. J., & Hogarth, R. M. (1975). Unit weighting schemes for decision making. *Organizational Behavior and Human Performance, 13,* 171–192.

Einhorn, H. J., & Hogarth, R. M. (1978). Confidence in judgment: Persistence of the illusion of validity. *Psychological Review, 85,* 395–416.

Einhorn, H. J., & Hogarth, R. M. (1981). Behavioral decision theory: Processes of judgment and choice. *Annual Review of Psychology, 32,* 53–88.

Einhorn, H. J., & Hogarth, R. M. (1982). Prediction, diagnosis, and causal thinking in forecasting. *Journal of Forecasting, 1,* 23–36.

Einhorn, H. J., & Hogarth, R. M. (1986). Judging probable cause. *Psychological Bulletin, 99,* 3–19.

Einhorn, H. J., & Hogarth, R. M. (1987, January–February). Decision making: Going forward in reverse. *Harvard Business Review, 87,* 66–70.

Einhorn, H. J., & McCoach, W. (1977). A simple multi-attribute procedure for evaluation. *Behavioral Science, 22,* 270–282.

Epstein, S. (1994). Integration of the cognitive and the psychodynamic unconscious. *American Psychologist, 49,* 709–724.

Epstein, S. (1998). Cognitive-experiential self-theory. In D. F. Barone, M. Hersen, & V. B. Van Hasselt (Eds.), *Advanced personality.* New York: Plenum.

Epstein, S., Denes-Raj, V., & Pacini, R. (1995). The Linda problem revisited from the perspective of cognitive-experiential self-theory. *Personality and Social Psychology Bulletin, 21,* 1124–1138.

Epstein, S., Lipson, A., Holstein, C., & Huh, E. (1992). Irrational reactions to negative outcomes: Evidence for two conceptual systems. *Journal of Personality and Social Psychology, 62,* 328–339.

Epstein, S., Pacini, R., Denes-Raj, V., & Heier, H. (1996). Individual differences in intuitive-experiential and analytical-rational thinking styles. *Journal of Personality and Social Psychology, 71,* 390–405.

Ericsson, K. A., & Charness, N. (1994). Expert performance: Its structure and acquisition. *American Psychologist, 49,* 725–747.

Ericsson, K. A., & Kintsch, W. (1995). Long-term working memory. *Psychological Review, 102,* 211–245.

Ericsson, K. A., Krampe, R. T., & Tesch-Römer, C. (1993). The role of deliberate practice in the acquisition of expert performance. *Psychological Review, 100,* 363–406.

Ericsson, K. A., & Lehmann, A. C. (1996). Expert and exceptional performance: Evidence of maximal adaptation to task constraints. *Annual Review of Psychology, 47,* 273–305.

Ericsson, K. A., & Smith, J. (Eds.). (1991). *Toward a general theory of expertise: Prospects and limits.* Cambridge: Cambridge University Press.

Estes, W. K. (1976). The cognitive side of probability learning. *Psychological Review, 83,* 37–64.

Fiedler, K. (1988). The dependence of the conjunction fallacy on subtle linguistic factors. *Psychological Research, 50,* 123–129.

Fiedler, K. (2000). Beware of samples! A cognitive-ecological sampling approach to judgment biases. *Psychological Review, 107,* 659–676.

Fiedler, K., Brinkmann, B., Betsch, T., & Wild, B. (2000). A sampling approach to biases in conditional probability judgments: Beyond base rate neglect and statistical format. *Journal of Experimental Psychology: General, 129,* 399–418.

Fischhoff, B. (1982). Debiasing. In D. Kahneman, P. Slovic, & A. Tversky (Eds.), *Judgment under uncertainty: Heuristics and biases.* Cambridge: Cambridge University Press.

Fischhoff, B., Slovic, P., & Lichtenstein, S. (1978). Fault trees: Sensitivity of estimated failure probabilities to problem representation. *Journal of Experimental Psychology: Human Perception and Performance, 4,* 330–344.

Fong, G. T., Krantz, D. H., & Nisbett, R. E. (1986). The effects of statistical training on thinking about everyday problems. *Cognitive Psychology, 18,* 253–292.

Fong, G. T., & Nisbett, R. E. (1991). Immediate and delayed transfer of training effects in statistical reasoning. *Journal of Experimental Psychology: General, 120,* 34–45.

Forgas, J. P. (1995). Mood and judgment: The affect infusion model (AIM). *Psychological Bulletin, 117,* 39–66.

Frabble, D. E. S., Blackstone, T., & Scherbaum, C. (1990). Marginal and mindful: Deviants in social interactions. *Journal of Personality and Social Psychology, 59,* 140–149.

Freud, S. (1953). *The interpretation of dreams.* In J. Strachey (Ed. & Trans.), *The standard edition of the complete works of Sigmund Freud* (Vols. 4–5). London: Hogarth Press. (Original work published 1900)

Funder, D. C. (1995). On the accuracy of personality judgment: A realistic approach. *Psychological Review, 102,* 652–670.

Garb, H. N. (1998). *Studying the clinician: Judgment research and psychological assessment.* Washington, DC: American Psychological Association.

Garb, H. N., & Schramke, C. J. (1996). Judgment research and neuropsychological assessment: A narrative review and meta-analysis. *Psychological Bulletin, 120,* 140–153.

Garcia, J. (1981). Tilting at the paper mills of academe. *American Psychologist, 36,* 149–158.

Garcia, J., McGowan, B., Ervin, F. R., & Koelling, R. (1968). Cues: Their relative effectiveness as reinforcers. *Science, 160,* 794–795.

Garcia, J., McGowan, B., & Green, K. (1972). Sensory quality and integration: Constraints on conditioning. In A. H. Black & W. F. Prokasy (Eds.), *Classical conditioning: Vol. 2. Current research and theory.* New York: Appleton-Century-Crofts.

Gardner, H. (1983). *Frames of mind: The theory of multiple intelligences.* New York: Basic.

Gardner, H. (1995). "Expert performance: Its structure and acquisition": Comment. *American Psychologist, 50,* 802–803.

Garner, W. R. (1970). Good patterns have few alternatives. *American Scientist, 58,* 34–42.

Gernsbacher, M. A. (Ed.). (1994). *Handbook of psycholinguistics.* San Diego: Academic.

Gigerenzer, G. (1991). How to make cognitive illusions disappear: Beyond heuristics and biases. *European Review of Social Psychology, 2,* 83–115.

Gigerenzer, G. (1996a). On narrow norms and vague heuristics: A reply to Kahneman and Tversky (1996). *Psychological Review, 103,* 592–596.

Gigerenzer, G. (1996b). The psychology of good judgment: Frequency formats and simple algorithms. *Medical Decision Making, 16,* 273–280.

Gigerenzer, G., & Hoffrage, U. (1995). How to improve Bayesian reasoning without instruction: Frequency formats. *Psychological Review, 102,* 684–704.

Gigerenzer, G., Hoffrage, U., & Kleinbölting, H. (1991). Probabilistic mental models: A Brunswikian theory of confidence. *Psychological Review, 98,* 506–528.

Gigerenzer, G., & Hug, K. (1992). Domain specific reasoning: Social contracts, cheating, and perspective change. *Cognition, 43,* 127–171.

Gigerenzer, G., Todd, P. M., & ABC Research Group. (1999). *Simple heuristics that make us smart.* New York: Oxford University Press.

Gilden, D. L., & Proffitt, D. R. (1989). Understanding collision dynamics. *Journal of Experimental Psychology: Human Perception and Performance, 15,* 372–383.

Gilovich, T. (1991). *How we know what isn't so: The fallibility of human reason in everyday life.* New York: Free Press.

Gilovich, T., Vallone, R., & Tversky, A. (1985). The hot hand in basketball: On the misperception of random sequences. *Cognitive Psychology, 17,* 295–314.

Goldberg, L. R. (1970). Man versus model of man: A rationale, plus some evidence, for a method of improving on clinical inferences. *Psychological Bulletin, 73,* 422–432.

Goleman, D. (1995). *Emotional intelligence: Why it can matter more than IQ.* New York: Bantam.

Goleman, D. (1998). *Working with emotional intelligence.* New York: Bantam.

Graham, T., & Ickes, W. (1997). When women's intuition isn't greater than men's. In W. Ickes (Ed.), *Empathic accuracy.* New York: Guilford.

Greenwald, A. G. (1992). New Look 3: Unconscious cognition reclaimed. *American Psychologist, 47,* 766–769.

Greenwald, A. G., & Banaji, M. R. (1995). Implicit social cognition: Attitudes, self-esteem, and stereotypes. *Psychological Review, 102,* 4–37.

Hall, J. A. (1984). *Nonverbal sex differences: Communication accuracy and expressive style.* Baltimore: Johns Hopkins University Press.

Hammerton, M. (1973). A case of radical probability estimation. *Journal of Experimental Psychology, 101,* 252–254.

Hammond, J. S., Keeney, R. L., & Raiffa, H. (1999). *Smart choices: A practical guide to making better decisions.* Boston: Harvard Business School Press.

Hammond, K. R. (1955). Probabilistic functioning and the clinical method. *Psychological Review, 62,* 255–262.

Hammond, K. R. (1996). *Human judgment and social policy: Irreducible uncertainty, inevitable error, unavoidable injustice.* New York: Oxford University Press.

Hammond, K. R., Hamm, R. M., Grassia, J., & Pearson, T. (1987). Direct comparison of the efficacy of intuitive and analytical cognition in expert judgment. *IEEE Transactions on Systems, Man, and Cybernetics, 17,* 753–770.

Hänze, M. (1997). Mood and the Stroop interference effect. *Psychologische Beiträge, 39,* 229–235.

Hänze, M., & Meyer, H. A. (1998). Mood influences on automatic and controlled semantic priming. *American Journal of Psychology, 111,* 265–278.

Harrison, A. A. (1977). Mere exposure. In L. Berkowitz (Ed.), *Advances in experimental social psychology* (Vol. 10). New York: Academic.

Hasher, L., & Zacks, R. T. (1979). Automatic and effortful processes in memory. *Journal of Experimental Psychology: General, 108,* 356–358.

Hasher, L., & Zacks, R. T. (1984). Automatic processing of fundamental information: The case of frequency of occurrence. *American Psychologist, 39,* 1372–1388.

Hendrickx, L., Vlek, C., & Oppewal, H. (1989). Relative importance of scenario information and frequency information in the judgment of risk. *Acta Psychologica, 72,* 41–63.

Herrnstein, R. J., & Miller, C. (1996). *The bell curve: Intelligence and class structure in American life.* New York: Free Press.

Hinton, G. E. (1990). Mapping part-whole hierarchies into connectionist networks. *Artificial Intelligence, 46,* 47–76.

Hogarth, R. M. (1974). Monozygotic and dizygotic twins reared together: Sensitivity of heritability estimates. *British Journal of Mathematical and Statistical Psychology, 27,* 1–13.

Hogarth, R. M. (1978). A note on aggregating opinions. *Organizational Behavior and Human Performance, 21,* 40–46.

Hogarth, R. M. (1981). Beyond discrete biases: Functional and dysfunctional consequences of judgmental heuristics. *Psychological Bulletin, 90,* 197–217.

Hogarth, R. M. (Ed.). (1982). *Question framing and response consistency.* San Francisco: Jossey-Bass.

Hogarth, R. M. (1987). *Judgement and choice: The psychology of decision* (2d ed.). Chichester: Wiley.

Hogarth, R. M., Gibbs, B. J., McKenzie, C. R. M., & Marquis, M. A. (1991). Learning from feedback: Exactingness and incentives. *Journal of Experimental Psychology: Learning, Memory, and Cognition, 17,* 734–752.

Hogarth, R. M., & Makridakis, S. (1981). The value of decision making in a complex environment: An experimental approach. *Management Science, 27,* 93–107.

Holbrook, M. B., & Schindler, R. M. (1994). Age, sex, and attitude toward the past as predictors of consumers' aesthetic tastes for cultural products. *Journal of Marketing Research, 31,* 412–422.

Hursch, C., Hammond, K. R., & Hursch, J. L. (1964). Some methodological considerations in multiple cue probability studies. *Psychological Review, 71,* 42–60.

Ickes, W. (Ed.). *Empathic accuracy.* New York: Guilford.

Isen, A. (1987). Positive affect, cognitive processes, and social behavior. *Advances in Experimental Social Psychology, 20,* 203–253.

Isen, A. (1993). Positive affect and decision making. In M. Lewis & J. M. Haviland (Eds.), *Handbook of emotions.* New York: Guilford.

Izard, C. E. (1993). Four systems for emotion activation: Cognitive and noncognitive processes. *Psychological Review, 100,* 68–90.

Jacoby, L. L., Lindsay, D. S., & Toth, J. P. (1992). Unconscious influences revealed: Attention, awareness, and control. *American Psychologist, 47,* 802–809.

Jung, C. (1926). *Psychological types* (H. G. Baynes, Trans.). London: Routledge & Kegan Paul.

Kagan, J. (1996). Three pleasing ideas. *American Psychologist, 51,* 901–908.

Kahneman, D., Slovic, P., & Tversky, A. (Eds.). (1982). *Judgment under uncertainty: Heuristics and biases.* New York: Cambridge University Press.

Kahneman, D., & Snell, J. (1992). Predicting a changing taste: Do people know what they will like? *Journal of Behavioral Decision Making, 5,* 187–200.

Kahneman, D., & Tversky, A. (1972). Subjective probability: A judgment of representativeness. *Cognitive Psychology, 3,* 430–454.

Kahneman, D., & Tversky, A. (1973). On the psychology of prediction. *Psychological Review, 80,* 237–251.

Kahneman, D., & Tversky, A. (1979). Prospect theory: An analysis of decision under risk. *Econometrica, 47,* 263–291.

Kahneman, D., & Tversky, A. (1982). On the study of statistical intuitions. *Cognition, 11,* 123–141.

Kahneman, D., & Tversky, A. (1996). On the reality of cognitive illusions: A reply to Gigerenzer's critique. *Psychological Review, 103,* 582–591.

Kaiser, M. K., Jonides, J., & Alexander, J. (1986). Intuitive reasoning about abstract and familiar physics problems. *Memory and Cognition, 14,* 308–312.

Kaiser, M. K., McCloskey, M., & Proffitt, D. R. (1986). Development of intuitive theories of motion: Curvilinear motion in the absence of external forces. *Developmental Psychology, 22,* 67–71.

Kaiser, M. K., Proffitt, D. R., & Anderson, K. (1985). Judgments of natural and anomalous trajectories in the presence and absence of motion. *Journal of Experimental Psychology: Learning, Memory, and Cognition, 11,* 795–803.

Kaiser, M. K., Proffitt, D. R., & McCloskey, M. (1985). The development of beliefs about falling objects. *Perception and Psychophysics, 38,* 533–539.

Kanter, R. M. (1993). *Men and women of the corporation* (2d ed.). New York: Basic.

Kareev, Y. (1995). Positive bias in the perception of correlation. *Psychological Review, 102,* 490–502.

Kareev, Y., Lieberman, I., & Lev, M. (1997). Through a narrow window: Sample size and the perception of correlation. *Journal of Experimental Psychology: General, 128,* 278–287.

Keeney, R. L., & Raiffa, H. (1976). *Decisions with multiple objectives: Preferences and value tradeoffs.* New York: Wiley.

Keren, G., & Wagenaar, W. A. (1987). Temporal aspects of probabilistic predictions. *Bulletin of the Psychonomic Society, 25,* 61–64.

Kihlstrom, J. F. (1987). The cognitive unconscious. *Science, 237,* 1445–1452.

Kihlstrom, J. F., Barnhardt, T. M., & Tataryn, D. J. (1992). The psychological unconscious: Found, lost, and regained. *American Psychologist, 47,* 788–791.

Kim, I. K., & Spelke, E. S. (1992). Infants' sensitivity to effects of gravity on visible object motion. *Journal of Experimental Psychology: Human Perception and Performance, 18,* 385–393.

Kirkpatrick, L. A., & Epstein, S. (1992). Cognitive-experiential self-theory and subjective probability: Further evidence for two conceptual systems. *Journal of Personality and Social Psychology, 63,* 534–544.

Klayman, J. (1995). Varieties of confirmation bias. In J. R. Busemeyer, R. Hastie, & D. L. Medin (Eds.), *Decision making from a cognitive perspective.* New York: Academic.

Klayman, J., & Ha, Y.-W. (1987). Confirmation, disconfirmation, and information in hypothesis testing. *Psychological Review, 94,* 211–228.

Klayman, J., Soll, J. B., González-Vallejo, C., & Barlas, S. (1999). Overconfidence: It depends on how, what, and who you ask. *Organizational Behavior and Human Performance, 79,* 216–247.

Klein, G. (1998). *Sources of power: How people make decisions.* Cambridge, MA: MIT Press.

Kleinmuntz, B. (1968). The processing of clinical information by man and machine. In B. Kleinmuntz (Ed.), *Formal representation of human judgment.* New York: Wiley.

Kleinmuntz, B. (1990). Why we still use our heads instead of formulas: Toward an integrative approach. *Psychological Bulletin, 107,* 296–310.

Kleiter, G. (1994). Natural sampling: Rationality without base rates. In G. H. Fischer & D. Laming (Eds.), *Contributions to mathematical psychology, psychometrics, and methodology.* New York: Springer.

Kmett, C. A., Arkes, H. R., & Jones, S. K. (1999). The influence of decision aids on high school students' satisfaction with their college choice decision. *Personality and Social Psychology Bulletin, 25,* 1293–1301.

Koestler, A. (1967). *The act of creation.* New York: Dell.

Kolb, D. A. (1984). *Experiential learning: Experience as the source of learning and development.* Englewood Cliffs, NJ: Prentice-Hall.

Kosonen, P., & Winne, P. H. (1995). Effects of teaching statistical laws of reasoning about everyday problems. *Journal of Educational Psychology, 87,* 33–46.

Krampe, R. T., & Ericsson, K. A. (1996). Maintaining excellence: Deliberate practice and elite performance in young and old pianists. *Journal of Experimental Psychology: General, 125,* 331–359.

Krist, H., Fieberg, E. L., & Wilkening, F. (1993). Intuitive physics in action and judgment: The development of knowledge about projectile motion. *Journal of Experimental Psychology: Learning, Memory, and Cognition, 19,* 952–966.

Krist, H., Loskill, J., & Schwartz, S. (1996). Intuitive physics in action: Perceptual-motor knowledge about projectile motion in 5–7 year old children. *Zeitschrift für Psychologie, 204*, 339–366.

Kruglanski, A. W. (1989). The psychology of being "right": The problem of accuracy in social perception and cognition. *Psychological Bulletin, 106*, 395–409.

Kunst-Wilson, W. R., & Zajonc, R. B. (1980). Affective discrimination of stimuli that cannot be recognized. *Science, 207*, 557–558.

Labouvie-Vief, G. (1989). Modes of knowledge and the organization of development. In M. L. Commons, J. D. Sinnott, F. A. Richards, & C. Armon (Eds.), *Adult development* (Vol. 2). New York: Praeger.

Labouvie-Vief, G. (1990). Wisdom as integrated thought: Historical and developmental perspectives. In R. J. Sternberg (Ed.), *Wisdom: Its nature, origins, and development.* New York: Cambridge University Press.

Langer, E. J. (1989). *Mindfulness.* Reading, MA: Perseus.

Langer, E. J. (1997). *The power of mindful learning.* Reading, MA: Perseus.

Larrick, R. P., Morgan, J. N., & Nisbett, R. E. (1990). Teaching the use of cost-benefit reasoning in everyday life. *Psychological Science, 1*, 362–370.

Larrick, R. P., Nisbett, R. E., & Morgan, J. N. (1993). Who uses the cost-benefit rules of choice? Implications for the normative status of microeconomic theory. *Organizational Behavior and Human Decision Processes, 56*, 331–347.

Lazarus, R. S. (1984). On the primacy of cognition. *American Psychologist, 39*, 124–129.

LeDoux, J. (1996). *The emotional brain: The mysterious underpinnings of emotional life.* New York: Simon & Schuster.

Lehman, D. R., Lempert, R. O., & Nisbett, R. E. (1988). The effects of graduate training on reasoning: Formal discipline and thinking about everyday-life events. *American Psychologist, 43*, 431–442.

Lehman, D. R., & Nisbett, R. E. (1990). A longitudinal study of the effects of undergraduate training on reasoning. *Developmental Psychology, 26*, 952–960.

Lewicki, P., Hill, T., & Czyzewska, M. (1992). Nonconscious acquisition of information. *American Psychologist, 47*, 796–801.

Lewontin, R. C. (1979). Sociobiology as an adaptationist program. *Behavioral Science, 24*, 5–14.

Liberman, N., & Klar, Y. (1996). Hypothesis testing in Wason's selection task: Social exchange cheating detection or task understanding. *Cognition, 58*, 127–156.

Lieberman, M. D. (2000). Intuition: A social cognitive neuroscience approach. *Psychological Bulletin, 126*, 109–137.

Livingston, J. S. (1988, September–October). Pygmalion in management. *Harvard Business Review,* 121–130.

Loewenstein, G. F., Weber, E. U., Hsee, C. K., & Welch, N. (2001). Risk as feelings. *Psychological Bulletin, 127,* 267–286.

Loftus, E. R. (1979). *Eyewitness testimony.* Cambridge, MA: Harvard University Press.

Loftus, E. R., & Klinger, M. R. (1992). Is the unconscious smart or dumb? *American Psychologist, 47,* 761–765.

Lopes, L. L., & Oden, G. C. (1991). The rationality of intelligence. In E. Eells & T. Maruszewski (Eds.), *Probability and rationality: Studies on L. J. Cohen's philosophy of science.* Amsterdam: Rodopi.

Luce, M. F., Bettman, J. R., & Payne, J. W. (1997). Choice processing in emotionally difficult decisions. *Journal of Experimental Psychology: Learning, Memory, and Cognition, 23,* 384–405.

Luce, M. F., Payne, J. W., & Bettman, J. R. (1999). Emotional trade-off difficulty and choice. *Journal of Marketing Research, 36,* 143–159.

Luchins, A. S. (1942). Mechanization in problem solving: The effect of Einstellung. *Psychological Monographs, 54*(6).

MacGregor, D. G. (in press). Decomposition for judgmental forecasting and estimation. In J. Scott Armstrong (Ed.), *Principles of forecasting: A handbook for researchers and practitioners.* Norwell, MA: Kluwer.

MacLean, P. D. (1970). The triune brain, emotion, and scientific bias. In F. O. Schmitt (Ed.), *The neurosciences: Second study program.* New York: Rockefeller University Press.

Maier, N. R. F. (1931). Reasoning in humans: 2. The solution of a problem and its appearance in consciousness. *Journal of Comparative Psychology, 12,* 181–194.

Marcus, G. F., Vijayan, S., Bandi Rao, S., & Vishton, P. M. (1999). Rule learning by seven-month-old infants. *Science, 283,* 77–80.

Maurer, A. (1965). What children fear. *Journal of Genetic Psychology, 106,* 265–277.

McArthur, L. Z., & Baron, R. M. (1983). Toward an ecological theory of social perception. *Psychological Review, 90,* 215–238.

McCloskey, M. (1983). Intuitive physics. *Scientific American, 248,* 122–130.

McCloskey, M., Caramazza, A., & Green, B. (1980). Curvilinear motion in the absence of external forces: Naïve beliefs about the motion of objects. *Science, 210,* 1139–1141.

McKenzie, C. R. M. (1994). The accuracy of intuitive judgment strategies: Covariation assessment and Bayesian inference. *Cognitive Psychology, 26,* 209–239.

McKoon, G., & Ratcliff, R. (1998). Memory-based language processing: Psycholinguistic research in the 1990s. *Annual Review of Psychology, 49,* 25–42.

McMackin, J., & Slovic, P. (2000). When does explicit justification impair decision making? *Journal of Applied Cognitive Psychology, 14,* 527–541.

Medin, D. L. (1989). Concepts and conceptual structure. *American Psychologist, 44,* 1469–1481.

Medin, D. L., Goldstone, R. L., & Gentner, D. (1993). Respects for similarity. *Psychological Review, 100,* 254–278.

Medin, D. L., & Smith, E. E. (1984). Concepts and concept formation. *Annual Review of Psychology, 35,* 113–138.

Meehl, P. E. (1954). *Clinical versus statistical prediction.* Minneapolis: University of Minnesota Press.

Mellers, B. A., & McGraw, A. P. (1999). How to improve Bayesian reasoning: Comment on Gigerenzer and Hoffrage. *Psychological Review, 106,* 417–424.

Mellers, B., Schwartz, A., Ho, K., & Ritov, I. (1997). Decision affect theory: Emotional reactions to the outcomes of risky options. *Psychological Science, 8,* 423–429.

Merikle, P. M. (1992). Perception without awareness. *American Psychologist, 47,* 792–795.

Merriam-Webster's Collegiate Dictionary (10th ed.). (1996). Springfield, MA: Merriam-Webster.

Merton, R. K. (1936). The unanticipated consequences of purposive social action. *American Sociological Review, 1,* 894–904.

Mervis, C. B., & Rosch, E. (1981). Categorization of natural objects. *Annual Review of Psychology, 32,* 89–115.

Meyers-Levy, J. (1998). Mixed messages: How men and women differ in their responses to marketing messages. *Capital Ideas, 1*(3), 7–8.

Meyers-Levy, J., & Maheswaran, D. (1991). Exploring differences in males' and females' processing strategies. *Journal of Consumer Research, 18,* 63–70.

Miller, G. A. (1956). The magical number seven, plus or minus two: Some limits on our capacity for processing information. *Psychological Review, 63,* 81–96.

Miller, P. M. (1971). Do labels mislead? A multiple cue study within the framework of Brunswik's probabilistic functionalism. *Organizational Behavior and Human Performance, 6,* 480–500.

Moore, O. K. (1957). Divination: A new perspective. *American Anthropologist, 59,* 69–74.

Murphy, A., & Winkler, R. L. (1984). Probability forecasting in meteorology. *Journal of the American Statistical Association, 79,* 489–500.

Murphy, G. L., & Medin, D. L. (1985). The role of theories in conceptual coherence. *Psychological Review, 92,* 289–316.

Murphy, K. M., & Becker, G. S. (1988). A theory of rational addiction. *Journal of Political Economy, 96,* 675–700.

Needham, A., & Baillargeon, R. (1993). Intuitions about support in 4.5-month-old infants. *Cognition, 47,* 121–148.

Neisser, U. (1963). The imitation of man by machine. *Science, 139,* 193–197.

Newell, A., & Simon, H. A. (1973). *Human problem solving.* Englewood Cliffs, NJ: Prentice-Hall.

Nisbett, R. E., Fong, G. T., Lehman, D. R., & Cheng, P. W. (1987). Teaching reasoning. *Science, 238,* 625–631.

Nisbett, R. E., Krantz, D. H., Jepson, C., & Kunda, Z. (1983). The use of statistical heuristics in everyday inductive reasoning. *Psychological Review, 90,* 339–363.

Ohlsson, S. (1992). Information-processing explanations of insight and related phenomena. In M. T. Keane & K. J. Gilhooly (Eds.), *Advances in the psychology of thinking* (Vol. 1). New York: Harvester Wheatsheaf.

Pacini, R., & Epstein, S. (1999). The relation of rational and experiential information processing styles to personality, basic beliefs, and the ratio-bias phenomenon. *Journal of Personality and Social Psychology, 76,* 972–987.

Pacini, R., Muir, F., & Epstein, S. (1998). Depressive realism from the perspective of cognitive-experiential self-theory. *Journal of Personality and Social Psychology, 74,* 1056–1068.

Payne, J. W., Bettman, J. R., & Johnson, E. J. (1993). *The adaptive decision maker.* New York: Cambridge University Press.

Peters, J. T., Hammond, K. R., & Summers, D. A. (1974). A note on intuitive vs. analytic thinking. *Organizational Behavior and Human Performance, 12,* 125–131.

Peterson, C. R., & Beach, L. R. (1967). Man as an intuitive statistician. *Psychological Bulletin, 68,* 29–46.

Piaget, J. (1971). *Genetic epistemology* (E. Duckworth, Trans.). New York: Norton.

Piaget, J., & Inhelder, B. (1958). *The growth of logical thinking from childhood to adolescence.* New York: Basic.

Pinel, J. P. J., Assanand, S., & Lehman, D. R. (2000). Hunger, eating, and ill health. *American Psychologist, 55,* 1105–1116.

Pinker, S. (1994). *The language instinct: How the mind creates language.* New York: HarperCollins.

Pinker, S. (1997). *How the mind works.* New York: Norton.

Ploger, D., & Wilson, M. (1991). Statistical reasoning: What is the role of inferential rule training? Comment on Fong and Nisbett. *Journal of Experimental Psychology: General, 120,* 213–214.

Poincaré, H. (1913). *The foundations of science* (G. B. Halsted, Trans.). New York: Science Press.

Proffitt, D. R., & Gilden, D. L. (1989). Understanding natural dynamics. *Journal of Experimental Psychology: Human Perception and Performance, 15,* 384–393.

Proffitt, D. R., Kaiser, M. K., & Whelan, S. M. (1990). Understanding wheel dynamics. *Cognitive Psychology, 22,* 342–373.

Raiffa, H. (1968). *Decision analysis.* Reading, MA: Addison-Wesley.

Reber, A. S. (1989a). Implicit learning and tacit knowledge. *Journal of Experimental Psychology: General, 118,* 219–235.

Reber, A. S. (1989b). More thoughts on the unconscious: Reply to Brody and to Lewicki and Hill. *Journal of Experimental Psychology: General, 118,* 242–244.

Reber, A. S. (1993). *Implicit learning and tacit knowledge: An essay on the cognitive unconscious.* New York: Oxford University Press.

Reeves, L. M., & Weisberg, R. W. (1993). Abstract versus concrete information as the basis for transfer in problem solving: Comment on Fong and Nisbett (1991). *Journal of Experimental Psychology: General, 122,* 125–128.

Reilly, B. A., & Doherty, M. E. (1992). The assessment of self-insight in judgment policies. *Organizational Behavior and Human Decision Processes, 53,* 285–309.

Rips, L. J. (1989). Similarity, typicality, and categorization. In S. Vosniadou & A. Ortony (Eds.), *Similarity and analogical reasoning.* Cambridge: Cambridge University Press.

Roese, N. J. (1997). Counterfactual thinking. *Psychological Bulletin, 121,* 133–148.

Rogers, C. R. (1961). *On becoming a person.* Boston: Houghton Mifflin.

Ross, L. (1977). The intuitive psychologist and his shortcomings: Distortions in the attribution process. In L. Berkowitz (Ed.), *Advances in experimental social psychology* (Vol. 10). New York: Academic.

Rowan, R. (1986). *The intuitive manager.* Boston: Little, Brown.

Rumelhart, D. E., & McClelland, J. L. (Eds.). (1986). *Parallel distributed processing* (2 vols.). Cambridge, MA: MIT Press.

Russo, J. E., & Schoemaker, P. J. H. (1989). *Decision traps: The ten barriers to brilliant decision-making and how to overcome them.* New York: Doubleday.

Salovey, P., & Mayer, J. D. (1990). Emotional intelligence. *Imagination, Cognition, and Personality, 9,* 185–211.

Savage, L. J. (1954). *The foundations of statistics.* New York: Wiley.

Sawyer, J. (1966). Measurement and prediction, clinical and statistical. *Psychological Bulletin, 66,* 178–200.

Schachter, S., & Singer, J. E. (1962). Cognitive, social, and physiological determinants of emotional state. *Psychological Review, 69,* 379–399.

Schank, R. C., & Abelson, R. P. (1977). *Scripts, plans, goals, and understanding: An inquiry into human knowledge.* Hillsdale, NJ: Erlbaum.

Schkade, D. A., & Kahneman, D. (1998). Does living in California make people happy? A focusing illusion in judgments of life satisfaction. *Psychological Science, 9,* 340–346.

Schneider, W., & Shiffrin, R. M. (1977). Controlled and automatic human information processing: 1. Detection, search, and attention. *Psychological Review, 84*, 1–66.

Schooler, J. W., & Dougal, S. (1999). The symbiosis of subjective and experimental approaches to intuition. *Journal of Consciousness Studies, 6*, 280–287.

Schooler, J. W., & Engster-Schooler, T. Y. (1990). Verbal overshadowing of visual memories: Some things are better left unsaid. *Cognitive Psychology, 22*, 36–71.

Schooler, J. W., Ohlsson, S., & Brooks, K. (1993). Thoughts beyond words: When language overshadows insight. *Journal of Experimental Psychology: General, 122*, 166–183.

Schütze, C. T. (1996). *The empirical base of linguistics: Grammaticality judgments and linguistic methodology.* Chicago: University of Chicago Press.

Schwartz, B. (1982). Reinforcement-induced behavioral stereotypy: How not to teach people to discover rules. *Journal of Experimental Psychology: General, 111*, 23–59.

Scribner, S. (1984). Studying working intelligence. In B. Rogoff & J. Lave (Eds.), *Everyday cognition: Its development in social context.* Cambridge, MA: Harvard University Press.

Seger, C. (1994). Implicit learning. *Psychological Bulletin, 115*, 163–196.

Seligman, M. E. P. (1970). On the generality of laws of learning. *Psychological Review, 77*, 406–418.

Seligman, M. E. P. (1971). Phobias and preparedness. *Behavior Therapy, 2*, 307–320.

Senge, P. (1990). *The fifth discipline: The art and practice of the learning organization.* New York: Doubleday/Currency.

Shafir, E., Simonson, I., & Tversky, A. (1993). Reason-based choice. *Cognition, 49*, 11–36.

Shanon, B. (1976). Aristotelianism, Newtonianism, and the physics of the layman. *Perception, 5*, 241–243.

Shanteau, J., & Stewart, T. R. (1992). Why study expert decision making? Some historical perspectives and comments. *Organizational Behavior and Human Decision Processes, 53*, 95–106.

Shiffrin, R. M., & Schneider, W. (1977). Controlled and automatic human information processing: 2. Perceptual learning, automatic attending, and a general theory. *Psychological Review, 84*, 127–190.

Shirley, D. A., & Langan-Fox, J. (1996). Intuition: A review of the literature. *Psychological Reports, 79*, 563–584.

Showers, J. L., & Chakrin, L. M. (1981). Reducing uncollectible revenues from residential telephone customers. *Interfaces, 11*, 21–31.

Shultz, T. R. (1982). Rules of causal attribution. *Monographs of the Society for Research in Child Development, 47*, 1–51.

Sieck, W. R., Quinn, C. N., & Schooler, J. W. (1999). Justification effects on the judgment of analogy. *Memory and Cognition, 27,* 844–855.

Simon, H. A. (1955). A behavioral model of rational choice. *Quarterly Journal of Economics, 69,* 99–118.

Simon, H. A. (1996). *The sciences of the artificial* (3d ed.). Cambridge, MA: MIT Press.

Simon, H. A., & Chase, W. G. (1973). Skill in chess. *American Scientist, 61,* 394–403.

Skinner, B. F. (1984a). The phylogeny and the ontogeny of behavior. *Behavioral and Brain Sciences, 7,* 669–711.

Skinner, B. F. (1984b). Selection by consequences. *Behavioral and Brain Sciences, 7,* 477–510.

Sloman, S. A. (1996). The empirical case for two systems of reasoning. *Psychological Bulletin, 119,* 3–22.

Slovic, P., Finucane, M., Peters, E., & MacGregor, D. (in press). The affect heuristic. In T. Gilovich, D. Griffin, & D. Kahneman (Eds.), *Intuitive judgment: Heuristics and biases.* New York: Cambridge University Press.

Slovic, P., & Lichtenstein, S. (1971). Comparison of Bayesian and regression approaches to the study of information processing in judgment. *Organizational Behavior and Human Performance, 6,* 649–744.

Slovic, P., Monahan, J., & MacGregor, D. G. (2000). Violence risk assessment and risk communication: The effect of using actual cases, providing instruction, and employing probability versus frequency formats. *Law and Human Behavior, 24,* 271–296.

Smolensky, P. (1988). On the proper treatment of connectionism. *Behavioral and Brain Sciences, 11,* 1–23.

Sniezek, J. (1986). The use of variable labels in cue probability learning tasks. *Organizational Behavior and Human Decision Processes, 38,* 141–161.

Spelke, E. (1994). Initial knowledge: Six suggestions. *Cognition, 50,* 431–445.

Spelke, E. (1998). Nativism, empiricism, and the origins of knowledge. *Infant Behavior and Development, 21,* 181–200.

Spelke, E., Breinlinger, K., Macomber, J., & Jacobson, K. (1992). Origins of knowledge. *Psychological Review, 99,* 605–632.

Staddon, J. E. R. (1988). Learning as inference. In R. C. Bolles & M. D. Beecher (Eds.), *Evolution and learning.* Hillsdale, NJ: Erlbaum.

Starkey, P., Spelke, E., & Gelman, R. (1990). Numerical abstraction by human infants. *Cognition, 36,* 97–128.

Sternberg, R. J. (1995). Theory and measurement of tacit knowledge as a part of practical intelligence. *Zeitschrift für Psychologie, 203,* 319–334.

Sternberg, R. J. (1997a). *Successful intelligence: How practical and creative intelligence determine success in life.* New York: Plume.

Sternberg, R. J. (1997b). Tacit knowledge and job success. In N. Anderson & P. Herriot (Eds.), *International handbook of selection and assessment.* New York: Wiley.

Sternberg, R. J., & Grigorenko, E. L. (1997). Are cognitive styles still in style? *American Psychologist, 52,* 700–712.

Sternberg, R. J., & Lubart, T. I. (1996). Investing in creativity. *American Psychologist, 51,* 677–688.

Sternberg, R. J., Wagner, R. K., Williams, W. M., & Horvath, J. A. (1995). Testing common sense. *American Psychologist, 50,* 912–927.

Sutherland, S. (1994). *Irrationality: Why we don't think straight!* New Brunswick, NJ: Rutgers University Press.

Swann, W. B., Jr. (1984). Quest for accuracy in person perception: A matter of pragmatics. *Psychological Review, 91,* 457–477.

Tarabulsy, G. M., Tessier, R., & Kappas, A. (1996). Contingency detection and the contingent organization of behavior in interactions: Implications for socioemotional development in infancy. *Psychological Bulletin, 120,* 25–41.

Taylor, S. E., Pham, L. B., Rivkin, I. D., & Armor, D. A. (1998). Harnessing the imagination: Mental simulation, self-regulation, and coping. *American Psychologist, 53,* 429–439.

Thaler, R. H. (1991). *Quasi rational economics.* New York: Russell Sage.

Thomas, L. (1983). *The youngest science: Notes of a medicine watcher.* New York: Viking.

Thorndike, E. L., & Lorge, I. (1944). *The teacher's word book of 30,000 words.* New York: Teachers College, Columbia University.

Timmermans, D., & Vlek, C. (1994). An evaluation study of the effectiveness of multi-attribute decision support as a function of problem complexity. *Organizational Behavior and Human Decision Processes, 59,* 75–92.

Tordesillas, R. S., & Chaiken, S. (1999). Thinking too much of too little? The effects of introspection on the decision-making process. *Personality and Social Psychology Bulletin, 25,* 623–629.

Tversky, A. (1977). Features of similarity. *Psychological Review, 84,* 327–352.

Tversky, A., & Kahneman, D. (1973). Availability: A heuristic for judging frequency and probability. *Cognitive Psychology, 5,* 207–232.

Tversky, A., & Kahneman, D. (1974). Judgment under uncertainty: Heuristics and biases. *Science, 185,* 1124–1131.

Tversky, A., & Kahneman, D. (1980). Causal schemas in judgment under uncertainty. In M. Fishbein (Ed.), *Progress in social psychology.* Hillsdale, NJ: Erlbaum.

Tversky, A., & Kahneman, D. (1981). The framing of decisions and the psychology of choice. *Science, 211,* 453–458.

Tversky, A., & Kahneman, D. (1983). Extensional versus intuitive reasoning: The conjunction fallacy in probability judgment. *Psychological Review, 90,* 293–315.

Tversky, A., & Kahneman, D. (1986). Rational choice and the framing of decisions. *Journal of Business, 59*(4, Pt. 2), S251–S278.

Vaughan, F. E. (1979). *Awakening intuition.* New York: Anchor/Doubleday.

Vicente, K. J., & Wang, J. H. (1998). An ecological theory of expertise effects in memory recall. *Psychological Review, 105,* 33–57.

von Winterfeldt, D., & Edwards, W. (1986). *Decision analysis and behavioral research.* New York: Cambridge University Press.

Vosniadou, S., & Brewer, W. F. (1992). Mental models of the earth: A study of conceptual change in childhood. *Cognitive Psychology, 24,* 535–585.

Wason, P. C. (1960). On the failure to eliminate hypotheses in a conceptual task. *Quarterly Journal of Experimental Psychology, 12,* 129–140.

Wason, P. C. (1966). Reasoning. In B. M. Foss (Ed.), *New horizons in psychology.* Harmondsworth: Penguin.

Wason, P. C., & Johnson-Laird, P. N. (1972). *Psychology of reasoning: Structure and content.* London: Batsford.

Watson, J. B., & Rayner, R. (1920). Conditioned emotional reactions. *Journal of Experimental Psychology, 3,* 1–14.

Wertheimer, M. (1959). *Productive thinking* (2d ed.). London: Tavistock.

Westcott, M. R. (1968). *Toward a contemporary psychology of intuition: A historical, theoretical, and empirical inquiry.* New York: Holt, Rinehart & Winston.

White, R. W. (1959). Motivation reconsidered: The concept of competence. *Psychological Review, 66,* 297–333.

Whitehead, A. N. (1911). *An introduction to mathematics.* New York: Holt.

Wilson, T. D., Kraft, D., & Dunn, D. S. (1989). The disruptive effects of explaining attitudes: The moderating effect of knowledge about the attitude object. *Journal of Experimental Social Psychology, 25,* 379–400.

Wilson, T. D., Lisle, D. J., Schooler, J. W., Hodges, S. D., Klaaren, K. J., & LaFleur, S. J. (1993). Introspecting about reasons can reduce post-choice satisfaction. *Personality and Social Psychology Bulletin, 19,* 331–339.

Wilson, T. D., & Schooler, J. W. (1991). Thinking too much: Introspection can reduce the quality of preferences and decisions. *Journal of Personality and Social Psychology, 60,* 181–192.

Yaniv, I., & Foster, D. P. (1995). Graininess of judgment under uncertainty: An accuracy-informativeness trade-off. *Journal of Experimental Psychology: General, 124,* 424–432.

Yaniv, I., & Hogarth, R. M. (1993). Judgmental versus statistical prediction: Information asymmetry and combination rules. *Psychological Science, 4,* 58–62.

Yaniv, I., & Meyer, D. E. (1987). Activation and metacognition of accessible stored information: Potential bases for incubation effects in problem solving. *Journal of Experimental Psychology: Learning, Memory, and Cognition, 13*, 187–205.

Yntema, D. B., & Torgerson, W. S. (1961). Man-computer cooperation in decisions requiring common sense. *IRE Transactions on Human Factors in Electronics, HFE-2*, 20–26.

Zacks, R. T., Hasher, L., Alba, J. W., Sanft, H., & Rose, K. C. (1984). Is temporal order encoded automatically? *Memory and Cognition, 12*, 387–394.

Zajonc, R. B. (1968). Attitudinal effects of mere exposure. *Journal of Personality and Social Psychology Monograph Supplement, 9*(2, Pt. 2), 1–27.

Zajonc, R. B. (1980). Feeling and thinking: Preferences need no inferences. *American Psychologist, 35*, 151–175.

Zajonc, R. B. (1984). On the primacy of affect. *American Psychologist, 39*, 117–123.